LO: TECH: POP: CULT

This edited collection assembles international perspectives from artists, academics, and curators in the field to bring the insights of screendance theory and practice back into conversations with critical methods, at the intersections of popular culture, low-tech media practices, dance, and movement studies, and the minoritarian perspectives of feminism, queer theory, critical race studies and more.

This book represents new vectors in screendance studies, featuring contributions by both artists and theoreticians, some of the most established voices in the field as well as the next generation of emerging scholars, artists, and curators. It builds on the foundational cartographies of screendance studies that attempted to sketch out what was particular to this practice. Sampling and reworking established forms of inquiry, artistic practice, and spectatorial habits, and suspending and reorienting gestures into minoritarian forms, these conversations consider the affordances of screendance for reimaging the relations of bodies, technologies, and media today.

This collection will be of great interest to students and scholars in dance studies, performance studies, cinema and media studies, feminist studies, and cultural studies.

Alanna Thain is Associate Professor of English, World Cinemas and Gender, Sexuality and Feminist Studies at McGill University.

Priscilla Guy is a Canadian artist and researcher holding a PhD in feminist screendance from Université de Lille.

ROUTLEDGE ADVANCES IN THEATRE & PERFORMANCE STUDIES

This series is our home for cutting-edge, upper-level scholarly studies and edited collections. Considering theatre and performance alongside topics such as religion, politics, gender, race, ecology, and the avant-garde, titles are characterized by dynamic interventions into established subjects and innovative studies on emerging topics.

An Actor Survives
Remarks on Stanislavsky
Tomasz Kubikowski

Black Women Centre Stage
Diasporic Solidarity in Contemporary British Theatre
Paola Prieto López

Meaning in the Midst of Performance
Contradictions of Participation
Gareth White

Burning Man
Learning from Heterotopia
Linda Noveroske

Screened Stages
On Theatre in Film
Rachel Joseph

Of Kings and Clowns
Leadership in Contemporary Egyptian Theatre Since 1967
Tiran Manucharyan

Female Playwrights and Applied Intersectionality in Romanian Theater
Cătălina Florina Florescu

For more information about this series, please visit: www.routledge.com/Routledge-Advances-in-Theatre–Performance-Studies/book-series/RATPS

LO: TECH: POP: CULT

Screendance Remixed

Edited by Alanna Thain and Priscilla Guy

With contributions from

Addie Tsai, Alanna Thain, Anatoli Vlassov, Anna Macdonald, Camille Auburtin, Cara Hagan, Claudia Kappenberg, Emilie Morin, Hilary Bergen, Jessica Jacobson-Konefall, Karla Etienne, Kijâtai-Alexandra Veillette-Cheezo, Luce deLire, Manon Labrecque, Nadège Grebmeier Forget, Priscilla Guy, Ryan Clayton, Sonya Stefan and Yutian Wong

LONDON AND NEW YORK

Cover: Image courtesy of Emilie Morin and Ryan Clayton, *The Spectre Animates Our Bones* (2023)

First published 2024
by Routledge
4 Park Square, Milton Park, Abingdon, Oxon OX14 4RN

and by Routledge
605 Third Avenue, New York, NY 10158

Routledge is an imprint of the Taylor & Francis Group, an informa business

© 2024 selection and editorial matter, Priscilla Guy, Alanna Thain; individual chapters, the contributors

The right of Priscilla Guy, Alanna Thain to be identified as the authors of the editorial material, and of the authors for their individual chapters, has been asserted in accordance with sections 77 and 78 of the Copyright, Designs and Patents Act 1988.

All rights reserved. No part of this book may be reprinted or reproduced or utilised in any form or by any electronic, mechanical, or other means, now known or hereafter invented, including photocopying and recording, or in any information storage or retrieval system, without permission in writing from the publishers.

Trademark notice: Product or corporate names may be trademarks or registered trademarks, and are used only for identification and explanation without intent to infringe.

British Library Cataloguing in Publication Data
A catalogue record for this book is available from the British Library

Library of Congress Cataloging-in-Publication Data
A catalog record has been requested for this book

ISBN: 9781032364612 (hbk)
ISBN: 9781032372150 (pbk)
ISBN: 9781003335887 (ebk)

DOI: 10.4324/9781003335887

Typeset in Sabon
by Taylor & Francis Books

To the culture workers, the movers, and the artists

CONTENTS

List of figures x
List of contributors xii
Foreword xvi
Acknowledgments xviii

Introduction 1
Alanna Thain and Priscilla Guy

PART I
Onsceneity: Glitching Visions 23

1 "Let Me in Through Your Window": Dancing with Kate Bush and Hatsune Miku 25
   Hilary Bergen

2 The Queer Art of Hospitality: "If You Can Fuck, You Can Dance!" 45
   Luce deLire

3 Kinesthetic Empathy as Human Connection in Digital Space 70
   Cara Hagan

4 The Value of a Cheap Trick: Reverse Motion from Lo-Tech SFX to Speculative Spectacle 85
   Alanna Thain

5 Little Visions and Grandiose Perceptions: An Interview with Manon Labrecque 104
   Priscilla Guy

PART II
Touching Time: Histories Beyond the Binary 111

6 Canonising BTS: FOMO in the Archives of
   Digital Convenience 113
   Yutian Wong

7 Keeping in Time: Mastery, as a Condition of Colonial and
   Patriarchal Discourse, and the Temporality of Screendance 133
   Anna Macdonald

8 Bill Robinson: Icon of Dignity 153
   Karla Etienne

9 The Ghost(s) of Alice Guy: Reminiscences of a Feminist
   Screendance Pioneer 161
   Priscilla Guy

10 In a World of Dancing Waves and DIY Addiction: An
   Interview with Sonya Stefan 177
   Priscilla Guy

PART III
Kinetics and Politics of Ephemerality and Ownership 187

11 "Take Me to the Place Where the White Boys Dance":
   Tom Hanks's Manchild 189
   Addie Tsai

12 Traces, Memories, and Rediscovered Gestures: A Creative
   Practice of Archiving and Sensitive Writing 209
   Camille Auburtin

13 Terrance Houle's Ghost Dancing in a Wagon
   Burner Landscape 228
   Jessica Jacobson-Konefall

14 Desire to Heal; Desire to be Seen; Desire to Dance: An
   Interview with Kijâtai-Alexandra Veillette-Cheezo 245
   Priscilla Guy

PART IV
Technology; Technics; Tenderness 253

15 From _ Ryan Clayton To _ Emilie Morin 255
   Ryan Clayton and Emilie Morin

16 Filming Consciousness: Between Phonesia® and Talking Camera—Organological Cinema 268
Anatoli Vlassov

17 The Matter of Analogue Media Technologies in Screendance, Post Martin Heidegger and Post Hito Steyerl 286
Claudia Kappenberg

18 Moving Mirror: Screendance as Performance Methodology: An Interview with Nadège Grebmeier Forget 308
Alanna Thain

Index 322

FIGURES

0.1 Emilie Morin and Ryan Clayton, *The Spectre Animates Our Bones* (2023)   1
1.1 Hilary Bergen dances the choreography for Kate Bush's "Wuthering Heights," facing the Alienware computer, the Microsoft Xbox 360 Kinect, and a YouTube tutorial video. Technician Michael Li watches   26
1.2 Computer monitor with MMD in choreography mode, with avatar's "bones" highlighted   31
1.3 MMD in video capture mode, with avatar in red kimono standing in an urban green space setting   32
1.4 Four of the bodies involved in this dance translation perform the gesture of pressing palms to window: Myself, in a still from the video tutorial for Bush's choreography posted to YouTube (upper left); Miku's avatar performing Bush's choreography via my motion data fed into MMD (upper right); Bush in a YouTube still from her 1979 music video for "Wuthering Heights" (bottom left); Miku from her single "Hibikase" in her 2015 live show (bottom right).   37
1.5 Still from the final product of my MMD dance translation project, "Let Me in at Your Window" (2016), featuring Miku's glitching body   40
2.1 Still from: Santiago Tamayo Soler, *Retornar*, 2021   45
2.2 Still from: Santiago Tamayo Soler, *Retornar*, 2021   61

7.1	Performer Terrance Houle stands next to a swimming pool wearing pow-wow first nation regalia	137
7.2	Performer Concha Vidal is seen face down in a pool filled with white polystyrene balls	143
12.1	Micheline Auburtin image from a Super 8 home movie captured by Michel or Pierre Auburtin in the 1980s	214
12.2	Camille's hands handling a family photo showing her as a baby and her grandmother Mimi, framed by Camille with a rostrum camera stand	217
12.3	Micheline Auburtin surrounded by her daughter Marjorie Auburtin and Camille in her nursing home in Sélestat, framed by Christophe Hanesse	223
13.1	Terrance Houle. 2013. Film still. *Isstahpikssi (ghost) part 1*	233
15.1	*SkypeDuet* performed at Regards Hybrides International Forum, Montreal (QC), Canada in November 2019	255
15.2	*SkypeDuet* performed at Hexagram GALA, Montreal (QC), Canada in December 2021	256
16.1	Tess Vlassov and Anatoli Vlassov, *Phoné-Scopie*, 2015, photo from a shot of the film	269
16.2	Tess Vlassov and Anatoli Vlassov, *Phoné-Scopie*, 2015, photo from a shot of the film	270
16.3	Tess Vlassov and Anatoli Vlassov, *Phoné-Scopie*, 2015, photo from a shot of the film	273
16.4	Tess Vlassov and Anatoli Vlassov, *Phoné-Scopie*, 2015, photo from a shot of the film	274
16.5	Tess Vlassov and Anatoli Vlassov, *Phoné-Scopie*, 2015, photo from a shot of the film	276
16.6	Tess Vlassov and Anatoli Vlassov, *Phoné-Scopie*, 2015, photo from a shot of the film	279
16.7	Tess Vlassov and Anatoli Vlassov, *Phoné-Scopie*, 2015, photo from a shot of the film	281
16.8	Tess Vlassov and Anatoli Vlassov, *Phoné-Scopie*, 2015, photo from a shot of the film	282
18.1	*Inside-Outside, Off & On* (2020)	308
18.2	*Re-Reflecting On…* (2016)	311
18.3	Stilled as Marilyn stilled by Bert as Marilyn Behind a White Veil (March 6), from *Hier est Aujourd'hui* (2016)	316
18.4	Still from *Some Kind of Game* (2020)	320

CONTRIBUTORS

Ivanie Aubin-Malo is a Wolastoq and Quebecois dancer, choreographer and curator who invests herself in projects that reflect on ecology and human ethics regarding our environment. She has also danced Fancy Shawl, a powwow style, since 2015, connecting with the spirit of transformation and celebrating women's audacity. Her artistic research as a creator aims to shed light on the beauty of the Wolastoqey language and its relation to the land and the body.

Camille Auburtin is a video artist, performer and director based in Bordeaux, France. Auburtin's work considers image, body, and movement through different filmic objects: art documentaries, experimental films, commissioned films for dancing, co-creations, and mediation tools. Her work includes *Les Robes Papillons* (2020), *Méandre(s)* (2022), and other filmic creations currently in production for the choreographer and anthropologist Sylvie Balestra – SYLEX.

Hilary Bergen is an FRQSC postdoctoral researcher at The New School in New York where she studies dance, digital animation and virtual bodies. A dancer and a writer, Bergen has published work with *PUBLIC*, *Word and Text*, *Culture Machine* and *Screening the Past*. She is currently organizing an international conference called "Dance and/as Technology" (with VR scholar Philippe Bédard) and writing a book called *Dance Anima: More-than-Human Choreography from Loie Fuller to Boston Dynamics*, under contract with Oxford University Press.

Ryan Clayton is an artist working in New Media. Since 2017, Clayton and Emilie Morin have maintained a collaborative performance practice focusing primarily on consumer telecommunication technologies such as Skype, Twitch, and Zoom.

List of contributors xiii

Luce deLire is a ship with eight sails, and she lies down by the quay. As a philosopher, she publishes on the metaphysics of infinity but also on queer theory, anti-racism, postcolonialism, and political theory. In her performances, she embodies figures of the collective imaginary. For more (including booking), see getaphilosopher.com.

Karla Etienne is a dance artist, curator and cultural manager. She has devoted herself to advancing the cause of anti-racism and inclusion in the arts, at all levels of practice, management and dissemination. Etienne is interested in her dance and writings on the persistence of the body in space as an act of resistance and of sublimation of the self.

Nadège Grebmeier Forget is an interdisciplinary artist, best known for her live and private durational performances. She critically reflects on the medium, questioning its presentation devices, documentation, and the potential of its mediation. Her work is influenced by feminisms, her own body and personal psyche as mediums of observation, research, and transformation. http://www.nadege-grebmeier-forget.com/.

Priscilla Guy is a performer, choreographer, filmmaker, curator, and scholar. She holds a PhD in feminist screendance and is the co-founder of Regards Hybrides. She has contributed to several screendance media and books such as *The International Journal of Screendance* and *The Oxford Handbook of Screendance Studies*. She is working on a few forthcoming screendance publications projects, notably with Routledge, les Presses du réel, and Presses de l'Université de Montréal. http://www.collection.regardshybrides.com/.

Cara Hagan (she/they) is a mover, maker, writer, curator, champion of just communities, and a dreamer. Hagan is editor and contributor to the anthology *Practicing Yoga as Resistance: Voices of Color in Search of Freedom* (Routledge, 2021). She is also the author of *Screendance from Film to Festival: Celebration and Curatorial practice* (McFarland, 2022).

Jessica Jacobson-Konefall is an assistant professor of Canadian art at the University of Lethbridge. Her current work focuses on care and vulnerability as well as settler colonialism in Canadian contemporary art, politics, and life.

Claudia Kappenberg is an artist, writer, curator and Honorary Fellow at the University of Brighton, UK. She led the International Screendance Network and co-founded the International Journal for Screendance in 2009. Her writing has been published in *MIRAJ* (2021), *Performing Process: Sharing Dance and Choreographic Practice* (Intellect, 2018), *Syncope in Performing and Visual Arts* (Éditions Le Manuscrit, 2017) and *The Oxford Handbook of*

Screendance Studies (Oxford University Press, 2016). In 2020 she co-curated the online Screendance season with Fiontán Moran.

Manon Labrecque was a multidisciplinary artist based in Montreal, Canada. A true polymath, Labrecque eludes categories and labels. Her work is an encounter between the banal and the grandiose; the human body and the machine; the useless and the essential. She passed away in August 2023, leaving behind a massive body of work, as well as an indelible imprint on Canadian video art.

Anna Macdonald is a dance artist/scholar and Course Leader for MA Performance: Society at UAL: Central St Martins, London. Macdonald's work focuses on the relationship between the body, time, and affect to expose the resonance of simple movements. Her work is regularly exhibited and has generated interdisciplinary findings in the fields of health, science, and law, within large-scale projects funded by AHRC, Arts Council England, and Wellcome Trust.

Emilie Morin is a dance and new media artist. Since 2017, Ryan Clayton and Emilie Morin have maintained a collaborative performance practice focusing primarily on consumer telecommunication technologies such as Skype, Twitch, and Zoom.

Sonya Stefan is a media and dance artist specializing in 16mm film. Her work has contributed to build screendance practices and discourses over the past 20 years in Canada. Her films are screened worlwide and won several prizes.

Alanna Thain is a professor at McGill University, Tiohtià:ke/ Montreal/ Mooniyang, Canada. Director of the Moving Image Research Lab and CORÉRISC (Collective for Research on Epistemologies of Embodied Risk), her research concerns embodiment, risk, survival and time in media and performance. She is the author of *Bodies in Suspense: Time and Affect in Cinema* (Minnesota UP, 2017).

Addie Tsai (any/all) is an artist and writer who teaches Creative Writing at William & Mary University and Regis University. Tsai is the Fiction Co-Editor and Editor of Features & Reviews at *Anomaly* and Founding Editor in Chief at *just femme & dandy*. They have authored the novels *Dear Twin* (Metonymy Press, 2019) and *Unwieldy Creatures* (Jaded Ibis Press, 2022) as well as many scholarly publications.

Kijâtai-Alexandra Veillette-Cheezo is a filmmaker and journalist based in Montreal, Canada. Their short films speak to Indigenous realities in Canada from a personal point of view, weaving together political concerns with their singular perspectives. As an activist, they use words and images to create bridges between communities and support their Indigenous peers.

Anatoli Vlassov is a talking dancer, choreographer, and videographer. He has created choreographies with street cleaners, people with autism, and danced with a wireless endoscopic camera. He developed a new performative technique, Phonesia®, enabling the simultaneous articulation of dance and speech. Vlassov has authored the manifesto *TENSER* (Éditions Jannink) and his thesis *PHONÉSIE* is under consideration for the collection *Gestures* (Les presses du réel).

Yutian Wong is a professor of dance in the School of Theatre & Dance at San Francisco State University. Wong has authored *Choreographing Asian America* (Wesleyan, 2010), edited *Contemporary Directions in Asian American Dance* (Wisconsin, 2016), and co-edited *The Routledge Dance Studies Reader 3rd Edition* (2018), "Dancing in the Aftermath of Anti-Asian Violence" for *Conversations* (2023), and *Bangtan Remixed: A Critical BTS Reader* (Duke, 2024).

FOREWORD

Three Poems by Ivanie Aubin-Malo[1]

Translated by Cath Marceau

Balmoral Hotel[2]

    The raven dances.
    The black Stain,
        Somewhere in the identity,
            Flaps its wings...
    The beating hearts of streets
        Find refuge
            At the Balmoral Hotel.

Wamin (The Apple)[3]

    The colour sticks to my hands.
    It veils my prints
    Regularly,
    I take off this strange peel.
        From the core to the tip of the sepals,
    The one you call Wamin
    Has never taken her eyes off
    The fruit she chooses to become.

Kijâtai[4]

    My voicemail is full.
        Full of love,
        Of land,
        Of memories.
    From Lac-Simon to Montreal,
        I hear once again the voices that have preceded.
    The drum and the hearts align to open the way for me...
        To guide me towards the lost memories.
    Leave me a message,
        I will invite them near the water,
        In the air that smells of sage.

Notes

1 In 2021, artist Ivanie Aubin-Malo was invited by curator Priscilla Guy to write poems in reaction to screendance works directed by Indigenous artists from different nations. These poems were first published in French on La Fabrique culturelle's website, as an accompaniment for the videos that were available for viewing online as part of a series called Indigenous Voices, copresented by Regards Hybrides and La Fabrique culturelle.
2 The title of this poem refers to the title of a screendance work directed by Wayne Wapeemukwa that inspired this poem: *Balmoral Hotel* (2015).
3 The title of this poem refers to the title of a screendance work directed by Katherine Nequado that inspired this poem: *Wamin (The Apple)* (2018).
4 The title of this poem refers to the title of a screendance work directed by Kijâtai-Alexandra Veillette-Cheezo that inspired this poem: *Kijâtai* (2019).

ACKNOWLEDGEMENTS

This book initially stemmed from our experience with the second edition of Regards Hybrides' International Forum/Rencontres Internationales Regards Hybrides (RIRH), that we organized in 2019, as well as from the encounters we made and the discussions we had on that occasion. We wish to acknowledge the support of Tangente Danse (Montreal) and their whole team for welcoming us in their venue and providing us with essential resources and support, making this gathering possible. Special thanks to Dena Davida, whose trust in this project, as well as interest in art curation, encouraged us to move forward with the publication.

We also want to thank Douglas Rosenberg for his presence at the 2019's edition of the Forum. We appreciated his spontaneous enthusiasm for this publication, and his dedication to screendance development, notably by opening the way to publishing major reference books that weave together discourses by artists, curators, theoreticians and cultural workers. His vision of screendance has been a springboard from which we were motivated to push the boundaries of the field with challenging ideas.

We wish to thank the contributors to this volume, which largely took shape during the COVID 19 pandemic and its often relentless challenges, ones that we have attempted to register rather than overlook or power through. We thank them for their patience with the length of this process, and the limits of our editorial energy, and we acknowledge the vast and varied circumstances in which their writing came to be. The work gathered here testifies to an unimaginable wealth of insight, experience and intelligence, and the affective labour of engagement in deeply embodied forms of thought. Our contributors write from many different places, often all at once: as artists, curators, programmers, fans, dancers, choreographers, filmmakers, spectators, academics, across precarious positions and from the stability of institutional affiliation. Such differences of access, resources and time are often opaque in finished formats, and so we highlight them here.

We also wish to thank all those who provided critical support in the production process. Many thanks to Dominic Corti, Swati Hindwan and Laura Hussey at Routledge for their precious support. Many hands shaped these materials, including our copyeditors at the press, as well as Nived Dharmaraj, Sarah Osment and our subtle translators Cath Marceau and Violette Drouin. We acknowledge the financial support of the Social Sciences and Humanities Research Council of Canada and Thain's research project "Anarchival Outbursts", the Fonds de Recherche du Québec—Society and Culture, and Hexagram: Network in Research-Creation in Arts, Culture and Technology. This book also benefited from financial and production support by Mandoline Hybride, a non-profit art organization founded by Guy producing Regards Hybrides' International Forum and a key partner in the realization of this initiative. From this team, we wish to thank Marie-Charlotte Castonguay-Harvey and Clotilde Dyotte-Gabelier for their administrative and production work in the process of putting this project together and for their support for screendance development in general in Québec. Bridging artistic and academic approaches has been at the core of our motivations and we are glad to confirm that such partnerships between research labs and art organizations are not only possible, but also extremely fruitful. Thanks as well to Public Journal for permission to include adapted material in the chapters by Hilary Bergen and Alanna Thain from previously published work.

Finally we want to acknowledge that much of the editorial work for this project, as well as Regards Hybrides' International Forum, took place in Tiohtiá:ke/ Mooniyang/ Montreal on the traditional and unceded territory of the Kanien'kehà:ka. We recognize with gratitude that they are the traditional custodians of the lands and waters on which we meet, live and dance. Tiohtiá:ke has long served as a site of meeting and exchange amongst many First Nations including the Kanien'kehá:ka of the Haudenosaunee Confederacy, Huron/ Wendat, Abenaki, and Anishinaabeg peoples. In the spirit of DIY production that animates this book, we want to highlight Wapikoni Mobile for their transformative work training Indigenous youth in Quebec in telling their own stories through screen media, including the films *Kijâtai*, *Odehimin*, and *Wamin*, directed by Kijâtai-Alexandra Veillette-Cheezo and Katherine Nequado, discussed in this volume.

Alanna wishes to thank first and foremost Priscilla Guy, whose art is not only on screen or on stage but in fabricating community and collectivity. A militant and expansive feminist, her keen intelligence and generous spirit has shaped this book in every way imaginable. She also wishes to thank the many people with whom she has thought through dance on and around screens for more than a decade, including Lynne Joyrich and the Pembroke Centre for

Research and Teaching on Women at Brown University. She thanks brilliant students and postdocs who are cherished colleagues in dance and movement research and queer and feminist art and media: Noémie Solomon, VK Preston, Catherine Lavoie-Marcus, Diego Gil, Stefanie Miller, Ayanna Dozier, Hilary Bergen, Philippe Bédard, Antoine Damiens, Dayna McLeod, Resat Fuac Cam, Celia Vara and Carolyn Bailey. She thanks her colleagues in particular in feminist research circles in Montreal, at the Feminist Media Studio (Concordia), in the Réseau québécois en études féministes and above all at the Institute for Gender, Sexuality and Feminist Studies at McGill University, in particular Alexandra Ketchum, Carrie Rentschler and Mary Bunch. Many dancers, filmmakers, students and colleagues have shared their work and time at the Moving Image Research Lab at McGill, which is dedicated to the study and care for bodies in moving image media; she is grateful for the continued support of the MIRL as infrastructure and ever changing community. Thanks as well to dear friends and colleagues at McGill always up for dancing and writing: Jenny Burman, Bronwen Low, Fiona Ritchie, Monica Popescu and Katie Zien. She thanks her family, especially her mother Linda Thain and partner Nik Forrest, who has taught her so much about the elegant art of queer survival. Lastly, she wishes to thank the Montreal dance scene for everyday joy, in particular the amazing space of Studio 303 and Myriam Ginestier and Ami Shulman as well as Montreal Danse and Kathy Casey, in particular their annual Choreographic Workshop, and to all the makers and artists in this city constantly reinventing ways to share art widely and hold open spaces of practice and performance under the increasingly challenging conditions of precarity and unsustainable, fickle and inadequate support, who act with such generosity and a very Montreal DIY/ DIT spirit!

Priscilla wishes to thank Alanna for her friendship and for countless inspiring conversations throughout the years, but also for her exceptional ability to support one through the sometimes thick meanders of a publishing process. Her guidance was key to this whole project, and is characterized notably by an extremely humble approach that gives way to taking risks and asking difficult questions, while simultaneously showing a great deal of confidence, which is essential to putting together such an ambitious book. Alanna's vivid ease at making links between ideas and themes, as well as her strong sense of dramaturgy, has allowed Priscilla to feel at home within this first experience at editing an international book of reference. She also wants to thank her colleagues from the international screendance network, an ever growing group of people whose thinking and artwork have shaped her vision of screendance for the past fifteen years. Special thanks to Douglas Rosenberg, again, not only for offering the first international screening of one of her films in 2011, but also proving her with a very first experience writing a chapter for a major book with *The Oxford Handbook of Screendance Studies* (2016), which surely fed the desire to engage in the publication of *Lo*

Tech Pop Cult and offer other artists and thinkers the opportunity to share their voice. To Emilie Morin, artist and colleague of numerous screendance adventures, for participating in this dialogue between art and theory throughout the years, in so many ways. To Catherine Lavoie-Marcus, for opening up together new feminist screendance territories through creation and writing around the project *Singeries*, a turning point in Priscilla's creative approach to theory. To all the artists who contributed from far or from close to Regards Hybrides and its various extensions (workshops, conferences, screenings) thank you for your insights, trust and enthusiasm. Finally, to Claudia Hébert, co-founder of Regards Hybrides in 2012 who made it possible to imagine a space that would welcome both academic and artistic interrogations; a space for holding together our thoughts and aspirations for screendance discourses and practices.

INTRODUCTION

Alanna Thain and Priscilla Guy

In Our Bubble

What is this creature moving onscreen? A shambolic assemblage of an electrical substation, a mobile home, a pair of pink doll legs with metal claws helplessly suspended at the top of the body and a bottom pair of chicken legs clad in gold metallic spandex: this propositional body is exposed in its struggles as it spins and stumbles on an unstable dancefloor of bubbles

FIGURE 0.1 Emilie Morin and Ryan Clayton, *The Spectre Animates Our Bones* (2023)
Source: From the video *The Spectre Animates Our Bones*, Emilie Morin and Ryan Clayton, 2023.

DOI: 10.4324/9781003335887-1

floating in a black void. Legs suspended from utility swing wildly and seek purchase on other surfaces. The sheer implausibility of this surprisingly stable form (a small television set plays on, implacably, perched on the roof of the caravan) exacerbates the kinesthetic experience of this dance that, in the end, feels familiar despite its unknown nature and meaning. The avatar moves in a cloud of smooth and shiny floating spheres that always seem at the edge of a real colour—beige, caramel, grey, and a murky lilac—against a black background lost in space. In this world, every movement initiates a reactive response that ripples the environment and destabilizes any attempt to differentiate the capacities of this form from the world it moves through. The overall agitation that characterizes this piece is accomplished through the assemblage of eccentric movements that asks the viewer to spin around on their own axis, and, in following the action, to lose the singularity of vision. Indeed, in their artist statement, Emilie Morin and Ryan Clayton note that here: "what contemporary artist Brendan Fernandes calls the 'footmade' is as valuable as the 'handmade.'"[1] The whole piece plays off a core joy (in Spinoza's sense) of screendance: the opportunity to recompose and experiment with what a body can do.

The Spectre Animates our Bones (2023) is a digital animation and collaboration between Morin, a professional dancer, and Clayton, a visual artist and performer, that they have termed a "braided dance." Here, a duet emerges after the fact of performance: each recorded the same choreography with motion capture technology, and then mapped these onto the same virtual object. Their careful attempts at precision in following the performance score cannot disguise the failure to homogenize movement. The resulting avatar is a testament to this attempt to mimic and honor each other, while at the same time acknowledging the uncanny and imperfect, hilarious and grotesque outcome. The duet asks: "can virtual movement stand-in for individual human bodies?" But in its clumsy and lurching explorations of the world, driven by movement and a wobbly sense of balance rather than any evident sensory perceptions, we identify this thing immediately as a body *because* it moves. In this work of screendance, the stand-in maps the more urgent question of standing-up as the lurch of creative survival in this world.

The work is an alluring and visually sophisticated piece that at the same time retains a strong sense of bricolage, of the DIY, of imperfection and rough edges. In many senses, it is a work of "making do," both in the collage form of the avatar body and in the impulsive animation of the work itself. Indeed, as a viewer, you also have to make do, as behind your back and across from the monitor is a second image with the view from behind the camera. Across the shared forms of embodiment of this work is what Peter Sloterdijk calls "foam sociality": "an aggregate of micro-spheres ... of different formats that are adjacent to one another like individual bubbles in a mound of foam and are structured one layer over/under the other, without really being accessible to or separable from one another."[2] Towards the end of the piece, massive waves of red eyeballs flow across the scenery, mixing with the white and pale smooth spheres, suggesting perhaps millions of other points of view on this dancing body. Powered by mimeticism as the primary mode of relation, this foamy world is barely holding it together, and can never be separated out. As Amélie Wong-Merseau describes this:

> Morin and Clayton used consumer telecommunication technologies like Skype, Twitch, and Zoom to think about our relationships to one another as they are affected by these tools. The artists continue their exploration here using motion capture technology and animation to consider how the body is a communally mediated experience.[3]

In their single channel work, *Faz que Vai* [*Set to Go*] (2015), one of their earliest works of screendance, Bárbara Wagner and Benjamin de Burca similarly explore bodies moving at the edges of sociality and how "vernacular knowledge and culture reach a level of being recognized."[4] One of their research materials was a Brazilian documentary about the roots of frevo, a frenetic dance rooted in cultures of resistance to colonialism and slavery, recently consecrated as cultural heritage. In the film, bodies fill the street as history mingles with contemporary citizen dancers. Curiously, the end credits cut between a meticulous accounting of everyone who worked on the film, and a single female dancer energetically performing on the steps of a building. She is uncredited. When Wagner and de Burca began their research, they

> were living close to an artisanal shop where young frevo dancers from the area would perform for tourists intermittently, and [...] could always hear bars with frevo music playing. [Benjamin] said to Bárbara, "You know, it's really nice to hear the music and know what's happening but not see it and leave it to the imagination."[5]

Something of this discretion remains as a speculative impulse in the final work, challenging a simple politics of representation through the movement impulses of screendance. Leonel Brum cites Ana Paual Nunes, speaking to the significance of screendance in Brazilian culture: "videodance is a privileged space for the debate on body representation in contemporary society."[6] Wagner and de Burca note that many of the dance forms they have researched –frevo, brega, and maloya—live in the bodies of dancers who expertly perform for tourists while simultaneously making and distributing their own YouTube and Instagram videos for a more ambiguous audience, via the mediation of the screendance and the re-production of their own image. In "tak[ing] this work, typically shot on a smartphone, and giv[ing] it the production value of cinema,"[7] Wagner notes a double effect: increased access of these artists—often queer, trans, racialized and minoritarian—to elite spaces of galleries, museums, and festivals, and increased accessibility for audiences habituated to the language—and production values—of cinema.[8] Here, they reframe the (gendered) anonymity of the documentary dancer into a gesture of control at the edge of relation. In one sequence in *Faz Que Vai*, an irresistibly smiley dancer, Bhrunno, emerges onto a rooftop, his festival costuming at odds with the everyday surroundings where no audience is to be seen. He clearly performs "for us" engaging the camera with charm and precision, and simultaneously summons another sphere, in another of screendance's leaky sociabilities. At one point, he simply pauses, pulls out a phone, and starts taking selfies, redirecting his laser charm into the smartphone's screen and, presumably, beyond. It's a gesture of non-absolute refusal, one that lives somewhere other than on a clear borderline between the live and mediated. Instead of refusal, we might think of it as an insistence on *an other* time, *an other* place, a more to life. This is making do as both working with what you have and a propositional way of moving in the world.

Between these two contemporary captures at either end of the Americas, screendance makes do both *with* and *in* the world. Screendance is often taken to refer to an ever-evolving and mutating form of choreographic and dance works created for screens rather than intended for the stage as live performance. Across its many aliases, each speaking to braided histories and genealogies, screendance names the practices and discourses that interweave the potentials, actualized and otherwise, of dance and moving image media.[9] Ever present throughout film history, the availability and affordances of newer technologies of video and digital media have nurtured the emergence of screendance as its own genre and as a subject of academic inquiry in the twenty-first century. While screendance in popular media, in particular mainstream narrative feature films, has been an important concern for screendance studies, popular culture itself as an accessible reservoir of *somatechnical* embodiments has been less central to the field's development and conceptualization, with a focus on dance *in* popular culture, rather than *as* popular culture in all of its demands, potential, and ambivalences.

Lo: Tech: Pop: Cult is a prismatic take on how screendance already understands the body as an intimate, DIY technology that assembles with recording and playback technologies (including choreography and dance training), as well as the unruly archive of popular media, in unpredictable ways. Beyond the relation between live bodies and their mediated images, we reframe this concern through the access points of lo-tech creation, on the one hand, and popular culture as remixable cultural commons. In attending to the specificity of this emergent field, the question of screendance's relation not only to cinema and media history, but also to live performance and interpretation, remains an underexplored field. While video as a new vernacular for dance documentation, as well as the affordances of cutting edge and experimental technologies, have both been the subject of much attention, this collection excavates a parallel track in the history and practice of screendance—its connection to experimental live performance, lo-fi, DIY techniques in both media and movement, as it intersects with popular culture. How can the affordances of technological constraints create scenes of radical reimagination? How do dancing bodies glitch the polish of the popular and participatory movements of fan cultures, remaking, remixing, and more? Drawing on the legacy of feminist theory and cultural studies, which have centered DIY and lo-tech interventions as acts of speculative resistance, this book explores the question: how do lo-tech approaches and popular culture create a zone of free play that opens new directions in screendance research? Indeed, while we navigate the sea of digital innovation that delivers dance in novel forms, it remains immensely productive to tackle the implication of DIY and lo-tech approaches as strategies of resistance to mainstream discourses and as a counterpoint to dominant film culture.

In this collection's interdisciplinary approach, we seek to draw on the affordances of popular culture as a site of imaginative worldmaking, accessed through production, but also practices of fandom, copying, remixing, and as ambient media, to place it in conversation with screendance's legacy as a practice of experimental and avant-garde approaches. *Lo: Tech: Pop: Cult* asks: what are the methods, epistemologies, aesthetics, and practices of screendance that have emerged from feminist, decolonial, and minoritarian perspectives? How does work at the intersection of lo-tech approaches (grounded in DIY and experimental traditions) intersect with popular culture (as a movement and media practice of complex accessibility to those on the margins of social and artistic inclusion) to reveal the working methods and subversive tactics that have underpinned screendance's recent meteoric expansion and visibility? Critical theories address crucial social concerns in the studies of humanities and through fine arts criticism, while arts practitioners rework struggle and desire into the materials of imagination and expression. How does screendance activate the urgent questions of our moment around how we want to live, through the lens of our exposure to screens and the way our moving bodies interact with moving images? It is little wonder that Maya Deren's foundational work of screendance, *At Land* (1944), opens with a body trailed by the foam of the waves, bringing the dancing body always closer to the edge of endless recomposition.

The authors in the collection articulate a common sense that screendance is a pedagogy for renewed perceptions and sensations: for seeing, feeling, and moving differently (as a spectator, curator, artist, researcher) and in the process, for attending to the relations that compose us and our ways of moving in the world. While we see the relation between live performance and mediated screens as a continuum rather than a binary, we also acknowledge that the spatial and temporal coordinates on screendance offer novel ways to stretch out, deform, massage, and replay our habitual ways of translating perceptions and sensations into ways of knowing. One of the key ways that such shifts have been tracked is through the attempts to articulate the state of an emergent field. While screendance scholars and practitioners have articulated the field by differentiating it from other disciplines and highlighting its specificities, they have defined and dreamed the form of the field through manifestos, formats that describe and demand in equal measure. Such approaches aim to keep screendance away from reproducing dominant forms of commercial cinema and to inscribe its hybrid signature through DIY approaches. In 1999, then again in 2006, and 2015, manifestos were produced by different screendance communities to define its aesthetics, politics, and/or epistemologies, as well as to identify collective hopes for the form. Katrina McPherson explores such manifestos in screendance history in the second edition of her book *Making Video Dance*,[10] launched to celebrate the twentieth anniversary of this publication, and as does Noël Carroll in *Philosophy and the Moving Image*.[11] Points of reference include two manifestos from 1999: *Dance/Technology Manifesto*[12] by Douglas Rosenberg in which he calls for "more ideas and fewer technological tricks in screen dance"[13] and *Dogma Dance Manifesto*,[14] first circulated online and disseminated via email by artists Deveril, McPherson, and Litza Bixler.[15] *Dogma Dance*, which repurposed the Dogma95 manifesto, insists on several elements or creative constraints, such as only shooting with one camera, only using handheld shots, having just one light or using only natural light, etc., to emphasize and value a lo-tech approach that foregrounds human bodies. While, as with the original Dogma95 manifesto, such rules were made to be broken, and the actual work of screendance cannot be limited to human bodies on screen, the manifesto evinces an attempt to ensure human conditions for production, articulating care and aesthetics to keep screendance to a "human" scale. Other examples include *(Hu)Manifesto: Possibilities for Screendance* co-authored by the participants of a Scottish symposium on screendance and published as part of *Opensource (videodance)*[16] or *How to film the moving body in an hostile world?*, put together in Mexico by a group of interdisciplinary artists, whose very title articulates the stakes of screendance beyond representation of the status quo.[17] The title also recalls Donna Haraway's position in *Staying with the Trouble*, to cultivate "the possibility of life in capitalist ruins" as a pragmatic approach to survival.[18]

Such manifestos are pedagogical tools for the milieu itself, orienting screendance practices towards urgent stakes. Screendance as pedagogy has been largely unexamined in screendance literature, despite the growing number of university programs dedicated to it and the numerous workshops existing around the world. In this volume, Cara Hagan and Yutian Wong explicitly take up these questions in professional pedagogical practice, but almost all pieces foreground the challenge to established modes of perception that pedagogy poses and what it takes to learn to think otherwise. Practical guides on screendance production often fail to raise questions around why one makes such works, beyond aesthetic concerns. This book explicitly invites reflection, by authors and by readers, on the ethics and politics of screendance. We make and write about screendance because we need to watch/see things other than the flood of images, brutal and banal, that we are exposed to everyday. In a podcast conversation on screendance practices with Priscilla Guy, the renowned Canadian dancer and choreographer Louise Lecavalier describes feeling "hurt" by the careless onslaught of images in everyday life; for instance, how the bodies or faces of politicians are captured with little care for their impact.[19] All that matters is the speed and volume of the production of images. Lecavalier craves images of human bodies in motion that address her sense of the world with some sort of hopeful or utopian quality. How can screendance offer a platform to welcome and discuss a variety of moving bodies and images that open onto ontological considerations about how we perceive each other and experience the world, while sharing space and time?

In the DIY of making, or being moved through a full-bodied somatic attention, screendance has a capacity to reconcile us with the tools of power, as a countertechnique (of dance or media, but also of the power of images) for using such tools. An oft-cited impulse that screendance evokes is the contagious mirroring of movement itself. Across this book's contributions are accounts of the audacious and radical ways to learn and teach within the vast spectrum of practices screendance offers. Most critically, we address the need to unlearn some of the bodily discipline dance curriculums imposes on artists, reflecting wider constraints and habits in society. If screendance as a practice see dance everywhere it looks, it also asks: what are the ways in which we can cultivate practices of freedom? In their testimonies in this book, many artists describe the move to screendance as a practice of unlearning their dance training (as in our interview with Sonya Stefan). Other chapters explore how to retrain the human eye (and our philosophical privileging of the distance sense of vision) to counterbalance the controlling gaze of the camera or interrogate the concept of dance canon through the rewritable lens of popular culture (as in Yutian Wong's work in this book). Undoing hierarchies that remain dominant in the film and media industries as well as the arts scene, lo-tech screendance is a rich playground for dance artists who often develop impressive abilities at manipulating cameras and composing the frame of the screen, whose counteractions with technology unfold new effects and affects through its rebellious utilization. This collection thinks with such moves.

As such, we offer the following propositions as a preliminary score for moving with this book, and in the spirit of the speculative manifesto.

Use the "at-hand" (or "at-foot"): Though it may seem that lo-tech creation and popular culture are opposites, what connects them in this book is a concern for the intimacy of the close-at-hand: the everyday whose familiarity also and often fails to register in its specificity and strangeness. Screendance uniquely reframes a moving moment of encounter with the tools we have to both take up and take on the world around us. The question of how artists have managed to appropriate, pirate, upend, and also honour popular culture through screendance's creative practices remains a vital and provocative field of investigation.

Follow the impulse: This collection assembles practices—of making, but also of spectatorship and curation—beyond those forms of digital and other media that captivate the eye and the mind. Instead, *Lo: Tech: Pop: Cult* foregrounds techniques and analyses that are closely attentive to how media images are part of our collective consciousness and ecologies of existence.

Take up space: Our expansive approach to screendance is rooted not only in the specific legacy and contemporary rearticulations of expanded cinema, but in a hospitable (see Luce deLire's chapter) engagement. We borrow from the ubiquity of popular culture the insight that screendance can be found in all kinds of contexts for those who know how to look. What kind of expanded capacities does screendance demand from viewers as participants in the action?

Cherchez les femmes: Screendance is more present in academic discourses since the turn of the twenty-first century. Whether as curators, scholars, artists, or producers, it remains a field where the representation of women is significantly higher than in mainstream media production, and where minoritarian subjects can experiment with taking up space through dance in ways that are often constrained in everyday life. We remain committed to the insights around the limits of "representation" tracked by feminist, queer, trans, racialized, disabled, and other screendance artists and scholars, when we note that this specialized field often described as "dominated by women" offers close to no possibility to make a living out of screendance production and lacks the cultural capital prestige of other artistic fields such as narrative feature cinema or the visual arts. This tension asks us to reflect on the powers at play in mixed media production, and what recognition means if it occurs in an invisible field. How can we stay attentive to the differences between working in the margins and working as a minority?

Go Lo: Without fetishizing specific technological forms, we see "going lo" as a movement practice that enables stealth, sneaking past barricades, and grounding. We don't forget that even prosumer technologies like cell phones remain out of reach for much of humanity. Likewise, popular culture, so often linked to inertia and the homogenization of affect and thought, remains a potent arena for shared experience, an expansive dancefloor. Screendance as a practice of kinesthetic empathy, also asks how spectatorship is an art of remixing what a body can do.

Hybridize care: As a field, screendance requires critical contributions centring intersectional, feminist, decolonial, and inclusive perspectives, voices that refuse to ignore the political implications of the multiplication of screens and images in our daily lives. While aesthetic concerns and cross-disciplinary endeavours are at the core of this collection, it remains closely tied to the politics of moving bodies on screens. How do we pay attention, as curators, artists, and viewers, to the way our perceptual capacities and visions are socially constructed? How much care are we able to put into retraining how we perceive, visually and kinesthetically, the world around us through images of mediated bodies? We think this effort of reimagining our relationship to moving images can be facilitated by encountering discourses and practices that challenge dominant forms of perception.

We call this screendance *remixed*. Building on the foundational cartographies of the field that attempted to sketch out what was particular to screendance, and without assuming such questions are settled, we make a lateral move to consider the affordances of screendance for reimaging the relations of bodies, technologies, and media today. Across these chapters echo approaches that sample and rework established forms of inquiry, artistic practice, and spectatorial habits, suspending and reorienting gestures into minoritarian forms. Our authors, like the artists they take up, remix the key insights of a field that has troubled the live/recorded distinction to ask new questions about the politics of representation, archives, memory, somatics, aesthetics, and more from the point of view of those for whom *to make is to make life possible*—where lo-tech, DIY and popular culture meet as a demand to make do. This work also speaks back to and with the wider constellation of related fields from which screendance has sought to distinguish itself—cinema and media studies, dance studies, performance studies, cultural studies—bringing new perspectives from the intersections of media, movement, memory, and embodiment to how we navigate our mixed media realities.

Screendance remixed is a propositional form for bodies that are—maybe—as yet unliveable, or that may sometimes feel that way. It is a way of making material both the urgency of desires to move, live, and feel, and the forces that constrain or contain such impulses through the demands and violences of normativity. No wonder then that these works showcase a body at the edge of livability—an avatar whose puppet strings threaten to pull her apart, an erotic bloodbath where "instead of bodies caressing each other, hands now enter places that are not meant to provide safe passage" (see Luce deLire's chapter) and bodies violently suspended between flight and capture. This book has four sections—"Onscenity: Glitching Visions," "Touching Time: Histories Beyond the Binary," "Kinetics and Politics of Ephemerality and Ownership," and "Technology; Technics; Tenderness"—through which authors explore with vigor the potential of remixed ideas and practices.

Our first section, "Onsceneity: Glitching Visions," considers how foundational notions in cinema and media studies (such as the dominant paradigms of visibility, the gaze, and ocularcentrism), widely taken up by performance, decolonial, and feminist studies, are rethought through the radical embodiment of dance media. These essays and interviews explore how screendance's kinesthetic transferences of somatechnical practices between the audiovisual and the body complicate and suspend stereotyped perceptions, shaking up the archive and what stands at the centre of perceptions. How do minoritarian approaches to screendance refuse a logic of loss or mourning that has so often accompanied the transition from the live to onscreen body? Against finality, these chapters explore logics of potential that erupt in the evasions of control. Such methods for making do include obsolete desktop computer and glitchy movement (Bergen), the scene of screendance writing and curating (Hagan), end of the world hospitality (deLire), a cheap trick beyond measure (Thain), and ways of getting high by going lo (Labreque)—attending closely to the materiality of media and the scene of production, to find capacitation in the face of technologies that are often cut to the measure of a body not our own.

Screendance is marked by a history of hungry ghosts where the screen is imagined as a window that re-places the urgency of live, intimate, sweaty, and present bodies in a mediated beyond. Screendance theory is haunted by these forms of half-life and their implications. Bergen's "Let Me in Through Your Window: Dancing with Kate Bush and Hatsune Miku" imagines a more companionable approach to screendance creation that reads the real and the rendered as differences of degree, not kind. Through a DIY-embodied experimentation with avatars and choreographic software, along with the contagious impulses of pop music videos, Bergen charges a feminist reimagining of posthuman network theory with complex desires for relation and collectivity in the many bodies and embodiments that meet in this scene. Bergen's (auto)ethnography reflects on her choreographic "collaboration" with the Vocaloid character and Japanese hologram popstar Hatsune Miku, through MikuMikuDance (MMD), a freeware program where 3D digital models can be choreographed into various dance sequences through the use of motion data and keystroke animation. Amidst the ambient echoes of Kate Bush's "Wuthering Heights" video, Bergen dances her "own" extracted choreography of this work for a YouTube tutorial and a reperformance via the Microsoft Kinect with Miku. She indexes the "unruly bodies" producing the onscreen choreographic image and—more importantly—a glitched image operative beyond normative metrics of correctness, control, and ownership. Tracking how the "ragdoll physics" of the original software (designed to simulate realistic death scenes in video games) become a site for contagious forms of care and confrontation danced with and through the avatar body that is both her and not her own, she asks, what happens "when we stretch the idea of 'unison' to encompass digitally inflected concepts of time and space?" In this "exercise in letting go of control" Bergen outlines "a new methodology for disrupting both the immaterial associations with dance and digital bodies, *and* the sexual and economic exchanges in which MMD is normally embedded."

Bergen concludes by identifying dance as an instance of what Legacy Russell calls glitch activism, an "activism that unfolds with a boundless extravagance."[20] Our next chapter takes up the question of how to disrupt the deathliness of sexual and economic exchanges in favour of such abundance. Luce deLire's "The Queer Art of Hospitality: If You Can Fuck, You Can Dance!" engages in edge play at the threshold of hospitality and hostility—what Derrida terms *hostipitality*—in two queer visions of dance at the end of the world: the music video for Alice Glass's "Love is Violence" and Santiago Tamayo Soler's *Retornar,* a queer Latin American post-apocalyptic fantasy video game. deLire argues that dancing is a practice of hospitality, an "antidote ... to the toxic logic of private property," as the hegemonic form of social relations in Western culture. Away from a logic of mastery, control, and ownership, deLire reads dancing's pop cultural potential as a form of "unlearning" via a social relation we already know. As she describes: "Private property cannot simply be unlearned *conceptually*. It has to be unlearned *corporeally*, as a habit, as a physical disposition, as a way of embodiment." In this way, she speaks to the promises of pop culture that have heartbreakingly informed its fraught position in theories and logics of resistance. Exploring two works of screendance that enact the "freedom to be a host," deLire offers a novel take on questions of agency and embodiment apt for the current moment and for the complex captures of screendance. Dance is in essence a hospitable form, and expanded screendance its mobile home. For deLire, these works embody the "profound DIY quality" of flirtatious dancing as a practice of hospitality, played out on screen as training videos for a post-capitalist imaginary. The circulation of images on screen is not inherently revolutionary, but for deLire, screendance and social media might nonetheless "offer cues that we should observe carefully, appropriate, and possibly de-commodify."

From kinesthetic empathy and the way that dance moves us, to the replayablility of choreographic notation and shared embodiment, dance is made to be shared, and yet is so frequently re-privatized, hoarded, ex- and ap-propriated. Even as digital technologies have wildly accelerated the pace of circulation and exchange of dance media, the persistent recapture of dance's energetic impulses puts the lie to any simple association of dance with freedom. Cara Hagan's "Kinesthetic Empathy as Human Connection in Digital Space," shifts our attention from dance scenes to scenes of screendance—in the classroom and at the festival. Attending to the curation of encounter as an enabling mediation, Hagen explores the question of care through screendance as an antidote to the loneliness and disconnection that too often characterizes digital spaces. If for deLire, flirtatious dancing is a practice for a more hospitable future, for Hagan, a dancer, filmmaker, teacher, author of *Screendance from Film to Festival: Celebration and Curatorial Practices*, and founder of the Movies by Movers film festival, screendance too is a practice of desire as "a bridge between the poles of the algorithmic and the material." Her deeply personal and professionally informed reflection takes up kinesthetic empathy, or mirroring movement as the key to screendance's vitality. Kinesthetic empathy here reveals a layering of epistemologies that foregrounds sensations and affects in the understanding of the discourses that underlie moving images. Centering human experience as an integral part of making and programming screendance, the author presents two experiences that help to demonstrate a premise from the digital poetics community: that no screen space is complete without each other. Hagan looks at these scenes of feeling—a classroom survey of dance students watching screendance, and her program for a screendance festival built around the search for "traces of human residue"—for what they tell her about how and why screendance feels the way it does. As a practice primarily concerned with "imparting embodied experiences to other human beings through the screen," Hagan argues that "screendance makers have an opportunity to make the screen space more human through their pursuits because of the visceral nature of dance-making and the prioritization of non-verbal communication over dialogue as a driver of narrative." While screendance may seem to be a niche or marginal genre, for Hagan its implications are exemplary and urgent in relation to the spatio-temporal dominance of screen-based encounters today.

A non-verbal communication is precisely one of affective forces at work in Alanna Thain's "The Value of a Cheap Trick: Feeling Backwards Across Screendance." Thain offers a speculative fabulation of screendance history rooted in the legacy of the first "special effects" film—the Lumière Brothers' "Demolition of a Wall." In that film she identifies a recompositional impulse of refusal and reanimation located between the human and inhuman, cinematic and kinetic in a shared space of magic, as the ritual of desire. She proposes, through a reading of queer, feminist and minoritarian works from 1895 to 2023 that play with the oldest trick in the book—reversed movement—to consider the politics and aesthetics of reversal not simply as the other side of binaries beholden to dominant norms, but as a practice of making do. Reverse movement is the antithesis of restorative; instead, it is the very capacitation of perception as expanding the world. The special effect of reverse movement, a subgenre of time-travel movies, operates across bodies and technologies to explore the speculative force of utopian thinking, to pry open the question—through the rewind—of how this could be otherwise: the fixity of technology, the politics of movement between dancefloors and across borders, the deathliness of violence and the intimacy of companionability. What is critical in these examples is that the aberrance of backwards movement, its artificial animism, releases capture from the body to reanimate all aspects of the scene, and to shift the certain grounds of causality and control. If it doesn't actualize another world, it points to the conditions for something else to become possible.

This section concludes with Priscilla Guy's interview of Quebecoise artist Manon Labrecque and her practices of self-representation. Through glitching, remixing, distortion, and suspense, Labrecque plays with the edges of hospitality through the risk of self-destruction. "By removing the image, we look inwards. But what's inside, we don't know that in advance!" Like Bergen, Labrecque describes her practice of solo creation in collaboration with autonomous machines, like a camera that rotates on its own. "Afterwards, when I film before this new device, I see things, and that's what guides me into the unknown. We move forward together." Ceding ground to other impulses, she rediscovers a certain freedom of dispossession that is reflected in the extreme gestures and contortions of her own body on screen. Like Hagan, Labrecque is deeply concerned with the question of the human in her practice and situates this as an exchange of energies, or the creation of affects. "You put yourself in a predisposition, even for a task that may seem as technical as editing: a predisposition, a ritual."

Screendance was born at the paradoxical intersection of dance's presumed ephemerality and cinema's art of record. Section Two, "Touching Time: Histories Beyond the Binary," takes up time as material—embodied, valued and archived in time-based media—to rework this founding siting of the field. In particular, personal histories and affective encounters bring the temporal politics of memory and labour into sharper view. Confounding metrics of near and far as ways of measuring time, these chapters focus on the heterochronic potential of screendance as record the encounter with world historical events and the archive (Wong), of one's own work (MacDonald), of history alongside trauma and community (Etienne), with sociocultural norms and institutional (mis)recognitions (Guy), of one's own body and/or family life (Stefan). This section begins with three field notes, so to speak, that rethink the live/mediated binary that shaped many early conversations of screendance, with the more nuanced stakes of lived experience.

Few pop cultural phenomena have shaped the contemporary moment like K-Pop, and in particular the Korean boy band phenomenon, BTS. Yutian Wong's "Canonising BTS: FOMO in the Archives of Digital Convenience" reports back on pedagogical practices during the pandemic, rethinking canonicity and expanding our sense of dance's liveness as she traces her recruitment into the Pandemic Army of BTS. BTS serves as a nexus for thinking about the relation between the live and mediated, understood less as a relation between body and screen, and more as a network of flows, replays, exchanges, and movements. Prompted by the immediate experience of moving dance class online during the pandemic, as well as the ambient atmospherics of social media, Trumpism, anti-Asian racism, toxic masculinity, and xenophobia, BTS provided Wong with a "rabbit hole" of accelerated archiving. K-pop reaction videos serve as the gateway drug for remixing the flattened anxiety of pandemic life: "While the channel is designed to promote K-pop, the videos also serve the pedagogical function of teaching viewers how to deploy music theory to analyze popular music," in a space where "analysis and pleasure co-exist seamlessly." Wong traces a pedagogical method for "getting past the wow factor without losing enthusiasm for the wow"—a different form of liveness. Regarding fannish attention, she writes:

> To pay such close attention that one can identify minute variations in choreographic structure, movement quality, and the difference between improvisational moments and accidents across a decade's worth of different recordings of live performances, demonstrates a level of movement analysis usually associated with academically institutionalized practices such as Laban movement analysis. If a canon is a body of work designated as exemplary of a set of principles that are perceived as essential to training, the acquisition of vocabulary and skill, or the accumulation of knowledge about a subject, then the BTS archive is exceptional in the sheer amount of material (official, unofficial, and re-mixed) that functions as evidence of its own relevance as screendance.

Wong's reflections testify to the value of pedagogical practices of *taking time* as the counterpoint to the idea of digital convenience as simply "easy access." The scramble to find a toehold in the novel screen environments of pandemic teaching requires new ways of navigating the familiar and the novel, of navigating risk. For Wong, the volatility of the BTS archive as a site of attention and engagement generates a canon relevant and responsive to the demands of the contemporary moment. What is valuable is that time is material—from standing in line, to the blankness of hours that blink back into life from screentime.

From a different professional perspective, dancer, screendance artist, and theorist Anna Macdonald also takes up the question of time, specifically the "quality of timelessness that mastery generates, a sense that things are unchangeable" as an operation of colonial and patriarchal discourse within screendance practice. In her chapter "Keeping in Time: Mastery as a Condition of Colonial and Patriarchal Discourse, and the Temporality of Screendance," Macdonald situates herself as a white, middle-aged woman who benefits from both a scholarly and an artistic background and considers the merits of positionality as a tonic for mastery. Macdonald exercises herself at interrogating unexamined habits in her approach to art, movement, and mastery, starting from the premise that screendance has the capacity to generate an affective sense of the body as mutable, temporally situated, and with the potential for change. As both spectator and artist, her practice-led discussion addresses three screendance works that use similar lo-fi methods to intensify an affective sense of the body moving in and through time: Terrance Houle's *Friend or Foe* series (2010–2015), Concha Vidal's *Diving into your absence* (2014), and McDonald's own video, *I made everything* (2019). At stake is the question of how to avoid what Macdonald, citing Douglas Rosenberg, terms screendance's "gravitational pull": "a desire to master the body, the environment, technology, and time." Beginning by tracing how screendance's recapacitation of the body through the expansive possibilities of technology has often generated "a continued emphasis on flawless, hi-res, spectacular movement that transcends the effects of age, capacity and context," Macdonald then turns towards works that offer a different temporality of precarity, foregrounding qualities of "dependency, relatedness and failure." This in itself is not revolutionary, but in reminding us of the body's capacity for change, Macdonald makes an argument for films that participate in a rehearsal for living otherwise. In particular, she showcases the friendliness of lo-fi technologies for generating other affects, more hospitable to bodies frayed at their edges.

The last of this section's field notes is Karla Etienne's "Bill Robinson: Icon of Dignity." Through a double lens of dancer and spectator, Etienne pays homage to the tap-dancing legend perhaps best remembered through his performances of Hollywood's Golden Age cinema. Etienne argues for Robinson's impact and inspiration beyond the debates around stereotyping, complicity, and resistance that surround his legacy, or perhaps precisely *through* these ambiguities. Building on previous analysis of the famous "stair dance" performed by Robinson and Shirley Temple in the movie *The Little Colonel* (1935), Etienne broadens our gaze to embrace the complicated and powerful posture adopted by Robinson. For Etienne, Robinson is a *vision*— both in the film, but also beyond the character Robinson plays—of inspiration and uplift for Black communities and individuals. In this moment, where the attempts to decolonize the gaze are multiplying, Etienne mobilizes her twenty years of practice and research in African and Neo-African traditions to excavate what she argues is the essence of dignity in Robinson's dance, in a poetic and personal response to the film excerpt. In her reparative reading, Etienne uses screendance as a lens that allows for both precision and expansiveness in how we understand the work of emancipation, arguing that the trace dance leaves in our memory has the potential to generate new ontological embodiments through time. Dance's emancipatory force is not that it is synonymous with liberation but how it enacts "struggle not as an ultimate battle, but as a way of being in the world, as an uplifting celebration"—in other words, a practice.

Priscilla Guy's "The Ghost(s) of Alice Guy: Reminiscences of a Feminist Screendance Pioneer" also looks backwards from the perspective of the current moment, in a forensic investigation of the repeated disappearance of Alice Guy from the record of film history, as well as through the recent history of screendance, in which her work and contribution is barely acknowledged. The world's first female filmmaker and a strong candidate as the first person to make fiction films, Alice Guy has only slowly begun to be restored to her rightful place in how we tell the story of film. Alice Guy constantly turned her gaze towards dancing bodies, innovating a language for how to film female and gender non-conforming bodies and desires. While Priscilla Guy argues for understanding Alice Guy as a precursor to screendance and a pioneer in this field, her focus in this chapter also concerns the wider implications of what it takes to make a figure like Alice Guy disappear. Less concerned with simply filling in the blanks, the author shines a light on regimes of knowledge and gatekeeping that predetermine what constitutes the seeable and the sayable. She proposes a feminist methodology that goes beyond supplanting great men with great women, weaving together instead the personal, social, and aesthetics histories of Alice Guy's career, the limitations of the archive and the need for what Donna Haraway terms SF practices of speculation and fabulation to do justice to the past. If Etienne employs a speculative spectatorial practice in view of Robinson, arguing that his onscreen legacy must be supplemented by an appreciation of his wider practice on stage (a scene of greater freedom of expression) that authorizes her spotlight on Robinson's performing body, Priscilla Guy demands that the perhaps never-to-be-determined scope of Alice Guy's impact still inform our sense of her legacy, in order to ask better questions about what we want from film history.

Many of the texts in this section reflect on the constraints and demands of training: as a scholar, dancer, community member, woman, etc. To close this section, Priscilla Guy interviews Sonya Stefan, a Montreal-based screendance practitioner whose experimental DIY videos often explore questions of self-fashioning in dialogue with training practices from exercise videos to family affairs and more. Stefan discusses, amongst other things, touching time through her own affinity for lo-fi technologies: "I'm addicted to older technologies because when I touch film objects, it always feels like there's a history or a presence within that object. It's gone through its own voyage, its own world, and once it arrives into my hands then we continue our duet."

Stefan's trifecta of screendance impulses—energy, agency, and movement—also serve as a bridge to our book's third section, "Kinetics and Politics of Ephemerality and Ownership." This section considers how the archive—personal, somatic, cinematic, state, and aesthetic—can be remobilized through screendance practice. It is here that the at-hand quality of lo-tech production meets the "in the body" memory of popular culture as a replayable archive of inspiration and movement. Beyond the idea of capture and attentiveness to the work of presence, how do screendance works reanimate political and somatic potential through redistributing movement, at times by releasing it from the constraints of ownership, at other times reinforcing novel versions of normativity? As well, how do certain bodies archive—that is to say, make legible and legitimate—certain ideas about race, gender, sexuality, and capacity through their onscreen repetition and rehearsal?

Addie Tsai opens these questions through an exploration of a key thematic they have identified in their wider research into American pop cultural dance on screen, the "white men can't dance trope." This trope both serves as a site where whiteness, unusually, is re-marked in a performance of non-mastery, in this case during the shifting place of white masculinity during the 1980s–2000s. Tsai reads across a series of media movement sequences featuring Tom Hanks, "America's dad"—from his role in the early 80s' cross-dressing sit-com *Bosom Buddies*, his age-swapping comedy *Big* (1988), Carly Rae Jepsen's music video for "I Really Like You" (2015), and various appearances on YouTube—to track how Hanks exemplifies the white man dance trope by deploying an understated and non-threatening display of masculinity. However, even within this framework, Tsai suggests that Hanks complicates his gendered position within white American masculinity and in relationship to the white man dance trope as he sits firmly within it, coming to embody a novel "everyman" embodiment that comfortably appropriates other gendered and racialized qualities without risk. A novel homosociality emerges, "sensitive, vulnerable, and unafraid to show emotion," where white cis mastery is assured through mis- and under-performance.

Part of Tsai's argument is that Hanks's "everyman" is at once in control of itself, even in situations of crossing genders and generations, and yet unthreatened by such forms of "hospitality." Here, dance's cross-body contagions remain a site of control that continue to uphold normative relations of social power. Choreographer and filmmaker Camille Auburtin offers a unique perspective on bodily memory, transmission, and heritage that explore the delicate risks of shared embodiment through gestures of care, completion and companionability. Auburtin revisits her 2020 documentary film, *Les Robes Papillons*, in which the artist used archival footage from her childhood, as well as documentation of her visits to her grandmother Mimi, who suffers from Alzheimer's. A former ballet dancer for some of the most renowned European companies, Mimi struggles to remember faces, events, and places even as her body archived the many dances she learned in her career. Glimpses are revealed, and witnessed by the camera, when these traces are reactivated by music, touch, movement, and sensations. In this chapter, Auburtin steps back to explore her process, the poetic reconstructions of images that tackle the idea of time passing. For her, screendance is a speculative method to accurately evoke intangible phenomena: the devastating and emotional loss of someone's memory, history, or traces. Privileging experimental and DIY approaches to image making and editing, combined with Auburtin's compelling narrative, the film reaffirms the strength of dance and how our bodily memory persists even when everything else seems lost. Auburtin's deeply personal account offers a sensitive voyage through the entanglements of mind and body and questions of how we (re)collect individual and collective memories, beyond historical facts and the documentary archive. Here, movement and images are deeply interconnected. Auburtin's film requires a method of accompaniment to navigate the gaps between herself and her grandmother, between past and present, between what was, what is lost, and what might still be danced. Auburtin does not simply film, but experiments with expanding perception, to make perceptible her grandmother's memories with and through, not simply in spite of, gaps, omissions, and losses. Much like Guy argues for new speculative methods for feminist historiography in screendance that allows for a double vision of both an obscured past and the power moves that continue to block our view, Auburtin's work, in a different register, is a touching across time.

While "ghostcatching" names one of the founding works of digital screendance, it also is a material practice of such unsettled adhesions to time, animating an essential affordance of screendance: its temporal volatility.[21] In "Terrance Houle's Ghost Dancing in A Wagon Burner Landscape," Jessica Jacobson-Konefall unpacks Kainai artist Terrance Houle's lo-fi Super 8 methods for enacting the Kainai (re)creation story through their offerings of the play of light on the screen. Houle's films are a different kind of family movie, one where "artist, family, ancestors, and community meet spectators through the dynamism of electrical energy and presence." His practice aims to, as she describes this, "redraw perceptual boundaries with dance." Jacobson-Konefall traces across Houle's practices, her own embodied response, and the work of what Susan Foster calls "writing dance," a decolonial sensorium of "listening to images" as "a practice of looking beyond what we see and attuning our senses to the other affective frequencies." Houle's works offer an alternative portrait of masculinity as a practice of connection and care, reinscribing the male dancing body within "what Cree-Metis-Saulteaux scholar Jas Morgan calls 'being as kinship.'" If Houle's work is twice the focus of attention in this book, it is because the movement practices proposed by his works are a delicate and powerful medicine.

This section concludes with the medicine of kinship and kindness to oneself, through screendance's potential to unsettled learned histories of trauma and alienation. Priscilla Guy interviews Kijâtai-Alexandra Veillette-Cheezo, a Two-Spirit Annishnaabe artist, who describes filmmaking as a healing practice. In their films *Odehimin* and *Kijâtai*, the artist plays with "making images dance" as a means of redressing gendered and colonial violence, and of self-expression as the capacitation of the body's freedom to move and hold space, beyond dominant beauty canons.

The final section, "Technology; Technics; Tenderness," carries forward the conversation this book has aimed to generate about our technological intimacies in relation to the transformative potential of lo-tech screendance practices and twenty-first-century pop culture's promise of representation. Here, our authors consider how the emphasis on lo-tech approaches requires other relations to technology beyond progress and innovation. How do screendance's other rhythms deploy more quotidian forms of what Bernard Steigler calls "technics and time," attentive to the aesthetic and political therapeutics of media movements?[22] Across four texts working from a post-digital moment, authors consider the relays between analogue and digital movements, technologies and affects. The emphasis on lo-tech approaches requires other relations to technology, beyond progress and innovation.

Emilie Morin and Ryan Clayton propose a tender incursion into their creative process in their chapter "From_Ryan Clayton To_Emilie Morin." The topic under discussion is *SkypeDuet*, their collaborative live and mediated performance using the conversational software of Skype as an artistic medium: both artists use props, filters, and green-screen effects in a conceptual and at times abstract dialogue of movements, colours, and words. One performs in front of a live audience while the other appears onscreen, performing remotely before their computer. Reevaluating this work from a distance—from each other but also from the moment of performance itself—the two artists continue their exploration of technological mediation in their conversation, as the interface of email exchange remediates their Skype-based performance. While most of their collaboration happens online, Morin and Clayton successfully centre care and tenderness in their collaboration, notably through the inclusion of personal anecdotes, everyday challenges, etc. While the way they envision dance in their collaboration is fully imbricated in technological softwares—from its creation to its performance, and even through its postmortem—kindness drives their creative process. Technology is reimagined not as oppositional to connection nor as a transparent facilitator, but as available for emotional modulation. The duet moves together to invent a space that fluidly crosses physical and virtual worlds, offering a reality that gently binds together bodies, discourses and spaces that don't necessarily belong to each other, but make kin.[23]

Similarly, the duet composed of artist and researcher Anatoli Vlassov and his daughter in the playful work *Phoné-Scopie* also proposes this combination of domestic and commercial technology with movement creation to disrupt expectations of high-tech tools: both *SkypeDuet* and *Phoné-Scopie* interfere in the conventional use of cameras, computers or software. In a dance designed like a game, Vlassov and his daughter both wear GoPro cameras on their foreheads and start by filming each other, face to face.

When the two performers eventually separate to take their own journey, one appears in the frame of the other from a distance, or the same spaces are filmed from different angles by the two cameras, a split-screen presentation enabling simultaneity. Drawing on this intergenerational collaborative work, Vlassov's chapter "Filming Consciousness: Between Phonesia and Talking Camera—Organological Cinema" searches for a vision of moving images that belongs to the body and its sensation, taking place in, on, and around the body, as an extension of human consciousness. Here again, tenderness— notably in the playful exchange between Vlassov and his daughter—functions as a generative counterpoint to normative modes of seeing and the commodification of images. *SkypeDuet* and *Phoné-Scopie* use technology for alternate purposes, unafraid of glitches and errors and offering a new, lo-tech, sophistication; a different technique that requires training and strategies, notably strategies to undo the expected use of said technology.

Claudia Kappenberg's "The Matter of Analogue Media Technologies in Screendance: Post Martin Heidegger and Post Hito Steyerl" also poses the question of progress and technology, but through the lens of analogue devices as springboards to reflect our capacity to react to social and environmental changes in a direct manner. While dance and the human body are approached in this book as lo-tech methods and tools to undo preconceived visions of the world, Kappenberg revisits Heidegger's take on technology as a way to engage Steyerl's concept of the "poor image" and to think technology through its very deterioration, that is, through its potential for failure and surprising outcomes. Kappenberg suggests that "screendance technotopia can be a sphere in which technology is dance and dance is technology, and perhaps we may even invent new analogue technologies that bring us back to the matter of matter." Remixing discourses from the twentieth century and engaging with current issues in the digital world of art, Kappenberg proposes an incursion into some of the most pressing challenges screendance practitioners face, while at the same time taking a distance from the production aspects of the field by positioning herself through philosophical interrogations.

We conclude with Alanna Thain's interview of Montreal-based artist Nadège Grebmaier-Forget. Her practice has long confounded disciplinary boundaries but has consistently remained concerned with the relations of bodies and screens, the intimacies of mediation, affect as movement, and the radical plasticity of the body itself. Tracing a long legacy of feminist work that sees the metaphor of the screen as mirror as a space to recompose the self, her work makes provocative demands on spectators to abandon their own passivity, animating and activating a dynamic of vulnerability and control. Often using lo-tech affordances such as live streaming and Skype, Grebmeier Forget's work is perfectly adapted to the ecosystem composed of online archives of the self, social media, and the makeover as a making do.

Across these works is a rich investment in the potential of screendance in and for twenty-first century concerns. Rooted in a multiplicity of practices and perspectives—conceptual, pragmatic, pedagogical, and spectatorial—*Lo: Tech: Pop: Cult: Screendance Remixed* explores the question: how do lo-tech approaches and popular culture create a zone of free play that opens new directions in screendance research?

Notes

1. Ryan Clayton and Emilie Morin, "Exhibition Description," Concordia University, https://www.concordia.ca/finearts/facilities/fofa-gallery/exhibitions/2023/ryan-clayton-emilie-morin.html.
2. Peter Sloterdijk, cited and translated in Christian Borch, "Organizational Atmospheres: Foam, Affect and Architecture," *Organization* 17:2 (2009), 223–241, 226.
3. Amélie Wong Merseau, "Pas de deux," Concordia University, https://www.concordia.ca/finearts/facilities/fofa-gallery/exhibitions/2023/ryan-clayton-emilie-morin.html. See also Morin and Clayton's chapter reflecting on their own collaborative work with Skype in this collection.
4. Margot Norton, "Staying with the Tension," in *Bárbara Wagner and Benjamin De Burca: Five Times Brazil*, eds. Margot Norton and Bernardo Mosquiera (New York: New York Museum, 2022), 13; *Faz Que Vai* [*Set To Go*], directed by Bárbara Wagner and Benjamin de Burca (2015).
5. Norton, "Staying with the Tension," 13.
6. Leonel Brum, "Brazilian Videodance: A Possible Mapping," in *The Oxford Handbook of Screendance Studies*, ed. Douglas Rosenberg (Oxford University Press, 2016), 105–24.
7. Norton, "Staying with the Tension," 17.
8. Norton, "Staying with the Tension," 17.
9. These include "dance for the camera," "videodance," "screen choreography," "camera choreography," "screendance," etc.
10. Katrina McPherson, *Making Video Dance*, 2nd ed. (New York and Oxon: Routledge, 2019).
11. Noël Carroll, *Philosophy and the Moving Image* (Oxford: Oxford University Press, 2021).
12. International Dance and Technology Conference, 1999, Arizona State University, USA.
13. Carroll, *Philosophy and the Moving Image*, 291.
14. McPherson, *A Space of Time: The Evolution of a Screendance Practice*, PhD diss., Edinburgh Napier University, 2023.
15. Dogma95 was written in Denmark in 1995 by several Danish filmmakers, including Lars Von Trier and Thomas Vinterberg. In the wake of new digital technologies, it proposed new rules (often immediately broken by the filmmakers) based on traditional cinematographic values of story, acting, and themes, and prioritizing low budget film productions.
16. Katrina McPherson and Simon Fildes, *Opensource* [videodance] (Lulu Publishing, 2007).
17. Ladys Gonzales et al., "How to film the moving body in an hostile world," *Comunidades Híbridas*, accessed June 17, 2023, http://comunidadeshibridas.weebly.com/manifiesto-en.html.
18. Donna Jeanne Haraway, *Staying with the Trouble: Making Kin in the Chthulucene* (Durham: Duke University Press, 2016), 36.

19 Charlotte Dronier, "Le balado *Camera lucida*," L'Observatoire du cinéma au Québec, accessed June 17, 2023, https://ocq.umontreal.ca/le-balado-camera-lucida/.
20 Legacy Russell, *Glitch Feminism: A Manifesto* (London: Verso, 2020), 55.
21 *Ghostcatching*, directed by Paul Kaiser and Shelley Eshkar, choreographed by Bill T. Jones (San Francisco, CA: Riverbed Media, 1999).
22 Bernard Stiegler, *Technics and Time 1: the Fault of Epimetheus* (Stanford, CA: Stanford University Press, 2022).
23 Harraway, *Staying with the Trouble*.

Bibliography

Brum, Leonel. "Brazilian Videodance: A Possible Mapping." In *The Oxford Handbook of Screendance Studies*, edited by Douglas Rosenberg, 105–124. Oxford: Oxford University Press, 2016.

Carroll, Noël. *Philosophy and the Moving Image*. Oxford: Oxford University Press, 2021.

Clayton, Ryan, and Emilie Morin. "Exhibition Description." Concordia University. https://www.concordia.ca/finearts/facilities/fofa-gallery/exhibitions/2023/ryan-clayton-emilie-morin.html.

Dronier, Charlotte. "Le balado Camera lucida." L'Observatoire du cinéma au Québec. https://ocq.umontreal.ca/le-balado-camera-lucida/.

Eshkar, Shelley and Paul Kaiser, *Ghostcatching*. Choreographed by Bill T. Jones. San Francisco, CA: Riverbed Media, 1999.

Gonzales, Ladys, Priscilla Guy, Emilie Morin, Camille Auburtin, Jean-Baptiste Fave, Benito González, Rocío Becerril Porras, Yolanda M. Guadarrama, Ximena Monroy, Laura Ríos, Paulina Ruiz Carballido, Alfredo Salomón, and Laura Vera. "How to film the moving body in an hostile world." Comunidades Híbridas. http://comunidadeshibridas.weebly.com/manifiesto-en.html.

Haraway, Donna Jeanne. *Staying with the Trouble: Making Kin in the Chthulucene*. Durham: Duke University Press, 2016.

McPherson, Katrina. "A Space of Time: The Evolution of a Screendance Practice." PhD dissertation. Edinburgh Napier University. 2023.

McPherson, Katrina. *Making Video Dance*. 2nd ed. New York and Oxon: Routledge, 2019.

McPherson, Katrina, and Simon Fildes. *Opensource* [videodance]. Lulu Publishing, 2007.

Merseau, Amélie Wong. "Pas de deux." Concordia University. https://www.concordia.ca/finearts/facilities/fofa-gallery/exhibitions/2023/ryan-clayton-emilie-morin.html.

Norton, Margot. "Staying with the Tension." In *Bárbara Wagner and Benjamin De Burca: Five Times Brazil*, edited by Margot Norton and Bernardo Mosquiera. New York: New Museum, 2022.

Russell, Legacy. *Glitch Feminism: A Manifesto*. London: Verso, 2020.

Stiegler, Bernard. *Technics and Time 1: the Fault of Epimetheus*. Stanford, CA: Stanford University Press, 2022.

Wagner, Bárbara, and Benjamin de Burca, dirs. *Faz Que Vai [Set To Go]*, 2015.

PART I
Onsceneity: Glitching Visions

1

"LET ME IN THROUGH YOUR WINDOW"

Dancing with Kate Bush and Hatsune Miku

Hilary Bergen

Introduction: Dancing with/in the Assemblage[1]

I am standing in a production suite at Concordia University's Milieux Institute, in front of a large computer monitor propped up on a low desk, performing the choreography for Kate Bush's iconic song, "Wuthering Heights." The cement floor is cold and hard underfoot—not ideal for dancing—and a white scrim behind me curves where it meets the floor, to give the appearance of a non-background: a vacuum-like space. I am wearing black tights and a leotard so that the Microsoft Xbox 360 Kinect, which is balanced on another table just under the computer monitor, can better recognize my body and read my movements (see Figure 3.1).

The room fills with a deep, powerful hum as the heavy Alienware computer—the only one at Milieux outfitted with Windows 7, which is required to run the Kinect—powers on. The computer's black aeration flaps that resemble aquatic gills flare open as the sound gets louder, funneling hot machine breath into the room. The computer is huge and feels ancient and, in order to transport it to the production suite, my collaborator Michael Li and I had to heft it onto a metal dolly and steer it carefully through hallways and into elevators. It seems fitting that I, a dancer, should be collaborating with such an enormous and outdated machine; the awkwardness of the computer is a good metaphor for my own discomfort at entering this endeavour with subpar tech literacy—after all, it is common for dancers to acquire access to certain technologies only once they are somewhat obsolete. Once the computer powers on, we navigate to the interface for a freeware choreographic program called MikuMikuDance (MMD),[2] the tool I am relying on to carry out this dance experiment. The monitor displays a two-dimensional cartoon

DOI: 10.4324/9781003335887-3

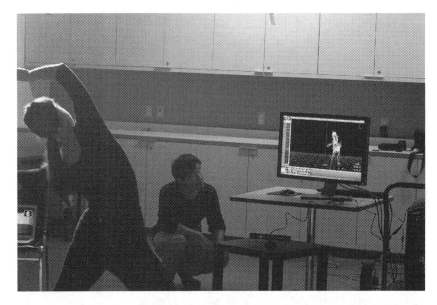

FIGURE 1.1 Hilary Bergen dances the choreography for Kate Bush's "Wuthering Heights," facing the Alienware computer, the Microsoft Xbox 360 Kinect, and a YouTube tutorial video. Technician Michael Li watches
Source: Photograph by Darren Wershler, Concordia University, 2016.

girl standing against a grid behind which recedes a black void. A series of dots mark the joints of her body and her facial features, and these points are tethered by neon lines to various points on the grid. Like a reverse marionette, her body is controlled not from above, but from below, where the bright threads attach her to the ground. Next to the monitor, my Mac laptop rests open on a plastic office chair. It displays a YouTube video tutorial for the choreography for Kate Bush's song "Wuthering Heights."[3] This video is paused, suspending the dancer on screen in mid-twirl. The dancer on screen is also me.

I am initiated into this gathering of screens and apparatuses as I begin to perform the choreography for "Wuthering Heights." I glance periodically at *myself* in the YouTube instructional video in order to dance the sequence as accurately as possible, aware of the uncanny interplay between multiple bodies, images, and selves. Bush's original video and dance is the ghostly "origin" for the project, yet it is already receding into the network of videos and screens imbricated in the project's assemblage; my immediate interface here is the instructional video, which was released in preparation for an international yearly flash mob called "The Most Wuthering Heights Day Ever"—an event I helped organize in 2016 for Montréal participants. In order to make the dance legible to participants with little-to-no dance training, I adapted Bush's dance from her music video, stripping away the original video's multiple cuts and changes of scale and flattening the choreography into a single-take, front-facing version, shot in the same studio I am currently dancing in. As I stand against the same empty scrim, wearing similar tight black clothes to those I wore in the video, my body begins to trace the steps I have rehearsed so many times before. This time, the idea is to feed the choreography to the animated dancer in MMD, via the Microsoft Kinect. The little avatar on screen responds immediately to my dancing, but only by jerking spasmodically. She cannot mirror me (she is not naturally mimetic), and it seems as though her limbs are tied down to the ground.

Michael and I quickly realize that the Kinect works better with less light. When we turn off the spotlights in the production suite, my gestures are more legible to the camera. Zeynep Gunduz writes about motion capture and dance, stating that "even the most sophisticated technologies lack the complexity of the human body and require certain adaptations from the dancer [to] help the computer-based system 'recognize' the dancer," such as "by accentuating extremities of the body."[4] Likewise, I find myself performing Bush's dance moves more "loudly" than is correct in order to have the Kinect read me the way I want it to. I throw my arms up into an exaggerated V, and I resist letting my limbs swing and fall with gravity, instead holding the shape of a high kick one second longer. It feels as though my body is being shaped, mechanized even, by the assemblage I am dancing within. And yet, this also gives me pause to reflect upon the difference between what feels mechanized and what feels "natural" in my dancing body. Why does the force of gravity on my body feel more natural or neutral than the influence of the Kinect? Perhaps the discomfort of dancing with the Kinect comes from my having to actively resist the habitual body gestures (or release with gravity) that years of repeated dance technique has instilled in me. Because its repetition has made it quotidian for me, that mechanized technique feels neutral and even *natural*, and yet the durational repetition has also turned my body machinic, in a sense. I am like a choreographic interface, waiting to receive direction and perform gesture in the way I have been programmed to, which feels natural to me. This tension in my own body draws technique and technology together, highlighting the porous relationship between humans and machines, and calling preconceived notions of human agency into question. In this way, my project proposes dance as a crucial intervention into discourses of *posthumanism* and asks what a posthuman dance choreography might look like, given the power dynamic inherent to choreographic practices. In this chapter, I integrate the idea of the posthuman network (most commonly popularized by Bruno Latour's Actor Network Theory)[5] into a discussion of collectivity and *relationality*, through the idea of many "bodies" (human and non-human) that dance together and influence one another, kinetically, affectively, and philosophically.

Mine is but one of the many bodies involved in this dance experiment, and I myself am more than one. Other bodies include:

- The corporeal presence of Kate Bush, who was eighteen when she wrote "Wuthering Heights," and collaborated on the choreography for the accompanying music video.[6]
- The filmic presence of Kate Bush, whose music video I have watched repeatedly, to learn her dance.[7]
- My dancing body, which is technically trained (in Limon-influenced contemporary dance technique) and has rehearsed Kate Bush's choreography countless times.
- My body in the YouTube tutorial, which has now been viewed over 176,000 times.[8]
- The manipulatable digital avatar body displayed on the computer monitor against the grid in MMD.
- The "hologrammatic" body of Hatsune Miku—the Japanese popstar who is choreographed via MMD and regularly tours the world performing a live stage show.[9]
- The bodies of the fans at Miku's show, many of whom help create her choreography using MMD.
- The clunky, loud "body" of the Alienware computer.
- The sensing body of the Kinect.
- The body of Michael Li: my technician and collaborator/MMD expert.
- The many other bodies that have inhabited and will inhabit Kate Bush's choreography, especially at the international yearly event, the "Most Wuthering Heights Day Ever," where thousands of fans come together to dance in red dresses, *en masse*.[10]

It was precisely in order to engage with this multi-bodied swarm that I enacted this dance translation project, bringing Bush and Miku—two influential yet disparate pop stars—to meet my own dancing body in a constellation of techniques and technologies. Even with this expanded notion of "body," my list does not encapsulate all of the agents, or active processes, that contribute to this assemblage.[11] In an exchange of gestures that travels across space and time via screens, code, algorithmic media, technical training, and biometric data, my dance translation project explores the ways in which dance movement passes between bodies, both virtual and organic, in order to disperse agency often attributed to the human body alone. Choreography is one mode of relation between the dancing bodies in my project, and although Bush's choregraphed dance is the basis of translation here, mine is also an experiment that asks what choreographic transmission might look like outside of human control.

By allowing my datafied gestures to dance through and *with* Miku's avatar, thereby relinquishing the traditional power of the choreographer who positions and directs dancing bodies with precision, I embrace the lively, glitchy, posthuman output of the choreographic translation. My project uses an embodied, situated method and a DIY approach to attend to the porous nature of bodies—filmic, digital, and organic—and the constant imbrication of humans with non-human objects, processes, and forms. Dancing bodies are just one part of a posthuman assemblage of performative actants, like lights, costuming, and music. In this case, the dance assemblage expands to include avatars, computer programs, and instruments of digital capture. Choreography, whose etymology references both the act of writing and the Greek, *khoreia*, meaning to "dance in unison," is often seen as a human endeavour, but what if it was the non-human technology of the Kinect or the MMD interface that was responsible for the choreography at least in part, or collaboratively? What is the effect of *khoreia* when the unison dance is enacted between my own, human, body and Miku's avatar, or when we stretch the idea of "unison" to encompass digitally inflected concepts of time and space? How might this type of choreography be understood not just as a method of writing, organizing, and controlling bodies, but as an exercise in letting go of control?

Miku: The Modular Girl-Image

In order to start exploring this project's complex, posthuman network, we might consider, in greater detail, the body of Hatsune Miku (初音 ミク): a virtual Japanese pop star with turquoise pigtails, saucer eyes, and long, spidery limbs. Created by Crypton Future Media in 2007, she regularly tours the world as a 3D image, performing on stage to sold-out shows. Miku is marketed as a hologram, but in reality, her body is not a laser-projected, 3D clone but a video cast onto a curved screen.[12] She is described as 5'2", 92 pounds, and sixteen years old. As a virtual star, she will never age.[13] This constant youth is reminiscent of Bush's music video, which freezes her in teenage-hood, and the way that video capture in general stalls time and mortality, but Miku—because her body has the capacity to be animated and perform live—is truly forever young. Miku may have been invented by Crypton, but her persona is maintained through collaborative engagement by her fans, who work to "produce content with the Hatsune Miku VOCALOID or anime character … compose and upload songs, animate music videos and produce drawings" as well as "participate in dialogues … submit reviews and rate [content], and join communities such as fan sites and chat forums."[14] The content produced by these fan-collaborators—such as videos created with MMD—are regularly uploaded to websites like Nico Nico Dōga, Japan's version of YouTube, where they are disseminated to other fans and even entered into competitions to animate Miku in her live performances.[15]

Crypton presents Miku as a girl, but she is actually a product: a plug-in for a music synthesizer software called Vocaloid, made by Yamaha in 2004. Miku's voice is a digital modulation of the voice of Japanese voice actress Saki Fujita, and her songs, like her choreography, are modular: composed from Vocaloid database of instruments, melodies, vocal tones, and lyrics. This means that a recording of Fujita's voice has been broken into individual phonemes—or "digitized separable and transportable fragments of recorded voice"—that can be concatenated by the Vocaloid user into unique melodic, rhythmic, and syntactic phrases.[16] The technology gives creators access to a professional singer without having to pay one, and it also affords composers of Miku's songs greater control over her vocal output, without the obstacles an organic singer might present. Fujita's voice once emanated from a live human body, and now it exists timelessly in the Vocaloid database as a series of parts—which when put together sound synthetic and very high in pitch, giving the voice an uncanny, doll-like quality.[17] I, too, have become modular as I participate in this choreographic translation and my danced gestures mobilize Miku's avatar, limb by limb. Fujita and I both contribute to Miku's essentially collaged identity, which is compiled of pieces drawn together from across a web of codes, texts, images, and platforms. Given that her movements and songs are user-generated by a large collective of fans, some view Miku as a "nonorganic embodiment of an organic subjectivity."[18] This is true to the extent that Miku is a digital assemblage who contains traces of human bodies and collective activity, and her hologrammatic presence acts as a nexus of human fantasies about ownership, control, femininity, and the pliable body. Miku has no organic body, yet her modifiable image reinforces unrealistic expectations of suppliant plasticity that impact the human bodies of girls and women. As I dance facing Miku's avatar, I am well aware of the cartoonish beauty standards she reinforces (her extremely long legs, her very slim waist), and I experience the discomfort of controlling such a body when I manipulate her gestures later, in the MMD choreographic interface, causing her body to contort, albeit painlessly.

I first learned about MMD through my conversations with Mike Li at Concordia's Technoculture Arts and Games Lab (TAG). Mike is something of an expert in MMD, having spent hours honing his skills in creating choreographies and videos in the program. Originally created by HiguchiM (Garnek), MMD is a Japanese freeware animation program that enables users to create music videos for Hatsune Miku by maneuvering, posing and choreographing 3D models—many of them resembling Miku herself—using digital puppetry and the application of motion data. MMD users can customize backgrounds, add sound and music with the Vocaloid voice bank, and manipulate every one of the thirty or more "bones" in the figure's body (see Figure 3.2). The model's facial expressions can also be altered, and her hairstyle and clothing are highly customizable. For our project, we found a red kimono with a black sash to approximate Bush's famous red dress (see Figure 3.3).[19]

MMD uses the Bullet physics engine to simulate the movement of the figure's hair and costume. It also mimics "soft body dynamics" through "ragdoll simulation," in which the animated body is made up of multiple rigid objects tethered to the body's core, so that in instances of falling and kinetic gesture, the movement looks more organic or human.[20] Ragdoll physics was originally developed to simulate realistic death scenes in video games by mimicking body kinetics associated with dying or collapsing. I find the link between dying and dancing interesting here: video game death sequences, like dance scenes on screen, are a kind of spectacle that invites the gaze and solicits affective response; in both cases, the pain of the body (through violent death or the physical intensity of dance) is rendered spectacular and becomes a kind of performance. And because Miku's immortality is innately linked to her elastic physical form (performed through ragdoll physics)—it is ironically the impossibility of her death that also imparts a sense that her body is alive.[21]

As real as she is to her fans, Miku is first and foremost an image. She is a digital rendering in humanoid form, referred to as a "*moe* anthropomorph" on her Wikipedia page.[22] According to Patrick W. Galbraith, *moe* is a Japanese slang word that indicates a "response to fantasy characters," primarily based on "two dimensional images."[23] Galbraith writes that "*moe* characters

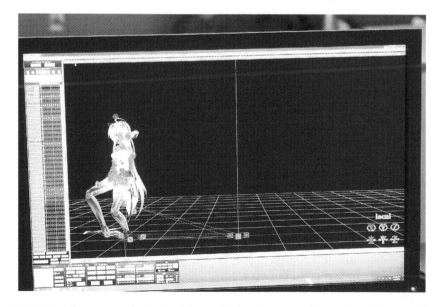

FIGURE 1.2 Computer monitor with MMD in choreography mode, with avatar's "bones" highlighted
Source: Photograph by Hilary Bergen, 2016.

FIGURE 1.3 MMD in video capture mode, with avatar in red kimono standing in an urban green space setting
Source: Photograph by Hilary Bergen, 2016.

are fantasy forms animated by fluid desires, and as such cannot easily be divided into static categories."[24] He explains that fans of anime and manga "access *moe* in what they refer to as pure fantasy (*junsui na fantajii*), or characters and relationships removed from context, emptied of depth and positioned outside reality."[25] Galbraith explains that the desire to nurture *moe* characters is extremely common among fans: "The *moe* target is dependent on us for security (a child, etc.) or won't betray us (a maid, etc.). Or we are raising it (like a pet) [sic]."[26] Because her body is made of manipulatable data, Miku is not just two-dimensional or static, but what Jørgensen et al. define as an "uncertain image": one that is desired, and which itself desires.[27] Miku presents a dream of fluidity and virtual potential for her creator-fans, who can project their own desires onto her, and act them out through her plastic form. As a fantasy, Miku can be anything to anyone, but in reality, she is limited by (and to) her visual identity as a sexualized teenage girl. This limitation in turn tends to dictate her role as a "pet" or "child" under the control of her fans—a control that is justified by fans as a kind of "nurturing" or paternal orientation. Miku is given an identity, lyrics that read like diary entries, and an overall semblance of interiority, and yet she has no agency—no control over her image whatsoever. As I interacted with Miku's image in my own experimentations with MMD, I was struck by how the practice of dance choreography can mirror this dynamic. The traditional power imbalance between choreographer and dancer is magnified in the space of the choreographic interface, and upon the digital body of the teenage girl.

In *Girlhood and the Plastic Image* (2014), Heather Warren-Crow references female characters like Alice in Wonderland, Tinker Bell, and German theorist Siegfried Kracauer's Tiller Girls to show how their compulsively transforming bodies reflect "key attributes of digital images: malleability, transmediation and instability."[28] Warren-Crow's analysis demonstrates the influence of representational frameworks upon certain governing ideologies about girlhood, namely how "nothingness and its corollaries, openness and potentiality, have become attached to girls and images in the first place."[29] Dance plays a pivotal role here, in relation to Miku, because like digital media and the figure of the (*moe*) girl, *dance* is also often associated with malleability and the almost-impossible body. Traditional Western definitions of ballet and early modern dance commonly align with fantasies of virtuosity and superhuman weightlessness; in *Time and the Dancing Image* (1988), American dance historian Deborah Jowitt writes of the airy, supernatural quality prized by classical dance in the romantic era where "insubstantiality [was] close to godliness."[30] Yet the power to be ethereal (or perform ethereality) is rarely attributed to the *skill* of the dancer who has trained their body to do so. Dance is often seen as a quality that can be lifted off the body, meaning it can move between and reside fleetingly in other bodies—or that dance does not necessarily need a concrete, material body to exist. This associates dance, like the digital image, with immateriality. And so it becomes clear that Miku's persona is manipulatable in a number of ways: as a digital dancer with virtuosic plasticity; as a teenage girl; as a cute, *moe* entity, whose fans remove her from reality, constructing her as a vessel for overdetermined fantasies about trust and stewardship; and as a dancer with a biometrically-determined interface that facilitates her fans' power over her body, making her puppet-like. But I want to suggest that her lively, dancing body is not just material to be choreographed, but also holds a kind of kinetic potential or agency that challenges the very biometric process that governs her.

Choreography as Control

MMD is primarily used by Miku's fans to choreograph synchronized dance sequences intended for her music videos and live shows. Fans enter their choreographies into the MMD Cup, a bi-yearly competition that determines which dances Miku will perform, and where fans compete to win exclusive models for use in future MMD videos. These fan-made videos—generally running up to three minutes in length—usually require a week or two of editing within the MMD spreadsheet. Given that MMD is free, open-source, and available for all to use, it presents a democratic, collective approach to technological creativity. As Laurel Halo and Mari Matsutoya write, Miku "is both the receptive and reflective vessel of her fans; a depository for the emotions, ambitions and talents of would-be pop songwriters, producers and recording artists; a voice singing songs written by the masses, for the masses."[31] The interactive project of MMD, in which fans carry out an impressive "compromise between creativity and intellectual property, between preventing piracy and promoting creative endeavors," can conceal the power dynamic that MMD reinforces, in which a teenage girl dancer (albeit in image form) is like a puppet, trapped within a grid of control, who must obey the choreography her fans impose upon her.[32] Miku's novel existence is clearly profitable, given that she generated more than 10 billion yen (or approximately US $120.28 million) in the first five years after her release.[33] However, questions around *who* profits from Miku are rarely raised. As Miku is licensed under creative commons,[34] it is possible for Crypton to benefit financially from the unpaid labour of her fans.[35] Miku is unabashedly branded as a teenage girl (an identity that serves to excuse her symbolic exploitation), and yet she is often defined not as a girl but as a "socially networked phenomenon" who is produced through "endless circulations of different modes of participation and communication" by her "ever-increasing fan base."[36] She has, therefore, become an interesting case study for examining the complex relationship between digital bodies, gender biometrics, ownership, and profit.

Certainly, Miku herself does not benefit financially. Even Miku's fan-invented lyrics often self-consciously express discomfort and anxiety at her lack of control over her own digital body, referencing the powerful "masters" who create her songs and choreographies. In one of Miku's live performances from 2015, the stage features a large scrim lit with a projection of a computer screen. The screen displays a loading icon for Vocaloid software, and a black-and-white Miku appears, pressing her palms to the screen, as if she is trapped within the computer. She picks up an antique hammer and begins to swing at the screen, which eventually "breaks," signified by the sound of shattering glass as Miku, freed from the screen, tumbles out of the computer onto the stage, becoming three-dimensional and colourized as she does. This hyperreal design by Crypton not only facilitates Miku's ability to move between virtual realms, but also betrays the irony of the fact that Miku (much like most celebrities) will never escape life as a screened entity.

My engagement with MMD establishes a new methodology for disrupting both the immaterial associations with dance and digital bodies *and* the sexual and economic exchanges in which MMD is normally embedded. The kind of project I have created in MMD is rare. People do not tend to use this software experimentally, nor is it common to use the Kinect or other mo-cap systems to mine body motion for MMD choreography. Michael and I attempted to use MMD's built-in program for translating my motion data to the model's body, but it was stubborn and slow, so we settled on a lesser-known application called MikuMikuCapture (MMC), which Michael found after some searching. That this application was so difficult to find suggests that, generally, people are not as interested in using it, or perhaps that the app is used for dancing (or exercise), but not for choreographing. Rather, MMD users often choreograph Miku by copy-pasting dance sequence data from other, pre-existing projects, focusing most of their time on costuming, sets, camera angles and fine-tuning the execution of their dancers. Generally, fans who make videos using MMD want to do well in the video contests, earn votes, and win bragging rights, but we knew that our video would never impress in these types of contests. Instead, I was interested in how, using the Kinect, Miku's body became mobilized by my own gestural input, turning her from a symbolic image, or an icon, into an indexical body. Rather than conceiving the indexical here as linear or leading back to *one* original source body that "inscribes the sign at a specific moment of time," I wanted to map out the *many* bodies that leave "a mark or trace of [their] physical [or virtual] presence," thereby layering gesture and multiplicity through time and space.[37] This multiplicity index is further textured in my project through the appearance of the glitch, a consequence of using rudimentary mocap technology and little-to-no editing to polish the choreography in my project. The glitch, which Dutch artist Rosa Menkman calls an "unstable process" of "shock," is the moment where the assemblage asserts its nonhuman agency.[38] The glitches in the dance are, for me, cracks in the "window" or screen behind which Miku dances—a window that looks in on the assemblage of gender, technology and viral, monetized social media that comprise this form of dance.

Thousands of Kates: Screen / Window / Threshold

I chose the choreography for Kate Bush's "Wuthering Heights" as my input for the MikuMiku project precisely because it has already passed through so many bodies over time and space and reflects the posthuman politics of relational collectivity that I wished to explore. Written by Bush at just eighteen years of age, "Wuthering Heights" was her breakout single on her debut album, *The Kick Inside* (EMI Records),[39] which went on to top the UK charts for four weeks. It remains her most successful song. Novelist David Mitchell remembers when the song was released in January 1979. He recounts how "the following morning all the girls at my small rural primary school were dancing around the yard like twenty Kate Bushes, ... trailing half-remembered lyrics and clouds of frosted breath."[40] The song's iconic status and imitability persist today largely thanks to screen-based social media and the popular show, *Stranger Things*, which featured another of Bush's most charted songs (her 1985 single "Running up that Hill") on season 4, episode 4.[41] Every summer for the last five years, an international event called "The Most Wuthering Heights Day Ever" brings together thousands of international participants to re-produce the choreography of "Wuthering Heights" as a group number, in their respective cities. As the organizer of the Montréal edition of this event in 2016, I danced in the instructional video posted to YouTube. Thousands of participants have since learned the dance using my body as a guide, mirroring my movements with theirs, just as I learned by watching Kate Bush on my laptop screen. In translating the choreography from screen to my body, I extracted only Bush's body gestures (not the camera angles, cuts, and zooms), making the choreography transferrable from one body to another, and inserting my own body (and interpretation of the dance) into the network as I did so. The ritual of acquiring gesture or choreography by way of screen engagement is more commonplace today, where YouTube videos are often used, in the words of Thomas DeFrantz, as "video games that require participation" and where communities form around fan discourses within the comments sections of these videos.[42] Like Miku's persona, Bush's song is viewed as a kind of collaborative hub—a center for communal activity that occurs across screens and bodies. My dance translation project adds another layer to this collectivity, asking Miku and Bush to dance together, through and with me.

Miku and Bush seem to be linked, symbolically and gesturally, through their choreography and surrounding narratives. The lyrics and music video for Bush's "Wuthering Heights" tie her to discourses of nature, spectral Gothic themes, and bodies haunted by madness. Similarly, Miku, who is immortal and whose many forms haunt her present iteration, has been referred to by Ken McLeod as a "holographic ghost," one who is virtually trapped in between digital and material worlds.[43] During the choreography for the chorus of "Wuthering Heights," Bush pushes the palms of her hands against an invisible pane of glass as she sings, "Let me in at your window." This is a key gesture in the choreography, and Bush's lyrics—a reference to Brontë's Gothic novel,[44] in which Heathcliff begs Cathy's ghost to stay when there is no evidence she exists—gives agency to the ghost and sets up the window as a threshold between the world of the living and the world of the dead.[45] Miku coincidentally performs a similar gesture in her live show when she "breaks" into 3D space, and in a song created for her 2015 live show—a mashup of Gumi's "Echo" and Miku's "Hibikase"—when she holds her palms up against the screen of the computer, expressing her despair at being unable to break through and fully inhabit the space of the living. Miku and Bush are twinned in their stance, pressing against the invisible pane. They both pass through this choreographic pose, which evokes entrapment and supplication in addition to ghostly agency. This gestural relation between these bodies, which have never technically occupied the same space, is made possible through and in the space of my dancing body, and through the mediating space of the screen (Figure 3.4).

"Let Me in Through Your Window" 37

FIGURE 1.4 Four of the bodies involved in this dance translation perform the gesture of pressing palms to window: Myself, in a still from the video tutorial for Bush's choreography posted to YouTube (upper left); Miku's avatar performing Bush's choreography via my motion data fed into MMD (upper right); Bush in a YouTube still from her 1979 music video for "Wuthering Heights" (bottom left); Miku from her single "Hibikase" in her 2015 live show (bottom right)
Source: Hilary Bergen.

The repeated pose here draws together window and screen, and hints at the potential permeability of both, as portals of contagious gesture. The dancers' palms, pressed against the invisible barrier, signal the containment of their bodies within the various screens they inhabit, screens that both separate them from the viewer and allow that viewer to gaze in. Yet, even as the gesture communicates a feeling of containment, it also expresses a dynamic longing to interact, or *relate*. The repeated pose I detail above—in which the dancer invents a pane of glass using her hands—summons the referential, metaphorical, and symbolic window as a dance motif that draws attention to the larger framework of mediation happening around these dancing bodies. The repeated gesture also brings many different bodies together in asynchronous synchronicity or mirroring—a function only possible through a complex chain of mediation. Synchronicity is crucial to the success of events like "The Most Wuthering Heights Day Ever", where people spend weeks learning the choreography to Bush's song and then gathering to dance in step together, and unison group dancing can be a source of great power and joy (again, the Greek *khoreia* links choreography and unison dancing). However, Bush and Miku never technically dance together in the same space, and this unexpected moment of synchronicity (described above) is at odds with the overall lack of synchronized movement my dance translation in MMD produces. The window motif displays the capacity of these dancing bodies to be in relation with one another—in collectivity across space and time—while remaining at the threshold between worlds, thereby amplifying the complexities of the posthuman assemblage that my dance translation introduces.

Glitch as Dance

After recording the motion data, Mike and I dragged the computer and equipment back upstairs and returned to the lab, where he aided in adding a background for our video and experimented with costuming. Even with the approximate details in place, the video does not look the way it is "supposed to," according to the unspoken performance codes of MMD. It is glitchy and abject and lacks the polished aesthetic of other MMD videos achieved through long hours of editing. In popular MMD videos, the dancers approximate agency by moving to the rhythm of the song with measured and contained fluidity. In the video for "Echo," for example, the camera begins on the ground, in an up-skirt shot, "filming" three dancers as their hips sway back and forth (Figure 3.5). The program's physics engines ensure that their long hair and short skirts also swing to the beat. The camera often tilts or zooms quickly. It appears to have limitless mobility within the space of the screen, unencumbered by the laws of gravity or the restrictions of technical equipment. The effect is dizzying and hypnotic. It mimics the music video dance moves, which often feel stilted and lacking in weight (perhaps unsurprisingly, since they are orchestrated by digital bodies). My video, on the other hand, is not heavily edited nor does it feature a lot of camera choreography. The addition of the Kinect also allows for emergent, unexpected behaviour. My dancer looks as though she has lost control of her body and is just realizing this. The dance moves through her like a river. It pushes and pulls her body, and her sickled ankles drag behind. Witnessing this spectacle, I did not have the urge to manipulate her into pretty positions. Instead, I turned towards my own dancing body. I wondered about my own level of control over my limbs and gestures. After all, dance is about toeing the line between doing and being done, between moving and being moved along the current.

Upon seeing my dance translation, an established Montréal-based Mohawk artist who works with digital avatars and machinima asked me, "why did you do this to her?" This particular artist has a very nurturing and intimate relationship with her own avatars and felt that I had not shown enough care for Miku's precarious body. Perhaps she was right. In relinquishing control, I had allowed the mechanics of Miku's digital form, programmed into her code, to act unchecked, to bend and collapse and hyperextend, or rather to react to my own movements, uncensored. I may not have "done it to her," but I did let it happen. This artist's objection was to the images I had permitted to form—the symbolic violence done to Miku's body looked to be my careless doing (or perhaps my secret wish). Or perhaps—given the common equation with dance and self-expression—the artist's objection was to my forcing Miku into a situation where she appeared to be expressing pain, awkwardness, and discomfort.

But are Miku's contortions merely a symptom of action done to her or choreography imposed upon her? Or does the glitch itself contain a kind of agency? Could giving Miku permission to glitch also, conversely, be seen as a kind of care? In her book, *Glitch Feminism*, Legacy Russell writes that "the etymology of glitch finds its deep roots in the Yiddish *gletshn* (to slide, glide, slip) or the German *glitschen* (to slip). Glitch is thus an active word, one that implies movement and change from the outset; this movement triggers error."[46] And yet, glitch is also "celebrated as a vehicle of refusal, a strategy of non-performance."[47] Glitch is both action and stillness/resistance, and both are a kind of dance that reveal the impossibility of the demands of performance on the body. Russell continues: the glitch "aims to make abstract again that which has been forced into an uncomfortable and ill-defined material: the body."[48] The vulnerability of my avatar's "uncomfortable" digital body becomes exaggerated in my dance translation, but this vulnerability can finally be diagnosed, not as a quality inherent to her teenage girl identity, but as a symptom of her imbrication within the spreadsheet of MMD's choreographic interface. German media theorist Bernhard Siegert writes that the invention of the grid combines the representation of human bodies with operations of "governance."[49] Between the "sixteenth and eighteenth century," Siegert explains, "grid-shaped control becomes the universal practice that constitutes the basis of modern disciplinary societies."[50] In MMD, the spreadsheet, in which each cell corresponds to the avatar's body position at a given time, organizes the dancing body within the logic of the grid, a technique that Siegert argues is "capable of turning humans into retrievable objects."[51] The MMD grid serves a diagrammatic and choreographic function, as well as enacting a delineation of space where there is none. Hatsune Miku's avatar stands on the grid against the vacuum of digital space, waiting to be danced. The grid marks all coordinate potentialities for her body positions and gestures; it delineates the possibility of her movement. But Miku's glitches in my project reveal themselves as a series of cracks in the seamless ideology of control that MMD proposes. Her glitches expose the unknown or surprising mechanisms of the interface that manifest through *failed* operations—or failed choreography. Miku's glitching resonates with dance as a kind of "self-expression" that is neither fully natural, nor fully mechanized. Her glitches are both errors *and* affective-gestural outburst or danced protests that are determined by, and nonetheless exceed, the choreographic governance of the grid.

In considering a posthuman aesthetics of dance, I feel the "unruly edges" of my dancer are crucial to her liveliness and potential for relation. Her resistance to perfect execution of choreography, her failure to perform accurate mimesis, and her resulting glitchy expression repels the predominantly male gaze of MMD fans as well as the practice of biometrics that scaffolds her interface and holds within it a desire for "progress" or improvement by virtue of aggregated knowledge and power over the body. And yet her own gaze is powerful and unwavering. One feature of MMD's software is that the model's eyes are always trained on the viewer. Even when you turn her body away with your cursor, Miku's gaze remains fixed. As uncanny as this gaze may be, it also provides an intimate space of recognition: a counterpoint to the practice of surveillance biometrics which use visual identification to categorize, classify and "pin a multivalent subject to a dataset."[52] Because Miku's pupils track front, they facilitate a strange power shift whereby the subject under surveillance or choreographic control gazes back, her pool-like eyes locked in the direction of the user, again conveying a desire to be in

FIGURE 1.5 Still from the final product of my MMD dance translation project, "Let Me in at Your Window" (2016), featuring Miku's glitching body
Source: Screen capture by Hilary Bergen, 2016.

relation. The dancing avatar in my project is posthuman in a number of ways: her digital body is moved by code—making her posthuman in a literal sense of the term, implying a shift away from privileging hierarchies of organic bodies and "natural" origins—but she also holds within her an assemblage of relation, a genealogy of many other dancing bodies (including her own) that move in response to one another. Miku's glitches in my project are my feminist intervention into the presumed flattened network of posthumanism. Her glitches are an act of resistance, but I do not see them as a non-performance. Because, as Russell writes, "Glitching is a gerund, an action ongoing"; my dancer's defiant, agentic glitches call choreographic power into question while participating relationally in the game of dance telephone I have staged.[53] My MMD project reveals a fundamental tension between dance and choreography, and proposes *glitch as dance* and as a kind of "activism that unfolds with a boundless extravagance."[54] In carrying the trace of both my organic body and Kate Bush's screen body in tandem with the glitch response of her interface, Miku's avatar performs a drive towards posthuman *relation*, conjured through dance.

Notes

1 Parts of this chapter appear in Hilary Bergen, "Animating the Kinetic Trace: Kate Bush, Hatsuke Miko and Posthuman Dance," *PUBLIC Biometrics: Mediating Bodies* 30, no. 60 (2020): 188–207.
2 Higuchi Yu, "Mikumikudance," *Softonic*. 2008, https://mikumikudance.en.softonic.com/.
3 Kate Bush, "Wuthering Heights," *The Kick Inside*, EMI Records, 1977.
4 Zeynep Gündüz, "Digital Dance: Encounters between Media Technologies and the Dancing Body," *At the Interface / Probing the Boundaries* 85 (2012): 309–33.
5 See Bruno Latour, *Reassembling the Social: An Introduction to Actor-Network Theory* (Oxford University Press, 2005), 17.
6 Margaret Talbot, "The Enduring, Incandescent Power of Kate Bush," *The New Yorker*, December 19, 2018, https://www.newyorker.com/culture/culture-desk/the-enduring-incandescent-power-of-kate-bush.
7 There are actually two music videos for Bush's "Wuthering Heights": the "red dress" version, shot on a foggy, verdant moor, and the "white dress version," shot in an empty studio. Both videos are directed by Keith MacMillan and choreographed by Bush with help from one of her dance tutors, Robin Kovac. See Min Chen, "Roll And Fall In Green: Kate Bush's 'Wuthering Heights' video is still moving," *Proxy Music*, August 20, 2018, https://proxymusic.club/2018/08/20/kate-bush-wuthering-heights-video/.
8 Wuthering Heights Montreal, "Kate Bush Wuthering Heights Choreography," June 30, 2016, accessed January 23, 2023, YouTube video, 4:27, https://www.youtube.com/watch?v=IziOMwBu7ws.
9 "Hatsune Miku," Vocaloid Wiki, accessed August 4, 2021, https://vocaloid.fandom.com/wiki/Hatsune_Miku.
10 I was the organizer of the first Montréal edition of this event, in 2016.
11 Again, see Bruno Latour, *Reassembling the Social*.
12 Marketing Miku as a hologram makes it seem as though there is a 3D object to clone, when really, she has always been a 2D image.

13 "Who is Hatsune Miku?," Crypton Future Media, INC., accessed December 5, 2018, https://ec.crypton.co.jp/pages/prod/vocaloid/cv01_us.
14 Stina Marie Hasse Jørgensen, Sabrina Vitting-Seerup, and Katrine Wallevik, "Hatsune Miku: An Uncertain Image," *Digital Creativity* 28, no. 4 (2017): 318–31.
15 Nico Nico Dōga, the most popular video sharing website in Japan, launched in 2006. It now has more than 23 million registered users. Many of its design features resemble YouTube, but a significant difference is its ability to allow users to add comments in direct overlay atop the videos at specific playback times.
16 Ka Yan Lam, "The Hatsune Miku Phenomenon: More Than a Virtual J-Pop Diva," *The Journal of Popular Culture*, 49, no. 5 (2016): 1107–24.
17 Kate Bush is also known for her high singing register and sometimes-ghostly tone.
18 Lam, "The Hatsune Miku Phenomenon," 1109–10.
19 We also approximated the grassy English moors of Bush's music video setting for the video, trying out various in-app background such as an urban park/greenspace and a lush Japanese forest.
20 David M. Bourg and Bryan Bywalec, "Chapter 14: Physics Engines," Physics for Game Developers 2nd ed. (O'Reilly Media, Inc., 2013), https://www.oreilly.com/library/view/physics-for-game/9781449361037/ch14.html.
21 For an exploration of this link in greater depth, see Roger Copeland, "The Best Dance Is the Way People Die in Movies (or Gestures Toward a New Definition of 'Screendance')," *The Oxford Handbook of Screendance Studies*, ed. Douglas Rosenberg (Oxford University Press, 2016), 225–42.
22 "Hatsune Miku," Wikipedia, https://en.wikipedia.org/wiki/Hatsune_Miku.
23 Patrick W. Galbraith, "Moe: Exploring Virtual Potential in Post-Millennial Japan," *Electronic Journal of Contemporary Japanese Studies* 31 (October 2009), http://www.japanesestudies.org.uk/articles/2009/Galbraith.html.
24 Galbraith, "Moe."
25 Galbraith, "Moe."
26 Galbraith, "Moe."
27 Jørgensen et al., "Hatsune Miku," 318–31.
28 Heather Warren-Crow, *Girlhood and the Plastic Image* (Hanover: Dartmouth College Press, 2014), xiv.
29 Warren-Crow, *Girlhood and the Plastic Image*, 11.
30 Deborah Jowitt, *Time and the Dancing Image* (William Morrow & Company, 1989), 39.
31 Laurel Halo and Mari Matsutoya, "Still Be Here: The Multiplicity of Hatsune Miku," *Interface Critique Journal* 2 (2019): 143–49.
32 Linh K Le, "Examining the rise of Hatsune Miku: The first international virtual idol," *The UCI Undergraduate Research Journal* (2014): 1–11.
33 Crystalyn Hodgkins, "Interest SankeiBiz: Hatsune Miku Has Earned US$120 Million+," *Anime News Network*, March 27, 2012, https://www.animenewsnetwork.com/interest/2012-03-27/sankeibiz/hatsune-miku-has-earned-us%24120-million+#:~:text=The%20SankeiBiz%20news%20website%20posted,first%20introduced%20five%20years%20ago.
34 Miku is licensed as Attribution-NonCommercial 3.0 Unported (CC BY-NC 3.0) and the license can be read in its entirety here: https://creativecommons.org/licenses/by-nc/3.0/legalcode.
35 Fans put up with this unpaid labour because the freeware aspect of MMD allows them to infuse each version (song, dance, video) of Miku with some of their own dreams, aspirations, and creative talent. They may not profit off of her performances, but MMD creators are proud of their creations, as displays of talent.
36 Jørgensen et al., "Hatsune Miku," 323.
37 Laura Mulvey, *Death 24X a Second: Stillness and the Moving Image* (London: Reaktion Books Ltd., 2006), 9.

38 Rosa Menkman, "The Glitch Art Genre," *O Fluxo*, July 2012, https://www.ofluxo.net/the-glitch-art-genre-by-rosa-menkman/.
39 Kate Bush, *The Kick Inside*, EMI Records, 1978.
40 David Mitchell, "Kate Bush and Me," *The Guardian*, December 7, 2018, https://www.theguardian.com/books/2018/dec/07/david-mitchell-kate-bush-lyric-poetry.html.
41 This occurrence has resulted in a new wave of Kate Bush fans: teenagers who had never heard of Bush before this episode of *Stranger Things* are now taking to TikTok to proclaim her genius.
42 Thomas DeFrantz and Philipa Rothfield, eds., *Choreography and Corporeality: Relay in Motion* (Basingstoke: Palgrave MacMillan, 2016), 212.
43 Ken McLeod, "Living in the Immaterial World: Holograms and Spirituality in Recent Popular Music," *Popular Music and Society* 39, no. 5 (2016): 501–515.
44 Emily Brontë, *Wuthering Heights* (London: Thomas Cautley Newby, 1847).
45 See Lorraine Sim, "Wuthering Heights and the Politics of Space," *Limina: A Journal of Historical and Cultural Studies* 10 (2021): 32–51.
46 Legacy Russell, *Glitch Feminism: A Manifesto* (London and New York: Verso, 2020), 18.
47 Russell, *Glitch Feminism*, 16.
48 Russell, *Glitch Feminism*, 16.
49 Bernhard Siegert, *Cultural Techniques: Grids, Filters, Doors, and Other Articulations of the Real*, trans. Geoffroy Winthrop-Young (New York: Fordham University Press, 2015), 97.
50 Siegert, *Cultural Techniques*, 97.
51 Siegert, *Cultural Techniques*, 97.
52 Kirstie Ball, Kevin Haggerty and David Lyon, eds., *Routledge Handbook of Surveillance Studies* (Abingdon: Routledge, 2012), 1.
53 Russell, *Glitch Feminism*, 30.
54 Russell, *Glitch Feminism*, 30.

Bibliography

Ball, Kirstie, Kevin Haggerty and David Lyon, eds. *Routledge Handbook of Surveillance Studies*. Abingdon: Routledge, 2012.
Bourg, David M. and Bryan Bywalec. "Chapter 14: Physics Engines." *Physics for Game Developers*, 2nd ed. O'Reilly Media, Inc., 2013. Accessed February 8, 2019. https://www.oreilly.com/library/view/physics-for-game/9781449361037/ch14.html.
DeFrantz, Thomas and Philipa Rothfield, eds. *Choreography and Corporeality: Relay in Motion*. Basingstoke: Palgrave MacMillan, 2016.
Galbraith, Patrick W. "Moe: Exploring Virtual Potential in Post-Millennial Japan." *Electronic Journal of Contemporary Japanese Studies* 31 (October 2009). http://www.japanesestudies.org.uk/articles/2009/Galbraith.html..
Gündüz, Zeynep. "Digital Dance: Encounters between Media Technologies and the Dancing Body." *At the Interface / Probing the Boundaries* 85 (2012): 309–333.
Halo, Laurel and Mari Matsutoya. "Still Be Here: The Multiplicity of Hatsune Miku." *Interface Critique Journal* 2 (2019): 143–149.
"Hatsune Miku." Vocaloid Wiki. Accessed August 4, 2021. https://vocaloid.fandom.com/wiki/Hatsune_Miku.
"Hatsune Miku." Wikipedia. https://en.wikipedia.org/wiki/Hatsune_Miku.
Hodgkins, Crystalyn. "Interest SankeiBiz: Hatsune Miku Has Earned US$120 Million +." *Anime News Network*, March 27, 2012, https://www.animenewsnetwork.com/interest/2012-03-27/sankeibiz/hatsune-miku-has-earned-us%24120-million+#:~:text

=The%20SankeiBiz%20news%20website%20posted,first%20introduced%20five%20years%20ago.

Jørgensen, Stina MarieHasse, Sabrina Vitting-Seerup, and Katrine Wallevik. "Hatsune Miku: An Uncertain Image." *Digital Creativity* 28, no. 4 (2017): 318–331.

Jowitt, Deborah. *Time and the Dancing Image*. New York: William Morrow & Company, 1989.

Lam, Ka Yan. "The Hatsune Miku Phenomenon: More Than a Virtual J-Pop Diva." *The Journal of Popular Culture* 49, no. 5 (2016): 1107–1124.

Latour, Bruno. *Reassembling the Social: An Introduction to Actor-Network Theory*. Oxford: Oxford University Press, 2005.

Le, Linh K. "Examining the rise of Hatsune Miku: The first international virtual idol." *The UCI Undergraduate Research Journal* (2014): 1–11.

McLeod, Ken. "Living in the Immaterial World: Holograms and Spirituality in Recent Popular Music." *Popular Music and Society* 39, no. 5 (2016): 501–515.

Menkman, Rosa. "The Glitch Art Genre." *O Fluxo*, July 2012.

Mitchell, David. "Kate Bush and Me." *The Guardian*, December 7, 2018, https://www.theguardian.com/books/2018/dec/07/david-mitchell-kate-bush-lyric-poetry.html.

Mulvey, Laura. *Death 24X a Second: Stillness and the Moving Image*. London: Reaktion Books Ltd., 2006.

Russell, Legacy. *Glitch Feminism: A Manifesto*. London and New York: Verso, 2020.

Siegert, Bernhard. *Cultural Techniques: Grids, Filters, Doors, and Other Articulations of the Real*. Translated by Geoffroy Winthrop-Young. New York: Fordham University Press, 2015.

Talbot, Margaret. "The Enduring, Incandescent Power of Kate Bush." *The New Yorker*, December 19, 2018, https://www.newyorker.com/culture/culture-desk/the-enduring-incandescent-power-of-kate-bush.

Warren-Crow, Heather. *Girlhood and the Plastic Image*. Hanover: Dartmouth College Press, 2014.

"Who is Hatsune Miku?" Crypton Future Media, INC. Accessed December 5, 2018. https://ec.crypton.co.jp/pages/prod/vocaloid/cv01_us.

Wuthering Heights Montreal. "Kate Bush Wuthering Heights Choreography." June 30, 2016. Accessed January 23 2023. YouTube video, 4:27. https://www.youtube.com/watch?v=IziOMwBu7ws.

Yu, Higuchi. 2008. "Mikumikudance." *Softonic*. https://mikumikudance.en.softonic.com/.

2
THE QUEER ART OF HOSPITALITY
"If You Can Fuck, You Can Dance!"[1]

Luce deLire

FIGURE 2.1 Still from: Santiago Tamayo Soler, *Retornar*, 2021
Source: Santiago Tamayo Soler.

Introduction

"Love is Violence."[2] The camera pans down. A person lays in bed smoking, dressed in early 2000s DIY punk aesthetic, matching the interior design of a room where we watch a drama between two teenagers unfold: they both get up, undress each other, and start making out, captured in a highly erotic manner. Then things take a turn. Up to this point, hands were caressing skin, lips kissing; now a loving bite is pulling flesh away from a body. What started as a music-induced amorous tête-à-tête becomes a blood bath. Instead of bodies caressing each other, hands now enter places that are not meant to provide safe passage, pulling out guts and intestines. Yet, next to the romantic scene turning into a teenage horror movie, a TV screen shows Alice Glass dancing the survival dance, dressed in a latex goth outfit: gently swinging from left to right, a flirtatious look giving way to hands symbolically pushing the viewer away. Glass insists that there is something beyond the tragedy. It's the ~~future~~ you see at any queer party, any serious rave:[3] a community driven by indeterminacy, despite colonial violence, unaffordable housing, looming ecological collapse and financial crises, violence in the streets, micro aggressions at the work place, and all the other miseries that make queer and trans lives harder than they should be.[4] Santiago Tamayo Soler's *Retornar* articulates this ~~future~~ in an extreme case when in the face of the complete ecological collapse of the earth, Ricorica, ambassador of an alien species, proclaims: "In the meantime, dance and enjoy. Like there is no tomorrow. We have to celebrate."[5]

In this text, I investigate Alice Glass's "Love is Violence," a dark pop song and its accompanying video about two lovers taking each other's intestines out, and Santiago Tamayo Soler's *Retornar*, a queer Latin American post-apocalyptic fantasy video game that tells of the last nine people (all queer and/or trans) on earth after planetary ecological collapse. I claim that we can find conditions for a life after capitalism spelled out in dance on screen in terms of *hospitality*. Along the way, I will argue the following:

a   Hospitality turns into hostility when it takes on the form of private property.
b   Extending and intensifying practices of hospitality can therefore help us *unlearn* private property and thus transform the hegemonial kind of social interaction in our immediate environment.
c   Social institutions that extend and intensify hospitality must nevertheless be developed in order to de-institutionalize private property as a primary kind of inter-personal relation.
d   Sexual intimacy is a form of extreme hospitality and can be used as a widespread paradigmatic practice of hospitable action.
e   We should understand sex as a kind of dancing because (flirtatious) dancing as a way to make desire intelligible exists on a continuum with sexual intercourse.
f   The most inhospitable (and most un-ethical) action damages or destroys the conditions of hospitality, namely the host and/or guest themselves. In terms of intimacy, I suggest to call this inhospitality "toxicity."
g   However bad the damage may be, dancing preserves a relation to an indeterminate, unactualized ~~future~~ (a strange *a-venir*, about which I shall say more later on).

I Hospitality and Private Property

In this section, I first argue that capitalism is set to produce misery for internal, structural reasons and that private property is a main ideological cover for this systemic dysfunctionality. I then move on to present hospitality as a counter-paradigm, an antidote of sorts, to the toxic logic of private property.

I.a Private Property

Every problem, every crisis, every damage calls for a remedy. Under conditions of neo-liberal capitalism, every remedy comes in the form of private property, and such property inspires spending. Where there's spending, however, there's accumulation of capital. Now, capitalism in general aims at accumulating capital. Thus, capitalism has no interest in anything ever getting any better. Misery generates profit, while happiness does not. This counts especially for neo-liberal capitalism, understood as an advanced level of universalization of capital as a motivational force on all levels (individuals, collectives, the state, international relations, etc.). In fact, neoliberal capitalism has a systemic interest in perpetuating misery, selling more prescription drugs, more holiday trips, more once-in-a-life-time chances that get you out of the mud they make you call life – maybe. Neoliberal capitalism wants you to drag on with maximum stress and minimal joy so as to maximize spending and minimize resistance.[6]

The primary ideological cover for neoliberal capitalism is the idea of private property as a manifestation of negative freedom. Negative freedom is the absence of external interference – freedom *from* taxes means that taxes do not interfere with my income, freedom of movement is absence of external interferences with my physical position (such as a wall or travel restrictions), etc. Inversely, positive freedom is a productive interference – a friend telling me about their breakup story for hours might seem like a taxing investment of my time, yet it interpellates me *as* their friend, thus constituting a social relation that could not exist otherwise. That fifteenth breakup conversation thus *is* my freedom.[7] Ideologically speaking, private property is the manifestation of negative freedom in an object.[8] For allegedly, private property is reserved exclusively for your use, while everybody else is excluded from it. My matcha latte and my transparent dresses are *mine* in that *I alone* decide if, how, and when they are being used (including all the notable exceptions, of course).[9]

I.b Hospitality

Private property is a hegemonic form of social relations all over the Western world. In fact, this is just what happens when the economic sphere is allowed to substantiate all other spheres of life, meaning that love, friendship, politics, medical care, justice, etc. start functioning according to market rules.[10] Yet life is not commodified all the way down just yet. Besides the hegemonic form, there are other paradigms of social relations. These *counter paradigms* provide alternative kinds of interaction that we are already familiar with. We thus do not have to learn anything from scratch. We just need to turn up the volume on these aspects of social life so as to try and drown out private property as a primary way of dealing with one another. This is how we *unlearn* private property as the principal form of social interaction. I pointed out above that capitalism has no interest in producing conditions for happiness just because problems and misery are so much more profitable. I also argued that private property is the cornerstone of capitalistic ideology. We are thus looking for a social paradigm that can help us unlearn private property in particular.

I want to suggest hospitality as a paradigm of this kind. Judith Still defines hospitality as follows:

> Hospitality is by definition a structure that regulates relations between inside and outside, and, in that sense, between private and public. Someone or ones, categorised as 'outside', as not necessarily, by right or legal contract, part of the 'inside', is temporarily brought within.[11]

Practices of hospitality, then, would be catalysts of belonging, of inclusion and exclusion. Do you bring wine for dinner? Do you take a third serving? Into which languages does a country translate its immigration forms? Do refugees have to be grateful for political asylum or do they merely exert their rights? Questions like these are answered by different inflections of hospitality as cultural institutions. Yet there is another layer of meta-hospitality within each act of hospitality, where we are interpellated to figure out what hospitality is to mean *in this instant*. Everything else would be a suspension of hospitality on a meta level, excluding the guest, for example, from co-determining the rules of hospitality currently in place. Yet these rules are not and cannot be written down in some large almanac of hospitality. For that would yet again coagulate the process of hospitality into solid rules, inhospitable to re-negotiation. There is thus no legal code of hospitality. I thus disagree with Still about the nature of hospitality. I do not believe that hospitality is restricted to a mediation between inside and outside. And neither do I believe that hospitality must be a temporary affair. Hospitality is above all a practice of negotiation and improvisation around insufficiently determined guidelines. In fact, I want to suggest that genuine hospitality is an experience of indeterminacy. Imagine a dinner party where someone suddenly exclaims: "it's midnight already!" The forgetting of time indicates that genuine hospitality as experience of indeterminacy (of time). Consequentially, hospitality cannot be said to be "temporary" in any meaningful way, given that the duration of the hospitable condition is itself subject to indeterminacy, hence negotiation and improvisation. The same counts for the indeterminacy of inside and outside: Where the inside/outside is should itself be subject to the hospitable practice. Hospitality, I say, is a practical confrontation with indeterminacy, hence negotiation and improvisation. It is not, however, without guidelines altogether. As a *practice*, it engages with given conditions, needs, desires, rules, fears etc. It is not altogether *beyond* rules. And yet indeterminacy marks the space where hospitality actually happens. It marks the space of an embodied encounter between particular people where a genuine connection in a particular moment remains possible. There is, in principle, no pre-established value here, no predetermined tenure over this or that set of things. And this is what distinguishes hospitality from private property as the manifestation of negative freedom: where the latter knows only yours/mine, inclusion/exclusion, inside/outside, private/public, the former knows variously grained and stratified shades of gray that reside outside, in between, or in spite of these binary distinctions. *Mi casa es su casa*. Hospitality allows to *live inside the problem of ownership* because who owns what, who is who, may always be suspended. It *stages* this problem (*who owns what?*) instead of solving it into binary oppositions such as yours/mine, here/there, inside/outside etc.

In this sense, hospitality is not an *interference* with your ownership of your house, your food, your time. Hospitable giving is not understood as giving something *away* but as mutually benefiting both guest and host, not as an interference with my freedom to own but as a privilege to share. Offering someone a cup of tea is not taking that tea *away* from someone. Rather, it serves to establish a particular social relation – that of a host, a friend, a parent, a lover, etc. Here then we have a case of transforming a kind of negative freedom into a kind of positive freedom in the sense defined above. It is not about the having or not having of some particular object. It's about the way in which ownership is negotiated, shared, protected, or dispersed. Hospitality, understood in this way, offers a soft alternative to expropriation, the classical demand of leftist politics. It is, however, not meant to replace it. No matter the degree of hospitality, the one percent will have to be (partially) expropriated. However, just like private property, hospitality structures our relation to one another through particular things – tea, beds, cookies, etc. And it can be applied to nonmaterial things as well, such as time, attention, affection, etc. Just as one may offer a cup of tea, one may offer to listen to someone's concerns or be affectionate with someone either in the logic of private property *or* in the logic of hospitality, either as something that is taken away from me *or* as something joyfully shared.

II Hospitality against Private Property

Private property cannot simply be unlearned *conceptually*. It has to be unlearned *corporeally*, as a habit, as a physical disposition, as a way of embodiment. For the body has its own properties and resistances. It is, as Linda Martín Alcoff puts it, "a dynamic material domain."[12] The body is not a vessel for the intentions, concepts, or critical interventions of some ruling consciousness. Rather, "the materiality of the body itself is [...] volatile."[13] Its "[m]otion is material."[14] The body is being "organized" through concrete activities, meaning that it becomes *this particular* body, with *these particular organs*, through surroundings that cause it to tendentially behave in this or that way – in conversation with, but irreducibly to conceptuality.[15] Capitalism is thus *habituated, embodied*. It goes without saying, without thinking, without resistance regarding action or inaction. It is a naturalized way of behaving, of standing back, of turning towards or away from something or somebody. Capitalism is visceral, affective. It makes us fear, desire, and hope in particular situations and particular ways. Capitalism is corporeal all the way down. In this sense, capitalism is a way of life, constituting our every motion. And that is why it must be unlearned *physically*, it must be dishabituated, replaced with alternative kinds of embodiment. Dance as a practice of embodiment, of holding your body in this or that way, is one way of doing this. In this section, I exemplify this claim along the continuity between dance, flirtation, and sex as practices of hospitality.

In order to understand hospitality and its embodiment we need to understand the limits of hospitality. The music video to "Love is Violence" (2022) by Alice Glass is a great example of such limits. The video shows two people watching a video of Alice Glass dancing to her song "Love is Violence," embracing each other lovingly, then slowly taking each other's intestines out. There are thus *two* scenes on *two* screens going on here: the screen that we are looking at and the screen that the protagonists are looking at. In what follows, I argue that (i) hospitality dissipates where the host becomes the property of the guest (while people can be simultaneously guest and host in different respects, as is the case in "Love is Violence"). I also suggest (ii) hospitable sex and flirtatious dancing as sites for pre-enactments or rehearsals of a world beyond capitalism. I then investigate (iii) the industrialization of dance through its recordability, before turning to (iv) the screen within the screen, which articulates an indeterminate ~~future~~ that terminally resists the hostile logic of private property, preserving an indeterminate hospitality besides and in spite of the slaughter.

II.a Love is Violence

"Two bodies press outward from each other into each other."[16]

Physical intimacy is one of the most delicate and most widespread kinds of hospitality: hospitality to other bodies. Instead of sharing tea, shelter, or passports, physical intimacy – be it sex or cuddling or otherwise – means to share your very own body with others, that is to say, you are sharing yourself. Intimacy is an extreme kind of hospitality, where the host is not sharing some external thing, but is sharing themselves instead. Intimacy is *embodied* hospitality. A host may, for example, let someone (or something) *into themselves*. Yet all hospitality may turn into hostility. The reason is that just like every invention produces its own accident, every success lives on conditions of its potential breakdown.[17] The train produces the train wreck, crypto currency produces crypto theft, the compliment harbours the possibility of the insult, and truth harbours the possibility of falsity. In the same way, hostility lives at the heart of hospitality. Picking up on a term coined by Jacques Derrida, we may call this particular condition, where hospitality is enabled by its relation to hostility (and vice versa), *hostipitality*.[18] It is the condition both of hospitality and of hostility, itself a state of indeterminacy at work in every actual hospitality/hostility. It is *because* the guest resides in the custody of the host while the latter suspends their power that hospitality occurs. Inversely, the host lets down their guard, their defence is suspended, danger is imminent, and damage may occur. Yet the guest does not exploit this vulnerability. And that is where hospitality occurs.

"Love is Violence" depicts *hostipitality* as follows: an invitation into a bedroom through text message is followed by the protagonists inviting each other into each other's bodies through gentle touch and French kisses (entering that large cavity called "the mouth"). Next, they go under each other's shirts (taking their shirts off), sharing intimacy through skin-on-skin contact. Then hospitality turns into hostility: an affectionate bite becomes destructive when skin is ripped off a body, hands enter the body and *take possession* of its insides, literally turning the body of the other inside out. Physical borders are crossed, ending in the death of both lovers, blood spilled all over the carpet. The possibility of hostility (violence) lives within the most hospitable act (sex). The transformation is seamless. That moment of the loving bite is especially an expression of true *hostipitality*: what first looks like a generous act of giving/receiving love turns out to be a destructive intrusion. That bite expresses the indeterminate tipping point between hospitality and hostility. Yet the whole sequence – invitation by text message, communal watching on one protagonist's TV, then turning towards each other, making out, physical intimacy turning into violence, mutual gutting, death – displays the spectrum between hospitality and hostility on a temporal scale in the form of continuous transformation, where the transition is seamless because the possibility of violence establishes the reality of love just as the possibility of hostility establishes the reality of hospitality and vice versa.

Glass's lyrics tell a similar story. The chorus goes: "Love is violence / 'Cause I don't even know what the fuck we've become / You're bleeding me dry, is it enough? / I don't even know if I'll make it through the night / Still I wonder why I feel release."[19] It's namely the indeterminacy between hospitality and hostility, love and violence in suspension ("I don't even know what the fuck we've become" – lovers or enemies?), while death is imminent ("I don't even know if I'll make it through the night"), yet more hospitality is being offered ("[...], is it enough?"), becoming an instrument of the violence/hostility that is being enacted. Nevertheless, affection prevails ("Still I wonder why I feel release"), verbally mirroring the protagonists' erotic bliss which we see on screen.

II.a.i Toxicity

What though is the hinge between hospitality and hostility, between love and violence? Glass's lyrics capture it as follows: "You just take from my body / Is it pleasing to defile inside?"[20] Just as the protagonists in the video literally *take from* each other's bodies (their intestines), the addressee of the lyrics *takes from* a body through rape. We can see that hospitality turns into hostility exactly when it enters the logic of private property ("You just *take* from my body", my emphasis), when it becomes a form of negative freedom ("You *just* take [exclusively]", my emphasis) where someone takes something into their own private possession. Especially when a host is sharing themselves in physical intimacy, such hostility is not just breach of contract or offence but an attack on the condition of hospitality itself, namely an attack on the hostness of the host, meaning her very existence.[21]

In this way, "Love is Violence" manifests the extreme form of what one may call a *toxic love*: eroticization of mutual disembowelment, the romanticization of private property driven to an absolute extreme. Hospitality becomes *impossible* when both protagonists, hosting one another, murder one another. This, then, is the negative limit of hospitality: its incapacitation in the erosion of the *conditions* of hospitality, which in this case ends in the death of both hosts. Yet this is not just some random fantasy. It is a common formation of neoliberal love: questions of private property are negotiated through separation anxieties, shared practices, mutual disciplining, etc. They perforate and constitute intimate relations under neoliberal capitalism.[22] When jealousy, breakup dramas, and attachment issues are primary topics of pop music, movies, literature, and other kinds of cultural production, we should assume that commodified love is often taken to be the natural form of romantic love. "Love is Violence" therefore does not just depict some individual person's sad story. It manifests a cultural paradigm. And insofar as physical intimacy is embodied hospitality, toxicity is the embodiment of the property form of hostility. In this sense, toxicity is a symptom of neoliberal capitalism, be it in friendships, in sexual, romantic, business, or other relationships. "Love is Violence" depicts its embodiment as violent intrusion, holding on to vital parts, then taking them out and incapacitating them. This behaviour is toxic, *never mind the invitation* and the direct response (in this case: smiling faces). The reason is that it undermines the conditions of the hospitality that had been offered: it damages and ultimately destroys the host.

II.a.ii Fucking, Flirting, Dancing

How can we learn to avoid, tendentially at least, this collapse of hospitality into private property? Intimate hostility (that is, domestic violence) in the wake of the property form is often romanticized, eroticized.[23] Given the embodied, habituated dimension of private property under neoliberal capitalism touched on earlier, we need to ask: how can genuine hospitality be eroticized? How can hospitality become *hotspitality*, the hot, desired, longed for kind of interaction? This question is inherently queer in that queer desire eroticizes what is usually thought to be undesirable or at least not meant to be desired. And my suggestions consequentially emerge from the repertoire of queer and trans lives, such as dance and sex.

At a conference in London in 2016, dancer Alkistis Dimech emphatically exclaimed: "If you can fuck, you can dance!"[24] Why is that? There are of course many dances – religious dances, communal dances, acrobatic dances, dance as work outs, etc. Yet one very common version of dancing in the twenty-first century – and dancing on screen in particular – is essentially extended flirtation,[25] which expresses desire for another and/or expresses availability to the desire of another. It is dance as the *display of intelligibility* to the desire of another and the desire to be desired. That is to say, in flirtatious dancing, I function as the reflector of someone else's desire.[26] In "Love is Violence," this happens particularly in the screen-on-screen part of the video: Glass, dressed in tight black latex that shows a lot of skin of her upper body, especially highlighting her décolleté, looks into the camera, turning her head to the right ever so slightly in an inviting gesture as if to ask us to come closer. We then find ourselves looking up to a Glass kneeling halfway above the camera as if topping the viewer (sexually speaking). A little later (after another scene showing the main protagonists caressing each other), we see Glass kneeling in front of the camera, pushing her palms forward with her elbows pointing outwards as if she was pushing the viewer away. This play on invitation and rejection is essentially flirtatious: Glass makes herself intelligible to our libidinal leanings – we might find her hot, toxic, silly or might not respond to the latex outfit. We might want to wear that outfit ourselves, might want to be her or want to imitate or avoid the moves she is making. Desire,[27] however, will play a role in our affective relation to her performance. This effect happens on a regular dance floor just as well: I might move smoothly or ferociously, with eyes closed thus allowing another's gaze to take me in or locking eyes with someone so as to meet their intrusive gaze, or to invite more proximity. Yet dance on screen allows for a particular kind of libidinal intelligibility because the screen-dancer does not actually engage with me. Whatever I do, they will not find it intrusive. Flirtatious dance on screen thus (in most cases) invites a gaze that might otherwise be interpreted as an intrusive stare (which in real life of course happens as well, especially along social hierarchies). Compared to a dance floor situation, the distance brought about by the transmission of an image on screen thus heightens the aspect of libidinal *intelligibility* central to flirtatious dancing in general.

Now, even the body engaged in actual sexual activity *still* makes itself recognizable *as desiring*, desirable, etc. – or not (note that the success of these acts of communication is another question). That is to say, there is no real distinction between (flirtatious) dancing and actual sexual activity. Dimech is right: "If you can fuck, you can dance."[28] The reason is that (flirtatious) dancing exists on a continuum with the kind of seductive performance displayed during sexual intercourse (whatever you may think counts as such). While Glass is filmed from below with a shaky hand camera as if she was topping the audience, a grainy aesthetic and occasional glitches intensify the impression of distance, highlighting the fact that we are looking at a transmitted image. Cut to the music and juxtaposed with other scenes, the moment becomes an element of (digitally) choreographed dancing. However, someone may well perform in the exact same way during a sexual act, the head slightly leaning to one side, mouth half open with slow and rhythmic movement. The flirtatious performance, the seduction, does not stop when the sexual act begins (whatever you think is required for an act to count as such). Sex is just the continuation of seduction, neither its end nor its objective (and vice versa). There will still be invitations to play, avoidance and articulations of disinclination. While having sex, we still make ourselves *libidinally intelligible*, meaning that we are readable as flings, as long-term partners, as pillow queens or vanilla tops. While having sex, we are still read for what we dis/like – we never stop performing, we never stop dancing. For this reason, we can understand libidinally oriented movement paradigmatically (though not exclusively) as a kind of dance. We should thus understand the two protagonists in "Love is Violence" who first undress and then kill each other, as two dancers, engaged in an embodied performance of toxic love.

Moving on the dance floor, moving through the street, moving along, winking, turning away, circling around one another, looking at each other in intervals, undressing each other to the sound of music or to the sound of one's breath, exploring each other's bodies with eyes, hands, mouths, tongues, sex toys, genitals, etc. – all of these actions are rhythmic expressions of desire or the lack thereof to the ongoing beat of seduction. They are dance moves, parts of libidinal DIY dances. They follow the rhythms of particular moments, cultural backgrounds and largely unscripted experiences, determined by very particular circumstances. They're often clumsy, besides the beat, full of mistakes or not recognized as elements of flirtatious dancing at all. Yet these aspects of imperfection, their profound DIY quality, also make up their particular charm. More often than not, some flirtatious move occurs *in spite of* its foreseeable imperfection. Desire is expressed *although* there's a good chance that it will not be reciprocated. These dances thus ask for hospitality. They ask for a generous response in spite of their clumsy imperfection, in spite of being uncalled for, in spite of lacking skill, rehearsal, courage, and everything that makes dance stunning, acrobatic, impressive, etc. Yet these dances are themselves acts of hospitality, invitations to interact or to interact differently. For the flirtatious dance move can be dismissed, can come off as rude or be altogether ignored. (Flirtatious) dancing is thus an encounter on the territory of hospitality, negotiating social indeterminacy – who we are, will be, or want to be with and for one another – in a way that is decidedly not governed by private property. In this way, flirtatious dancing (on stage, on screen, in the sheets, etc.) is a site where we can learn or rehearse hospitality and thus unlearn private property. In other words, we can unlearn private property through hospitable dancing and through hospitable sexual encounters. If "communism" names a world beyond private property, we can conclude: if you know how to fuck hospitably, you know how to be a communist.

Is the screen a preferred site of de-commodification? It is not. Dance on screen offers a particular repertoire of moves, of flirtatious interventions that we may mime – and probably fail at repeating. It can thus add to our own reservoir of flirtatious interactions, poised for failure and inviting a hospitable response. And yet, watching a video more often than not inspires to remain *in*active, to delegate the move to the screen, absolve oneself from re-enactment, just sit back, relax, forget. Some, however, take to TikTok in actual re-enactments of choreographed sequences, thus turning themselves from spectator to spectacle. The citation of such moves also increasingly seeps into everyday interactions. Like a running gag or a figure of speech, running gestures and figures of movement evoke shared systems of embodied references. On the one hand, dancing to viral videos on social media allows corporate interests to live rent free in our minds, occupy our time, and influence our political leanings. On the other hand, the active, collectivizing embodiment of shared movements can function as a road sign that points away from private property as the substance of social relations and towards a more hospitable form of living together. Social media is not the revolutionary force we are looking for. It may even be an element of global warfare, inspired by geopolitical interests.[29] But it does offer cues that we should observe carefully, appropriate, and possibly de-commodify.

I pointed out earlier that private property is not a mere concept. It is also embodied, habituated, and permeates our every movement. Dancing and sexual encounters will not bring down capitalism. For that we need executive power, expropriation, abolition of inheritance, etc.[30] Yet in order to prepare for the time after capitalism, hospitable sex and flirtatious dancing may serve as pre-enactments. In this context, "Love is Violence" describes a useful limit case. Two protagonists engage in flirtatious dancing in its minimal DIY form. Yet their love becomes lethal when hospitality collapses into possessiveness. We learn that hospitality dissipates where it is excessively generous, where the host becomes the property of the guest (while people can be simultaneously guest and host in different respects, as is the case in "Love is Violence").

II.a.iii The Industrialization of Dance

Death as the result of hospitality turned into hostility, however, is contested on the TV screen in "Love is Violence." There, Alice Glass dances slowly, minimally. The camera reduces the movement, enables close up and zoom, thus allowing for smaller movements (which might otherwise be invisible) to have a larger effect. The minimal action on the small screen thus inverts the maximal action on the big screen – disembowelment and death are countered with small, smooth movements of the hands, a gentle swing towards the camera and back. The camera allows for contraction, pulling together what seems otherwise dispersed, distilling movements otherwise left unseen into an intensity that may be felt, but escapes tracking off screen. In doing so, the camera industrializes dance: just as the machine contracts many workers into one, video contracts many movements into few. To see this, consider the following quote from Karl Marx's *Capital, Volume One*:

> In the modern manufacture of envelopes, for example, one worker folded the paper with the folder, another laid on the gum, a third turned over the flap on which the emblem is impressed, a fourth embossed the emblem and so on; and on each occasion the envelope had to change hands. One single envelope machine now performs all these operations at once, and makes more than 3,000 envelopes in an hour.[31]

A central aspect of mechanization over against manual labour, then, is the *contraction* of various activities into one. In this case, at least four different operations are condensed into one single process. Yet Marx insists that mere contraction is not enough. It is important to integrate the principle of movement into the machine as well so as to take human force and agency out of the equation and degrade particular workers to elements of the machine, handlers rather than operators. "As soon as a machine executes, without human help, all the movements required to elaborate the raw material, and needs only supplementary assistance from the worker, we have an automatic system of machinery, capable of constant improvement in its details."[32] Such is the case in a factory. Here, a set of machines operates more or less on their own. The machines are handled and maintained by humans but exceed each individual human's intention and control as much as they exceed the sum total of intentions and controls of all humans involved. The machine is no longer an extension of human action. Rather, the machine itself becomes the main actor, while humans become extensions of the mechanized process, secondary to it, and ultimately replaceable.[33] In this sense, the factory gives rise to a different *kind* of labour, one where the machine part is primary, the human part is secondary. That is why the factory does not merely optimize manual labour. It really does mechanize or industrialize *labour itself*.

In a way similar to the industrialization of labour just described, the camera, along with the process of editing, industrializes dance: it contracts many small movements into one observable process. The replay allows the eye to wander, take in minuscule movements of lips and hair, the wrinkling of clothes, etc. Just as the envelope machine contracts five workers into one, the camera contracts a million eyes, many re-performances into one (or few). We may record ourselves, then watch, re-watch, do it again but differently. Dance on screen thus becomes a disciplining device that enables a stricter rehearsal. Note that in contemporary music videos, it is exactly the mishap, the mistake that is thus filtered out of an actual performance, made to disappear in practice, thus rendering hospitality towards a clumsy performance superfluous. Furthermore, however, the camera allows to edit many hours into just a few minutes or seconds. Hours and hours of footage may be filtered for the most sexy, most stunning, most weird moments and then edited accordingly.

Furthermore, the dancer becomes a mere element to the dance on screen. Just as the worker becomes an extension to the envelope machine, the dancer becomes an extension to the camera, to the editing process. The movements that we see are made *for* the camera – and often they are merely snippets of many more movements, filmed from various angles so as to provide material to be edited. The same counts for outfits, for light (which cameras need a lot of), for make up (which is often over-pronounced so as to cover what could never be seen in a physical encounter), etc. Here, another machine enters the equation: the computer with its digital image producing software. It's the possibilities of the *editing* process that dictates the number of repetitions during a recording session as well as positions, make up, etc. The dancer repeats their action or keeps improvising, while the camera changes position, moves in a different way, often only in order to get that *one shot* or set of shots that will eventually looks good for a few seconds at a video streaming platform. Yet again, the dancer (just as the worker) adheres to the logic of the machine and not the other way around.

This contraction, this condensation makes for another kind of dance, which inevitably takes hold of human movement off screen as well: all dance is screen dance. A filter of screenability, of adjustment to re-play lays over offline movements. Our own embodiment is at least in part shaped by the patterns of movement that we see and imitate. But more so, our habituation to *sit and watch* informs our ways of perceiving real-life interactions as well – we constantly perform little sketches for each other, a little dance, a little performance. There is thus no real distinction between on-screen and off-screen, insofar as the referential system of dance-on-screen guides our gestures, enables our rehearsal, and provides a background for our perception – not just of dance, actually, but of movement more generally.

This contracting, industrializing, condensing effect, however, is also why video lends itself to DIY aesthetics. In principle, it does not necessarily take much action to make an impressive image. It does take a lot of editing though, or the right kind at least. While the lovers outside the TV screen murder each other – the largest gesture in the game of love there is – the small screen allows for effect without damage, with simple cuts and simple moves. This industrialization of dance goes along especially well with Jupiter Io as guitarist in the background who barely moves at all, looking downward. We don't even see his face. He is barely doing anything. And yet he is arranged in the image in a way that makes him look withdrawn, mysterious, sometimes a bit scary. He's moving, dancing even, if ever so minimally. But it's the editing, the adjustment and positioning within the rhythm of the song as a sometimes-sudden occurrence that lets his withdrawal shine.

II.a.iv ~~Future~~

"Love is Violence" presents a dance on screen *within* the screen. Although the dance is minimal, it is unmistakably taking place. It resides in a space beyond or besides the main action. While the two lovers eviscerate each other, Glass dances *in a TV screen*. She resides elsewhere, industrialized, digitalized, forever removed. In fact, in 2022 (when the video went online), TV sets were very much out of fashion. Glass's dance is thus not merely stitched together by digital editing technique, but also projected back into a past that never took place. It is an impossible dance that in its full proportion can happen *only* in an impossible space, both spatially and temporally removed from reality. Now, this is an appropriate depiction of the nature of something I want to call ~~future~~ as a strange "a-venir"[34] it never actually arrives, remains irresolvably withdrawn, virtual, ghostly (appropriately, Glass and Io look like ghosts). This ~~future~~ as a strange "a-venir" is an indeterminate notion. Literally, "avenir" is French for "future." Yet written with a dash, it may also mean "that which comes/arrives" (reading "venir" as "to come" and "a" as a prefix signalling towardness as in "attention," which literally means "toward the stretch") or "that which never comes/arrives" (reading "a" as a negation as in "asocial," which literally means "opposed to the social" or "incapable of being social"). "A-venir" means *all of this*: a future that never fully arrives, that always remains in suspension, always at least partially indeterminate, but also always in a process of arrival, never out of sight, never disappearing completely. And really, this is how futurity works: there is always more of it, in itself it remains indeterminate, never mind how much of it manifests. ~~Future~~ is mere intelligibility of futurity without actualization. The ~~future~~ is queer – it dances on, looks for another expression, another embodiment, manifests difference without an end in sight, not even a next morning or a next minute. In their song "Mos Thoser," Hyperpop duo Foodhouse says it like this: "Tonight let's do shit that gets us in cringe comps / Make some new behaviors that straight people will infringe on."[35] A "cringe comp[ilation]" is a video that entails excerpts from other videos deemed "cringe," thus somehow strange, ridiculous, or else edgy and ethically dubious. Yet these actions, say Foodhouse, are exactly what "straight people will infringe on" – that which the mainstream is going to appropriate, internalize, and commodify. The consequence is, of course, that other "new behaviors" will be created, that queerness will migrate elsewhere, to other cringe territories, generate, *differentiate* culture for future mainstream appropriation.[36] Yet the queer activity is not directed towards this. It is mere differentiation, mere attempts to move on, to escape – colonial violence, unaffordable housing, looming ecological collapse and financial crisis, violence in the streets, micro aggressions at the workplace, and all the other miseries that make queer and trans lives harder than they should be. Consequentially, queer life has traditionally been associated with parties, with nightlife, with the transient zones of indeterminacy, without a clear image of tomorrow, dwelling in suspension of whatever comes next. These are the spaces and activities of ~~futurity~~, which act and subsist in difference from the given – *the end*.[37] The ~~future~~ is a baseline hospitality, minimal in its bare receptiveness for *something* that can never be actualized, never be filled.

When Glass dances in a space beyond the slaughterhouse of "Love is Violence," it's the survival dance, the dance of bodies aimlessly pushing forward.[38] There is no hope – *the end*. Just bare persistence, continuation, dancing-on. It is the mark of a "futurity" without a narrative, without a direction, which is why I choose to cross it out, calling it ~~future~~. The ~~future~~ is receptive to temporality but is not inherently linked to time understood as a continuity between temporal units such as moments, hours, days or segments of a life. In the ~~future~~, there will be no "future" in an emphatic, positively charged, or even hopeful sense. Its fate is not yet determined – in fact, it is that indeterminacy. The ~~future~~ is not even geared towards actualization. It's the bare intelligibility of an elsewhere. This indeterminacy is a genuine characteristic of creatures like us: we never know the full order of causes, we are always subject to surprises, to history taking yet another turn.[39]

However, as long as we remain in the space of intelligibility, the a-venir remains intact; things will go on, hope and fear may materialize. In "Love is

Violence," the TV on screen is the marker of this intelligibility as inevitable removedness.[40] For what is intelligibility if not doubling, distance, withdrawal, the capacity *not* to be present *while* one is present? Intelligibility makes the world go 'round because it grants it a breath, a gap, a pause through which existence can slip in and start moving. And likewise, TV runs on interruption (the commercial break, the end of an episode) and (almost) always represents an *elsewhere* (spatially), most often a replay of a past that never happened (a fictional scenario, even if it's live). Yet it nevertheless manifests an indeterminate ~~future~~.[41] In "Love is Violence," then, an animating gap occurs as the intelligibility (the screen on screen) that manifests an indeterminate ~~future~~ (that strange a-venir). Its inevitable receptivity for an elsewhere, an otherwise, etc., contests the violent collapse of hospitality into the hostility of private property. For the latter requires a level of *determination* that remains forever troubled by the ~~future~~, that strange intelligibility of an *indeterminate* elsewhere that continuously calls for re-negotiation, for re-invention, and for the failure thereof. Whatever grows out of this indeterminacy will be subject to it yet again. If "[t]he desire for communism is a desire without the present,"[42] it may be this aspect of survival preserved in dance on screen in all its ambiguity: an aspect that is not consumed in hospitality becoming hostility, never mind how violent that hostility is going to be – and yet doomed to be consumed by its own indeterminacy.[43] In the following section, I want to focus more on that aspect of survival.

II.b Ecological Collapse

Dance as a rehearsal of hospitality is expressed masterfully in Santiago Tamayo Soler's *Retornar*. The queer Latin American post-apocalyptic fantasy video game follows the trajectory of the last nine people (all queer and/or trans) on earth after the last war has ended. That war had been induced by ecological collapse, caused by brutally extracting whatever possible, turning it into private property.[44] Yet again, at the horizon of the scenario under investigation, private property is a driving force, though this time as a continuation of colonial appropriation sometimes called "original accumulation." For the material basis of capitalism is really not individual ownership as the institution of private property would have us believe, but centuries of large-scale theft of land and people.[45]

About 40 percent of *Retornar* is spent dancing to a remix of Nicki Minaj's "Did it On 'Em" by DJ Minas.[46] After a lengthy trip through deserted lands, main protagonist SSAANNTIIIAAGGOO climbs a staircase made of clouds and reaches a celestial dance floor, called *the Unknxwn*, where he is being warmly welcomed by three other survivors and a very tall creature called Ricorica, who explains that the dance floor was generated out of SSAANN-TIIIAAGGOO's brain waves in order to comprehend an alien presence.

Ricorica then adds: "[...] dance and enjoy. Like there is no tomorrow. We have to celebrate."[47] And so, they do. One by one, survivors arrive on the dance floor, while everybody is going all out in their pixelated dance performances. These performances are short clips in infinite loops in various speeds and of various styles from the repertoire of queer movement: some look like vogueing, some more like lab dance, some like regular club movements. The game is clearly queer coded: the majority of the story takes place in front of a pinkish background, the main protagonist gets in touch with aliens through a gigantic disco ball, and everybody is dressed in light weight club gear.

After five more survivors arrive, we learn that the alien presence sent humankind to Earth a long time ago and is now, after the effective collapse of humanity, going to try save the planet. The last nine people on Earth are thus being collected by alien overlords to serve as biological material to make the planet inhabitable again after its imminent ecological collapse. Effectively, in the very last minutes of humanity, we see them dancing – with each other, for one another, and for their own enjoyment – to a soundtrack by electronic music producer DJ Minas that invites us to join the post-apocalyptic party.[48] Here, then, Earth has become *inhospitable* to human life due to humankind's *hostile* actions. Within the logic of the game, the reason is the same as it is in actual reality: natural resources have been turned into private property and were, as a consequence, depleted for the sake of the accumulation of capital. In analogy with "Love is Violence," private property turns hospitality into hostility. But whereas "Love is Violence" focused on individual bodies as hosts for one another, *Retornar* focuses on planet Earth as the host of humanity as such. The last nine are being sacrificed in order for the lost

FIGURE 2.2 Still from: Santiago Tamayo Soler, *Retornar*, 2021
Source: Santiago Tamayo Soler.

hospitality to return (hence the title of the game: *Retornar*), in the hope that they may eventually transform into the soil from which new organisms will come to grow. The end of dancing, then, is the end of humanity as well. Yet it is also, arguably, the preservation of planet Earth. Thus, while in "Love is Violence" we see the destruction of the host as the ultimate limit case of embodied hospitality, *Retornar* shows us the opposite end of the spectrum: self-sacrifice in order to regenerate what little is left of the planet's hospitality to organic life in general, so as to eventually *extend* that hospitality to more and different forms of life.

However, through dancing, the last nine insist on hospitality for one another in the face of an ecologically ruined world. Even during this very last dance, the last nine people on Earth preserve an indeterminate, post-apocalyptic ~~future~~, a relation to one another and to a moment yet to come. This last dance captures yet again that ~~futuristic~~ indeterminacy that lives at the heart of human existence discussed above in the case of the TV screen in "Love is Violence."[49] And yet again, futurity is indicated by multiple layers of withdrawal: the game takes place in a retro look, reminiscent of pixelated games from the 1990s or early 2000s, yet it involves 3D scans of real people and their dance moves. Just as the grainy image of the TV set in "Love is Violence," *Retornar* thus indicates ~~futurity~~ by way of interpellating an impossible past. Note also that *Retornar* tells the story of the last people on Earth. Its ~~futurity~~ is thus the ultimate no-future-future: it is literally the end of humanity. The story told here cannot actually be told, because it is the end of all human storytelling.[50] Besides the temporal impossibility of the game (1990s aesthetic with 2020s technology), it also sustains a narrative impossibility: The premise that there will be no human storytelling after this story, notwithstanding that we perceive this post-apocalyptic scenario *as humans* and in a historical moment that calls for a fundamental U-turn regarding global measures against the ensuing ecological disaster. *Retornar's* ~~futurity~~ thus articulates another limit case: receptivity for an *elsewhere*, an *otherwise* where there are no resources for an *elsewhere* or *otherwise* left. And yet hospitality for that *elsewhere/otherwise* is hard wired into the nature of (particular) existence, which is why it remains a driving force even in the face of total ecological collapse.

In *Retornar,* hospitality extends beyond the gamescape. The in-game characters are, in fact, results of an open call on Instagram looking for Latin American/Latinx people that were interested in performing some actions in front of a green screen for a small fee.[51] Because of Covid-19 restrictions, it needed to be a local Montreal group. The dancers were asked to create characters based on a dystopian world set in Latin America. Some focused on physical skills and looks only, others wrote full biographies. The only restriction was not to wear anything that would interfere with the green screen during post-production. Tamayo then shot footage of them walking, crawling, jumping, sitting, greeting, and dancing on an axis from four "isometric" angles required to make everyone move around in the gamescape. These movement interpretations were specific to each dancer and their character. They included dance moves, which were performed to old school reggaeton with very defined bass and rhythm, that would later be easy to match with the music that Minas was working on. The models for the characters were mostly musicians, performers, visual artists, ballroom (vogue) dancers (one of them is the mother of House of Mulan in Montreal).[52] In this way, the hospitality performed within the gamescape extends to mutual real-life hospitality: Tamayo first hosts the dancers within a studio and then within his dystopian world. The dancers share their bodies, their movements, their characters to populate that world. In this sense, the production of a virtual hospitality generates actual, real hospitality.

From this, we can derive an anticapitalistic principle: enable more hospitality. For we have already seen how hospitality properly understood and private property are mutually exclusive, how hospitality turns into hostility once practiced within the confines of private property. In order to unlearn private property, we must thus enact hospitality in such a way that it does not merely please everybody involved, but facilitates an *extension* of the sphere of hospitality, inspires repetition of the experience of hospitality, nourishes and cultivates hospitality as a counter paradigm of social interaction. *Retornar* demonstrates a limit case: in a scenario where the hospitality of planet Earth for organic life in general is in jeopardy, the last nine offer their own bodies as the source material for a restart of organic life. The frontier between host (the planet) and guests (the inhabitants) collapses and the physical destruction of the latter serves to maintain the former and preserve an as-of-yet indeterminate future. This futurity however is independent of feasibility, independent of any possible outcome or potential happy end. It is a baseline of (particular) existence, a fact of reality. From a perspective of futurity, then, it is of no consequence whether planet Earth or humanity itself can be saved or not. The question of hospitality itself is not goal oriented. It may, however, have a beneficial effect on the ecological trajectory of planet Earth nonetheless.

The ethical question we can draw from all this is: how can we inspire an intensification and repetition of hospitality in our concrete, individual actions? The parallel political question is this: which social institutions encourage an extension of the sphere of hospitality and an intensification of hospitable acts? Both "Love is Violence" and *Retornar* suggest that we can use dance as a rehearsal space for anti-capitalistic hospitality. Yet as pointed out above, the concrete manifestations of these hospitable acts must remain indeterminate, to be specified in concrete interactions. And insofar as we already have a taste of the feeling of hospitality, we can already glance through the cracks of private property as the hegemonial kind of social relation under neoliberal capitalism. The future announces itself when we dance, when we flirt, when we have sex – but only as an echo from nowhere. Everything depends on our detailed study of these experiences, on intensifying them in our everyday lives, on insisting on their relevance and superiority over private property as a way of life, on producing (dramatic, architectural, poetic, entrepreneurial, visual, intellectual) works and designs that explore and propagate these practices, and on suggesting social institutions that encourage them long term.

"... if that's all there is my friend, then let's keep dancing."

Peggy Lee[53]

Notes

1. Alkistis Dimech, "202: The Occulted Body," May 5–6, 2016, in *Rendering Unconscious*, presented at the Psychoanalysis, Art & the Occult Conference, podcast, MP3 audio, 34:02, https://soundcloud.com/highbrowlowlife/ru202-butoh-dancer-alkistis-dimech-presents-the-occulted-body. Accessed October 1, 2022.
2. Alice Glass, "Love is Violence," Eating Glass Records, 2022.
3. I cross out "future" because although nominally pointing elsewhere in a loosely temporal sense, that elsewhere is not restricted to or even meant to actualize at some point in time, however imminent or far out. For more on this, see section II. a.iv, ~~Future~~.
4. For an alternative, though related perspective, see McKenzie Wark, *Raving* (London and Durham: Duke University Press, 2023), 19, 29, 92.
5. Santiago Tamayo Soler, "Santiago Tamayo Soler – G3: *Retornar*," PHI Foundation for Contemporary Art, September 22, 2021, accessed October 1, 2022, https://archives.fondation-phi.org/en/audio/phi-montreal-santiago-tamayo-soler/ Available at https://vimeo.com/786738025.
6. If now you think that you *do* enjoy your life, think again: how much could you enjoy your life if you did not have to spend much of it trying to chase money that pays the bills, social capital that will work as social security in case of emergency, or cultural capital that can be cashed in for the lack of finance or recognition that permeates your every day?
7. For more on this distinction, see Isaiah Berlin, *Two Concepts of Liberty* (Oxford: Clarendon, 1959).
8. In fact, however, private property is most often built on theft, conquest, oppression, and the like. See, for example, Brenna Bhandar, *Colonial Lives of Property* (Durham: Duke University Press Books, 2018); David Graeber, *Debt – The first 5000 years* (Brooklyn, NY: Melville House Publishing, 2012).
9. If positive freedom now sounds like the better deal, it does so only in a social formation where direct authoritarian acquisition is outlawed. For in a social order where basic means of survival such as food or shelter can be taken away from you by a feudal lord or a member of an authoritarian party, private property as the manifestation of negative freedom guarantees a minimal agency and recognition of one's existence as a person. Private property in fact promises some satisfaction of our desires and that is why we desire private property. In fact, this is the constant choir of the proponents of private property: they sing of authoritarian leaders, of medieval oppression, etc. In a situation under siege, where other people, countries, sexual orientations constantly want to take something away from you, private property as a

social institution seems like a great way to ensure your flourishing, survival, and enjoyment. Yet once the immediate threat of lethal dispossession is tamed, why not move on to overcome the structural troubles built into a social order based on negative freedom, such as the perpetuation of crisis mode and toxic relationships?

10 For the example of medical care, see exemplarily: Janine Marchessault and Kim Sawchuk, *Wild Science: Reading Feminism, Medicine, and the Media*, (London: Routledge, 2000); Fouzieyha Towghi, "The Re-colonization of South Asian Women's Bodies: Normalizing Off-Label Experiments in the Pharmaceuticalization of Homebirth," in *Negotiating Normativity: Postcolonial Appropriations, Contestations, and Transformations*, eds. Nikita Dhawan, Elisabeth Fink, Johanna Leinius, and Rirhandu Mageza-Barthel (Berlin: Springer, 2016), 113–30; Paul Preciado, "Pharmacopower," in *Testo Junkie* (New York: The Feminist Press, 2013), 144–235.
11 Judith Still, *Derrida and Hospitality* (Edinburgh: Edinburgh University Press, 2012), 14.
12 Linda Martín Alcoff, *Visible Identities: Race, Gender and the Self* (Oxford, New York: Oxford University Press, 2005), 185.
13 Alcoff, *Visible Identities*, 185.
14 Margaret Cavendish, *Observations Upon Experimental Philosophy* (New York: Cambridge University Press, 2003), 73. Spinoza's vision of the body would be consistent with this. See, for example, E2p13-E2p14 and E3p2s in Baruch Spinoza, *Oeuvres IV: Ethica / Éthique*, ed. and trans. Pierre-François Moreau (Paris: Presses Univeritaires de France, 2020). For more on a Cavendishian feminism, see Luce deLire, "Erotics as First Philosophy – Metaphysics and/of Desire between Aristotle, Avicenna, Cavendish and Spinoza," in *Libidinal Economies of Crisis Times*, ed. Ben Gook (New York: Columbia University Press, forthcoming).
15 The concept of "organization" is used in Gilles Deleuze and Felix Guattari, *Anti-Oedipus* (Minneapolis: University of Minnesota Press, 2003), 8, 27–28.
16 Wark, *Raving*, 45
17 Jacques Derrida, *Limited Inc* (Evanston, IL: Northwestern University Press, 1977).
18 Derrida, *Acts of Religion*, eds. Jaques Derrida and Gil Anidjar (New York and London: Routledge, 2002) 356.
19 Glass, "Love is Violence."
20 Glass, "Love is Violence."
21 Derrida, *Cosmopolites de Tous Les Pays, Encore Un Effort!* (Paris: Galilée, 1997), 42. "Hospitality is culture itself and not simply one ethic amongst others." The reason is that *everything* is always already involved in a negotiation about limits, about what belongs where. Hospitality thus permeates all ethical frameworks as its shaky ground. This is why rape is rightly thought to be one of the worst crimes: it attacks not only this or that ethical rule but is an affront against ethics itself. For more on the gendered dimension of hospitality, see Still, *Derrida and Hospitality*.
22 For more on this, see deLire, "Lessons in Love I: On Revolutionary Flirting," *Stillpoint Magazine*, December 15, 2022, https://stillpointmag.org/articles/lessons-in-love-i-on-revolutionary-flirting/; Comrade Josephine, "Full Queerocracy Now!: Pink Totaliterianism and the Industrialization of Libidinal Agriculture," *e-flux journal*, no. 117 (2021), https://www.e-flux.com/journal/117/386679/full-queerocracy-now-pink-totaliterianism-and-the-industrialization-of-libidinal-agriculture/.
23 For more on this, see deLire, "Lessons in Love II: The Erotics of Toxicity," *Stillpoint Magazine*, October 2022, https://stillpointmag.org/articles/lessons-in-love-ii-the-erotics-of-toxicity.
24 Dimech, "202: The Occulted Body."
25 Note that flirtation does not necessarily lead to sex. See deLire, "Lessons in Love I"; Jean Baudrillard, *Seduction* (London: Palgrave Macmillan, 1991).

26 For more on libidinal intelligibility, see deLire, "Catchy Title[1]: Gender Abolitionism, Trans Materialism, and beyond," *Year of the Women Magazine*, September 4, 2022, https://yearofthewomen.net/en/magazin/catchy-title-1-gender-abolitionism-trans-materialism-and-beyond.
27 For my take on desire, see deLire, "Erotics as First Philosophy."
28 Dimech, "202: The Occulted Body."
29 Nita Farahany, "TikTok is part of China's cognitive warfare campaign," *The Guardian*, March 25, 2023, https://www.theguardian.com/commentisfree/2023/mar/25/tiktok-china-cognitive-warfare-us-ban. See also Farahany, *The Battle for Your Brain: Defending the Right to Think Freely in the Age of Neurotechnology* (New York: St. Martin's Press, 2023).
30 Luc Boltanski and Eve Chiapello, *The New Spirit of Capitalism* (London: Verso Books, 2018); Thomas Picketty and Arthur Goldhammer, *Capital In the Twenty-First Century* (Cambridge, MA: Harvard University Press 2018); Penny A. Weiss, *Feminist Manifestos: A Global Documentary Reader* (New York: New York University Press, 2018).
31 Karl Marx, *Capital Volume One*, trans. Ben Fowkes (New York: Penguin 1976), 500.
32 Marx, *Capital Volume One*, 503.
33 One might wonder why the physical set up of the machine does not figure more prominently in this description. In fact, I do believe that restricting the terms "mechanization" and "industrialization" to the development of machines falls prey to a bourgeois ideology of progress and misses the point about what industrialization really is.
34 For more about this, see Jacques Derrida, *The Politics of Friendship*, trans. George Collins (London: Verso Books, 2020) 29. See also Jacques Derrida, Jürgen Habermas and Giovanna Borradori. *Philosophy in a Time of Terror: Dialogues with Jürgen Habermas and Jacques Derrida* (Chicago: University of Chicago Press, 2003), 96.
35 Foodhouse, "Mos Thoser," Genius, October 27, 2020, https://genius.com/Foodhouse-mos-thoser-lyrics.
36 For more on queer and trans people as differentiators, see deLire, "Can the Transsexual Speak?," in "Intersectionality Today," special issue, *philoSOPHIA: Journal of Transcontinental Feminism* 13, 54 (2024).
37 For an alternative view, see Wark, *Raving*.
38 In the last interview with Derrida, see his thoughts around survival: Derrida, *Learning to Live Finally*, trans. Pascal-Anne Brault and Michael Naas (Hoboken: Melville House Publishing, 2011).
39 Both José Esteban Munoz and Ernst Bloch try to interpret this indeterminacy as a necessary hope. I disagree. Indeterminacy can only be hope if it is appropriated in a favourable way. Compare Jose Esteban Munoz, *Cruising Utopia – The Then and There of Queer Futurity*, 10th Anniversary ed. (New York: New York University Press, 2019); Ernst Bloch, *Das Prinzip Hoffnung* (Berlin: Walter de Gruyter, 2016); E3DA12, E4p47d, E3p50 in Spinoza, *Oeuvres IV*.
40 In the sense of a constitutive withdrawal. See Jacques Derrida, "Desistance," in *Typography: Mimesis, Philosophy, Politics*, eds. Philippe Lacoue-Labarthe and Christopher Fynsk (Cambridge: Harvard University Press 1989), 2.
41 See also Avital Ronell, "Trauma TV – Twelve Steps Beyond the Pleasure Principle," in *The ÜberReader*, eds. Avital Ronell and Diane Davis (Urbana, IL: University of Illinois Press 2008), 66–68.
42 Wark, *Raving*, 31
43 Derrida, *Learning to Live Finally*.
44 Santiago Tamayo Soler, "Santiago Tamayo Soler – G3: *Retornar*," PHI Foundation for Contemporary Art, September 22, 2021, https://archives.fondation-phi.org/en/audio/phi-montreal-santiago-tamayo-soler/. Accessed October 1, 2022. Available at https://vimeo.com/786738025.

45 See for example: Bhandar, *Colonial Lives of Property*; Silvia Federici, *Caliban and the Witch* (Brooklyn, NY: Autonomedia, 2004); Cedric J. Robinson, *Black Marxism* (Chapel Hill, NC: University of North Carolina Press, 2005); Eric Williams, *Capitalism and Slavery* (Morrisville, NC: Lulu Press, Inc, 2015).
46 DJ Minas, SoundCloud, accessed October 1, 2022, https://soundcloud.com/djminasecu.
47 Soler, *Retornar*, PHI Montreal 2021.
48 DJ Minas.
49 As I have argued elsewhere, such material indeterminacy is the core of politically explosive contemporary queer politics. See Luce deLire, "The New Queer – Aesthetics of the Esoteric Left and Virtual Materialisms," *Public Seminar*, August 19, 2019, https://publicseminar.org/essays/the-new-queer/. Accessed October 1, 2022. Note that what I call "indeterminacy" here is called "virtuality" in that essay.
50 Is there non-human storytelling? Possibly. But it's probably heterogenous to human storytelling, possibly hardly understandable. The end of humanity is therefore most probably the end of storytelling as we know it, if not the end of story telling altogether.
51 The following paragraph is an edited version of Santiago Tamayo Soler's responses to questions I posed through Instagram.
52 "The Imperial Dynasty House of Mulan," Toronto Kiki Ballroom Alliance, https://tkba.ca/mulan. Accessed October 1, 2022.
53 Peggy Lee, "Is that all there is?," Warner Chappell Music, Inc., 1969.

Bibliography

Alcoff, Linda Martín. *Visible Identities: Race, Gender and the Self*. Oxford, New York: Oxford University Press, 2005.
Baudrillard, Jean. *Seduction*. London: Palgrave Macmillan, 1991.
Berlin, Isaiah. *Two Concepts of Liberty*. Oxford: Clarendon, 1959.
Bhandar, Brenna. *Colonial Lives of Property*. Durham: Duke University Press Books, 2018.
Bloch, Ernst. *Das Prinzip Hoffnung*. Berlin: Walter de Gruyter, 2016.
Boltanski, Luc, and Eve Chiapello. *The New Spirit of Capitalism*. London: Verso Books, 2018.
Cavendish, Margaret. *Observations Upon Experimental Philosophy*. New York: Cambridge University Press, 2003.
Comrade Josephine. "Full Queerocracy Now!: Pink Totaliterianism and the Industrialization of Libidinal Agriculture." *e-flux journal*, no. 117 (2021). https://www.e-flux.com/journal/117/386679/full-queerocracy-now-pink-totaliterianism-and-the-industrialization-of-libidinal-agriculture/.
Deleuze, Gilles, and Felix Guattari. *Anti-Oedipus*. Minneapolis: University of Minnesota Press, 2003.
deLire, Luce. "Can the Transsexual Speak?" In "Intersectionality Today," special issue, *philoSOPHIA: Journal of Transcontinental Feminism* 13 (forthcoming).
deLire, Luce. "Catchy Title [1]: Gender Abolitionism, Trans Materialism, and beyond." *Year of the Women Magazine*. September 4, 2022. https://yearofthewomen.net/en/magazin/catchy-title-1-gender-abolitionism-trans-materialism-and-beyond.
deLire, Luce. "Erotics as First Philosophy – Metaphysics and/of Desire between Aristotle, Avicenna, Cavendish and Spinoza." In *Libidinal Economies of Crisis Times*, edited by Ben Gook. New York: Columbia University Press, forthcoming.

deLire, Luce. "LESSONS IN LOVE I: ON REVOLUTIONARY FLIRTING." *Stillpoint Magazine*. December 15, 2021. https://stillpointmag.org/articles/lessons-in-love-i-on-revolutionary-flirting/.

deLire, Luce. "LESSONS IN LOVE II: THE EROTICS OF TOXICITY." *Stillpoint Magazine*. October 2022. https://stillpointmag.org/articles/lessons-in-love-ii-the-erotics-of-toxicity.

deLire, Luce. "The New Queer – Aesthetics of the Esoteric Left and Virtual Materialisms." *Public Seminar*. August 19, 2019. https://publicseminar.org/essays/the-new-queer/. Accessed October 1, 2022.

Derrida, Jacques. "Desistance." In *Typography: Mimesis, Philosophy, Politics*, edited by Philippe Lacoue-Labarthe and Christopher Fynsk. Cambridge: Harvard University Press, 1989.

Derrida, Jacques. *Acts of Religion*. Edited by Jaques Derrida and Gil Anidjar. New York and London: Routledge, 2002.

Derrida, Jacques. *Cosmopolites de Tous Les Pays, Encore Un Effort!* Paris: Galilée, 1997.

Derrida, Jacques. *Learning to Live Finally*. Translated by Pascal-Anne Brault and Michael Naas. Hoboken: Melville House Publishing, 2011.

Derrida, Jacques. *Limited Inc*. Evanston, IL: Northwestern University Press, 1977.

Derrida, Jacques. *The Politics of Friendship*. Translated by George Collins. London: Verso Books, 2020.

Derrida, Jacques, Jürgen, Habermas and Giovanna, Borradori. *Philosophy in a Time of Terror: Dialogues with Jürgen Habermas and Jacques Derrida*. Chicago: University of Chicago Press, 2003.

Dimech, Alkistis. "202: The Occulted Body." Presented at the Psychoanalysis, Art & the Occult Conference. *Rendering Unconscious*. May 5–6, 2016. Podcast, MP3 audio, 34:02. https://soundcloud.com/highbrowlowlife/ru202-butoh-dancer-alkistis-dimech-presents-the-occulted-body. Accessed October 1, 2022.

DJ Minas. SoundCloud. https://soundcloud.com/djminasecu. Accessed October 1, 2022.

Farahany, Nita. "TikTok is part of China's cognitive warfare campaign." *The Guardian*. March 25, 2023. https://www.theguardian.com/commentisfree/2023/mar/25/tiktok-china-cognitive-warfare-us-ban.

Farahany, Nita. *The Battle for Your Brain: Defending the Right to Think Freely in the Age of Neurotechnology*. New York: St. Martin's Press, 2023.

Federici, Silvia. *Caliban and the Witch*. Brooklyn, NY: Autonomedia, 2004.

Foodhouse. "Mos Thoser." Genius. https://genius.com/Food-house-mos-thoser-lyrics.

Glass, Alice. "Love is Violence." Eating Glass Records, 2022.

Graeber, David. *Debt*. Brooklyn, NY: Melville House Publishing, 2012.

Lee, Peggy. "Is that all there is?" Warner Chappell Music, Inc., 1969.

Marchessault, Janine, and Kim Sawchuk. *Wild Science: Reading Feminism, Medicine, and the Media*. London: Routledge, 2000.

Marx, Karl. *Capital Volume One*. Translated by Ben Fowkes. New York: Penguin, 1976.

Munoz, Jose Esteban. *Cruising Utopia – The Then and There of Queer Futurity*. 10th Anniversary ed. New York: New York University Press, 2019.

Picketty, Thomas, and Arthur Goldhammer. *Capital In the Twenty-First Century*. Cambridge, MA: Harvard University Press, 2018.

Preciado, Paul. "Pharmacopower." In *Testo Junkie*, 144–235. New York: The Feminist Press, 2013.

Robinson, Cedric J. *Black Marxism*. Chapel Hill, NC: University of North Carolina Press, 2005.
Ronell, Avital. "Trauma TV – Twelve Steps Beyond the Pleasure Principle." In *The ÜberReader*, edited by Avital Ronell and Diane Davis, 63–88. Urbana, IL: University of Illinois Press, 2008.
Soler, Santiago Tamayo. *Retornar*. PHI Montreal 2021.
Soler, Santiago Tamayo. "*Santiago Tamayo Soler – G3: Retornar.*" PHI Foundation for Contemporary Art. September 22, 2021. Accessed October 1, 2022. https://archives.fondation-phi.org/en/audio/phi-montreal-santiago-tamayo-soler/.
Spinoza, Baruch. *Oeuvres IV: Ethica/Ethique*. Edited and translated by Pierre-François Moreau. Paris: Presses Universitaires de France, 2020.
Still, Judith. *Derrida and Hospitality*. Edinburgh: Edinburgh University Press, 2012.
"The Imperial Dynasty House of Mulan." Toronto Kiki Ballroom Alliance. https://tkba.ca/Mulan.
Towghi, Fouzieyha. "The Re-colonization of South Asian Women's Bodies: Normalizing Off-Label Experiments in the Pharmaceuticalization of Homebirth." In *Negotiating Normativity: Postcolonial Appropriations, Contestations, and Transformations*, edited by Nikita Dhawan, ElisabethFink, Johanna Leinius, and Rirhandu Mageza-Barthel, 113–130. Berlin: Springer, 2016.
Wark, McKenzie. *Raving*. London and Durham: Duke University Press, 2023.
Weiss, Penny A. *Feminist Manifestos: A Global Documentary Reader*. New York: New York University Press, 2018.
Williams, Eric. *Capitalism and Slavery*. Morrisville, NC: Lulu Press, Inc, 2015.

3
KINESTHETIC EMPATHY AS HUMAN CONNECTION IN DIGITAL SPACE

Cara Hagan

As a point of entry into speaking about kinesthetic empathy as human connection in digital space, it is necessary to situate myself within the field of screendance (also referred to as *dance film*), the genre of digital creation this chapter is concerned with. I have been working as a maker of screendance since 2007 and have created more than twenty short films, many of which have traveled the screendance festival circuit. I began curating screendance in 2009 and founded the Movies by Movers film festival (subsequently American Dance Festival's Movies by Movers) in 2010. I directed and curated for the festival for thirteen years, before handing the directorial reins to fellow curator Jennifer Scully-Thurston in the fall of 2022. Since 2015, I have been an educator of screendance in both collegiate and community settings, having developed curricula pertaining to practice, history, and theory. I began my work as a scholar of screendance in 2015, publishing my first essay in 2016. I have since published a book on the topic of screendance and curatorial philosophy, from which I take this definition of screendance that serves as the undercurrent to my understanding of the genre and the lens through which I consider topics related to the experiences of making, watching, and curating:

I hold that screendance is one, some, or all of the following:

1. Site-Specific – meaning that we bring viewers into spaces where we may not otherwise be able to because of accessibility, geography, or the actual existence of a space prior to our imagining and creating it. Ideally, work is not simply transposed onto a space, but informed and driven by its inherent elements including but not limited to architecture, energy, history, and socio-cultural matter.

DOI: 10.4324/9781003335887-5

2. Camera-Specific – meaning that the camera is not a mere bystander capturing an event for posterity, rather it is an active participant in an effort to focus the eye of the viewer, accentuate kinetic experience as made possible by directors, choreographers, and performers, and appear as a character unto itself in the work through its contributions made possible by the cinematographer(s).
3. Edit-Specific – meaning that the final choreographic act in a dance film is that of arranging and rearranging mediated material for the purpose of constructing a work impossible to experience outside of the screen.[1]

I always say that I love being a maker of screendance because I believe it is magic. Having power over the laws of time and physics, the ability to reimagine the world or to create new ones, and the privilege of focusing the eye of the audience intentionally as a way of inviting spectators into a non-verbal experience makes creating these hybrid pieces of art deeply satisfying. It feels like an important mode of communication in a world where digital space has become a large part of many of our lives, but the need for human connection persists. Screendance for me, exists as a bridge between the poles of the algorithmic and the material.

When I occupy the role of the spectator – which is often, and with pleasure – I can appreciate the experience of being invited to walk this bridge. One of the things I love most about watching screendance is the *kinesthetic empathy* that occurs as part of the viewing process. If you are new to the term or concept, "kinesthetic empathy describes the ability to experience empathy merely by observing the movements of another human being."[2] Kinesthetic empathy isn't just a simple, mimetic response. Kinesthetic empathy employs *both* our physical and emotional bodies. It is rooted in science and is made possible by the very structure of our brains. Kinesthetic empathy is an important part of our ability to connect with each other as humans, and to connect with, and make sense of, aesthetic experiences. *Mirror neurons* are a class of brain cells found in animals and humans that are "activated, both when an action, such as grasping or gesturing is executed by one human being and *observed* by another."[3] Further, it has been found that these cells fire even when another human being is not present, for example, in the case of hearing a piece of music. In fact, the brain can intuit movement even if there is only an allusion to it, for instance when one observes the presence of brush strokes in a painting – the viewer can intuit the motion needed to create the strokes, eliciting a mirror response in the brain.[4]

As exciting as the discovery of mirror neurons is, more recent research on our brains suggest that the mirror neuron concept only partially explains our ability to connect actions observed or allusions to actions, to experiences within our own bodies. In his book, *The Myth of Mirror Neurons: The Real Neuroscience of Communication and Cognition*, Gregory Hickok highlights the limitations of the mirror neuron theory as lacking nuance with regard to the spectrum of human experience, which involves both motor and non-motor sensory and empathetic experiences:

> Although there is currently plenty of love between mirror neuron and embodiment theorists, the union is not without some tension. For example, the broader embodied cognition view holds that conceptual knowledge is grounded in the sum total of one's sensory, motor, and emotional experience...This is theoretically confusing because when researchers talk about functions that have little motor involvement, such as reading emotions or feelings for others, they invoke "mirror mechanisms" in nonmotor systems...thus endorsing the broader embodiment view.[5]

Science aside, humans have intuited the inherent empathetic connections between us and have utilized these connections in the pursuit of socialization and well-being. Cultures across the globe engage in shared, embodied experiences as vehicles for understanding, group learning, spiritual uplift, inspiration, and general well-being.

One of the most recognized practices cultivated for such purposes in the West would be Dance Movement Therapy (DMT in the US, DMP – Dance Movement Psychotherapy – in the UK). Marian Chace began her pioneering work in developing and codifying the practice of DMT in the 1940s in Washington, DC, while working in clinical settings. "Mirroring movement was key to Chace's method...Chace was aware that answering movement in similar forms dissipates the feeling of apartness...Empathy meant sharing the essence of all non-verbal expression resulting in what she called 'direct communication.'"[6] In essence, Chace used kinesthetic empathy to peel back the layers of verbal communication, societally inherited cues, and social politics to allow our most visceral impulses and feelings to emerge in communication. Through her work in various mental health facilities Chace recognized the inherent value of observing the movements of others and moving together writing, "rhythmic action in unison with others results in a feeling of well-being, relaxation and good fellowship. Even primitive man understood that a group of people moving together gained a feeling of more strength and security than any one individual could feel alone."[7]

In the twenty-first century, where we spend countless hours in front of screens, and most especially since the start of the Covid-19 pandemic, apartness and barriers to open communication are experiences we are intimately acquainted with. As more of our lives move onto internet platforms, and those platforms and the parameters of their uses blur, we are reminded how digital space simultaneously has the potential to be both a connecting force and a lonely void.

In the field of screendance, many artists are in the business of imparting embodied experiences to others through the screen via choreographic exploration on other human beings, which may include solo or group work in settings specific to the concepts being presented by the makers, alongside music or other sound specific to the work at hand. These aspects of screendance as I have described them may open the door for spectators to "feel into"[8] the work. This may in turn evoke emotions, memories, or other responses in the audience due to the ways our brains process information as briefly explained above. The challenge is immense: translating the sensations of touch, breath, bodily heat, and other corporeal experiences onto a screen. Even so, screendance makers have an opportunity to make the screen space more human through their pursuits because of the visceral nature of dance-making and the prioritization of non-verbal communication over dialogue as a driver of narrative. Additionally, "narrative" is a loose term when applied to screendance, which often finds its arc in the liminal space of abstraction where the screen acts as a sort of dream space where sensorial intuition drives imagery and pacing. Screendance aside, those in the field of cinema broadly conceived have recognized the power of screen-based work to inspire kinesthetic empathy in viewers. Adriano D'Aloia writes that "the most effective cases of empathetic relation in the film experience are those in which the movement of the represented body...creates a field of energy that vitalizes the space between the character's body and the spectator's body."[9] Given these aspects of screendance and film more broadly, I argue that kinesthetic empathy is not only a matter of course in the viewing experience, but that it is a necessary consideration in how many artists, scholars, and curators create, study, and program screendance. Thus, while it is not the express purpose of screendance to combat loneliness and disconnection, the genre can be seen as a powerful site for humanistic affinity. As articulated by Marian Chace, encountering rhythm and movement as a social or collective experience engenders empathy among human beings such that these experiences are profound enough to play a role in ameliorating mental illness like depression and anxiety, both of which are common ailments in contemporary society.[10] In the case of screendance, we might consider the gathering of people in a theater to be such a collective experience, or perhaps the meeting of the eyes of one person and a screen featuring other human (and non-human) beings as another kind of gathering unique to humans as the only species that makes content for the screen.

In my role as a screendance curator – which engages my experiences as a spectator, a researcher, and a steward of the form – I tend to find myself concerned with the possibility of energetic exchange in screendance on a screen where there are no actual humans present. The challenge here lies in the inability to make energetic exchanges with audience members in the ways they may occur in live theatrical performance which may include direct eye contact, three-dimensionality, and real interaction, to name a few. How do we maintain some residue of human interaction on the screen, where there is only light and pixels? What does it mean to be able to impart some deep feeling or stirring in a living spectator, when the very definition of watching something on screen means that they do not enjoy a two-way energetic exchange? What does it mean to inspire sensory investment when spectators are rendered more or less inert as they watch their screens? Although I recognize that viewers are also often inert while watching live performance too, the lack of two-way energetic exchange seems to amplify the experience of sitting (relatively) still.

As a partial answer to these questions, I am inspired and encouraged by those in the fields of digital platform development and digital poetics, who remind us that no screen space is complete without each other. Scholar Judith Donath for example, writes about the quest for humanness online in her text, *The Social Machine: Designs for Living Online*. She argues that for online spaces to truly engage us, they need to be attuned to the human experience. She says,

> We are embodied beings, who have evolved in the physical world; our thoughts and imagination are rooted in the sensory experience of our physical surroundings. Online, there is no body; there is only information. We comprehend abstract ideas by reframing them in metaphoric terms that ultimately derive from physical experience.[11]

Reading this quote some years ago, I was inspired to dig deeper into the politics of humanness in digital space from the vantage point of screendance and by extension, kinesthetic empathy. Though I had already recognized the presence of kinesthetic empathy in the experience of making and watching screendance prior to reading this quote and the literature that follows it in Donath's work, I had yet to make connections between kinesthetic empathy and the role of human connection in an increasingly digitized world. I had yet to fully appreciate the opportunity I have as a curator of screendance, to consider the possibilities of an experience in kinesthetic empathy for audiences who may have wildly varied experiences depending on what I choose to program, and how that material is presented.

To get to the point of being able to more aptly employ an understanding of kinesthetic empathy in my curatorial practice, I was inspired – in part by the work of Dee Reynolds and Matthew Reason referenced in this piece, in part by my curiosity as to how my knowledge of audience response could bolster my ability to be a better custodian of screendance – to conduct a small, qualitative study for the purpose of cultivating a better understanding of just *how* spectators experience kinesthetic empathy. How do physical sensations inform emotional experiences in individuals? How does emotional content drive one's experience of the body? How does an awareness of one's body during an aesthetic encounter help to paint a more holistic picture of the experience? An invitation to a small group of students helped me to begin to answer these questions.

Studying the Presence of Kinesthetic Empathy in Screendance

In the spring of 2018, I ran my study with 45 students across two sections of a freshman-level general education dance class. In that study I endeavored to illuminate how these students – the vast majority of whom would not describe themselves as artists or arts enthusiasts – experienced watching pieces of screendance as a visceral encounter. Given the nature of their existence as digital natives, and their varied experiences with embodiment practices, I was curious to see the range of responses they might have to watching people move on screen with choreographic intention.

Before presenting the findings of my study, I must name the limitations of such an endeavor. Although it was articulated to the students that their responses were not tied to their grade and therefore not mandatory to pass the class, many may have felt the need to respond positively (or at all) to the study because of the power dynamics at play in a collegiate classroom. Having introduced the study by having a conversation about what screendance is, and what kinds of sensations they may want to be aware of while viewing the works chosen for the study, some students may have been influenced in their responses by our classroom discussion. With regard to the bodily sensations I reference in the study, I had no equipment with which to measure the participants' bodily functions, meaning that changes in heart rate, breath, temperature, and amount of bodily movement could not actually be measured. Yet, while I acknowledge that this study is entirely anecdotal from a scientific standpoint, from a curatorial standpoint, I do believe there is valuable information here.

To carry out the study, I showed each group three short dance films over three separate days. These films were chosen from the vast collection of the Screendance Collective archive publicly available on Vimeo. One film, called *Believe* (2017), directed by James Lees, follows a wise and whimsical little boy as he turns soldiers in a war zone into a group of dancers through his own infectious movement. Another film, *I Got You* (2017), directed by Yagaboo, is a duet featuring a pair of synchronized swimmers in a dynamic and virtuosic choreography. The final film, *Wheelchair Dance* (2016), directed by Yasuhiro Tamura, is a "piece created in anticipation of the 2020 Olympics and Paralympics by interested Japan-based creatives, inspired by the wheelchair and contemporary dance" (Vimeo, 2017). In sum, the collection of films featured different genres of dance, bodies that are different from each other, and different subject matter and aesthetic styles. After watching each film, I asked the students to respond to the following prompts in a survey:

1. In one sentence, describe what the film is about.
2. Write three adjectives that you feel describe the film.
3. What is the overarching emotion you perceive in the film?
4. In one sentence, describe how you feel after watching the film.
5. During the film, did you notice any physical changes within yourself?

It came as no surprise that the answers to the first four questions ran the gamut of possibility. It was abundantly clear that the students responded to those questions based on first impressions (naturally), their level of exposure to the arts, their world view, their varied ability to articulate their thoughts and feelings in writing, and how they were feeling the day they watched each film. For example, where one student described *Wheelchair Dance* as "inspiring, emotional, and full of passion," another described the film as "somber, thrilling, and mysterious." Yet another described the same film as "daring, courageous, and fearless." It is evident that although there are some similarities between their answers – one can draw thematic connections between words like passion, thrilling, and daring, for example – these students all experienced this film very differently from one another, from emotional and cultural standpoints.

In fact, responses that alluded to a student's possible cultural experiences and worldview were most glaring among the prompts that asked the participants to speak to their interpretation of the film. Speaking about *Wheelchair Dance* again, students' responses ranged from being able to articulate thoughts about their own awareness of how the film affected them energetically, to those articulating thoughts about the film in a societal context, to those articulating thoughts based on stereotypes or pre-conceived notions of how someone different from themselves experiences their life. The following quotes help paint a picture of the range of responses students wrote on their questionnaires:

> "I feel like I want to release all of my stress I have been feeling this week through dance in that way."
> "The film brought an energy that translated well with me and I felt very passionate for this man's love of dance and how it helps him channel his emotions."
> "After watching the film, I felt myself desiring to know the fate of the man in the wheelchair and the woman from the coffee shop and if dance is something that connects them."
> "I feel much more aware of ableism and the stereotypes of dancers. Like when we picture an average dancer, we think of a skinny tall person that

moves gracefully. But this is so limiting to so many people who want to dance and don't fit this stereotype."

"When he was headed to the ocean I was on my seat because it looked as if he was going to kill himself."

The final quote was as jarring to me, as I imagine it is to you, but demonstrates how a student who may not have had much exposure to diverse groups of people might feel like the dancer's situation is so hopeless that he may actually endeavor to end his life. This was not at all the premise of the film, to be clear.

Although it would be easy to assume that emotional and physical responses to the films would align logically with how students interpreted them, this was not at all true. Many of the responses felt incongruous at first glance. After reading through the questionnaires several times, I once again had to remind myself that for many of these students, becoming aware of and expressing something about an encounter with a piece of art was quite new to them.

Though all of the prompts help paint a holistic picture of the experience of the films for each student, the question I was most interested in was the one about bodily sensations or changes. When I culled the answers to that question, I expected to read that many of the students found themselves swaying to the music, tapping their feet, or nodding their heads as they watched other humans moving their bodies across the screen. This did, in fact, happen. What was most interesting though was that the second-most reported sensation across all the films was feeling one's heartbeat fluctuate. More than one student reported "feeling my heartbeat racing." Some students noted more than one change in heart rate, writing responses like, "my heart started beating slower, then faster." It is interesting to note here that *heart rate variability*, or the time in between individual beats within a heart rate can "serve as an indicator of the functioning of brain regulatory systems,"[12] meaning that our heart rate, and changes to heart rate, can help us understand when sympathetic (fight or flight, arousal) and parasympathetic (rest) responses to both outer and inner stimuli are being activated within a person. Heart rate variability also "influences brain and emotional function" meaning that the rate of our heart and changes in heart rate can impact the way we feel emotionally and are able to function physically.[13] Perhaps some of the students were becoming aware of their own heart rate variability, in response to content that stimulated them.

On a scale of most to least frequent sensation reported, students reported bodily movement the most, accounting for 33% of all the responses tallied. Changes in heart rate accounted for 25% of the responses. Changes in breath, which included changes in breath rate and other breath experiences like sighs or gasps, accounted for 17% of responses. Other sensations, like goosebumps, smiling, and crying, accounted for 15% of responses. Responses that reported no change in bodily sensation at all accounted for 10% of responses. Several of those responses that reported no mention of bodily sensation *did* report emotional changes like feeling uplifted, peaceful, sad, excited, or anxious. In these instances, though I could not count their emotional responses as physical ones, I imagine that it could have been hard for some students to be aware of their bodies enough to notice the physical changes that may accompany emotional ones. I also recognize that the material may not have been of high interest to some of them and their actual attention (watching without distraction or letting their minds wander) may have been low. In contrast to this, about one quarter of the students noted more than one bodily sensation on their questionnaire, writing responses like, "I felt my heartbeat, and my fists clenched up."

As another aspect of the students' experience of empathy, I was delighted to find that several of the students – many of whom claimed multiple times over the course of the semester to have no artistic sensibilities – responded poetically to the films. For example, one student considers their experience of watching the synchronized swimmers in the water, writing, "It felt like a rush that one gets when they are in love, like having your breath taken away." Poetic response to a piece of art has long been recognized as an important form of empathetic response in the field of expressive arts therapy (multimodal creative therapy that may include dance, visual art, drama, music, poetry, and other forms of expression). It suggests that the viewer or participant has made a meaningful connection with the work that presents a generative opportunity for the emotional well-being of the viewer-artist.

There were no students in either class that had no response to the material at all. As mentioned, most of those questionnaires that indicated no physical changes within the participant did list some emotional or aesthetic response to the films. There were no students in either class that did not indicate some sort of aesthetic opinion about the work, even if they thought it was to express a level of neutrality about the work ("I thought this film was boring"). What bubbles to the surface for me in this experience is the disconnect Western society perpetuates between the mind and the body, between verbal and written language and the aesthetic. If nothing else, the study demonstrates the importance of energetic interplay between the viewer and the art. As Reason and Reynolds point out in their work, the relationship between the art and the audience can be strengthened through empathetic responses. Empathetic responses are integral to the audience's enjoyment of the art and their motivations to continue consuming art.[14]

Circling back to my role as a curator, I am invested in not only cultivating audiences for single events but encouraging individual audience members to become regular supporters of the arts. Based on this study, I decided to make an awareness of kinesthetic empathy in spectators of screendance a more critical concern in my curatorial practice in an effort to realize this vision in part, coupled with the necessary activities of marketing, promotion, community exposure and education, and garnering various forms of community support.

Curating for Kinesthetic/Empathetic Impact:

Following the experience of the study, I was contacted by Priscilla Guy of Regards Hybrides in the spring of 2019 with a request to guest-curate a block of films for an event taking place that November. When I received the curatorial prompt, the part of it that stood out to me the most was, "in a sea of technological innovation, what becomes of creativity on a human scale and its impact on our relationship with the world on a daily basis?" My mind turned to our quest for humanness in digital space and a set of burning questions emerged:

- Despite the end product of screendance existing in digital space, what is still *human* about the creative process with regard to screendance?
- What human residue does that process leave on the final product?
- What analog tools do we employ that are indispensable parts of making screendance?
- How do those tools serve to engender empathetic responses in spectators viewing the final product?

Following some consideration of these questions, a list of tools and experiences emerged that I felt would signal a strong empathetic response in the final product. My list included things like collaboration, the exploration of human conundrums like the difference between justice and injustice, answering the call to carry culture forward within our digital existence, explorations of our relationship to nature as humans, and the very human experience of introspection.

Thus, all of the films in the block I curated for the Regards Hybrides are ones where I considered both the final product and the process taken to create the films. For example, *Ground Swell*, directed and performed by JACKS (Kelsey Kramer and Lexie Thrash), is one created through a "multidisciplinary production and a collaborative round-robin editing process." Hannah Hamalian's *Aquarium*, a stop-motion animation "seeking unity between mind and body," was necessarily one that was created through a time-intensive process that would have employed both close planning and intuition. *Apariciones*, by Carolina Caycedo and Marina Magalhães, "depicts ghost-like dancers inhabiting the historic Los Angeles landmark, The Huntington Library ... centered on brown, black, and queer bodies ... the gaze of the dancers, or phantoms, holds the viewer accountable, something that is too often missing from history and art."[15]

All the films screened were as follows, in this order:

Ground Swell (2018), by JACKS (Kelsey Kramer and Lexie Thrash)
Women in Cities (2017) by Rosie Trump
Don't Miss It (2018) by Teddy Tedholm
Strategic Retreat (2018) by Marta Renzi
Aquarium (2018) by Hannah Hamalian
HOME (2017) by Jenny Larsson
Apariciones (2018) by Carolina Caycedo and Marina Magalhães
Piñata (2018) by LROD y Artistas (Laura Rodriguez)

In choosing to present the films in this order, I hoped to usher the audience through an intentional, energetic arc. That arc is one meant to prioritize physical and emotional awareness as a challenge to notions of the separation between art and spectator, and an intermingling of analog and digital experience.

How the Films Feel

Now, I take the liberty to creatively express how each film in the block I curated engenders empathy in me. I do this as a way of demonstrating the energetic arc I describe above, without having the films to show here on the page. As writing is for me yet another way to communicate felt experiences, this collection of impressions is both a translation of the filmic experience and a collection of small pieces of art, unto itself. Though objectivity is a useful and often called-upon tool in my curatorial work, I honor that our humanness is an inexorable part of ourselves, in all endeavors.

Ground Swell: The opening scene is like opening your eyes after taking a long nap out in the sun. It's late afternoon and your skin is hot. The light feels harsh as the scene comes into focus. My brow furrows. The sound of a ticking clock draws me immediately to the rhythm of my own heart. I hear the sounds of the woods – wind, rustling trees, water, the hum of insects – and realize I am humming softly, under my breath. Among the many shapes the bodies take on screen, I am most affected by the tension of a spine, isolated by the camera lens, curved as its body pulls against another. My spine curves a tiny curve, in recognition. A bow of respect from one set of searching bones, to another.

Women In Cities: Thrown, throwing, thrown again. My eyes are playing a little game, knocking around in their sockets as my attention is drawn to multiple parts of the screen at once. Three women jerk and stagger in a stark, shadowless world. When the extremities of their bodies are not flung to some part of the empty space, the women float from the top of the screen to the bottom. They rotate as if on a lazy Susan. They could be on display in a showroom, or in a museum. "Judge me," they say, as they pass in and out of view. Instead, I revel in the irreverent toss of a head of hair, in the disobedient rumple of a jacket in motion. I want to toss and rumple too, so I cross my legs, and give the edges of my cardigan a snap.

Don't Miss It: Watching a reiterated Teddy Tedholm make punctuated gestures that give way to tenuous release, my shoulders struggle to soften but I begin to sway anyhow. I take many deep breaths. In my chest, I feel the pangs of nostalgia, and the weight of melancholy. A simultaneous pressure and hollowness. Is it because the film is rendered in black and white? Is it the frames that falter like a skipping record? Maybe it's the lyrics of the song by James Blake: "When you stop being a ghost in a shell/And everybody keeps saying you look well/Don't miss it." Audible sighs as my body attempts to fill the void.

Strategic Retreat: The click-click-click of bicycle wheels calls my attention. Two people escape the world of concrete, bronze, and knotty histories to a haven under a canopy of old trees, and a soft bed where gentle sun welcomes tender touch. Tip-toeing fingers and roving noses on exposed skin engender warm feelings. I want to linger here. Images and sounds of societal strife break my reverie: news reels, raised voices, drums, and marching feet. Pulse erratic. Mixing emotions. Yet, there is hope. Bright colors invite me to play. I do.

Aquarium: a series of angular, animated shapes become a body made up of pieces and parts. They sit, stand, walk, collapse, and expand to the furthest reaches of the screen. Watching this body compose, crumble, scramble, explore the world in disarray, and recompose itself, I can feel the ways my own body is destroyed, reconfigured, and restructured in cycles – the shedding and regrowth of cells, parts of me injured and healed. I feel the spaces between my breaths lengthen and I feel a longing in the cavity where my heart lives. How does one reorganize a body when the body and disorder have become good friends?

HOME: Blurred visions reveal the shimmer of the sun, embodied. She shines on the grasses and the muck of the wetlands. I'm not sweating, but I could be. I can smell the rich earth material of the Everglades: peat and silt. Slick mud pressed and turned between palms. When's the last time I held mud in my own hands? The dryness of the skin between my fingers becomes impossible to ignore. The sun finds a perch on the grounded trunk of a rotting tree. Surely her sparkle is a welcome contribution to the sacred process of decay. I close my eyes and listen for a moment: "The golden one, a shapeshifter, a speedster, a trickster."

Apariciones: The persistent image of dancers shaking in place makes my breath feel shallow and my skin feel electric. I remember times when I have quaked with anger at injustices close to me and far away. The dancers' breath is audible and as they swirl among structures, spill down grand staircases, and twirl under the confinement of fishing nets. I feel tension move into my jaw. Reprieve comes when the dancers connect to the earth. Tree bark, water, stone. They stand still and stare. Their energy penetrates the barrier of my skin. I cannot blink when my breath is in limbo.

PIÑATA: The first sensation I feel is a shiver as a fan blows colored streamers hung from the ceiling in a windowless room. The faint light of the candles on the ofrenda evoke the smell of burning wax and smoke. All the times I have smelled that smell in my life collide in my mind. Dancers switch positions on a dime – the result of stop motion. They break the rules of rhythm and disrupt space-time as they multiply, become transparent, and speak in gesture. My heart tries to keep pace. Frantic levity – my feet wiggle and tap – becomes kaleidoscope – I catch my breath but my eyes keep darting.

In conclusion

Kinesthetic empathy is a human experience that is physically complex and plays a large role in our lives as sentient, intelligent beings. As humans, we seek to harness the power of empathetic response to make connections across space, including digital space. As our lives become more intertwined with digital platforms, our challenge is to continue to center the humanness of our interactions. Screendance emerges as one way we can explore the possibilities of raising our awareness and practice of empathy in digital space. As makers, educators, and curators of screendance, we are uniquely positioned to support audiences and fellow artists to encounter works that may elicit experiences of kinesthetic empathy. Connecting people to works and the artists that make them is essential to the health of the field of screendance because profound empathetic experiences keep people coming back to view and support the work. Like Marian Chace, Judith Donath, Dee Reynolds, and other thinkers, I believe that embodied experiences between people serve as connective tissue in societies. Hence, not only is the presence of kinesthetic empathy necessary to the ecosystem of the arts, it is integral to our very existence and survival.

Notes

1 Cara Hagan, *Screendance from Film to Festival: Celebration and Curatorial Practice* (Jefferson, NC: McFarland Publishing, 2022).
2 Dee Reynolds and Matthew Reason, *Kinesthetic Empathy in Creative and Cultural Practices* (Bristol: Intellect, 2012).
3 Carol S. Jeffers, "Within Connections: Empathy, Mirror Neurons, and Art Education," *Art Education* 62, no. 2 (2009): 18–23, https://doi.org/10.1080/00043125.2009.11519008.

4 Jeffers, "A Still Life Is Really a Moving Life: The Role of Mirror Neurons and Empathy in Animating Aesthetic Response," *The Journal of Aesthetic Education* 44, no. 2 (2010): 31, https://doi.org/10.5406/jaesteduc.44.2.0031.
5 Gregory Hickok, *The Myth of Mirror Neurons: The Real Neuroscience of Communication and Cognition* (New York: W.W. Norton & Company, 2014).
6 Bonnie Meekums, "Kinesthetic Empathy and Movement Metaphor in Dance Movement Psycho-Therapy," in Reynolds and Reason, *Kinesthetic Empathy*, 51–66.
7 Harris Chaiklin, *Marian Chace, Her Papers* (Kensington, MD: American Dance Therapy Association, 1975).
8 Susan Marie Lanzoni, *Empathy: A history* (New Haven: Yale University Press, 2018).
9 Adriano D'Aloia, "Cinematic Empathy: Spectator Involvement in the Film Experience," in Reynolds and Reason, *Kinesthetic Empathy*, 91–109.
10 Chaiklin, *Marian Chace, Her Papers*.
11 Judith Donath, *Social Machine: Designs for Living Online* (Cambridge, MA: The MIT Press, 2014).
12 Mara Mather and Julian F. Thayer, "How Heart Rate Variability Affects Emotion Regulation Brain Networks," *Current Opinion in Behavioral Sciences* 19 (2018): 98–104, 94 https://doi.org/10.1016/j.cobeha.2017.12.017.
13 Ibid.
14 Reason, Matthew, and Dee Reynolds. "Kinesthesia, Empathy, and Related Pleasures: An Inquiry into Audience Experiences of Watching Dance." *Dance Research Journal* 42, no. 2 (2010): 49–75, https://doi.org/10.1017/s0149767700001030.
15 These quotes are from the blurbs sent by the directors. They aren't published anywhere per se but are essentially everywhere the films go.

Bibliography

Chace, Marian. *Marian Chace, Her Papers*. Kensington, MD: American Dance Therapy Association, 1975.

D'Aloia, Adriano. "Cinematic Empathy: Spectator Involvement in the Film Experience." In Dee Reason and Matthew Reynolds, *Kinesthetic Empathy*, 91–109. Bristol: Intellect, 2012.

Donath, Judith. *Social Machine: Designs for Living Online*. Cambridge, MA: The MIT Press, 2014.

Hagan, Cara. *Screendance from Film to Festival: Celebration and Curatorial Practice*. Jefferson, NC: McFarland Publishing, 2022.

Hickok, Gregory. *The Myth of Mirror Neurons: The Real Neuroscience of Communication and Cognition*. New York: W.W. Norton & Company, 2014.

Jeffers, Carol S. "Within Connections: Empathy, Mirror Neurons, and Art Education." *Art Education* 62, no. 2 (2009): 18–23. https://doi.org/10.1080/00043125.2009.11519008.

Jeffers, Carol. "A Still Life Is Really a Moving Life: The Role of Mirror Neurons and Empathy in Animating Aesthetic Response." *The Journal of Aesthetic Education* 44, no. 2 (2010): 31. https://doi.org/10.5406/jaesteduc.44.2.0031.

Lanzoni, Susan Marie. *Empathy: A History*. New Haven: Yale University Press, 2018.

Mather, Mara, and Julian F. Thayer. "How Heart Rate Variability Affects Emotion Regulation Brain Networks." *Current Opinion in Behavioral Sciences* 19 (2018): 98–104. https://doi.org/10.1016/j.cobeha.2017.12.017.

Meekums, Bonnie. "Kinesthetic Empathy and Movement Metaphor in Dance Movement Psycho-Therapy." In Dee Reason and Matthew Reynolds, *Kinesthetic Empathy*, 51–66. Bristol: Intellect, 2012.

Reason, Matthew, and Dee Reynolds. "Kinesthesia, Empathy, and Related Pleasures: An Inquiry into Audience Experiences of Watching Dance." *Dance Research Journal* 42, no. 2 (2010): 49–75. https://doi.org/10.1017/s0149767700001030.

Reynolds, Dee, and Matthew Reason. *Kinesthetic Empathy in Creative and Cultural Practices*. Bristol: Intellect, 2012.

4

THE VALUE OF A CHEAP TRICK

Reverse Motion from Lo-Tech SFX to Speculative Spectacle

Alanna Thain

In Yinka Shonibare MBE's 2004 work of screendance, *Un Ballo in Maschera* (*A Masked Ball*), dancers perform and rewind the 1792 assassination of the Swedish king Gustav III (played in this film by a female dancer) at a masked ball in Stockholm, over a thirty-two minute duration.[1] There is no music at this ball, or in the digital video; only the sounds of embodied movement—breath, step, swish of costumes (Shonibare's signature Dutch wax fabrics), creak of floor, pistol shot, applause. The soundtrack itself is doubled between signification (a swooning sigh by two women fainting after the king falls) and the signaletic (the dancers' embodied labour rippling the closed and extravagant perfection of the mise en scène, a tableau come to laborious and at times creepy life). The video's circular structure is itself a layered and cumulative one, what Rebecca Schneider terms a "living loop": it begins with the assassin entering a palace and ends with her reversing out of the same place. In between, the action races towards the moment of assassination and collapse, only for the king to rise again to continue dancing, three times, before the same scenes play again in reverse.[2] This replay recurs, and reversal takes place both across human bodies, performing a rewind, and through a technological reversal of the image played backwards, in a hybrid choreography by Lisa Torun. As Schneider notes,

> it is the strength of the choreography that successfully and quite subtly poses and reposes the question of whether the movement is technologically replaying (that is, through the film) or bodily replaying (that is, through the dancing body). Technology and the body both are here interinanimated as repetition machines.[3]

DOI: 10.4324/9781003335887-6

To which I would add: it is an affordance of moving image technology that a special effect can come to be uncertainly perceived as (un)lived. The disorientations of reversal thus accumulate in a careful meditation on history, power, and evidence, and the stakes of life itself.

Across his works, Shonibare has repeatedly employed Dutch Wax print cloth, brightly coloured and highly patterned "fabric influenced by Indonesian design, produced by the Dutch, who tried it on the West African market, where it was appropriated as African," to insistently complicate and retrace the colonial histories that disguise a one way, extractive traffic in colonial economy as "discovery" and to make felt the spectres of unequal exchange.[4] Within the folds of the fabric at this masked ball, questions of colonial violence are raised and intensively suspended in the thick time of reversal itself. As Shonibare describes this:

> What I decided to do with this film was to ask all the actors to act the idea of the loop. What you see when the action comes around again is actually a reenactment of what went before; it's not an electronic loop, it's imitating one.[5]

Shonibare links this repetition to the "repetition of (imperial) power that always returns to the same point", noting that "my work comments on power, or the deconstruction of power, and I tend to use notions of excess as a way to represent that power."[6] Excess here is the work of reversal itself, which doesn't simply undo or invert the normativity of the forward or "progressive," but summons what David Wills terms the "dorsal chance…of what cannot be foreseen."[7] Dorsality, or the backwards turn, for Wills names the way that the technological is an affordance of the body itself: "In its guise of the technological, the dorsal therefore names, in a number of ways, what comes from behind to inhabit us as something other, some other thing, the other; an other beyond what can be conceived of within the perspective of our frontal relations".[8] A backwards troping is everywhere in Shonibare's film (which unfaithfully amplified eighteenth-century court choreography), perhaps nowhere more so than in the king's gestures, such as a repeated turning into a fourth position port a bras, but elsewhere: in a reverence hiccupped by a small rise and hop backwards, or the mimetic backwards collapse of dancers after the fall of the king. Reversal is thus a contagious, deranging, and disorienting movement impulse. Like dorsality, screendance is situated at the ambiguous imbrication of bodies and technologies, characterized by what I term an *anarchival* impulse to resist normative constraints of time, to animate instead a time in the making, as Shonibare does here.

During the 1990s, the radically pervasive impact of digital technologies, in particular of rendering rather than recording in cinema's new everyday, led critics like Lev Manovitch to declare that digital or contemporary cinema was merely "a particular case of animation."[9] This polemical claim was part of a longer retrospectation, or looking backwards, at a linear cinema history beyond the dominance of narrative cinema and the "guarantee" of the indexical, seeing the narrative fiction feature film not as the "evolution" of cinema, but perhaps simply a royal road. This included the history of the cinema of attractions as part of a backwards thinking through cinema's entire history, giving a renewed attention to spectacle and special effects, tracing cinema's lost highways and underground currents. The effect has not been to consolidate a singular story of cinema, but to better attend to the volatile conditions of preservation, desire, and emergence that put past, present, and future into a speculative and even fabulative relation. In this chapter, I align the spectacular and the speculative to start from the prompt: what if all cinema is a particular case of screendance? This chapter considers reversed and backwards motion across many iterations as lo-tech special fx—the cheapest of all cheap tricks—in post-digital screendance during cinema's second century. In the cases I examine here, reversal is not simply a property of the camera or technology, but of the body itself, where "the turn is the deviation from itself by means of which the human, in being or 'moving' simply human, is understood to become technological."[10] Dorsality thus names a condition in which the human and the technological are co-constituent, against an image of human will as a forward-looking autonomy. Traveling through time, reverse movement is not simply a mirror image: it creatively remakes the order of the world. For this reason, reverse motion can also serve as a means for exploring social and cultural forces that constrict and capture minoritarian movement, human and inhuman alike. Likewise, it brings to the fore stakes of analysis and assessment beyond the "progress narratives" of cinematic sense that discard aberrant movement. Finally, it echoes and displaces the tension between the live and the recorded that so critically marked the emergence of screendance as a field of research. Reverse motion doesn't copy anything actual, and as such it permits questions of survival and creation to go elsewhere.

An unexpected starting point might be the 1896 film by the Lumière Brothers, *Demolition of a Wall*, rather than early images of dance onscreen such as Thomas Edison's studio recordings of *Anabelle Butterfly Dance*, *Carmencita*, or the *Sioux Ghost Dance*, all from 1894. *Demolition of a Wall* contains nothing of a pre-existing dance form. It is sometimes described as the first special effects film, part of the enthusiasm for branding cinematic origin stories, but also a testimony to the thrilling nature of early cinema images in their effects on audiences.[11] Three workers and a boss are preparing to knock down the street-facing wall of a largely demolished house, open to the elements. Two men attack the interior base of the wall with pickaxes, while a third men manipulates a crank on a lever to exert force from outside. The boss stomps around, pointing and gesturing. At a certain moment, the men evacuate the interior space of the house, and one begins pushing from the street side. The thick wall collapses inward, kicking up a huge cloud of dust, ghosts escaping the ruins. Without waiting for it to clear, the men race in with pickaxes raised, hacking away to ensure the wall stays down, as if it might just be wounded, but still dangerous. Entering from another affective dimension than the frantic attack, two men stroll into the scene from screen left ...and then without missing a beat they exit the same way, walking backwards. The briefness of this incursion, as they reverse their way offscreen, introduces a world of altered dynamics. With each strike of the pick, clouds of dust are sucked into the tools, and the upward swing suspends action at the top as if to ensure disappearance. Debris races towards the tools charged with desirous magic and the balance tips agentively: from the human bodies breaking things down to non-human materials and forces ambiguously assembling for reasons all their own. The staged destruction, directed by Louis Lumière and starring Auguste Lumière as the foreman, was legendarily screened forward and then manually rewound through the camera while still projecting, causing an image of the world to be projected in reverse to the delight and astonishment of the spectators, in a radically novel rewinding of time.

How could we read this short *actualité* not simply as a special effect, but as a dance film, through the affordances unleashed by moving backwards? The dance film was a cherished subject of the early cinema of attractions. And the Lumières were notorious choreographers of everyday life: their documentary shorts staged quotidian movement for the camera's eye and the screen's frame, as they bossed their workers and families onto the scene. As Ian Christie notes, in a certain "yes" to spectacle: " But if the first successful moving picture demonstrations of Edison, Lumière and Paul impressed by their lifelike recording of normal movement, almost immediately viewers were equally intrigued by the abnormal movement of reverse motion."[12] The cinematographe, powered not by electricity but by the human body, also quickly begins to choreograph deviations and torsions in the bodies that it records, a doublemindedness of gaze and feet towards and away at once. These are early microchoreographies of screendance and are part of the deep fascination we feel for these images. Yet the pleasure and potential of a simple reversal is neither restoration nor recuperation. Instead, a world reprocessed by reversal reveals an entire optical unconscious of co-present yet elusive forces, matters and animacies, not simply revealed but generated.

Watching *Demolition of a Wall* as a dance film, I notice two main things. The first is that Auguste, as the boss, doesn't simply command the destruction: he paces and reverses in a small dance with the wall's immanent fall. Even before the film rewinds, his movements reveal the virtuality of the act of the irreversible fall—reversal animates suspension as the intensive force of time.[13] A reversed trajectory opens a world of possible motion through this embodied and intensified suspense, what in another context, drawing on Gilles Deleuze's work on cinematic time, I call aberrant movement. A first quality of reverse motion might then be that it challenges authority and direction. The second quality concerns how the stability of objects and subjects in the frame are made strange, becoming instead an inhuman ecology of forces and matterings. In reverse, dust particles move with the intention of a body. Released from normative directionality, time, gravity, and composition are made apparent. The effect is so strong and magical that I have to disagree with Christie that this film "produced the specific effect of chaos seeming to revert to order."[14] As Alexander Tohline notes in his historical study of reverse motion in cinema: "Reverse motion lays bare the contingent and the chaotic, rendering even sections of the past unpredictable by denying us the security of recalling causes as we witness effects."[15] Such chaos is not simply in a binary relation to order, but instead affectively re-charges the world: "a shot of reverse motion moves from effects to causes, but it does not necessarily move from the unknown to the known. That which has already happened un-happening is often stranger than that which has not happened happening."[16] In *Demolition of a Wall*, what dances in the image becomes molecular, troubling stable relations of scale and capture. The special effect of reverse movement, a subgenre of time travel movies, operates across bodies and technologies to explore the speculative force of utopian thinking, to pry open the question—through the rewind—of how this could be otherwise? What is critical in these examples is that the aberrance of backwards movement, its artificial animism, releases capture from the body to reanimate all aspects of the scene, and to shift the certain grounds of causality and control. If it doesn't actualize another world, it points to the conditions for something else to become possible.

Tohline calls reverse motion's effect "temporal plasticity," one which, like screendance, contributes to a heterogenesis of cinema. Tracing the origins of reverse motion both forwards and backwards from *Demolition of a Wall*, he essentially concludes (as does Christie) that reverse motion has a brief heyday during the cinema of attractions but largely disappears, with a few exceptions in experimental and avant-garde cinema, from a prominent place in cinema history, at least until the digital turn. In part, this move comes as the "spectacle" of reverse motion as interesting in itself gets "downgraded" to special effect, restricted to a single shot or sequence rather than the entirety of the film. Nonetheless, attending to this cheap trick, the easiest version of which is simply to turn the film camera upside down and splice the resulting image back to front, to the use of optical printers, to the simple scrub on a timeline in non-linear editing, means that "recentering film history and aesthetics upon reverse motion deterritorializes the primacy of narrative and affords a new perspective from which we may understand the new revelations of reality made possible by temporal plasticity."[17] In the few examples he discusses from cinema between narrative integration and the digital turn, he gives pride of place to Maya Deren, who found in reverse motion a properly cinematic kineticism. Deren, herself a pioneer of screendance, perhaps saw in reverse motion a choreographic capacitation of the cinematic body, akin to how the dancing body itself is a recording and playback device. Instead of alienated from its potential by technology, reversal amplifies a cinechoreographic collaboration with a body's "originary technicity," to borrow a term from Gilbert Simondon.[18] Here is also where I depart from Tohline's analysis in considering reverse motion through the conceptual lens of screendance. He writes: "The reverse motion establishes onscreen a virtual temporal space the like of which we can never physically inhabit, making us suddenly and vertiginously cognizant of the permanent structural immiscibility of audience space and screen space."[19] What is kinesthetic empathy, a central quality of screendance, in the face of reversal? As we will see in my brief survey of recent works of backwards movement, reversal is a minoritarian form well suited to bodies that have never been quite at home, queerly incommensurable and immiscible only in their volatility. Rather than an empathy predicated in syncing up or mapping onto, how might reverse motion, as "chronokinetically dissident," expand our sense of kinesthetic empathy or perhaps better, kinesthetic experience, to include a different, companionable otherness?[20]

Chronokinetic dissidence is the quality that dance theorist André Lepecki, writing about Renate Lorenz and Pauline Boudrey's 2019 screendance installation *Moving Backwards*, discussed in this chapter, sees as the importance of reversal in that work, part of what he calls a

> generalized minoritarian interpellation of the supposed non-political nature of the physical sciences...Only by questioning its supposedly 'natural laws,' its supposedly 'universal laws' can we finally fulfill the beautiful promise that nature, in its queer, deviant, desiring, untamed, fugitive, and incalculable pulse always already offers us.[21]

Moving backwards is a ritual endeavour that energizes extant, but often latent, animacy, a countercurrent of sense that shifts the normative and causal sense of movement. South African filmmaker and animator William Kentridge is the direct heir of the filmmaker who, one year after *Demolition of the Wall*, would become known as the first special effects filmmaker: magician turned director Georges Méliès. Méliès' cinema of attractions, predicated on the spectacularism and solicitation of the gaze, deployed special effects to take us to fantastical realms. His faith in magic led him to relentlessly stage the visibility of the illusion—the special effect—with full confidence in its persistent affect. His was a world for the making and it was through the body, often his own, that Méliès staged the cinematic magic of ephemeral affect and material effect. Kentridge, who in recent years has increasingly become a modest dancer in his own works, deploys reverse motion to call into question authority and progress in his long standing investigation of the legacy of apartheid in South Africa, world histories of failed utopian projects, and of death, violence and social division.[22] Kentridge uses reverse motion in his work as a fabulative technique for generating intensity, critiquing narratives of progress, capture and control.

In 2003, Kentridge made *7 Fragments for Georges Méliès* and its companion film, *Journey to the Moon*, a multiscreen installation that used a variant on what Kentridge terms his "stone age" technique of frame-by-frame hand-drawn charcoal animation to explore the still effective wonder of Méliès' suspension of habitual rules of space-time, as in his 1902 film *Le Voyage dans la Lune*. For Kentridge, as for Méliès, bodies serve as tiny time machines, not only carrying their history as an archive of memory but retaining an anarchival reserve of the unexpected. Sequences in *Journey to the Moon*, a hybrid of stop-motion live action and drawn animation, use reverse motion to trouble progress narratives and Kentridge's status as master magician, rewinding intentional gestures of discarding, drawing, and destruction. Fragments of things become agents, and the progress narrative of the journey to outer space becomes an intensive one of love and longing. A sketched portrait of Kentridge reassembles itself from torn pieces that fly towards the live Kentridge's hand and settle onto the wall with a smooth release. On the one hand, in this film Kentridge has a magical ability to call the world to him, but in that movement, the things equally take on a life of their own, in an agential ecology. Like the bosses of *Demolition of a Wall*, Kentridge's masterful figures, from the Soho Eckstein capitalist boss of his "Drawings for Projection" series to increasingly himself as the artist/ performer, are undone by the fractured intimacies of reverse motion.

More than a decade later, Kentridge produced *More Sweetly Play the Dance*, an eight-screen installation of a danse macabre, choreographed by his long-time collaborator Dada Masilo, best known for her mashups of African dance tradition such as gumboot dancing with classical ballet forms.[23] Kentridge's installation picks up on the repeated theme of the procession in his work, one he ties to a long history of thought from Plato onwards. The exhibition text also notes: "the procession reminds us of the media images of people fleeing from hunger, war or sickness. Moreover, it seems to hint at images of people protesting against political regimes, against corruption, and against political oppression."[24] The fourteen-minute piece is bookended by solo dancing bodies. I consider only the opening here, to note that origin and reversal are synonymous in this looped work. The film begins with a shamanic figure, who launches the work by moving against the grain of western legibility and its connotation of progress, entering from the far-right screen, and spinning his way across the installation alone in the installation's landscape. His own movement spiral switches directions at the last instant—in the transition between the final two screens—to launch a vertiginous plunge into the procession proper. His flip, propelled by the aberrant momentum of his right to left movement, occurs between the frames of the screen and glitches any continuous narrative. I read this opening figure as a time traveller, holding open an against-the-grain energy as the procession then marches on. Reverse movement here shifts the work away from historical representation, even as it presents us with fragments of a violent revolutionary past, towards fabulation. Kentridge's fabulations don't rewrite history, but serve a "people yet to come," responding to Deleuze and Felix Guattari's claim that

> creative fabulation has nothing to do with a memory, however exaggerated, or with a fantasy. In fact, the artist…goes beyond the perceptual states and affective transitions of the lived. The artist is a seer. How would he recount what happened to him, or what he imagines, since he is a shadow?[25]

Animation's longstanding relation conceptually and practically to forms of half-life, including shadows, underpins Kentridge's work where they exist in a dynamic exchange with the work of dance, understood conventionally as inherently ephemeral, in a different register. Kentridge's work consistently displays a tenderness for specificity of people on the move and the double temporality of the danse macabre, the finality and end point, the leveling of class and social distinction in a commons of mortality.

My next example is likewise concerned with the subversive force of reversal in the face of global geo-politics, and the tension between forced and tactical movement. For *Moving Backwards*, Pauline Boudry and Renate Lorenz converted the Swiss pavilion at the 2019 Venice Biennale into a dance club through screendance, one that "allows us to experiment with different forms of desire."[26] A large black box welcomes the audience, seated before a large screen with a shimmering curtain. When the curtain opens, we see the same space, now onscreen, and populated by a group of gender expansive dancers trying out various choreographies of reversal. Taking as their prompt the proposition "Let's collectively move backwards," dancers onscreen play with the perceptual wedge of reversal to unsettle habits of capture, comfort, and collectivity. In this work, backwards names not a single trajectory or reverse of motion, but a non-normative movement impulse carried between analog and digital effects, between bodies and technology, and between forms and feelings. As Boudry and Lorenz note: "Parts of the dances were reversed, and the performers learned to dance them that way. We reversed other parts of the film digitally, but in a subtle way, which requires attention to notice."[27] This extends a practice found across their other works that they call "temporal drag": the "co-presence of different temporalities, and of opening up a past moment that was not properly lived or actualised in the past, to give it another try."[28] Boudry and Lorenz's work takes it inspiration from the sense that we are living in a time of political regression, but one without easy or nostalgic recourse to the progress narratives so often affiliated to the "acceptance" of queer lives and the framing of the west as the avant-garde. Instead, they expansively trace how in the west we are moving backwards in the form of social gestures of sending back or refusal of boatloads of migrants, in the rise of xenophobia and homophobia that reverse hard won political rights. On this dance floor, they seek to explore how moving backwards can move from political regression to an act of resistance, embodying reversal to different ends. They take inspiration from female Kurdish guerillas of the YPJ, the women's protection unit in Rojava, Syria, who would wear their shoes backwards in snow to hide their trajectory from their enemies; in one sequence of the video, a dancer moves forward through the space, long hair disguising which is the front of face, in shoes that point in both directions at once. Another moves through space with shoes on their hands, making walking the first transformative technology of the body. Dancers hold backwards arches where the effort has gone elsewhere. To beats that remix the music of Terre Thaemlitz, a dancer in a modest pompadour shimmies across space with one shoulder clad in a long wig. Hair comes to serve as our best sense of when the images start to rewind, sprouting all over the dancers and creating small sensory glitches in perception, moving with the bodies rather than simply on them. Throughout the affect is attentive, collaborative, as if the dancers both move and perceive themselves moving, witness, like us, to an excess in the image.

This scene speaks to a key quality of reverse motion: its ephemerality that can only be accessed in a qualified way. *Moving Backwards* is a screendance installation, shot where it was initially screened. The choreography combines reverse motion both performed by dancing bodies and enacted through digital reversal, both lo tech and high impact. The pervasive queerness of the movement makes these hard to distinguish at time, and non-human actants in the form of clothes and materials, especially sequins that invite light into the movement, amplify and are amplified in this confound. For performance theorist José Muñoz, the dancefloor tells us something about "queering evidence, and by that I mean the ways in which we prove queerness and read queerness, by suturing it to the concept of ephemera. Think of ephemera as trace, the remains, the things that are left, hanging in the air like a rumor."[29] As an affective and political stake on the future, moving backwards sees the ephemeral quality of the dance floor—out of normative space and time—as a space for increasing "our tolerance for embodied practices. It may do so because it demands, in the openness and closeness of relations to others, an exchange and alteration of kinesthetic experience through which we become, in a sense, less like ourselves and more like each other."[30] In *Moving Backwards*, reverse motion, by assembling bodies moving and technology, is a gesture of transformation. About gesture, Muñoz writes:

> These acts are different, but certainly not independent, from movements that have more to do with the moving body's flow. Concentrating on gesture atomizes movement. These atomized and particular movements tell tales of historical becoming. Gestures transmit ephemeral knowledge of lost queer histories and possibilities within a phobic majoritarian public culture.[31]

Such atomization appears whenever reverse motion's strangeness and beauty opens our visual consumption to the stutter of a double vision—the movement and its effect generating a mutual suspense where we can no longer be sure about the order of things. Reverse motion is gestural. Even the shimmering curtain of the work as internal cut refuses a logic of division, lightly dancing in the breeze of bodies together in the space in a minor choreography of the fabulous.

The work explicitly links moving backwards to a variety of political struggles, and the exhibition catalogue includes letters from people such as Patrisse Cullors of Black Lives Matter, academics Judith Butler, Francoise Vergès, Eve Tuck, and others who critically unpack these ideas. In the film, everything unfolds without words and under the sign of the disco ball figuratively in the form of the night club, and in a redistribution that reminds me of the dust of the demolished wall, in the sparkles that dress the atmosphere via the shimmying curtain and the performers' costumes. It may seem profoundly frivolous, the sparkling call out to scenes of pleasure against the urgent matters of life and death that the work also calls in. But I want to take seriously the affordance of the sparkle as a sign of backwards movement, refracting directionality. In the careful delight of the dancers' performances is a feeling through reversal for elsewheres of action: each backwards step becomes the site of an explosion of potential where all bets are off.

Reverse movement activates what I call the anarchival quality of screendance, an anarchic archive of historical becoming, or the worldmaking capacities of the body in relation to a social archive of gestures, mediated and live.[32] In thinking through queer and feminist approaches to lo-tech screendance, I turn now to another dancefloor at a more intimate scale of queer life. Experimental video artist Nik Forrest's *Flip/Bend 1* (2012) explores the dynamic differential between their own, untrained body and that of dancer Sarah Williams, in a space that confounds percepts of normative orientation.[33] The black-and-white image of the video plays on a simplicity and reduction of the scene's elements to a series of twos—two bodies, two orientations, two colours—in order to transversally occupy the space in between. The camera frames the meeting point of a wood paneled wall and white floor, with the break between the mid-centre horizon of the image. Two bodies occupy the space, alternately seated or lying/standing directly on the floor, and the video is a set of explorations of the movement potential afforded by this space. It eventually becomes apparent that floor and wall are actually reversed and that the performers and spectators are disoriented in this lo-fi zero gravity chamber. Over the course of the film, the white wall and wood floor get remixed into redistributed squares, moving between quadrants and creating new zones of isolation and exchange. In this film, it is space, rather than time that is flipped, and yet it works affectively on our temporal orientation as well through suspense and confounded expectation. The effect is sustained and constantly surprising. Even when you get the "trick" of the image, its special effect continues to work affectively, unsettling questions such as what is the relation between these two people, or understanding the space as simply a support or background environment. In this anti-gravity film, the forces made apparent as the performers struggle to sit upright in a chair or crawl around on confounding trajectories in what appears to be scaling a wall, make the ecology active in an anarchic fashion. They learn and unlearn everyday gestures and movements, and anarchivally retrain themselves not through mastery of the environment, but through long sequences where little happens. Such pauses and delays are not simply the registration of not knowing how to move. They testify to reversal's expansion of time, which doesn't simply drag out accomplishment, but which luxuriates in attending to other pulls, other forces. The bodies work together, but in rarely in sync, and the video as a whole displays an ambiguous affect around how they relate to themselves, each other and the space. Often, Forrest and Williams mirror each other, but across a time lag that prevents a simple doubling. At other times they are on their own journeys; at one point Williams is elegantly playing with arching backwards in her chair and Forrest simply gets up and walks away. Near the end, they collaboratively remake the set, switching out the panelling and the floor. The result is not a transformation of bodies: it doesn't resolve into a new set of social relations. Indeed, the relation between performers remains opaque in this undone duet, that invites backgrounded forces to the dance. In this way, it queerly echoes Norman McLaren's classic work of live-action animated screendance, *A Chairy Tale* (1958), which already opened up the marriage plot of the fairy tale to other ends in its stop motion duet between a man and a chair that refuses to be sat on. At the same time, it goes beyond this, in swapping out the lo-fi effect of stop motion for a flipped set, which bends bodies and movements out of shape. Between body and room, the dorsality of what Sara Ahmed calls a "queer furnishing" emerges, which "might be about making what is in the background, what is behind us, more available as 'things' to 'do' things with."[34] The anti-gravitational images are not free floating but, coupled with the long takes and many pauses in movement, evoke an everyday extraterrestriality: not the heroic bodies of astronauts floating in slow motion in outer space, but the everyday aliens of queer lives, moving through reversal as a portrait of life on the flip side of gender and sexual binaries, working it out on a handmade dance floor. Such work casts a picture of the labour of making a life, what José Muñoz terms "queer thought":

> Queer thought is, in large part, about casting a picture of arduous modes of relationality that persist in the world despite stratifying demarcations and taxonomies of being, classifications that are bent on the siloing of particularity and on the denigrating of any expansive idea of the common and commonism. Within the category of human intraspecies connectivity, we feel the formatting force of asymmetrical stratifications both within humanity and outside it. The incommensurable thought project of inhumanity is the active self-attunement to life as varied and unsorted correspondences, collisions, intermeshings, and accords between people and nonhuman objects, things, formations, and clusterings.[35]

Through the lo-tech strangeness of reverse motion, we can access the work of self-attunement to what we haven't yet sorted out. In the end, *Flip/Bend 1*'s movements of reversal retain an anarchival force of potential, with a strongly ludic quality that is, at the same time, deeply moving. The work models reversal as a queer strategy for enlarging existence. Forrest's film embodies what artist Jean Cocteau termed "direct magic," the expansive power of effects directly registered by the camera's eye. As Andrew Tohline describes the "direct magic" of reversal in Cocteau's queer epics:

> Cocteau advanced the idea that visual effects in cinema should only depict that which the camera-eye can see – no process shots, matte work, optical printing, or other pictorial manipulation. Cocteau believed that he could accomplish whatever effects he needed without undermining the basic indexicality of the camera. He argued that an effect fabricated according to this principle 'can be convincing, owing to the mere fact that it is seen.'[36]

Such a queer magic moves across many of the works under consideration here. This may even be what Sara Ahmed has termed queer disorientation as both "an ordinary feeling" and an "uncanny effect."[37]

In other works, reversal is rendered as a virtual co-presence. In this way, virtuality as the double of the actual displaces the opposition of live and recorded ghosting screendance, a foundational presumption that often failed to look beyond the edges of the human, or that dissociated humanity and technicity. Consider the ten-film experimental series *Brouillard* (Fog, 2008–15) by Alexandre Larose, whose serial essays in embodied repetition and recording, as well as his duets with inhuman bodies, make his work screendance.[38] Larose's work frequently stretches the technical affordances of media substrates to their limits in search of the edges of perception, bending affect to occupy a zone between urgency and the everyday, magic made visible. In a suite of works—*Ville Marie A* (2006–09) & *B* (2010–17), *La Grand Dame* (2014–22)—that involve dropping a camera from the top of Place Ville Marie high-rise in Montreal, Larose trusts the camera to step in for a fall he has only experienced in dreams, watching from a vanishing viewpoint as the high-frame rate of cameras registers a wild fall to the ground. In this destructive act of unmaking, energies are unleashed as an entire ecology intensifies. If for *Flip/Bend 1*, the ecology of reversal was a flipped set navigated by queer orientations, Larose's films often likewise amplify the disorientations of reversal—looking up while falling down, or in the case of his series *Brouillard*, through the disjunctive layering of a repeated walk and a rewound and layered image. Each film in this series was produced according to the same essential setup. Wearing a 35mm Arriflex camera strapped to his body, Larose repeatedly walked along the same path from his parent's home, through a forest, and out onto a pier leading into Lac Saint Charles. Each take, shot on a 1000ft roll of 35mm colour reversal film, was shot at high speed and with a small aperture. Different iterations of the series contain different numbers of repetitions, transforming images into synaesthetic sonic vibration.[39] He repeatedly walked back, removed the film from the camera and, doubling his own peripatetic rewind, carefully rewound the film in the dark, before reloading the camera and beginning again. Here, this doubled reverse movement appears in a different dimension, through the layered repetitions and overexposures that surprisingly, retains a discrete opacity. The image is both recognizable—a daytime walk in the woods, glamourized by the sparkle of light through the trees and on the water—and fantastically unreal, a live-action animation of things bursting at their edges in the mismatch of layered temporalities. In these films, Larose's weighted and measured steps counterpoint everything else: the landscape dances indiscreetly in, to recall the Muñoz quote from earlier, "an exchange and alteration of kinesthetic experience through which we become, in a sense, less like ourselves and more like each other." While Larose has described his practice as "trying to get out of the way," in these films and his other works, I often take that to mean getting out of the way as a singular subject whose body determines the action.[40] Larose makes himself a recording machine in *Brouillard* in an exchange of affordances with the film camera, amplifying its ability to witness the direct magic of life itself through his own mechanical consistency and the critical function of reversal. Here, he steps into the small dance of the men in *Demolition of a Wall*, suddenly at the service of other orientations unleashed by the rewind of perception. In these works, Larose indexes another affordance of reverse movement, that it always generates more to see rather than simply the other side of forward movement. We quite literally see instead the inbetween of movement itself.

My last example, which begins like Larose's films in the *Brouillard* series with the image of a path as an icon for one-way movement, is Ja'Tovia Gary's 2017 short film *Giverny 1 (Negresse Imperiale)*.[41] I see this as a work of screendance for the way it insistently foregrounds aberrant motion, for the undecidable exchanges between somatic, technological, and organic motion, and for the way that it builds the work around the movement impulse of reversal. Green letters on a black screen type out "Giverny 1"; we then briefly glimpse an overgrown path fringed in tall grasses and flowers, leading into a narrow break in the trees ahead. The canted angle lists to the left as a languorous and interrupted looping of Louis Armstrong's version of the song "La Vie en Rose" begins to play, in a soundtrack by Norvis Jr. The trampled path holds still even as the explosion of plant life at its edges trembles in the wind, an analog shimmer of the digital glitches that will recompose this film throughout. If Larose's films recode the analog as remixable through intensive layers, Gary's work also undoes a strict binary of digital and analog, situating these works within an ecology of living images that mark the distance between the spectacle of the early reversals of the cinema of attractions and a post-digital screendance that explores movement in intimate and often laborious relation with survival. Insistently interrupting and reframing images of "nature" with analog and digital effects, the film has an animatorly quality that speaks to the labour it takes to register the existence of Black lives. As Ayanna Dozier writes,

> these bugs are analog aberrations, achieved through cameraless footage, à la Stan Brakhage, of hand-pressed leaves, activated by light and movement. Gary troubles the mise-en-scène with these celluloid tears, fracturing the frame's capacity to hold a scene or body together. These schisms dominate the scenes of Gary in Monet's famous garden in Giverny, in northern France, drawing attention to the disjuncture her black body brings to a landscape exemplary of white European cultural production that emerged alongside brute colonialism.[42]

First at 52 seconds, and then again at the 1:20 mark, scenes of Claude Monet's garden with and without Gary, and the vegetal archive of leaves pressed into service as organic glitches, are interrupted by footage of the livestreamed recording of the 2016 murder by police of Philando Castile, shot during a traffic stop, narrated in desperate witness by his partner Diamond Reynolds. Cellphone footage reels wildly over sky and sidewalk as Reynolds insistently asks after her daughter and tries to speak to her experience. It is here that the film bends around a resistance to the police's command to Diamond Reynolds, to "face away from me and walk backwards." The film cuts to a long shot of Gary, discretely screened by overgrown plants at the edge of a pond, as she takes a few steps backwards onto a bridge, facing the camera. Cutting back to Reynolds approaching the police, who tell her to "keep walking," the film cuts again to Gary continuing to walk backwards and out of sight as this command repeats. The film then explodes into a tightly controlled chaos, graphically interrupting the indexical image in an insistence on crafted digital and hand-made effects. At the three-minute mark, Gary will reverse her own backwards step, walking back to the edge of the pond to suddenly crouch and scream, in a sound registered as a high-pitched electronic tone. The film warps time through the intensity of trauma and the long drag of a history of necropolitical racism. Repeatedly returning to its setting in Monet's garden, the scene of Gary's artistic residency, Gary reworks the extractionist and flattening capture of ephemerality that litter Monet's paintings and the privileged seclusion into the urgency of the glitch and in her embodied replay of the police's command. A political fabulation, Gary's film makes apparent an urgent ecology of precarious life. Reversal will not be restorative here; this wish can only fail. But fabulation, like reverse motion, works in a different register, trying to make more actionable the past in the service of a more to life to come.

Dozier writes:

> Artists like Gary are working against representation to reveal a way of feeling and responding to documentation of black life differently. Her aesthetics recall [Saidiya] Hartman on the urgency of scrambling the archival validity of representation: 'Narrative restraint, the refusal to fill in the gaps and provide closure, is a requirement of this method [fabulation], as is the imperative to respect Black noise—the shrieks, the moans, the nonsense, and the opacity, which are always in excesses of legibility and of the law and which hint at and embody aspirations that are wildly utopian, derelict to capitalism.'[43]

Gary's film has since been remixed into her longer project *The Giverny Document*; in fact, all of my examples are explicitly engaged with seriality and the remix, perhaps signaling an anarchic heterochronicity released by the excess of reversal itself, even an important part of its appeal.[44] Reversal is only one of the many movement impulses Gary deploys in the film—she runs, screams, lounges, looks—but it holds a special place as an image that shivers the imperative "walk backwards" with the maker's body and technology in a dorsal resistance. This is the opposite of a tendency that Tohline identifies as "wish-images", a "historiographical method" as "an ahistorical fantasy of nullification."[45] It likewise works to glitch the too-quick impulse of the "forward" as images of Black death and suffering circulate on social media. Reversal here, as in the other examples in this chapter, is generative in excess of what is reversed, an apparitional and summoning force. Across the minor key of reverse movement, an anarchival impulse takes form between past and future.

Notes

1. Yinka Shonibare MBE, *Un Ballo in Maschera (A Masked Ball)*, 2004, high-definition digital video, 32 minutes.
2. Rebecca Schneider, "Gesture to Opera: Yinka Shonibare's *Un Ballo in Maschera*," *The Opera Quarterly* 31, no. 3 (2015): 155–69.
3. Schneider, "Gesture to Opera," 157.
4. Lars Bang Larsen and Yinka Shonibare MBE, "1000 Words: Yinka Shonibare," *Artforum*, January 2005, https://www.artforum.com/print/200501/1000-words-yinka-shonibare-8113.
5. Anthony Downey, "Yinka Shonibare by Anthony Downey," *Bomb Magazine*, no. 93 (October 1, 2005), https://bombmagazine.org/articles/yinka-shonibare/#:~:text=In%20the%20museum%20setting%2C%20films,electronic%20loop%2C%20it's%20imitating%20one.
6. Downey, "Yinka Shonibare by Anthony Downey."
7. David Wills, *Dorsality: Thinking Back through Technology and Politics* (Minneapolis: University of Minnesota Press, 2008), 7.
8. Wills, *Dorsality*, 11.
9. Lev Manovich, *The Language of New Media* (Cambridge, MA: MIT Press, 2002), 301.
10. Wills, *Dorsality*, 4.
11. In Alexander Tohline's doctoral dissertation *Towards a History and Aesthetics of Reverse Motion,* he debunks the attribution of the "first" use of reverse motion to an "accidental discovery" by the Lumières: "reverse motion was not born by accident when a Lumière operator happened to crank *Demolition of a Wall* (1896) in reverse, but rather that reverse motion was first imagined by a French science writer named Édouard Hospitalier, who surmised that if sonic records of duration could be turned backwards on a phonograph, then visual records of duration on the cinématographe ought to have the same property." Alexander M. Tohline, *Towards a History and Aesthetics of Reverse Motion* (Ph.D. diss., University of Iowa, 2015), 254, http://rave.ohiolink.edu/etdc/view?acc_num=ohiou1438771690.
12. Ian Christie, "Time Regained: The Complex Magic of Reverse Motion," in *Projected Shadows: Psychoanalytic Reflections on the Representation of Loss in European Cinema*, ed. Andrea Sabbadini (Hove: Routledge, 2007), 168.
13. For a discussion of suspense in relation to intensive forms of time, see Alanna Thain, *Bodies in Suspense: Time and Affect in Cinema* (Minneapolis: University of Minnesota Press, 2017).
14. Christie, "Time Regained," 168.
15. Tohline, *Towards a History and Aesthetics*, 22
16. Tohline, *Towards a History and Aesthetics*, 34.
17. Tohline, *Towards a History and Aesthetics*, 11–12.
18. See Gilbert Simondon, *On the Mode of Existence of Technical Objects*. Translated by Malaspina Cécile and John Rogove. 1st ed. (Minneapolis, MN: Univocal Publishing, 2017.
19. Tohline, *Towards a History and Aesthetics*, 169.
20. André Lepecki, "Infinite Retrogression Backwardfoward: Motions for Another Life," in *Pauline Boudry/Renate Lorenz: Moving Backwards*, ed. Charlotte Laubard (New York: Skira Rizzoli, 2019), 83–87, 85.

21 Lepecki, "Infinite Retrogression Backwardfoward," 84; Pauline Boudry and Renate Lorenz, *Moving Backwards*, 2019, digital video and installation.
22 For a discussion of Kentridge as screendance artist, including *7 Fragments for George Méliès*, see Thain, "Wandering Stars: William Kentridge's Err(Ant) Choreographies," *Parallax* 14, no. 1 (2008): 68–81.
23 William Kentridge, *More Sweetly Play the Dance*, 2015, 8-channel high-definition video installation, 15:00 minutes.
24 Exhibition wall text at the Eye Film Institute, Amsterdam, "William Kentridge: If We Ever Go to Heaven", April 25–August 30, 2015.
25 Gilles Deleuze and Félix Guattari, *What Is Philosophy?* (New York: Columbia University Press, 1994), 171.
26 Hannah McGivern, "Interview: Pauline Boudry and Renate Lorenz on dancing in the Swiss pavilion," *The Art Newspaper*, June 11, 2019, https://www.theartnewspaper.com/2019/06/11/interview-pauline-boudry-and-renate-lorenz-on-dancing-in-the-swiss-pavilion.
27 McGivern, "Interview."
28 McGivern, "Interview."
29 José Esteban Muñoz, *Cruising Utopia, 10th Anniversary Edition: The Then and There of Queer Futurity* (New York: New York University Press, 2019), 65.
30 Muñoz, *Cruising Utopia*, 65.
31 Muñoz, *Cruising Utopia*, 67.
32 This discussion of Forrest's video is adapted from Alanna Thain, "Anarchival Impulses: A Performance Theory of Media," *Public* 29, no. 57 (2018): 27–35, with the kind permission of *Public* journal.
33 Nik Forrest, *Flip/ Bend 1*, 2012, single channel video, 8:33 minutes.
34 Sara Ahmed, *Queer Phenomenology: Orientations, Objects, Others* (Durham: Duke University Press, 2006), 165.
35 Muñoz, "Theorizing Queer Inhumanisms: The Sense of Brownness," *Glq: A Journal of Lesbian and Gay Studies* 21, no. 2 (2015): 209–10, 210.
36 Tohline, *Towards a History and Aesthetics*, 152.
37 Ahmed, *Queer* Phenomenology, 157, 162.
38 Alexandre Larose, *Brouillard*, 2008–15, series of nineteen 35 mm short films.
39 "No sound, Larose claims, works with the image to save the projector's metrical breath, relaying the performance quality of Larose's original slow dance with the camera to the new scenes of reception." Nicole de Brabandere and Alanna Thain, "Drawing light: Gesture and suspense in the weave," *Necsus*, December 21, 2019, https://necsus-ejms.org/drawing-light-gesture-and-suspense-in-the-weave/.
40 Brabandere and Thain, "Drawing light."
41 Ja'Tovia Gary, *Giverny I (NÉGRESSE IMPÉRIALE)*, 2017, single channel video, 6:18 minutes.
42 Ayanna Dozier, "Sound Garden: Ayanna Dozier on Ja'Tovia Gary's *The Giverny Document* (2019)," *Artforum*, February 3, 2020, https://www.artforum.com/film/ayanna-%20dozier-on-ja-tovia-gary-s-the-giverny-document-2019-82077.
43 Dozier, "Sound Garden."
44 Kentridge's films have repeatedly redeployed the same characters and objects across his works, such as the ambulatory surveyor's tools or out of scales megaphones found equally in *More Sweetly Play the Dance*. *Flip/Bend 1* is developed in the work *Flip/ Bend 2* and a host of short essays by Forrest, while *Moving Backwards* has been remixed in the 2022 installation *Les Gayrillères*. *Brouillard* names a series of multiple films, one of which is already a compilation. Michael Sicinski, reviewing *The Giverny Document*, writes that "After all, *The Giverny Document* (Single Channel) has, at its core, a re-edited, expanded version of the material from Gary's previous film, *Giverny I (Négresse Impériale)* (2017). In fact, much of

that original film appears in its original order within *The Giverny Document*, with one significant new element added into the mix. In light of this, an additional remix of the Giverny project, with additional monitors and sequencing, could very well allow Gary to introduce new threads of inquiry into the piece which, for formal or narrative reasons, could not fit easily into the flow of the single, linear, 43-minute film. One could imagine *Giverny* becoming a long-term, multimedia project for Gary, along the lines of Apichatpong's *Primitive* series, which also contained short films, features, and museum installations." Michael Sicinski, "Garden Against the Machine: Ja'Tovia Gary's *The Giverny Document*," *Cinemascope* 81 (February 2020).

45 Tohline, *Towards a History and Aesthetics*, 204.

Bibliography

Ahmed, Sara. *Queer Phenomenology: Orientations, Objects, Others*. Durham: Duke University Press, 2006.

Boudry, Pauline, and Renate Lorenz. *Moving Backwards*. 2019. Digital video and installation.

Christie, Ian. "Time Regained: The Complex Magic of Reverse Motion." In *Projected Shadows: Psychoanalytic Reflections on the Representation of Loss in European Cinema*, edited by Andrea Sabbadini. Hove: Routledge, 2007.

de Brabandere, Nicole, and Alanna Thain. "Drawing light: Gesture and suspense in the weave." *Necsus*. December 21, 2019. https://necsus-ejms.org/drawing-light-gesture-and-suspense-in-the-weave/.

Deleuze, Gilles, and Félix Guattari. *What Is Philosophy?* New York: Columbia University Press, 1994.

Downey, Anthony. "Yinka Shonibare by Anthony Downey." *Bomb Magazine*, no. 93. October 1, 2005. https://bombmagazine.org/articles/yinka-shonibare/#:~:text=In%20the%20museum%20setting%2C%20films,electronic%20loop%2C%20it's%20imitating%20one.

Dozier, Ayanna, "Sound Garden: Ayanna Dozier on Ja'Tovia Gary's *The Giverny Document* (2019)." *Artforum*. February 3, 2020. https://www.artforum.com/film/ayanna-%20dozier-on-ja-tovia-gary-s-the-giverny-document-2019-82077.

Forrest, Nik. *Flip/ Bend 1*. 2012. Single channel video, 8:33 minutes.

Gary, Ja'Tovia. *Giverny I (Négresse Impériale)*. 2017. Single channel video, 6:18 minutes.

Kentridge, William. *More Sweetly Play the Dance*. 2015. 8-channel high-definition video installation, 15:00 minutes.

Larose, Alexandre. *Brouillard*. 2008–2015. Series of nineteen 35 mm short films.

Larsen, Lars Bang, and Yinka Shonibare. "1000 Words: Yinka Shonibare." *Artforum*. January 2005. https://www.artforum.com/print/200501/1000-words-yinka-shonibare-8113.

Lepecki, André. "Infinite Retrogression Backwardfoward: Motions for Another Life." In *Pauline Boudry/Renate Lorenz: Moving Backwards*, edited by Charlotte Laubard, 83–87. New York: Skira Rizzoli, 2019.

McGivern, Hannah. "Interview: Pauline Boudry and Renate Lorenz on dancing in the Swiss pavilion." *The Art Newspaper*. June 11, 2019. https://www.theartnewspaper.com/2019/06/11/interview-pauline-boudry-and-renate-lorenz-on-dancing-in-the-swiss-pavilion.

Muñoz, José Esteban. "Theorizing Queer Inhumanisms: The Sense of Brownness." *Glq: A Journal of Lesbian and Gay Studies* 21, no. 2 (2015): 209–210.

Muñoz, José Esteban. *Cruising Utopia, 10th Anniversary Edition: The Then and There of Queer Futurity*. New York: New York University Press, 2019.

Schneider, Rebecca. "Gesture to Opera: Yinka Shonibare's *Un Ballo in Maschera*." *The Opera Quarterly* 31, no. 3 (2015): 155–169.

Shonibare, Yinka. *Un Ballo in Maschera* (A Masked Ball). 2004. High-definition digital video, 32 minutes.

Sicinski, Michael. "Garden Against the Machine: Ja'Tovia Gary's *The Giverny Document*." *Cinemascope* 81 (February 2020).

Tohline, Alexander M. Towards a History and Aesthetics of Reverse Motion. Ph.D. dissertation, University of Iowa, 2015. http://rave.ohiolink.edu/etdc/view?acc_num=ohiou1438771690.

Wills, David. *Dorsality: Thinking Back through Technology and Politics*. Minneapolis: University of Minnesota Press, 2008.

5

LITTLE VISIONS AND GRANDIOSE PERCEPTIONS

An Interview with Manon Labrecque[1]

By Priscilla Guy

Translated by Alanna Thain

Manon Labrecque was a multidisciplinary artist based in Montreal, Canada. Her work is an encounter between the banal and the grandiose; the human body and the machine; the useless and the essential. A true polymath, Labrecque eludes categories and labels. A fan of handmade work, her relationship with technology unfolds through a lo-tech, autonomous aesthetic that engages the whole body. In her work—whether experimental video or multimedia installation—life and death continually collide in an eloquent fashion, evoking in turn the value of human life and the programmed obsolescence of the technologies that populate our world. From an aesthetic of the ordinary, she brings out layers of meaning underlying the tidiness of everyday life, notably through various techniques of disrupting and glitching the image. A mischievous artist, Labrecque is interested the alternative beauty of failures and technical bugs. Her techniques of hacking and editing brings to the fore the fragility of video materials. In this way, the artist takes on the role of an image witch: her skillful technical hijackings reveal material-bodies and machine-bodies that bear the marks of fallible technology, while at the same time exuding an undeniable yet strange,even reinvented humanity

Guy: What would it mean to take control of one's image, but also to work on self-representation? Maybe we can start with that: [in your work] there is self-representation, but also self-deprecation, and there is also the automation of our own gestures, self-criticism, and self-destruction. What are these "selves"? It's oneself across the material, but it goes beyond an image.

Labrecque: Filming oneself allows me to externally gaze at myself, but at the same time, I am also a material [...] After almost 27 years [as an artist], I see how at first, it was really the image and the medium, and the more it

DOI: 10.4324/9781003335887-7

continues, the more I disintegrate, I remove the edges [...] Self-destruction of the image: I have always felt like a material, but I have always fully dedicated myself, with all my weaknesses and traumas.

Guy: Yes, because self-destruction is the self-destruction of images and pretense. It's the self-destruction of superficiality, but not of the self.

Labrecque: Right. That's what it is. The self-destruction of appearances. To have no more edges and to peel off the skin. I've always liked vulnerability, to talk about things that are emotionally taboo for people, but also a kind of "exposure." I've never filmed my best side.

Guy: But what does that mean, the best side?

Labrecque: I mean I sometimes see videos with "attitudes" where it's very... seductive, in a very limited sense. In order for the image to self-destruct, to go beyond appearance, you have to... When I say "exposure," I mean that I really filmed myself upside down, I turned myself upside down and I filmed myself from beneath my feet. It has to do with the image of myself, but also the image of the video. It's as if, through the video, I was trying to remove the layers to get to the essence of the human being.

Guy: It reminds me of your video "En deçà du réel (1997)." There already was a form of self-destruction, until the body itself disappeared. It seems that in this video, in the end, the moment of greatest intensity is when the body disappears. It's a difficult emotion to name, what happens at the end of the video.

Labrecque: It's because we associate ourselves with that image. Our eyes are turned outwards instead of inwards. By removing the image, we look inwards. But what's inside, we don't know that in advance! It's full of things, emotions, and struggle.

Guy: Do you think it's easier to access this interiority when you are with yourself and filming yourself, as compared to when someone else is filming us or we film someone else? Is this interiority different?

Labrecque: I think it depends on the person. It's better for me alone, because I am less inhibited. Whereas with another person, there is another dynamic. [...] I couldn't do that, not now, maybe one day... I'll start with animals and rocks first [laughs]!

Guy: What do you think would be a rock's interiority? How does a rock represent itself?

Labrecque: Oh that's a good idea. I'm going to film a rock and I'm going to try to see what happens...

Guy: You might think it's dull. But it can be really explosive: Manon's view of the rock!

Labrecque: Ah, I already have little images coming to me!

Guy: This brings me to the topic of "Carnet de Voyage" (Travelogue) (2007). Because even if it's not rocks that you film in "Carnet de voyages," the objects are hyper-present and animated, in a way. I'm thinking of the dog and the balloon, and also the way you find yourself "in" the objects, a shot from within a glass of water for instance. Objects that we imagine to be very small; so, there is a work of scale. What does self-representation mean to you, when there are never other humans in your videos, but there are all sorts of things that come to life; either the editing or the image itself comes to life and self-destructs or animals or objects? Is it to have company, to be less alone? How do these presences manifest themselves for you?

Labrecque: Yes, company! When I started making motorized or non-motorized recording devices, it was so I could film myself while the camera was moving. I made a film where the camera starts to turn very fast, until you lose the image. It started like that and then it continued. Different ways of auto-destroying your surface image.

Guy: So, the camera's animation camera serves this aim. It may seem like a distraction from your body, but it's a strategy to circumvent conventions?

Labrecque: With the objects in "Carnet de voyages" – the bag, the tomato, the ball – it was to show materiality, gravity, gravitational pull. We all belong to this; we all fall in the end! In the pot or in the vase full of water, at the beginning, it was really a question of scale. The very fact of shrinking myself to put myself in a pot is a way of challenging my body, or my body image. Then there are the devices. It's also about inventing new challenges, with the camera in motion. These challenges will eventually create new affects. For me, that's what is made possible by the devices, basically: when something is reanimated.

Guy: [In your work], we find ourselves in these fictions, fantastic universes, where the play of scale, the work on gravity, everything is transformed a bit. So, we arrive in very fictional universes and strangely, the emotions that it creates for us are really familiar: real emotions. It makes me think of dreams. In our dreams, all sorts of impossible things happen to us, but we experience emotions that are the same as in real life, in relation to impossible situations. There is a connection between fiction and reality, at the level of affects, as you say, the challenges of the image serve to create affects.

Labrecque: Yes, right. To ask again: "what affects?" When I'm working – and that's why I have to work solo – my curiosity leads me to think, "Ah! What would it look like if I filmed myself from underneath?" You know, it's like a little vision. Or "what if I made a device that spins slowly and then faster and faster?" How far could it go? It's curiosity. Afterwards, when I film before this new device, I see things, and that's what guides me into the unknown. We move forward together. I say to myself, "Oh yes! Oh, that's too much... I don't like that. Oh, that touches me." And then I go and "wring out" the business. I often do these "wringing out" processes, I don't know if it's called... [laughs] In any case, we'll invent it! I find something I'm attracted to, and then I'll destroy it or accelerate it. I want to see how far it stretches, and what's left when it stretches. So sometimes it's curiosity, my

DIY side, I like it for that. But sometimes it's also "little visions" that I have. It started with a coffee, I woke up one morning and I thought, "Ah, OK, we're on Earth, but the Earth is spinning fast, fast, fast, so what would it be like if all of a sudden, the Earth stopped spinning?" The kinetic energy would be propelled towards us. This little vision led me to build the device, and after that it's like a friendship with the tools... I couldn't do that with others. I couldn't work with a team. I like humanity. But working creatively, these moments are too precious, it's always an adventure; I take off and see what happens with it.

Guy: You talk about visions: [in self-representation] there is often a mystical or spiritual part that is unresolved, that is mysterious, that arrives via the image, in the process of creation, in editing, or in the viewing of images. It becomes almost a shamanic relationship with oneself, in a specific moment or sometimes over time. I'm curious to know how this is for you, as you are very down to earth, very hands on, but there is also a very, very mystical part in your work.

Labrecque: Yes, for me, it's really an existential quest in the end. Even though I'm a woman, I've never made a feminist video; it was always about humanity. When we work with the body, whether it's with dance or the body in front of the camera, when we work with our physical incarnation, there is necessarily a ricochet towards the mystical, the spiritual. I went to a ceremony with a shaman in the north of Mongolia, and I had asked to see a woman. But when I saw her there, when she was in front of us and she was doing her rhythms and all that, I said to myself, "Ah! Shamans are the origin of performance." Performance, or at least of the body, because shamans call the energies of the earth and the sky into their bodies, the rhythms. I found that performance, dance, all that is related to the body, to the rhythm; it is as if we were capable of materiality as well as immateriality. Because we have poles in opposition.

Guy: What are these poles for you? They are multiple, but which ones appeal to you the most?

Labrecque: I have worked a lot on gravitational attraction and weight, materiality, and the desire to escape it. Levitations: even in my kinetic installations, sometimes everything falls or floats, objects start to fly. I have worked with forms, with air as well: to leave behind weight. That for me is my strongest extreme. The second, for me, would be humour and drama. I like to create moments of humour, but often I like to put the humour at the beginning, because it opens people's hearts. After that, you can talk about more vulnerable things. Those are the poles for me. The light, the dark, but the light and dark side that we have inside us too, in relation to the humour. And movement and inertia, through devices of reanimation, installations. Adding images in movement. For me, they are poles. One would not exist without the other. It's part of our duality. But how do we use duality to talk about what is "in between" and what could be a middle ground?

Guy: In creative work, in contemporary art, many people use these poles to create effects, but you really use them to create affects. There is never an "effect" to trap the viewer or to corner them. I've often seen shows where you laugh and then you feel bad, because in the end it's tragic, but in a slightly artificial way. It's [...] so different to work on affects, on emotions, and not just on intellect and surprise.

Labrecque: Yes, there's a bit of all that going on. For me, it has to move, but what interests me more are the vulnerable affects: trying to create vulnerable situations, to better approach the inner center. To destroy the image, to create vulnerable situations to make a link with the other, not just the image of the other. With the heart of the other. Ideally. I will spend my life trying to do that. That's my goal.

Guy: [...] I think of your works "Carnet de voyage" and "En deçà du réel." There is obviously your body in action in the image. There is the editing and all the movements you make your body do. But it's true that by dint of seeing them – and also of hearing you speak – I see Manon's body moving and doing the editing. And there is a kind of choreography of the invisible. There's a bit of a "backstory" to your videos. Because you've already told me how you were with the machine, physically rewinding and fast forwarding. I imagine you leaning over your VCR. There's a kind of choreography of "making" that video. And we'll never see the "film" of you the maker, but I've seen it in my head a lot. So, I wonder: what is the value of the gestures that we see and the gestures that we don't see in the videos, but that contributed to making the video the way it is? Do you still feel these gestures?

Labrecque: For me it's linked. When I'm editing, I play the image and then – "there it is!" That's when I have to stop. Sometimes with the sound, it's like a little dance that enters my body and I start editing with the images. When you talk about choreography, yes; when I work with sound it is really present, the energy of the choreography. Also, because when I work, my tools are important, so there is the physical side. Even with the cameras in the jar, all that, I need to have a presence when I shoot. It all adds up, everything is important to carry out the affect.

Guy: [...] It's as if, deep down, this relationship to being is also that, as an artist, there is no beginning and no end. We exist through our works, but the works are like little vehicles that take you on a journey. In the way you describe it, there is no glorification of the works or of your art. It's as if it's a path that renews curiosity.

Labrecque: I always use what I'm experiencing to create. Sometimes they are questions. Sometimes, it's things I've seen that have touched me; I note it down, I come back to it. But it's always driven by the idea of being in touch with what is. Otherwise, I wouldn't be driven. My curiosity goes hand in hand with where I am. That's why I like to use what we call weaknesses. For me, they are not weaknesses. And I like to use what happens in my life:

states, emotions, questions. Often these are states. In my body, what do I have in my body? I'll go with that.

[...] Each project, for me, is a relationship with myself, and also with life, it's like a quest. It's continuous curiosity. You know, when you experience something, if you pretend nothing happened, you won't know the "thing." But if you are inspired by the thing inside you, you create from that; it's like looking at it in all sorts of ways, facing what is inside you. In the process, there is learning. An inner discovery, for me. Even with my moving objects, even if sometimes I struggle with a movement: I want it to work, I want it to work so badly, and it doesn't work. And then facing that, at some point, I gave up, let go and found new ways! After several years, I really see that what I do, the creation, is really perfect for me. To live and know myself, and deal with life, and experiences. It's really perfect. I couldn't find anything else like that.

Guy: It's like you're practicing life in your art, and you're drawing inspiration from your art for your life. There's a kind of ping-pong movement.

Labrecque: It's like two intertwined aspects. It's a ball rolling on an axis. Both of them are breathing in, both of them are injecting energy, receiving the injection... just this little movement [intertwining hand movement].

Guy: I'll try to put it into words! [...] A lot of hand gestures! But that's why when I imagine you editing, I imagine you being agitated!

Labrecque: Yes, but when I was teaching video, I tried to tell them, "for editing, put both feet down." You know, some of them were doing it on the end [of the table], trying to find out when the image is finished! I would say to them, "No, get both feet on the ground, both hands ready, PLAY, and then react. But you have to have your feet planted so that the whole body can be ready." I made them laugh. But for me, when it didn't work for them – one of them was a student who made me laugh quite a bit, she always had her feet up, one toe touching the ground, one elbow touching the ground. Then she said, "it's difficult to make a video." We had a good laugh about it. But she admitted that when she put her two feet on the ground, it was better. It was a position of confidence. For me, the body is also that. You put yourself in a predisposition, even for a task that may seem as technical as editing: a predisposition, a ritual.

Guy: There is this energy, I think, when I look at your editing, there is such a strong kinesthetic relationship that it surely speaks of the body. It's not just interrupting the movement, it's not just always letting it finish. It's a response that is kinesthetic, that seems very intuitive.

Labrecque: Oh yeah, when I was teaching too, I used to say, "one frame of difference can really matter." Sometimes I do a rough edit, but when I get into a transition, I can work for hours on that. Changing the sound... For me, there is something physical, but also musical. It's a syncopation. A beat and… and, and… Maybe. Sometimes I cut things into "and, and." [laughs] I'm excited now!

Guy: But yes, it's the editing. I feel that every time we sit down to edit, especially if we're alone at the editing table, and it's our images that we know and that we're going to rediscover, and that we're in front of the unknown, and at the same time, in front of the known, in general, we sit there because we have planned a time, so we have time. But you quickly become irritated. There's a contrast between the fact that you settle in and you have time, but in the end you want to react quickly. But I like that, that excitement, and sometimes you can feel it in the films.

Labrecque: I know that I often use rising sounds, then a zero cut, as if to pull the rug out from under you. Repetition too, it has something. Because once, OK; twice, well…; three times, ah…; Four times, it starts to be funny. But when you persist five times, six times… Sometimes it's in the slowness, the cuts, the repetition; there's something weird too, to bring the audience in. You have to read the same thing again. The same thing, the same thing, the same thing, the same thing. For me, repetition is like a kind of experiment, a discovery and transformation of emotion, of affect over time.

Guy: Repetition as a discovery. You would imagine the opposite, but in fact it works.

Labrecque: But in fact, that's it, it's more of an introspective discovery.

Note

1 This interview was conducted on August 10, 2020, on Zoom. It was held as part of Priscilla Guy's doctoral research on feminist screendance self-representation (Université de Lille, France). It has been lightly edited for clarity and relevance.

Bibliography

Labrecque, Manon. *En deçà du réel*. 1997. Single channel video, 11:43 minutes.
Labrecque, Manon. *Carnet de voyages*. 2005. Single channel video, 25.29 minutes.

PART II

Touching Time: Histories Beyond the Binary

6
CANONISING BTS

FOMO in the Archives of Digital Convenience

Yutian Wong

Introduction

In 2002, I submitted an article to a journal proposing the idea that at some point in the near future, the canon of dance history, as it was understood up until that time, would one day be replaced by an electronic canon. This canon would be a canon of digital convenience. In other words, what often gets taught as dance history is often based on how difficult or easy it is to acquire audio-visual material to show in class. The article was informed by my experience creating a new course on Asian American dance history. As a newly minted Ph.D. in my first academic job, I wanted to expand course content beyond the material I had already collected in the process of research for my dissertation. I wrote to choreographers asking if they would be willing to share video recordings (still on VHS) for inclusion in a course syllabus. Quite often the answer was no. There was still distrust about what would happen to the material. Would the circulation of a video recording reduce touring opportunities? Would watching a video replace the need for and desire to see a live production in person?

That essay was rejected, and a reviewer commented that I failed to account for all the different ways dance historians teach dance history that does not exist on film or video. The ease of posting and viewing videos on streaming platforms such as YouTube would not become widely accessible for another three years and screendance as the intentional merger of dance/movement, choreography and film showcased in dance film festivals did not have the ubiquitous online presence it does today. Maybe the reviewers thought I was lazy or advocating for laziness? After all, the "real" work of research to produce knowledge about dance still existed as hours logged deciphering dance notation; seeing, doing, and recording dance in person; touching ephemera; knowing which libraries and archives housed reels of rare film footage, and who in one's professional network would allow access to bootleg video recordings. If knowledge production forming the canons taught as dance history must result from a confluence of scholarly and artistic effort, merit, and virtuosity – and not the crassness of accessibility – then the significance of works within a canon must be aesthetically self-evident, but also require translation in the form of explanation to cement canonicity as replicable in the teaching of dance history. Maybe I submitted to the wrong journal, maybe the article was poorly written, but it was obvious that most dance history was not captured *on* film or video. Having written a dissertation on a topic excluded from the canon of American dance history, and worked as a dance video librarian, I knew that what little was on commercially available film and video was always taught. Since the topic was tangential to my research at the time, the essay ended up buried and forgotten in the electronic dustbin of conference papers and first drafts that went nowhere.[1]

That is, until two decades later, when teaching dance and teaching about dance moved online in the middle of a global pandemic. The pandemic has taught us that the desire to see and experience things in person still exists. People still want to be in the same physical space with others experiencing the same event. This chapter is about teaching remotely due to a global health crisis. It is a report from working within the digital BTS dance archive that sustained teaching when access to public space was limited and, in many cases, foreclosed. As such, this chapter reflects on entanglements between pedagogy, dance history as a digital archive, and the making of dance canons via screendance; and how the accessibility of the archive cannot fully replace the desire to see live performance. Ease of access to digital materials stood in contrast to what was missing and absent from pandemic life. Missing people and bodies due to social distancing, sheltering-in-place, quarantines, lockdowns, and ultimately death generated a longing for pre-pandemic life. The desire to see things live is animated by memories of the past-as-history, and thus a digital archive in of itself. What was or could have been is removed from the present, such that desire operates as a longing for a future. The memory of the last performance, the last rehearsal, the last class together *in person* marked an end to or the beginning of an era.

A Concert

After twenty months of not seeing live performance in a theatre, I found myself in a crowd of 50,000 people singing, dancing, and waving light sticks at a football stadium in Inglewood, California. Yes, I will admit it. I went to the BTS *PERMISSION TO DANCE ON STAGE* concert at SoFi Stadium on

November 28, 2021, as did my sister, my hairdresser, my brother-in-law's coworkers, my best friend's friends and their offspring, their partners, at least two of my students, and a whole host of friends of friends and colleagues of colleagues who I later discovered were also at the concert. Much has been written in the popular press about the seven-member South Korean boy band BTS (*Bangtan Sonyeondan*, translated into English as Bulletproof Boys Scouts or simply referred to as the Bangtan Boys), their meteoric rise in the global popular music industry, the role that the ever-growing international fanbase called ARMY plays in their popularity, BTS's ubiquitous presence on social media, and their ability to exploit the full potential of the platformization of K-Pop.[2]

It is a well-known fact that BTS is prolific even by the standards of the K-Pop industry in which idol groups are expected to release content on a regular basis in order to maintain visibility and relevance within a crowded field of competitors. Less has been written about their production and release of content as an archive of screendance. If screendance is traditionally viewed through the lens of Western experimentalism as work that explores choreographic sensibilities or choreography that harnesses the artistic possibilities and impossibilities enabled by cinematography or film/video editing, framing BTS's dance repertory as screendance disrupts the corpus of the screendance canon as a series of singular artistic achievements that double as historical artefacts. Official music videos, official and unofficial video footage of performances at live concerts and awards shows, rehearsal footage, multiple versions of dance practice videos, and behind-the-scenes videos make up a body of material that fans use to create new pedagogical content that teaches viewers how to watch and analyse BTS repertory. And this is just the performance-related content that does not include the reality television shows, radio and television interviews, commercials, photoshoots, public service announcements, and other content related to K-Pop idol culture and BTS's specific role as South Korean cultural ambassadors.

In the week leading up to the PERMISSION TO DANCE ON STAGE concert, BTS attended the 2021 American Music Awards show in Los Angeles where they won all three awards that they were nominated for, including the award for Artist of the Year as well as awards for Favourite Pop/Rock Duo/Group, and Favourite Pop/Rock Song for "Butter." This would be the first time in history that an Asian pop music act, and one who sings predominantly in Korean, would win an award in a general category at an American music award show. Two days later, on November 23, 2021, video footage of BTS in Los Angeles flooded my phone as I drove south on Interstate 5 on my way to Southern California for the Thanksgiving weekend. BTS had been spotted at the intersection of Beverly Boulevard and Genesee Avenue, dancing to their three English-language singles, "Dynamite," "Butter," and "Permission to Dance."[3] Filmed for a segment of *The Late Late Show with James Corden* called

Crosswalk Concert that would be aired at a later date, the comedic sketch features the members of BTS being less-than-enthusiastic over having to perform in the middle of traffic next to a gas station.[4] On the evening of the same day BTS was spotted filming the Crosswalk Concert, BTS would appear on *The Late Late Show* for an interview. Looking calm, cool, and collected, RM, the leader of BTS, would tease (albeit diplomatically) an awkward public non-apology from Corden, the host of the show, over a poorly received joke that Corden made about the BTS fandom.[5] A few days later, fans would also be treated to a *Bangtan Bomb* (behind-the-scenes footage) of the band sitting on a couch on the set of *The Late Late Show* during a break. Wearing the black suits with yellow accents seen in the video footage taken by fans of the Crosswalk Concert, the seven members are crowded around a tablet to watch the announcement of their second Grammy nomination for Pop Duo/Group Performance, after which they would drink champagne and banter nervously about the competition.[6]

To say that the anticipation surrounding the BTS concert was palpable is an understatement, and no amount of pre-concert archival research – watching fan cams of live stadium concerts; watching news reports and fan cams of lines of concert goers snaking around Oakland Arena (Oakland, CA), Citi Field (New York City), the Rose Bowl (Pasadena) and Soldier Field (Chicago); reading advice columns on fan sites, or even reading Chapter 5 of Suk Young Kim's *K-pop Live* (2018) – would prepare me for the physical experience of being at a BTS concert.[7] Trying to collect, sort, and organize in real time all official and unofficial material generated by HYBE (BTS's company) and fans in just the few days before the start of the concerts felt almost impossible. FOMO (fear of missing out) is real when the archive of the live concert extends beyond the actual event itself. The amount of archival material produced and made publicly available requires the viewer/participant to keep track of time in order to reconstruct where and when things happened both virtually and in-person.

News reports about people showing up to the stadium the day before the concert was scheduled to begin, just to stand in line to buy official merchandise or on the off-chance of hearing BTS rehearse, were not exaggerated.[8] BTS fan sites such as usbtsarmy.com posted checklists on what to expect and how to prepare for a BTS concert.[9] It became clear that one did not just show up thirty minutes or even an hour before the show. Attending the concert would be an all-day affair requiring stamina, patience, nutrition, hydration, the right gear, logistics, official documents, and a good attitude.

After reading fan sites, forwarded twitter posts, and hearsay, I made a list of what to bring:

a   A clear 12x6x12 clear bag (required)
b   Proof of COVID-19 vaccination or proof of negative COVID-19 test (required)
c   Mask (required)

d   Hand sanitizer (habit)
e   Smartphone (required)
f   Digital ticket (required)
g   Digital parking pass (required if necessary)
h   Earplugs (required if aural health is a concern)
i   20 oz sealed water bottle (recommended)
j   Light stick aka ARMY bomb (optional, but not really)
k   Sweater (optional but recommended)
l   Comfortable shoes (recommended based on priorities)
m   Binoculars (recommended depending on where one's seat is)

I felt like I was packing to go on a camping trip, even though according to Google Maps, SoFi Stadium was only a ten-minute drive from my brother's house.

Armed with a clear backpack, fully charged phone with storage memory cleared out, musician's ear plugs, digital ticket, and vaccine card, I... stood... in... line... for hours... before entering into a space in which pure joy, delight, and pleasure, amidst the deafening roar of a crowd on their feet and a glittering expanse of twinkling lights would momentarily eclipse the tragedy of Astroworld, news of a recently discovered COVID-19 variant, reinstated border closures, continued efforts to dismantle Roe vs. Wade, rising inflation, and the ongoing destruction of the planet.

After spending two years avoiding crowds, the physical experience of being in the middle of a stadium concert was overwhelming. But this was fieldwork and as a dance scholar who writes about race and representation, BTS concerts had joined productions by Shen Yun Performing Arts as one of the two most highly visible spectacles of Asianess circulating on stage in the United States. Armed with my notebook and a pen, I was going to take notes in situ. I didn't write a thing. Outside the stadium, K-Pop dance cover crews performed for crowds waiting in line, cosplayers dressed as different eras of BTS looks and memes, and fans distributed handmade gifts. One had to keep moving in order to take in the entire experience. I had even done a reconnaissance trip by attending the *PERMISSION TO DANCE – LIVE PLAY* (simultaneous live stream of the concert) the night before at the YouTube Theater located next door to the stadium. Even after watching the entire concert on a screen in a 6,000-seat theatre that included indoor fireworks, confetti, and the synchronized ARMY bomb light show, there was still a palpable difference between the resonance of 6,000 people versus 50,000 people performing fanchants in an ocean of undulating light. Inside the stadium, it was impossible to write, dance, record, and wave a lightstick, while processing the fact that the seven people on stage, who are featured in a near constant stream of images and videos released by their company, are real. Suk Young Kim has written about K-Pop concerts as a mediated liveness given that the scale of performance venues means that one is more likely to watch the Jumbotron behind the performers rather than the performers themselves. This might be true depending on where one sits, but stadium concerts and music festivals are about rocking out to music played at a volume irreproducible elsewhere and so I danced for three hours next to complete strangers. The person to my left streamed the concert to a friend over a FaceTime video call, while the person to my right was visibly distraught that their lightstick was not connecting to the app that enables the crowdsourced light show. The people in front of me had the time of their lives and sang at the top of their lungs in a language they did not speak.

The Pandemic

I am what is referred to as Pandemic ARMY,[10] someone who fell into the BTS rabbit hole during the pandemic when the news cycle in the United States was a never-ending stream of social and environmental disasters. Many other US-based writers have written about taking the dive into the BTS-world as an escape from the toxic masculinity and xenophobia that was a daily feature of American public life, and which came to define the Trump administration.[11] I was no exception, and escalating anti-Asian violence resulting in the mass murder of six Asian women working at a spa outside of Atlanta, Georgia, on Tuesday, March 16, 2021, almost exactly one year after San Francisco shut down due to COVID-19, was yet another reason to feel trapped indoors.[12]

My journey down the BTS rabbit hole began with the immediate needs of my job of converting in-person dance classes to online classes. BTS emerged in the chaos of moving from the embodied practice of sharing physical space with my students and all the attendant claims to pedagogical specialness that dance often affirms, to the disembodied practice of talking at a screen full of black rectangles. As a dance teacher I was no different than anyone else – not the chemistry teacher Zooming from the dining room upstairs or the 9th grade homeroom teacher on a screen in the bedroom behind the kitchen.

After reformatting my courses into the synchronous, bichronous, and asynchronous online formats that instructors at my institution were required to choose from, I still had to figure out how to teach movement analysis over a screen. My repertoire of in-class activities that I had created over the previous two decades of teaching had become obsolete overnight. I had to start over from scratch. Unfortunately, the jokes about 2020–21 as the year of Zoom/YouTube university are less of a joke and more of a reality than one might think. I was looking for video clips to use as an example to show the difference between just saying you like something because one is impressed with performance quality and evaluating dance using movement/choreographic analysis.

This is when I started watching a series of reaction videos on YouTube on a channel called ReacttotheK, run by a musician named Emma Chang who began the channel while she was a student at the Eastman School of Music in Rochester, New York. Known as Umu on the channel, Chang films and edits videos of her music school friends reacting to K-Pop music videos. While some, but not all, of the reactors fangirled or fanboyed over the K-Pop idols while watching the music videos, everyone applied their knowledge of music theory to analyse, describe, and debate the structure of the music composition. The reactors describe chord progressions, scales, changes in rhythm, use of tonic, the use of major and minor scale, choices in vocal technique, instrumentation, and how all of these elements affect the colour, mood, or storytelling of the music. While the channel is designed to promote K-Pop, the videos also serve the pedagogical function of teaching viewers how to deploy music theory to analyse popular music.[13]

Inevitably, the reaction videos registered in my YouTube search algorithm and the channel's entire series of "Classical Musicians React to BTS" videos made their way into my list of recommended videos. So, I watched one, and then another, and another. And then I watched the reaction to "'ON' Kinetic Manifesto Film: Come Prima," in which a jazz singer and French horn player named Brianna describes in great detail how the music and choreography acknowledged African American music and dance cultures by referencing the aesthetics of traditional drumline and marching band practices particular to Historically Black Colleges and Universities (HBCUs).[14] Excitedly, Brianna discussed the place of the dance break within the marching band music and described how the choreography for the film featured stepping, krunk, and the nae nae. The fact that the seven band members were Korean did not seem to faze Brianna as she oohed and aahed over the inclusion of the Blue Devils, an award-winning drum and bugle corps. I saved the video and made a note about how Brianna delivered a detailed analysis of the structure of the music and choreography and provided both historical and cultural context of its citations. That she did this without compromising her enthusiasm for fangirling over the Blue Devils or BTS was a bonus. I added the video to my playlist of things to consider for showing in class.

Media studies scholar Michelle Cho frames the reaction video as an archive of liveness that produces feelings of community in capturing shared feelings of awe. She argues that the feeling is doubled in reaction videos to dance videos because dance itself always elicits an embodied response.[15] And this is why Brianna's response was so captivating to watch. Unlike most dance reaction videos that focus primarily on feelings about how well a dancer executes a move or how hard a dance looks, the reaction to "'ON' Kinetic Manifesto Film: Come Prima" replicated a familiar teaching scenario in which an instructor shows a video in class and tries to tease out the difference between an analysis of a performance and analysis of feelings about a performance. The episode was a model for getting past the "wow factor" without losing enthusiasm for the wow. The reaction video supplements the experience of watching "'On' Kinesthetic Manifesto Film: Come Prima" as a dance film or screendance rather than a music video by calling attention to the fact there are two different film versions of "ON," one of which is referred to as the Official MV (music video) and features BTS as characters inhabiting a dystopian sci-fi future.

With nothing else to do and nowhere to go, I ended up watching the entire series of classical musicians reacting to BTS videos in the order of their release until I got to the reaction video of "Black Swan" Art Film.[16] I was initially confused, because the music video did not include any of the band members and was essentially a contemporary dance film featuring the MN Dance Company, a European dance company based in Slovenia. Working squarely within the tradition of European contemporary dance, the movement vocabulary and choreographic conventions were fairly standard in the context of concert dance, and not something I expected to see as a music video for pop music. The reactors had a lot to say about the orchestral music, the sound of Western stringed instruments, the Korean gayageum, the use of pentatonic scale, and moments of chaos in the composition of the music, but they had very little to say about the choreography other than the fact that it was very beautiful and went really well with the music. "Going really well with the music" is usually a shorthand for music visualisation.

The film opens with a quote from Martha Graham's autobiography *Blood Memory* (1991), "a dancer dies twice—once when they stop dancing, and this first death is the more painful." Graham's penchant for dramatic sentiments about dancing and dance-making as an act of inspired genius and tortuous suffering is part of her legacy and mythology. The quote is one of many in which Graham railed against the ravages of time on her ageing body, as she saw younger dancers dance the roles that she had authored. Unlike the tradition of ballet in which the role of the choreographer and dancer are separate, and often separated by age, gender, and hierarchy, modern dance was founded on the tradition of the dancer/choreographer. While the lyrics of "Black Swan" speaks to the fear of losing passion for music due to the pressure of BTS's fame and the expectations of their fans, Graham never lost passion. She was always the central character within her own choreography, whether it be the Newlywed Bride, the Frontier Woman, Jocasta, Electra, Medea, and so on and so forth. Graham's "first death" was her ageing body and having to give up dancing the title roles that were always in some way based on herself.

What follows the title card with Graham's quote is a dance film or screendance of contemporary dance choreography performed inside an abandoned shopping mall in Southern California. There are seven dancers, one male soloist dancing the role of the swan, and a chorus of six dancers who pursue, pull, menace, lift, or embrace the swan. At some point near the end of the choreography, the swan fights against individual members of the chorus and eventually succumbs to the group and is lifted up above them, as if he is about to take flight in a vertical jump. The majority of the movement vocabulary is made up of extensions, lunges, and lush sweeping motions. The soloist executes "swan-like" movements, citing conventions of swanliness from Petipa's *Swan Lake*, Fokine's *Dying Swan*, Matthew Bourne's sinister all-male swans, and Darren Aronofsky's 2010 film *Black Swan*, in which Natalie Portman portrays a ballerina cast in the lead role in *Swan Lake* as Odette/Odile, and whose obsession with perfection turns into psychosis.

Perhaps one could read the mythology of Graham as legend and her notorious descent into alcoholism at the end of her career as a parable of Aronofsky's "Black Swan." Or one could read the academic classicism of Petipa's pairing of Odette/Odile as the manifestation of classical ballet's emphasis on the prima ballerina's ability to perform 32 fouetté turns at the end of a two–three-hour performance. Fokine's *Dying Swan* is only one swan, but one on the brink of a slow drawn-out death. Bourne's all-male swans are sinister and aggressive, and they don't die. Thinking it might be useful to demonstrate how the canon of ballet and modern dance continue to appear in contemporary culture, I added the video to my playlist thinking I can show it along with the music video for Queen's "I Want to Break Free," which features a cast of fauns piled on top of one another dressed in the spotted unitards from Nijinky's *Afternoon of the Faun*; the trailer for Francesco Vezzoli's homage to Sergei Diaghilev's *Ballets Russe* starring Lady Gaga playing piano for the company members of the Bolshoi Ballet; and a recording of Lil Buck's Memphis jookin version of Fokine's *Dying Swan* danced in tandem with former prima ballerina Nina Ananiashvili.

And so, my attention wandered away from the immediate needs of pandemic teaching, of logging off one Zoom class only to begin preparations for the next, towards the larger question of how to create a lecture around "Black Swan." Which version would I show? There were so many. Going on research trips, travel for conferences, and attending live performances were replaced with the compulsion to make sense of all the different versions of "Black Swan" performed by BTS: the official music video featuring all seven BTS members that was released after the version performed by the MN Dance Company; BTS's live performance on *The Late Late Show* danced in bare feet on a set reminiscent of *Swan Lake*; the interlude at the 2020 Melon Music Award (MMA) award show featuring the members of the band dancing in pairs to a purely instrumental orchestral arrangement of "Black Swan;" the multiple rehearsal videos in dance studios for these different performances; and the myriad other versions of "Black Swan" that kept appearing in my feed. There were so many different versions, and each was slightly different, such that the proliferation of variations meant that there were enough that one could find two that shared certain motifs but looked nothing alike, from the choreography, the costuming, the set design, or even the version of the song itself.[17]

Keeping track of all the different versions of "Black Swan" became a task not unlike other things I was doing, or had done in the past, such as trying to find all the YouTube clips of Dance Theatre of Harlem's (DTH's) *Creole Giselle* and *Firebird*. Like every other major dance company during the pandemic, DTH hosted virtual dance concerts by posting videos on their website and YouTube channel. After years of searching for excerpts of *Creole Giselle* online, DTH streamed the 1987 recording on their website, which was actually a link to a YouTube video, so it felt like a small victory for obsessive YouTube-watching. In some ways, the pandemic was a bonanza for access as dance companies in their rush to remain visible and relevant posted otherwise unavailable recordings of full-length works online. Finding a copy of DTH's *Firebird* still remains elusive.

I referred to my search for "Black Swan" videos as a task-like compulsion since I didn't necessarily listen to the song for the sake of listening to the song. Like most K-Pop music, a song is not complete without a corresponding visual element – the choreography. It was the presence of seven Korean men on an American late night talk show looking like modern dancers, dressed all in black, dancing hip-hop-inflected modern dance choreography in bare feet on a set made to look like a forest, singing in Korean about art and fear, that held my attention. In "Black Swan" was a compelling nexus of ideas linking popular culture, modern dance, gender, Asianness, and language. The version of "Black Swan" performed at the 2020 MMA show dispensed with hip-hop altogether and featured a series of duets between the members of the group, who emerge in pairs from what is essentially a corps de ballet. One of the duets is choreographed as a pas de deux in which one member lifts another in a classic fish lift commonly found in classical ballet. Performed to an instrumental track of "Black Swan" without vocals, the emphasis was solely on the dancing itself. And this is what drew me in – the citation of ballet, the use of contemporary dance vocabulary, the mixing of high and low, the multiple versions utilising different choreography and different movement vocabularies. In some versions, the members are the white swans surrounded by a corps of black swans. In other versions, the members are the corps of black swans, such that the narrative links between movement and lyrics (or lack of lyrics) are not consistent.[18] At some point while watching the 2020 MMA version, I thought to myself – they should take their shoes off, the black soles on those stiff-looking white ankle boots are not doing any favours for their leg line. Watching "Black Swan" had become no different than watching any of the pre-recorded live streamed dance concerts I was invited to attend. Regardless, I save all versions of "Black Swan" to my playlist. Maybe they would be useful examples for initiating a class discussion on the ontology of choreography.

And suddenly I was deep into the archive watching the behind-the-scenes videos of BTS shooting the official music video for "Black Swan," the dance practice video of BTS in sweatpants and tee shirts rehearsing "Black Swan" in a dance studio, the *Bangtan Bomb* of the seven members goofing off pretending to be opera singers during the shooting of the "Black Swan" music video, and finally a *Bangtan Bomb* of the members sitting on the floor gathered around a small screen reacting to the music video of "Black Swan."[19]

> I was watching … BTS watching themselves.
> And this is the moment I knew I had lost it.
> I was sucked in.
> Fallen into the deep end.
> Completely and utterly seduced by … BTS.
> Any pretence that I was still watching BTS videos as a purely pedagogical enterprise had now disappeared.
> Stop.
> There is a break here. A screeching halt. A shifting of gears.
> A turn around.

Canonising BTS

The absence of differentiation between private and public life, bled into the absence of differentiation between research, teaching, and "doing nothing." This is where pedagogy refashions itself as research in the return to the beginning of this chapter. Dance scholar Jens Richard Giersdorf once described being left in darkness while working alone in a West German archive. Absorbed in perusing archival documents, he sat in one place too long and the motion sensor lights turned themselves off.[20] I had those moments too, but I was at home clicking through a digital archive of screendance. With multiple windows open on my laptop, I would lose track of time before realising the sun had gone down and I too was sitting in the dark. It was easy to get lost in the BTS dance archive, which I discovered not because I was looking for BTS, but because I was looking for something to help teach students how to do dance analysis. This pedagogical labour, structured by the need to teach online, was enabled by an archive that was readily accessible and convenient.

Accessibility itself does not guarantee visibility or impact without the work of the musicians, dancers, vocal coaches, video editors, and producers who deploy their expertise to canonize BTS in the form of reaction videos to both official material and fan edited compilation videos. Titles such as BTS singing high notes, BTS rap line singing, BTS vocal line rapping, j-hope's best dance breaks, Jin's dance improvement, Taehyung doing body rolls in "Mic Drop," and Jungkook dancing to RM's line compile for the viewer fan-juried evidence of BTS's excellence and virtuosity. While some of the material is mostly concerned with the hotness of the moves, the fan edits do the work of drawing viewers' attention to specific elements of a performance as screendance. To pay such close attention that one can identify minute variations in choreographic structure, movement quality, and the difference between improvisational moments and accidents across a decade's worth of different recordings of live performances demonstrates a level of movement analysis usually associated with academically institutionalized practices such as Laban movement analysis. If a canon is a body of work designated as exemplary of a set of principles that are perceived as essential to training, the acquisition of vocabulary and skill, or the accumulation of knowledge about a subject, then the BTS archive is exceptional in the sheer amount of material (official, unofficial, and re-mixed) that functions as evidence of its own relevance as screendance.

The pedagogical labour of working my way through this archive of screendance would eventually turn into a scholarly object – the ultimate form of canonization. The archive would include the field notes, videos, photos taken while watching a live performance of "Black Swan" in person, as well as a research trip to see yet another screendance version on exhibit at the HYBE INSIGHT museum in Seoul. Dance history is made, in this case, in the form of a book chapter that reads the themes of ageing and death in "Black Swan" through the lens of Cold War dance history.[21] The chapter already assumes the body of work that makes up "Black Swan" is worthy as a set of objects that can be used to reflect on the legacy of American cultural diplomacy, the imposition of American modernism on Asian artists, and the inevitability of military conscription as the direct result of the still unresolved Cold War. That this reflection happens from the space of popular culture is significant in a historical moment in which the world bears witness to the stakes of unresolved military conflicts.

With over 43 million views on YouTube of the "'Black Swan' Art Film," 469 million views of the "Black Swan" official music video, 8.1 million views of BTS watching the "'Black Swan' Art Film," and 13 million views of BTS watching the "Black Swan" official music video, ease of access has proven to generate more interest by creating its own history as viewers instruct each other on how to watch, reassemble, and redistribute the archive of screendance, and in doing so, crystalize the canon.[22]

Notes

1 The article, "Technological Canons: Inventing Asian American Dance History in the Twenty-First Century," was first presented as a conference paper at the 2002 Association for Asian American Studies Meeting in Houston, Texas. I would like to thank Michelle Cho, Alanna Thain, and Priscilla Guy for the opportunity to resurrect this essay and Rani Neutill and Mim Thi Nguyen for their generous feedback.

2 See Patty Ahn, et al., eds., *Bangtan Remixed: The Critical BTS Reader* (Durham: Duke University Press, 2024).
3 I was driving to Los Angeles on November 23, 2021, when I started receiving notifications that fan cams of BTS performing on the streets of LA were posted on Twitter. Fan cam footage started showing up on YouTube soon after. The Hollywood Fix, "BTS & James Corden Perform Butter, Dynamite, and Permission to Dance for Fans on the Streets of LA," November 24, 2021, YouTube video, 9:22, https://www.youtube.com/watch?v=1ayOfSTTsco. Accessed November 24, 2021.
4 The segment aired on December 16, 2021. The Late Late Show with James Corden, "BTS Performs a Concert in the Crosswalk," December 16, 2021, YouTube video, 9:57, https://www.youtube.com/watch?v=A8KQhwmdZIw. Accessed December 16, 2021.
5 The Late Late Show with James Corden, "BTS and Papa Mochi are Reunited," November 23, 2021, YouTube video, 10:10, https://www.youtube.com/watch?v=pRl2tawentY. Accessed December 14, 2021. On September 21, 2021, James Cordon made a joke about BTS's address to the United Nations General Assembly (UNGA) saying that it was unusual that BTS was speaking at the UNGA. Cordon went on to say that it was the first time in history that "15-year-old girls everywhere found themselves wishing they were the Secretary General of the United Nations António Guterres." Vanessa Jackson, "James Corden is Getting Called Out for Making an Ageist Joke About BTS Fans…and Yikes," *Buzzfeed*, September 22, 2021, https://www.buzzfeed.com/vannessajackson/james-corden-called-out-by-bts-fans. Accessed December 14, 2021.
6 Bangtan Bombs are behind-the-scenes videos of BTS members goofing around backstage, in their dressing rooms, on set, or in rehearsal before or after performances, music video shoots, and other public events. Videos are posted to the official BTS YouTube Channel BANGTANTV. BANGTANTV, "[BANGTAN BOMB] Grammy Nomination Night-BTS (방탄소년단)," November 26, 2021, YouTube video, 1:28, https://www.youtube.com/watch?v=xlG2ZtnVSNI. Accessed December 14, 2021.
7 ABC7 News Bay Area, "K-pop band BTS draws massive line at Oakland's Oracle Arena," September 12, 2018, YouTube video, 2:05, https://www.youtube.com/watch?v=CG2YIvQbT_I. Accessed December 14, 2021; Billboard News, "BTS Fans Camp Out For Citi Field Show," October 5, 2018, YouTube video, 3:22, https://www.youtube.com/watch?v=7nCl_IjdbGk. Accessed December 14, 2021; CBS New York, "BTS Fans Gather For Concert," October 6, 2018, YouTube video, 1:58, https://www.youtube.com/watch?v=Xc24Ts2D8RQ. Accessed December 14, 2021; KTLA 5, "BTS Fever Descends on the Rose Bowl in Pasadena," May 6, 2019, YouTube video, 2:35, https://www.youtube.com/watch?v=F1bxFcFMNIY. Accessed December 14, 2021; Mikey's Basement, "BTS Live in Soldier Field – Speak Yourself World Tour – Day 1," May 28, 2019, YouTube video, 1:27:44, https://www.youtube.com/watch?v=kAFfR4OCAd4. Accessed December 15, 2021; "Tips for First time Concert Attendees," Reddit, accessed December 15, 2021, https://www.reddit.com/r/bangtan/comments/awuw4v/tips_for_first_time_concert_attendees/; "BTSARMYGuide," BTSARMYGuide, accessed December 15, 2021, http://bts-nynj.info/prudential.html; "BTS Announce 'BTS Permission to Dance on Stage – LA' Coming to SoFi Stadium for Four Nights," SoFi Stadium, September 28, 2021, https://www.sofistadium.com/bts/. Accessed December 15, 2021; "BTS LIVE PLAY KNOW BEFORE YOU GO," accessed December 15, 2021, https://www.youtubetheater.com/bts; Suk-Young Kim, "Chapter 5: Live K-pop Concerts and Their Digital Doubles," in *K-Pop Live: Fans, Idols, and Multimedia Performance* (Palo Alto, CA: Stanford University Press, 2018), 161–98.

8   Selome Hailu, "BTS Draws Thousands of Fans to L.A.'s SoFi Stadium Ahead of First Live Concert Since Start of the Pandemic," *Variety*, November 27, 2021, https://variety.com/2021/music/news/bts-concert-sofi-stadium-los-angeles-1235120579/; City News Service, "K-Pop's BTS Set for First Concert Since 2019 Tonight at Sofi Stadium," *NBC Los Angeles*, November 27, 2021, https://www.nbclosangeles.com/news/local/k-pops-bts-set-for-first-concert-since-2019-tonight-at-sofi-stadium/2767734/; Ashley MacKey, "BTS fans line up at SoFi Stadium in the middle of the night to wait for merchandise," *ABC7 Eyewitness News*, November 30, 2021, https://abc7.com/bts-concert-army-fans-kpop/11285987/.
9   "Concert Survival Checklist," US BTS ARMY, accessed December 15, 2021, https://www.usbtsarmy.com/concert-survival-checklist.
10 ARMY (Adorable Representative M.C. for Youth) is the official name of the BTS fandom.
11 Personal accounts of how BTS helped people get through the COVID-19 pandemic are not limited to the United States. The following list is but a fraction of the writing that has been published online about listening to and watching BTS content as a coping mechanism during the pandemic. Tan, "A First Encounter: Discovering BTS how I gained my happiness back," *Medium*, January 14, 2021, https://medium.com/planet-serotonin/a-first-encounter-discovering-bts-c49dea894179. Accessed December 16, 2021; Lenika Cruz, "The Astonishing Duality of BTS," *The Atlantic*, December 26, 2020, https://www.theatlantic.com/culture/archive/2020/12/bts-2020-borahae/617521/. Accessed December 16, 2021; Cruz, "BTS's 'Life Goes On' Did the Impossible," *The Atlantic*, November 30, 2020, https://www.theatlantic.com/culture/archive/2020/11/bts-life-goes-on-be-album/617244/. Accessed December 16, 2021; Arabelle Sicardi, "The Dark Side of K-Pop was what Drew me to the Genre," *Allure*, April 15, 2020, https://www.allure.com/story/k-pop-stardom-dark-side. Accessed December 16, 2021; Gabe Bergado "K-Pop Helped me Reconnect with my Asian American Identity," *Teen Vogue*, October 23, 2019, https://www.teenvogue.com/story/k-pop-reconnect-asian-american-identity. Accessed December 16, 2021; Helen Chen, "What K-Pop Taught Me About Xenophobia," *BKReader*, November 16, 2020, https://bkreader.com/2020/11/16/what-k-pop-taught-me-about-xenophobia/. Accessed December 16, 2021; Valerie Wu, "K-Pop Stars are Redefining Mainstream for Asian American Youth," *Mercury News*, June 23, 2018, https://www.mercurynews.com/2018/06/23/opinion-k-pop-stars-are-redefining-mainstream-for-asian-american-youth/. Accessed December 16, 2021; Lucia Ruan, "How BTS helped fans find community throughout the pandemic," *USC Annenberg Media*, November 30, 2021, https://www.uscannenbergmedia.com/2021/11/30/how-bts-helped-fans-find-community-throughout-the-pandemic/. Accessed December 16, 2021; Mariam Khan, "Being part of the BTS ARMY fandom held me together during the Covid pandemic," *i News*, October 3, 2021, https://inews.co.uk/opinion/bts-army-fandom-held-me-together-covid-pandemic-1224967. Accessed December 16, 2021; The Masked Writer, "How BTS helped me," *Medium*, December 27, 2020, https://medium.com/@nimishkasharma2019/how-bts-helped-me-43328f2734d2. Accessed December 16, 2021; Jerilyn Mae Precious Rosal Mansueto, "How BTS helps me through the pandemic," *Lifestyle Inquirer*, November 28, 2020, https://lifestyle.inquirer.net/375236/how-bts-helps-me-through-the-pandemic/. Accessed December 16, 2021; Karishma Shetty, "Exclusive: ARMY share how BTS is helping them cope with anxiety during the lockdown period due to COVID 19," *Pinkvilla*, April 1, 2020, https://www.pinkvilla.com/entertainment/exclusives/exclusive-army-share-how-bts-helping-them-cope-anxiety-during-lockdown-period-due-covid-19-520707. Accessed December 16, 2021; Hannah Yoon and Kat Moon, "These Portraits Show that the BTS ARMY is not a Monolith," *Time*, November 24, 2021, https://time.com/6122609/bts-arm

y-photos/. Accessed December 16, 2021; Guardian readers and Hibaq Farah, "'BTS taught me that I am worthy': readers on why they love the K-pop superstars," *The Guardian*, December 14, 2021, https://www.theguardian.com/music/2021/dec/14/bts-taught-me-that-i-am-worthy-readers-on-why-they-love-the-k-pop-superstars. Accessed December 16, 2021; Naila Syed, "How music and Kpop stars BTS helped Canadians' mental health in the pandemic," *The Toronto Observer*, October 10, 2021. https://torontoobserver.ca/2021/10/10/music-therapy-bts/amp/. Accessed December 16, 2021; Padya Paramita, "How Park Jimin of BTS Helped Me Feel Seen in my Brown, Queer Body," *Them*, February 2, 2021, https://www.them.us/story/park-jimin-bts-padya-paramita-personal-essay. Accessed December 16, 2021; Sara Kabir, "How BTS is Changing the World, One Song at a Time," *The Daily Star*, January 1, 2021, https://www.thedailystar.net/star-youth/news/how-bts-changing-the-world-one-song-time-2020593. Accessed December 16, 2021; Yoon, "BTS returns to the stage reuniting their ARMY of fans after a 2-year hiatus," *NPR*, December 4, 2021, https://www.npr.org/sections/pictureshow/2021/12/04/1060539313/bts-returns-to-the-stage-reuniting-their-army-of-fans-after-a-two-year-hiatus. Accessed December 16, 2021; Pranjal, "Footy, friends, and a little BTS," StudyAdelaide, accessed December 16, 2021, https://studyadelaide.com/student-stories/pranjal-footy-friends-and-little-bts; Dara David Roa, "9 Adorable Reasons Why This Mom Loves BTS," *Modern Parenting*, July 16, 2021, https://modernparenting.onemega.com/9-adorable-reasons-why-this-army-mom-loves-bts/. Accessed December 16, 2021; Rhian Daly, "How RM's 'mono' became a lighthouse in the pandemic's darkness," *NME*, October 23, 2021, https://www.nme.com/features/music-features/how-rms-mono-became-a-lighthouse-in-the-pandemics-darkness-3077124. Accessed December 16, 2021; Natalie Morin, "BTS Helps the World Feel a Little Smaller—& We Need it More than Ever," *Refinery29*, December 2, 2020, https://www.refinery29.com/en-us/2020/12/10163161/bts-be-album-songs-pandemic-group-interview. Accessed December 16, 2021; Antonia Haynes, "I Purple You: An In-Depth Look at the BTS ARMY and Their Stories-Part One," *Tilt* (blog), October 1, 2021, https://tilt.goombastomp.com/blog/i-purple-you-an-in-depth-look-at-the-bts-army-and-their-stories-part-one/. Accessed December 21, 2021; Tamara Fuentes, "BTS 'Fly to My Room' Lyrics Give Light to the Band's Struggles During Quarantine," *Seventeen*, November 20, 2020, https://www.seventeen.com/celebrity/music/a34740759/bts-fly-to-my-room-lyrics-meaning/. Accessed December 16, 2021; Bandwagon, "Titas of BTS on loving and supporting each other through the ongoing pandemic with music and stories," *Bandwagon*, June 3, 2021, https://www.bandwagon.asia/articles/titas-of-bts-army-philippines-filipino-fans-bangtan-anniversary-facebook-group-hybe-bighit-interview-2021.

12 Charmaine Chua, "Anti-Asian Violence," *Society + Space*, March 22, 2021, https://www.societyandspace.org/forums/anti-asian-violence. In the week following the murders of Daoyou Feng, Hyun Jung Grant, Suncha Kim, Paul Andre Michels, Soon Chung Park, Xiaojie Tan, Delaina Ashley Yaun, and Yong Ae Yue, Charmaine Chua invited Asian American scholars and organizers to contribute essays to contextualize the mass shooting that took place on March 16, 2021, in Atlanta, Georgia. Six of the eight victims were Asian women, and four of the six Asian women were of Korean descent. BTS would release a statement in response to the murders and Anti-Asian violence on March 29, 2021. See 방탄소년단 (@BTS_twt), "#StopAsianHate #StopAAPIHate," Twitter, March 29, 2021, https://twitter.com/BTS_twt/status/1376712834269159425?ref_src=twsrc%5Etfw%7Ctwcamp%5Etweetembed%7Ctwterm%5E1376712834269159425%7Ctwgr%5E%7Ctwcon%5Es1_c10&ref_url=https%3A%2F%2Fwww.buzzfeednews.com%2Farticle%2Feleanorbate%2Fbts-stop-aapi-asian-hate-racism-statement.

13 For a different reading of K-Pop reaction videos see Michelle Cho "3 Ways that BTS and Their Fans are Redefining Liveness." *Flowjournal*. May 29, 2018. https://www.flowjournal.org/2018/05/bts-and-its-fans/. Accessed August 29, 2022.
14 ReacttotheK, "Classical and Jazz Musicians React BTS: 'ON,'" October 5, 2020, YouTube video, https://www.youtube.com/watch?v=PhK_fScrGJc. Accessed December 14, 2021.
15 Michelle Cho, "3 Ways that BTS and Their Fans are Redefining Liveness," *Flowjournal*, May 29, 2018, https://www.flowjournal.org/2018/05/bts-and-its-fans/. Accessed August 29, 2022.
16 ReacttotheK, "Classical Musicians React: BTS 'Black Swan (Art Film),'" February 22, 2020, YouTube video, 16:27, https://www.youtube.com/watch?v=UAhtwpBDULE. Accessed December 14, 2021.
17 For a close reading of the different versions of "Black Swan," see Yutian Wong, "Martha and the Swans: BTS, 'Black Swan,' and Cold War Dance History," in *Bangtan Remixed: The BTS Critical Reader*.
18 For a discussion of modernism and "Black Swan," see Wong, "Martha and the Swans."
19 BANGTANTV, "[EPISODE] BTS 'Black Swan' MV Shooting Sketch," March 20, 2020, YouTube v ideo, 8:00, https://www.youtube.com/watch?v=hQH1LqAW5FQ; BANGTANTV, "[BANGTAN BOMB] Musical Actors BTS - BTS (방탄소년단)," October 24, 2020, YouTube video, 4:08, https://www.youtube.com/watch?v=lSK4Mvap5i0; BANGTANTV, "[BANGTAN BOMB] BTS 'Black Swan' MV Reaction – BTS (방탄소년단)," March 17, 2021, YouTube video, 4:08, https://www.youtube.com/watch?v=LQK7tF1vH2w.
20 Jens Richard Giersdorf, *The Body of the People* (Madison: University of Wisconsin Press, 2014).
21 Wong, "Martha and the Swans."
22 This is the number of views as of June 13, 2023. Between January 1, 2023, to June 13, 2023, views of the "'Black Swan' Art Film" increased by 1 million views, views of the "Black Swan" official music video increased by 54 million views, views of BTS watching the "'Black Swan' Art Film" increased by 100,000 views, and views of BTS watching the "Black Swan" official music video increased by 1 million views.

Bibliography

ABC7 News Bay Area. "K-pop band BTS draws massive line at Oakland's Oracle Arena." September 12, 2018. YouTube Video, 2:05. https://www.youtube.com/watch?v=CG2YIvQbT_I. Accessed December 14, 2021.

Ahn, Patty, Michelle Cho, Vernadette Vicuña Gonzalez, Rani Neutill, Mimi Thi Nguyen, and Yutian Wong, eds. *Bangtan Remixed: The Critical BTS Reader*. Durham: Duke University Press, 2024.

Bandwagon. "Titas of BTS on loving and supporting each other through the ongoing pandemic with music and stories." *Bandwagon*. June 3, 2021. https://www.bandwagon.asia/articles/titas-of-bts-army-philippines-filipino-fans-bangtan-anniversary-facebook-group-hybe-bighit-interview-2021.

BANGTANTV. "[BANGTAN BOMB] BTS 'Black Swan' MV Reaction – BTS (방탄소년단)." March 17, 2021. YouTube video, 4:08. https://www.youtube.com/watch?v=LQK7tF1vH2w.

BANGTANTV. "[BANGTAN BOMB] Grammy Nomination Night-BTS (방탄소년단)." November 26, 2021. YouTube video, 1:28. https://www.youtube.com/watch?v=xlG2ZtnVSNI. Accessed December 14, 2021.

BANGTANTV. "[BANGTAN BOMB] Musical Actors BTS – BTS (방탄소년단)." October 24, 2020. YouTube video, 4:08. https://www.youtube.com/watch?v=lSK4Mvap5i0.

BANGTANTV. "[EPISODE] BTS 'Black Swan' MV Shooting Sketch." March 20, 2020. YouTube video, 8:00. https://www.youtube.com/watch?v=hQH1LqAW5FQ.

Bergado, Gabe. "K-Pop Helped me Reconnect with my Asian American Identity." *Teen Vogue*. October 23, 2019. https://www.teenvogue.com/story/k-pop-reconnect-asian-american-identity. Accessed December 16, 2021.

Billboard News. "BTS Fans Camp Out For Citi Field Show." *L Billboard News*. October 5, 2018. YouTube video, 3:22. https://www.youtube.com/watch?v=7nCl_IjdbGk. Accessed December 14, 2021.

"BTS Announce 'BTS Permission to Dance on Stage – LA' Coming to SoFi Stadium for Four Nights." SoFi Stadium. September 28, 2021. https://www.sofistadium.com/bts/. Accessed December 15, 2021.

"BTS LIVE PLAY KNOW BEFORE YOU GO." YouTube Theater. https://www.youtubetheater.com/bts. Accessed December 15, 2021.

"BTSARMYGuide." http://bts-nynj.info/prudential.html. Accessed December 15, 2021.

CBS New York. "BTS Fans Gather For Concert." October 6, 2018. YouTube video, 1:58. https://www.youtube.com/watch?v=Xc24Ts2D8RQ. Accessed December 14, 2021.

Chen, Helen. "What K-Pop Taught Me About Xenophobia." *BKReader*. November 16, 2020. https://bkreader.com/2020/11/16/what-k-pop-taught-me-about-xenophobia/. Accessed December 16, 2021.

Cho, Michelle. "3 Ways that BTS and Their Fans are Redefining Liveness." *Flowjournal*. May 29, 2018. https://www.flowjournal.org/2018/05/bts-and-its-fans/. Accessed August 29, 2022.

Chua, Charmaine. "Anti-Asian Violence." *Society + Space*. March 22, 2021. https://www.societyandspace.org/forums/anti-asian-violence.

City News Service. "K-Pop's BTS Set for First Concert Since 2019 Tonight at Sofi Stadium." *NBC Los Angeles*. November 27, 2021. https://www.nbclosangeles.com/news/local/k-pops-bts-set-for-first-concert-since-2019-tonight-at-sofi-stadium/2767734/.

"Concert Survival Checklist." US BTS ARMY. https://www.usbtsarmy.com/concert-survival-checklist. Accessed December 15, 2021.

Cruz, Lenika. "BTS's 'Life Goes On' Did the Impossible." *The Atlantic*. November 30, 2020. https://www.theatlantic.com/culture/archive/2020/11/bts-life-goes-on-be-album/617244/. Accessed December 16, 2021.

Cruz, Lenika. "The Astonishing Duality of BTS." *The Atlantic*. December 26, 2020. https://www.theatlantic.com/culture/archive/2020/12/bts-2020-borahae/617521/. Accessed December 16, 2021.

Daly, Rhian. "How RM's 'mono' became a lighthouse in the pandemic's darkness." *NME*. October 23, 2021. https://www.nme.com/features/music-features/how-rms-mono-became-a-lighthouse-in-the-pandemics-darkness-3077124. Accessed December 16, 2021.

Fuentes, Tamara. "BTS 'Fly to My Room' Lyrics Give Light to the Band's Struggles During Quarantine." *Seventeen*. November 20, 2020. https://www.seventeen.com/celebrity/music/a34740759/bts-fly-to-my-room-lyrics-meaning/. Accessed December 16, 2021.

Giersdorf, Jens Richard. *The Body of the People*. Madison: University of Wisconsin Press, 2014.
Guardian readers and Hibaq Farah. "'BTS taught me that I am worthy': readers on why they love the K-pop superstars." *The Guardian*. December 14, 2021. https://www.theguardian.com/music/2021/dec/14/bts-taught-me-that-i-am-worthy-readers-on-why-they-love-the-k-pop-superstars. Accessed December 16, 2021.
Hailu, Selome. "BTS Draws Thousands of Fans to L.A.'s SoFi Stadium Ahead of First Live Concert Since Start of the Pandemic." *Variety*. November 27, 2021. https://variety.com/2021/music/news/bts-concert-sofi-stadium-los-angeles-1235120579/.
Haynes, Antonia. "I Purple You: An In-Depth Look at the BTS ARMY and Their Stories-Part One." *Tilt* (blog), October 1, 2021. https://tilt.goombastomp.com/blog/i-purple-you-an-in-depth-look-at-the-bts-army-and-their-stories-part-one/. Accessed December 21, 2021.
Jackson, Vanessa. "James Corden is Getting Called Out for Making an Ageist Joke About BTS Fans…and Yikes." *Buzzfeed*. September 22, 2021. https://www.buzzfeed.com/vanessajackson/james-corden-called-out-by-bts-fans. Accessed December 14, 2021.
Kabir, Sara. "How BTS is Changing the World, One Song at a Time." *The Daily Star*. January 1, 2021. https://www.thedailystar.net/star-youth/news/how-bts-changing-the-world-one-song-time-2020593. Accessed December 16, 2021.
Khan, Mariam. "Being part of the BTS ARMY fandom held me together during the Covid pandemic." *i News*. October 3, 2021. https://inews.co.uk/opinion/bts-army-fandom-held-me-together-covid-pandemic-1224967. Accessed December 16, 2021.
Kim, Suk-Young. "Chapter 5: Live K-pop Concerts and Their Digital Doubles." In *K-Pop Live: Fans, Idols, and Multimedia Performance*, 161–198. Palo Alto, CA: Stanford University Press, 2018.
KTLA 5. "BTS Fever Descends on the Rose Bowl in Pasadena." May 6, 2019. YouTube video, 2:35. https://www.youtube.com/watch?v=F1bxFcFMNIY. Accessed December 14, 2021.
MacKey, Ashley. "BTS fans line up at SoFi Stadium in the middle of the night to wait for merchandise." *ABC7 Eyewitness News*. November 30, 2021. https://abc7.com/bts-concert-army-fans-kpop/11285987/.
Mansueto, Jerilyn Mae Precious Rosal. "How BTS helps me through the pandemic." *Lifestyle Inquirer*. November 28, 2020. https://lifestyle.inquirer.net/375286/how-bts-helps-me-through-the-pandemic/. Accessed December 16, 2021.
Mikey's Basement. "BTS Live in Soldier Field – Speak Yourself World Tour – Day 1." May 28, 2019. YouTube Video, 1:27:44. https://www.youtube.com/watch?v=kAFfR4OCAd4. Accessed December 15, 2021.
Morin, Natalie. "BTS Helps the World Feel a Little Smaller—& We Need it More than Ever." *Refinery29*. December 2, 2020. https://www.refinery29.com/en-us/2020/12/10163161/bts-be-album-songs-pandemic-group-interview. Accessed December 16, 2021.
Paramita, Padya. "How Park Jimin of BTS Helped Me Feel Seen in my Brown, Queer Body." *Them*. Februrary 2, 2021. https://www.them.us/story/park-jimin-bts-padya-paramita-personal-essay. Accessed December 16, 2021.
Pranjal. "Footy, friends, and a little BTS." StudyAdelaide. https://studyadelaide.com/student-stories/pranjal-footy-friends-and-little-bts. Accessed December 16, 2021.

ReacttotheK. "Classical and Jazz Musicians React BTS: 'ON.'" October 5, 2020. YouTube Video, 24:55. https://www.youtube.com/watch?v=PhK_fScrGJc. Accessed December 14, 2021.

ReacttotheK. "Classical Musicians React: BTS 'Black Swan (Art Film).'" February 22, 2020. YouTube video, 16:27. https://www.youtube.com/watch?v=UAhtwpBDULE. Accessed December 14, 2021.

Roa, Dara David. "9 Adorable Reasons Why This Mom Loves BTS." *Modern Parenting*. July 16, 2021. https://modernparenting.onemega.com/9-adorable-reasons-why-this-army-mom-loves-bts/. Accessed December 16, 2021.

Ruan, Lucia. "How BTS helped fans find community throughout the pandemic." *USC Annenberg Media*. November 30, 2021. https://www.uscannenbergmedia.com/2021/11/30/how-bts-helped-fans-find-community-throughout-the-pandemic/. Accessed December 16, 2021.

Shetty, Karishma. "Exclusive: ARMY share how BTS is helping them cope with anxiety during the lockdown period due to COVID 19." *Pinkvilla*. April 1, 2020. https://www.pinkvilla.com/entertainment/exclusives/exclusive-army-share-how-bts-helping-them-cope-anxiety-during-lockdown-period-due-covid-19-520707. Accessed December 16, 2021.

Sicardi, Arabelle. "The Dark Side of K-Pop was what Drew me to the Genre." *Allure*. April 15, 2020. https://www.allure.com/story/k-pop-stardom-dark-side. Accessed December 16, 2021.

Syed, Naila. "How music and Kpop stars BTS helped Canadians' mental health in the pandemic." *The Toronto Observer*, October 10, 2021. https://torontoobserver.ca/2021/10/10/music-therapy-bts/amp/. Accessed December 16, 2021.

Tan. "A First Encounter: Discovering BTS how I gained my happiness back." *Medium*. January 14, 2021. https://medium.com/planet-serotonin/a-first-encounter-discovering-bts-c49dea894179. Accessed December 16, 2021.

The Hollywood Fix. "BTS & James Corden Perform Butter, Dynamite, and Permission to Dance for Fans on the Streets of LA." November 24, 2021. YouTube video, 9:22. https://www.youtube.com/watch?v=1ayOfSTTsco. Accessed November 24, 2021.

The Late Late Show with James Corden. "BTS and Papa Mochi are Reunited." November 23, 2021. YouTube video, 10:10. https://www.youtube.com/watch?v=pRl2tawentY.

The Late Late Show with James Corden. "BTS Performs a Concert in the Crosswalk." December 16, 2021. YouTube video, 9:57. https://www.youtube.com/watch?v=A8KQhwmdZIw. Accessed December 16, 2021.

TheMaskedWriter. "How BTS helped me." *Medium*. December 27, 2020. https://medium.com/@nimishkasharma2019/how-bts-helped-me-43328f2734d2. Accessed December 16, 2021.

"Tips for First time Concert Attendees." *Reddit*. https://www.reddit.com/r/bangtan/comments/awuw4v/tips_for_first_time_concert_attendees/. Accessed December 15, 2021.

Wong, Yutian. "*Martha and the Swans: BTS, 'Black Swan,' and Cold War Dance History*." In *Bangtan Remixed: The Critical BTS Reader*. Edited by Patty Ahn, Michelle Cho, Vernadette Vicuña Gonzalez, Rani Neutill, Mimi Thi Nguyen, and Yutian Wong. Durham: Duke University Press, 2024.

Wu, Valerie. "K-Pop Stars are Redefining Mainstream for Asian American Youth." *Mercury News*. June 23, 2018. https://www.mercurynews.com/2018/06/23/op

inion-k-pop-stars-are-redefining-mainstream-for-asian-american-youth/. Accessed December 16, 2021.

Yoon, Hannah, and Kat Moon. "These Portraits Show that the BTS ARMY is not a Monolith." *Time*. November 24, 2021. https://time.com/6122609/bts-army-photos/. Accessed December 16, 2021.

Yoon. "BTS returns to the stage reuniting their ARMY of fans after a 2-year hiatus." *NPR*. December 4, 2021. https://www.npr.org/sections/pictureshow/2021/12/04/1060539313/bts-returns-to-the-stage-reuniting-their-army-of-fans-after-a-two-year-hiatus. Accessed December 16, 2021.

방탄소년단 (@BTS_twt). "#StopAsianHate #StopAAPIHate." Twitter, March 29, 2021. https://twitter.com/BTS_twt/status/1376712834269159425?ref_src=twsrc%5Etfw%7Ctwcamp%5Etweetembed%7Ctwterm%5E1376712834269159425%7Ctwgr%5E%7Ctwcon%5Es1_c10&ref_url=https%3A%2F%2Fwww.buzzfeednews.com%2Farticle%2Feleanorbate%2Fbts-stop-aapi-asian-hate-racism-statement.

7

KEEPING IN TIME

Mastery, as a Condition of Colonial and Patriarchal Discourse, and the Temporality of Screendance

Anna Macdonald

Introduction: Mastery

> When films are made that are not mainstream, and not highly produced, and not heteronormative, and not fill-in-the-blank, the gravitational pull of screendance draws the field back into order. For every film that is 'outside the bubble' or moves the needle in a really aggressive way, there are a hundred films that pull that film back into orbit; that pull it back into maintaining the status quo.[1]

My experience of working as a screendance artist over the last twenty years resonates with my sense of what Douglas Rosenberg describes here, in an interview exploring the state of screendance in 2019. Despite many screendance festivals and publications working to include less seen bodies and more radical practices, through its enduring worship of whiteness, youth, beauty, technical expertise, high production values, and spectacular gesture, large parts of the screendance field continue to reproduce forms that perpetuate ideological and artistic stasis. What I suggest in this chapter is that one of the things at play within the "gravitational pull" of mainstream screendance is the pervasive allure of mastery: a desire to master the body, the environment, technology, and time. The writing explores how low fi methods of making, found within three examples of radical screendance, might work to resist mastery's pull.[2]

In her 2018 text *Unthinking Mastery*, Julietta Singh describes mastery as an "enduring ethico-political problem" whose prolific forms continue to be reproduced within both anti-colonial and post-colonial discourses.[3] Singh argues that the fundamental mechanisms of mastery are that of division, hierarchy, and a sense of timelessness, a sense that the first two conditions

DOI: 10.4324/9781003335887-10

will always be so. It is not, as she points out, that things can't change; it's that within the enveloping discourses of mastery, it feels as if they can't change. And so, socio-political inequalities "come to be recognized as permanent,"[4] as if emerging in response to innate, transcendent conditions that operate beyond our control. From this we see that time, or, more precisely, a felt sense of time, is an important part of the way mastery reproduces itself.[5] Drawing on Singh's observation, this chapter starts from the premise that within the "status quo" of mainstream screendance, intersectional narratives of mastery are perpetuated not only through the reproduction of harmful stereotypes but within a celebration of movement that feels transcendent, idealized, and unchangeable.

Screendance has often used filmic devices of slow-motion and multiple edits, in ways that deliberately extend and reconfigure the temporality of the moving body. Rosenberg, for example, has described the screendance body as being taken out of time, fragmented, re-corporealized, and then put back together onscreen.[6] Screendance's emphasis on expanding the relationship of the body to time, perhaps influenced by originary attempts to distinguish itself from recordings of live dance, has produced extraordinary work that reveals something of the temporality of both movement and film. However, it has also led to a continued emphasis on flawless, hi-res, spectacular movement that transcends the effects of age, capacity, and context. As Claudia Kappenberg argues, the potential for the body to do anything, without the restrictions of being in lived time, can lead to a "[f]oregrounding of autonomy, freedom and mastery."[7] In an effort to expand time, screendance can appear temporally suspended with performers resisting, what Kappenberg goes on to describe as, the interconnected signs of "dependency, relatedness and failure."[8] This chapter uses the term "precarity" to collectively describe these qualities of dependency, relatedness, and failure, and precarity returns throughout this writing as a key temporal state with the potential to unsettle stasis and invite change.[9]

If mastery creates a sense that its inequities will "always be so," to resist it we need to believe in the potential for change. Change, as bound with the movement of time and the question of what operates beyond or remains subject to time, as located within Western philosophical and temporal concepts of immanence and transcendence, has been the focus of my screendance practice for several years.[10] Building on this, this chapter proposes that by generating an affective sense of itself as both temporally situated and precarious—by keeping in time—screendance can create a sense of potential change that resists the timeless stasis of mastery.

The wider potential for screendance to conjure an affective understanding of what Laura Cull describes as the body "as a site of lived change [...] as immanent or embedded in, rather than transcendent to, the world as change"[11] is explored though a discussion of the following three screendances. The first work is Terrance Houle's moving image series, titled *Friend or Foe* (2010–2015), which artfully dismantles the colonial positioning of indigenous culture as temporally static and unchanging. The second is one of my own works called *I made everything* (2019), which is constructed from a series of continuous end points that unsettle connections between time and progression. The third is *Diving into your absence* (2014) by Concha Vida, which I argue resists temporal closure, creating a "thickened" sense of present,[12] through its holding onto lost things.[13]

Houle's and Vidal's works operate, as does my own, across film, performance art, and installation practice, occupying a space on the edges of the screendance field. I explore these works because they act as a counterpoint to what seems to be a prevailing desire of much screendance to reproduce masterful transcendent forms within its "ongoing idealization of mobility."[14] Each work involves a solo performer, limited use of technical dance vocabulary, and is shot predominantly using natural light and a static, single shot. These low fi devices are focused upon here, in terms of their potential to create precarious and affective experiences of embodied presence, responsivity and interdependence. Rather than aiming to transcend the constraints of time, I suggest that these works use low fi devices to keep in time, generating a sense of precarity that unsettles the temporal stasis of mastery.

After a brief introduction to the themes of temporal affect and change, this chapter focuses on each screendance in turn, allowing overlapping and distinctive approaches to body, time, and affect in each work to be drawn out. For the last ten years, my screendance-based research has focused upon ways of working that intensify or negate a sense of the in-timeness of the onscreen body. Drawing on this practice, the discussion of each work moves between insider and spectator perspectives, examining my felt sense of the temporal effect of watching Houle and Vidal performing in their films, watching back my own, and referencing my experience of constructing screendance that explores its relationship to time. Change involves movement from one state to another and screendance is used here as a moving research method that responds to the world as a mutable phenomenon. Responding to an understanding of the affective possibility of change as something dialogically produced between viewer and artwork, and artwork and maker, I lean into the temporal and temporary nature of my responses, theorizing from embodied experience. I lean in carefully, mindful, as David Garneau points out, that "[f]eeling is often just embodied culture."[15] I lean in carefully, heeding Singh's warnings concerning the seductive, re-inscriptive power of mastery. Mindful of both potential pitfalls, these screendances are not explored as definitive answers to the problem of mastery, but as a way into understanding both its allure, and the wider potential for the field to resist, rather than reproduce, its practices.

Screendance, Time, and Affect

How can a screendance be more, or less, in time? Sondra Fraleigh, whose work focuses on the phenomenology of dance, describes dance as "the embodied art, of life and our living of time."[16] All events have duration of course but Fraleigh is not referring here to an awareness of the chronological or clock-based time that the dance takes up, but the lived, sensed experience of time it generates in those that watch it. Along with other somatic-based writers such as Jana Parviainen and Susan Kozel, Fraleigh argues that dance invites a phenomenological awareness of time, in both dancer and viewer.[17] This felt sense of time is described here as temporal affect, referring to an embodied sense of time's flow when we experience dance.

The temporal affect generated by dance is generally attributed to the fact that dance emerges, and more significantly, disappears, within time. Transience is often positioned as that which generates liveness, a temporal quality which seems to offer a privileged relationship to both authenticity and the possibility of change.[18] If something is live, then anything can happen: there is risk, but there is also potential. As an art form reliant on the indeterminate and mutable body, it could be argued that dance has a distinctive potential to invite states of precarity that can disrupt the temporal inertia of mastery. But what then of screendance, which is not transient or at least does not bring together the bodies of performer and viewer in the same spatio-temporal location? What is the capacity for the recorded moving body, for screendance, to invite an affective sense of the potential for change?

According to Singh, it is the feeling that things can't change rather than the material possibility of change where the power of mastery lays. Even though screendance, like all film perhaps, retains its ontic connection to events that have already happened,[19] over the last ten years, writers such as Philip Auslander, Harmony Bench, and Rebecca Schneider have all re-positioned liveness as an intensive quality rather than a condition that demands spatio-temporal connection between event and viewer.[20] Potentially, for screendance to resist mastery, what is important then is not the ontological status of recorded movement, which can or can't be changed, but the sense of potential for change created in the viewer when they watch it.

In talking of "feelings" and "intensive qualities," this writing is referring to an understanding of affect in screendance, and the wider field of cinema studies, as a fundamental dimension of its potential to operate in the world. Affect is understood here (after Brian Massumi's *Parables for the Virtual*) as an embodied intensity that operates before (and in and out of) language and is generated between bodies, materials, and things. Within film discourse, Vivian Sobchack collectively refers to an affective sense of the in-timeness of film and the connected sensation of duration in the viewer, as the "film's body."[21] Being able to generate an affective sense of the film's body, however, is not a guarantee of being able to create a sense of potential change. Lived time can feel unchanging or precarious, live dances static and recorded dances lively. The question I consider, through the following discussion of three specific works, is how and why some screendances make us feel a sense of precarity and possibility, more than others?

Friend or Foe

Terrance Houle is an interdisciplinary artist who works across the disciplines of performance, video/film, music, photography.[22] He is a member of the Kainai Nation and often employs, what Garneau refers to as, "non-colonial" practices, such as traditional aboriginal dance and art, as a de-colonial practice that unsettles colonial forms of mastery.[23] *Friend or Foe* is a series of films where Houle, and later others, performs messages using a gestural trading language developed by indigenous people to allow communication between tribes.[24] In the films, Houle delivers his signed messages straight to camera, wearing pow-wow first nation regalia of tail feathers and loin cloth. There is a striking contrast between the everyday sites in which the work is filmed, including outside a cinema, by a pool, and in the park, and Houle's appearance.

In one of the *Friend or Foe* series, Houle stands in the centre of the frame signing to the camera, cars go past reflected in the windows behind him. We hear traffic noise and conversation as a baby is pushed past in their pram, two cyclists pass by in matching tops, and a boy rushes past on his scooter.

FIGURE 7.1 Performer Terrance Houle stands next to a swimming pool wearing pow-wow first nation regalia
Source: Still from *Friend or Foe* #1.

Within all this movement and sound, Houle signs steadily and unhurriedly, looking resolutely forwards into the camera. At one point, Houle adjusts his tail feathers. One passing young girl turns to look at him just before the image fades. *Friend or Foe* is funny, beautiful, and startling. What follows is an exploration of the intense sense of presence and multiplicity I experience in the work, which I suggest act to disrupt a sense of timelessness.

"Hello friend. I am buffalo herder. I saw several battles here."[25]

At the end of each string of signs, Houle pauses. The pacing of his movement is calm and steady. My body settles in response to Houle's, and I am drawn into his intention to communicate: the care taken over each sign. There is no translation offered when Houle signs, which means, unless you already know this language, you wait and watch the entire statement without knowing what is being said.[26] When the translation comes in the form of English text on the screen, the text is surprisingly short compared to the length of the signing, a reminder of historical reduction, the capacity of words to compress events, bodies, and actions in time.[27] Houle invites us to listen to, and feel, the embodied duration of his signs. His invite intensifies my own sense of being in time, placing an emphasis on the time required for the narrative to be told rather than a temporality shaped by the narratives themselves or the duration of the recording. It creates a place, which geographer David Loy refers to as "event time," where time is generated by the actions that take place within it.[28]

The care that Houle takes over his gestures reminds me of a child carefully reading a poem, and it creates an attentive quality in me as I watch. It also generates a sense of precarity, a suggestion that care is needed because things could go wrong or be interrupted. This feels entirely possible because *Friend or Foe* is filmed in public spaces; we see traffic and people passing, and at one point a person comes up to Houle, interrupting his movement to ask for a picture. The careful, responding-in-the-present-moment-that-we-are-looking-at, movement in *Friend or Foe* intensifies a sense of in-timeness. I know that Houle's story has already happened, but I still feel as if something else could happen each time I watch.

Part of the in-timeness of this work is produced by its use of a single, static shot, which is a device often associated with low budget and low fi aesthetics. Mary Ann Doane argues that the use of single shots, embraces the contingent possibilities of the event, such as, changes in light, stumbles, and interruptions, that multiple shot constructions resist.[29] Single shots can create a sense of precarity, resisting a transcendent and singular version of events, by embracing the possibility that things could happen differently. With reference to Auslander, I argue that both Houle's film, and my own, which I write about next, feel like "live recordings"[30] of something that will not happen again – a singular iteration of a repeatable temporal event caught in a singular measure of time. Operating somewhere between presence and absence, they complicate traditional binary distinctions in screendance between "dance that is made for live performance and then filmed, and dance that is made for, and generated by, the apparatus of film."[31] Each version of *Friend or Foe* is singular, but it could be made again differently and has the possibility of change baked into the form.

The use of a single shot "measure of time"[32] in *Friend or Foe* is complex though because it also confers the image with a quality of authenticity, as if the camera is being used here simply to record, rather than generate, events. Houle's central position within these static shots, adds to this quasi-scientific feel, making him look like an object of study within a photographic portrait, and I am made aware of my own colonial gaze mastering his image, as I watch.[33] The existence of a "static, prior moment as the site of authenticity"[34] is continuously disrupted, however, by Houle's intensified present/presence, which is filled with multiple voices that he brings in from mythic filmic "Indians," long-dead elders, passers-by and ex-wives. Even the gestures Houle performs are both old and contemporaneous. According to his site, Houle learnt this signed language after coming across a book by George Fronval called *Indian Signals and Sign Language* (1992) before subsequently finding out that his own grandmother spoke it fluently and studying it with her. Houle's gestures operate beyond the stasis of historical re-enactment, challenging a "settler temporality where Indigenous people can only ever be 'authentic' in some faraway past."[35] *Friend or Foe*'s unsettles a linear sense of then and now, complicating colonial notions of change as a masterful and irreversible form of progression.[36]

Houle is centre stage but the dominance of the sound and movement of people around him, dead and alive, merge subject and environment. I see a resistance to mastery operating within Houle's refusal of, what Bracha Ettinger refers to as, the "notion of the discrete and singular subject formed by the establishment of the boundaries that distinguish it from an oceanic or undifferentiated otherness of the world."[37] *Friend or Foe* does not negate the world to a backdrop, as with so much screendance, or history to the past, but situates Houle's movement as part of that time and space, and other times and spaces before and after. Allowing the viewer to experience a body-in-time responding to events in time, as opposed to encountering an untouchable idealized form, emphasises a sense that Houle, and therefore me as I watch it, are vulnerable to events and have the potential for change. *Friend or Foe* feels like a care-full conversation rather than a masterful statement.

> I made everything
> I am interested
> I have balance
> In 1987 I began to be able to move objects with the power of thought

> I can dance like Andrea Buckley
> I discovered the periodic comet 35P/Herschel–Rigollet
> I have recovered from traumatic loss
> In the late 1600s I came up with the idea of gravity
> I am England's highest ranking operational Fire Fighter
> I created the Harvard System.[38]

I made everything is a single screen screendance that explores the complex relationship between integrity, validation, self-esteem, and visibility within women's art. In it I, as a female identifying artist, lay claim to a long series of culturally recognized artistic, social, and scientific masterly achievements, accomplished since time began, listing them as a series of captioned statements on the screen. During the film, which is an hour and a half long, I perform a series of physical tasks with clearly self-generated constraints, which make them hard to achieve. For example, I place a coke can behind me on the table and move the chair just far enough away so that I can't reach it. But I keep trying to reach it. These movements are small, dogged, and apparently pointless, offering a potential contrast with the "greatness" of the claimed achievements, in terms of mastery, scale, permanence, and grandeur.

The captions in the work offer a series of "firsts" and "pinnacles" that evoke a model of spatialized time where duration is divided into measurable sections of before and after. This linear temporality sits within masterful positivist frameworks where change consists of one truth replacing another within a progressive timeline of accomplishments. On one level, change is found in *I made everything* within the movement of erasure. But this teleological sense of change, where transformation is understood as a move from presence to absence to new presence, is undermined by the sheer volume of discoveries and pinnacles that are offered in the work without a sense of progression or hierarchy. Personal achievements are placed next to grand historical shifts, some of the claims are ridiculous, either in their specificity or unachievable nature, and one follows another without dynamic change or inflection. The aim was to make a work that kept on arriving, resisting a sense of mastery as an inevitable and completed end point of progress.

The sense of mastery within these pinnacles of human (often male) achievement is also undermined by the smallness of my actions. These movements happen in a different temporality to the captions, which are added afterwards and, like the event time I identify in Houle's work, take as long as they take to do. The difference here is that, unlike Houle's clearly articulated gestural phrases, these actions are set up to be unresolvable and so have no clear endpoint. In some ways, they resemble what Baraitser refers to as the maintenance practices associated with female labour, which are not predicated on ideas of outcome or progression.[39]

Like the other works discussed in this chapter, *I made everything* was filmed in a single shot and once the camera was set up, I was alone in the room. I remember that the thought of 90 minutes of improvisation with only a chair, table, and coke initially felt challenging, but the sense of space quickly became enjoyable. Unlike most repetitive female labour, I had a pleasing sense that I could finish these tasks when I had had enough, rather than when an imagined future viewer might tire. This taking up of time felt unusual for me as a screendance artist, where works are normally expected to be under ten minutes in length if they are to make the festival circuit. I remember luxuriating in the time as if it were water. This sensation invited a sense of play, a staying-with things and a general lengthening and ease within my movement. Time felt expansive, present, and all mine to stay within.

I do not gesture to the camera/viewer in this work, as Houle does in *Friend or Foe*. I ask, instead, for attention to be given to my own attention to self. As a middle-aged woman, bringing attention to yourself, staying in the frame, staying in time, is a political act. Staying resists the invisibility that descends upon women who are no longer of value (reproductive or otherwise) within the patriarchy.[40] Women of menopause age and onwards are conspicuously absent in screendance, appearing perhaps as part of a flashback to another dancer playing their younger self, or representing illness or featuring in an amateur capacity within community-based work.[41] In a field often focused on mastery, as I return to later when considering dance technique, it is not surprising that the abject, unreliable, and soft-boundaried bodies of older women are excluded.

I embrace my own sense of precarity in this work by performing small acts of failure, weakness, want, lack, powerlessness, defeat, frustration, amateurishness, clumsiness, and incompetence. I attempt to drink a can of coke without using my hands and inevitably at some point we see the cola can spill over a table and slowly drip down to the floor. I try and reach a table too far behind me whilst fraudulently claiming other people's achievements. I see my identity continuously undone, or brought into being, through the series of unreliable claims and truths confessed or stolen from hundreds of other people.[42] I am not always clear now when I watch where the truth lies as many things are now true, or untrue, four years later. The above list of dictionary antonyms for mastery describe practices that I actively embrace in my work as a radical screendance maker. But radical screendance presupposes a teleological binary of before and after, where it is possible to grasp the root of more masterful screendance and replace it with something else.[43] The slippery, intersectional complexity of mastery for me, as I go onto consider next, is that I can't uproot what I am part of.

I first encountered *Friend or Foe* when Houle and I were both invited to share our practice as part of Regardes Hybrid, an international screendance festival that, in 2019, focused on the critical relationship between screendance, low-tech creation, and postcolonial and feminist perspectives. When I watched Houle's work during the festival, I remember thinking "my work is so white."[44] I wasn't sure what I meant by that statement in that moment, but seeing Houle's work and encountering Singh's writing, some years later, offered me the opportunity to explore my attempts to resist masterful forms, which I consider central to my practice as a screendance maker, in light of the intersectional complexities of precarity and privilege at play in my work as a white, female practitioner within academia.[45]

The work was filmed in one day in a space I could get to and from in time to pick up the kids from school, a space that didn't cost me money because the work was unfunded. It is also true that it is filmed within a white box, a corporate space with the only colour provided by the red global capitalist symbol of the coke can. What I saw then as a non-space is also a white space, because these are the spaces I operate in. And, unlike the public spaces of *Friend or Foe*, this is a space where I won't be interrupted. Here, in this ideological and material white space, I am safe enough to be able to cultivate a somatic responsivity, to not be spectacular, because I am not under threat.[46] I am playing with precarity, Houle appears to play with precarity, but potentially only I can step back inside the refuge of academia, discourse, and privilege.

In *I made everything*, I am deliberately rejecting a sense of mastery of the body by doing things I cannot do. The difficulty being of course that I do things I cannot do extremely well and this masterful precarity has been an important part of my expert practice for fifteen years. Arguably, it is not possible for a white woman, sitting at the centre of the frame, to ever actually be off-balance, and this too is a fraudulent claim.[47] In performing my own failure to fail, I reveal an "abiding desire for mastery"[48] that returns despite my watchfulness. The title of my work, *I made everything,* is explicitly dual. It refers to the absence of women from culturally validated production but also to my own privileged capacity and desire to control everything that is done and seen, including my own failure.

Whilst the act of keeping in time felt both luxurious and important for me, it also suggests a belief that I have the right to ask audiences to stay with a single one-hour-and-24-minute shot that quietly focuses on small qualitative movement detail, and even more perhaps that it doesn't matter so much to me whether they do. This is partly because my work is of little consequence to the gravitational pull of mainstream screendance and partly because my privilege means that I can afford to keep in time or not.

Diving into your Absence

Concha Vidal is a Spanish artist who describes her work as bringing together the live and mediated forms of video art, dance, and performance. In her

Keeping in Time 143

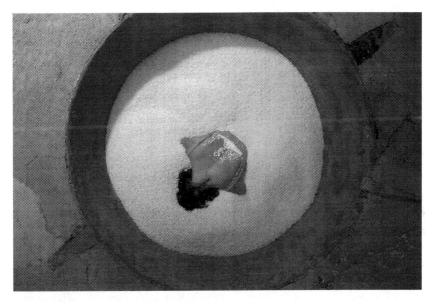

FIGURE 7.2 Performer Concha Vidal is seen face down in a pool filled with white polystyrene balls
Source: Still from *Diving into your absence*.

2017 work *Diving into your absence*, Vidal moves within a small circular structure, about the size and shape of a jacuzzi, filled with what look like tiny, white polystyrene balls. She circles round, diving into thousands of shifting spheres that are dry but move like liquid. It is a sensuous, fluid work. Sometimes the dancer looks like she is swimming, sifting through the dry water looking for things that elude her. Sometimes it looks like she is just trying to register the feeling of the materials against her skin, affirming their presence perhaps. At one point, she lets the balls flow right over her, filling her mouth.

Diving into your absence is mainly shot using a single overhead shot. Neither the polystyrene balls nor dancer leave the pool, but they move continuously throughout. The sound of plastic moving against metal sounds like the sea. The footage is run backwards at times making time appear to flow in different directions. It is a work about loss and is connected to another work by Vidal called *The Last dance* (2015). In this earlier screendance, we see Vidal dancing with a partner, wearing trousers and a suit jacket, who is made out of cloth and packing materials. Vidal continues to dance as her manikin partner dissolves into bits in her arms, changing from one state to another until we encounter these traces again as a white pool in *Diving into your absence*. This emphasis on both continuation and change, both within the film's movement and from one film to another, is unusual within screendance, which tends to favour discrete works rather than episodes or sequels. *Diving into your absence* performs change; like *Friend or Foe*, it brings together what was and what is in one place, holding movement in time up for us to contemplate. It works to resist masterful movement, which transcends the flow of time, by remaining connected to what has happened before.

In my experience, death rarely registers as a singular shift from presence to absence for those that are left. Vidal has lost someone but continues to be surrounded by them, diving and searching, perhaps unwilling or unable to accept their absence. Vidal's presence, and the presence of her lost partner, do not rely on spatio-temporal connection in this work. He is not there, and she is not there, for both are already, already gone and yet remain affectively present. In this sense, through its un-forming and re-forming, this film (and arguably Houle's and my own) move beyond simple binaries of liveness (movement) and non-liveness (stillness), re-positioning transience less as a movement from presence to absence and more as a movement from one state to another. This temporal quality is articulated here, drawing on Bergson's notion of durée, as a form of transience-as-change that is affectively experienced by the viewer.[49] Vidal moves and things change, but the absence remains. What this work offers is something that screendance scholar Bench might refer to as affective endurance, a moving form of time that refuses to move on.[50] There is movement here that, despite its lack of progression, resists the finality of mastery and will not be made still.

In *Diving into your absence*, as with the other two works, there is a notable absence of repeatable formal "steps," dance's key indicators of disciplinary mastery. Technical movement can of course be performed in a way that honors the temporal and cultural specificity of the performer, but movement that is not codified or performed in unison has a particular capacity to draw our attention to these qualities. Whilst acknowledging the complexity of relationship of technique and mastery, notably examined by writers such as Melrose and Sachsenmaier,[51] not using technical steps has political implications. As Bauer asserts,

> [w]e must not forget that until very recently dance rested on the idea of bodily control, simply putting the body to use in realizing its aesthetic goal. Furthermore, this concept of training literally gives substance to the general Western paradigm of the body as aesthetically mouldable matter. That which is mouldable is also meant to be devoid of cultural, aesthetic or subjective specificity. This in turn allowed the supremacy of [...] technique based on its presumed universality.[52]

Bauer's point is echoed by Kappenberg, in her essay "Does screendance need to look like dance" (2009), where she describes the ability of the trained dancer to be able to repeat things in time, to resist the mutability of the body, as using the "body as tool."[53] She contrasts this with working with the body-as-site where the choreographer responds to the specificity of the individual body-in-time. Houle and I both have overtly "specific" bodies by which I mean, in dance terms, where young, athletic bodies are celebrated, we look old. Also, Houle's stomach protrudes over his loin cloth, and I am not thin. Our bodies, whilst unremarkable within everyday life, are less expected in dance, offering, what Ann Cooper Albright refers to as "the disruptive presence of [...] a dancer's age or mortality."[54] Garneau talks about his preoccupation with Houle's belly in his work, describing its movement as "undisciplined irruptions" that have a peculiarly disruptive power to "intrigue the mental/sensual system more perplexingly than beauty or didacticism alone."[55] What I think Garneau describes here is the powerful and unsettling affect that un-mastered bodies can have.

The failures I chose to perform in *I made everything* did not include my undisciplined body. I remember carefully choosing a shirt that covered my belly, acutely aware of the transgressive nature of an uncontrolled (abject) female form. In *Diving into your absence*, however, Vidal performs in a brief satin slip, her body young and sleek. It is beautiful, Vidal is beautiful, and I remember initial feelings of disappointment that I was again watching a partially dressed woman dance onscreen.[56] However, this is maybe where mastery reasserts itself. Perhaps it is my internalized misogyny that seeps into in my perception of Vidal as a mastered object of the patriarchal gaze, rather than a mature artist making a choice, as Houle does, about the affective power of her body on film. For it is through being partially dressed in this work, that Vidal allows us to witness the sensuous encounter of her body upon materials. My imagined sense of what the polystyrene feels like on her skin intensifies my awareness of my own skin. Touch returns me to the present and I have a sense of occupying time with her as I watch. In a similar way to *I made everything*, there is a sense of luxuriating in time here, but rather than a conceptual choice to pass time unproductively, Vidal creates a more sensual and embodied temporal reverie in the film's body.

Earlier, I suggest that both the performers in *I made everything* and *Friend or Foe* have a sense of responsivity within their movement. I see this quality less in Vidal's movement because she seems out of my reach, locked behind a soft-focus lens and a sensuous soundtrack. The white balls cover her skin and every time Vidal's movement displaces the mass of tiny objects, they immediately re-form around her, flowing back into the space that's left and removing all trace of her actions. The text accompanying her work suggests that "the movement in the film evokes ideas of things un-forming as you reach out to grasp them."[57] Vidal is trying to hold onto things, and I am trying to hold onto her as I watch. Precarity, the affective sense that things might change, exists in this screendance on a level of belief. It concerns my effort to stay in time with Vidal – to maintain an affective sense of being with her.

Auslander argues that when we agree to the demands of the recorded artwork, to see it as live, we are complicit in engaging with its movement as if we are seeing it in the moment. He calls our ability to "hold on" to this sense of participatory liveness "a willed and fragile act" that requires constant attention to sustain.[58] *Diving into your absence* points us to one of the potential things at play within mastery's "gravitational pull" within screendance, because it reveals mastery as a desire to hold onto things. In this sense, we might usefully see mainstream screendance as an act of mourning for colonial, patriarchal, and heteronormative realities. Writing is also part of wanting to hold onto things, and the tenuous nature of affective connection Auslander describes is also found in my effort to try to stay in time with the sensation of seeing these films as I write about them now. As a screendance writer, the difficulty is in shifting from durational experience to communicable thought without slipping into reductive forms of mastery. As a screendance maker, the challenge is to find ways of holding movement up in time without idealizing it.

This chapter has explored some ways in which *Friend or Foe, I made everything*, and *Diving into your absence* resist the inherent sense that things cannot change. Rather than presenting a re-corporealized, transcendent dancing body onscreen, I have suggested that these films offer acts of re-membering and re-forming. I have argued that implicit in these works is the conceptual and affective understanding that they could be made again differently, that things could change. As the reflections upon my own desire for mastery suggest, it is important for artists to continue to try and resist the seductive power of mastery at play in the field of screendance. We need to understand better, as makers, the conditions our creative choices reproduce.

Notes

1 Douglas Rosenberg and Simon Ellis, "What Are We Doing?," *The International Journal of Screendance* 10 (2019): 161.
2 Radical screendance can be characterized as low budget, experimental work that is concerned with exploring the aesthetic and ideological possibilities of the form. See Anna Heighway, "Understanding The 'Dance' In Radical Dance," *International Journal of Screendance* 4 (2014): 44–62.
3 Julietta Singh, *Unthinking Mastery: Dehumanism and Decolonial Entanglements* (Durham and London: Duke University Press, 2018), 2.
4 Singh, *Unthinking Mastery*, 14.
5 Mastery is a vast area of study spanning geo-political and socio-cultural domains. Whilst acknowledging the lineage of discourse emerging from Mulvey's work on mastery and the gaze within film and Melrose's work on mastery and knowledge within dance – it is the relevance of thinking about the temporality of mastery within screendance that is the focus here. See Laura Mulvey, "Visual Pleasure and Narrative Cinema," *Screen* 16, no. 3 (1975): 6–18; Susan Melrose and Stefanie

Sachsenmaier, "Writing 'Practice' /Practising/ 'Writing' (in the doctoral research context)" in *Researching (in/as) Motion: A Resource Collection - Artistic Doctorates in Europe*, eds. Vida Midgelow and Jane Bacon (Helsinki: Theatre Academy, University of the Arts Helsinki, 2019), https://nivel.teak.fi/adie/writing-practice-practising-writing/.

6 Rosenberg, *Inscribing the Ephemeral Image* (New York: Oxford University Press, 2012), 57.
7 Claudia Kappenberg, "Does screendance need to look like dance?" *International Journal of Performance Arts and Digital Media* 5, no. 2–3 (2009): 103.
8 Kappenberg, "Does screendance need," 103. Kappenberg's observation is echoed by Nicolas Salazar-Sutil and Sebastian Melo, and still feels relevant a decade later. See Nicolas Salazar-Sutil and Sebastian Melo, "Exposed to Time," in *The Oxford Handbook of Screendance Studies*, ed. Douglas Rosenberg (New York: Oxford University Press, 2016), 143–65.
9 Precarity is a concept, which has received much attention within performance studies in recent years catalyzed by the work of Judith Butler, Rebecca Schneider, Tavia Nyong'o, and André Lepecki. See Judith Butler, *Precarious Life: The Powers of Mourning and Violence* (London and New York: Verso, 2003); Judith Butler, *Notes Toward a Performative Theory of Assembly* (Cambridge, MA, and London: Harvard University Press, 2015); Nicholas Ridout and Rebecca Schneider, "Precarity and Performance," *TDR: The Drama Review* 56, no. 4 (2012): 59; Tavia Nyong'o, "Situating precarity," *Women & Performance: A Journal of Feminist Theory* 23, no. 2 (2013): 157–6; André Lepecki, *Singularities* (New York: Routledge, 2016).
10 Anna Macdonald, "Going Nowhere: Screendance and the Time of Dying," *International Journal of Screendance* 8 (2017): 11–28; Macdonald, "Acts of Holding: Dance, Time and Loss," PhD Diss. (Manchester Metropolitan University, 2019). This work has focused on a particular quality of time, found in bereavement and grief, I articulate as stasis or a moving stillness, where time moves but does not progress. I use it in this chapter to think about the moving stillness of mastery, where it can feel as if things are unchangeable.
11 Laura Cull, "Attention Training," *Performance Research* 16, no. 4 (2011): 87.
12 Gary Peters, "Time to Die," in *Making Sense of Dying and Death Vol 1*, ed. Andrew Fagan (Amsterdam: Rodopi Press, 2004), 224.
13 The writing about Vidal's work is taken in part from an original review published in an online magazine accompanying International Screendance festival, *Movimiento en Movimiento*. See Macdonald, "Some thoughts about the Liquid body," *Movimiento en Movimiento*, no. 10 (2022): 26–29, https://issuu.com/yolanda.m.guadarrama/docs/revista_mov_en_mov_2022_parte_2.
14 Kappenberg, "Does screendance need," 103.
15 David Garneau, "Extra-Rational Aesthetic," *Fuse Magazine* 36, no. 4 (2013): 19. Garneau goes on to write that "Racism is a feeling; so is sexism, homophobia, xenophobia and all deep values that guide us without thinking."
16 Sondra Fraleigh, *Dance and the Lived Body*, (Pittsburgh: University of Pittsburgh Press, 1987), 181.
17 A phenomenology of time concerns how we experience time or how things appear to be temporal. See Jana Parviainen, *Bodies Moving and Moved* (Tampere: Tampere University Press, 1998), 41; Susan Kozel, *Closer* (Cambridge, MA: MIT Press, 2007), 76.
18 Parviainen, *Bodies Moving and Moved*, 173; Mary Anne Doane, *The Emergence of Cinematic Time* (Cambridge: Harvard University Press, 2002), 140; Lepecki, *Dance* (London: Whitechapel Art Gallery, 2012), 15.
19 Laura Mulvey, *Death 24x a Second* (London: Reaktion Books, 2006), 31.

20 See Philip Auslander, "Digital Liveness," *PAJ: A Journal of Performance and Art* 34, no. 3 (2012), 5; Harmony Bench, "'Complex Temporalities': digitality and the ephemeral tense in Adam H. Weinert's 'The Reaccession of Ted Shawn,'" in *The Routledge Dance Studies Reader 3rd edition*, eds. Richard Jens Giersdorf and Yutian Wong (London: Routledge, 2018), 369; Schneider, *Performing Remains* (Abingdon: Routledge, 2011), 7.
21 Vivian Sobchack, *The Address of the Eye* (New Jersey: Princeton University Press, 1992), xviii.
22 "Terrence Houle – IMDb," IMDb, accessed July 22, 2022, https://www.imdb.com/name/nm6364991/bio.
23 Garneau, "Extra-Rational Aesthetic," 17.
24 I focus here on *Friend or Foe #1 & #2* made between 2010 and 2013.
25 Extract from captioned text in *Friend or Foe*.
26 In the case of the first encounter with this work, it's not clear whether a translation will be offered at all.
27 Schneider's work on the archive and colonial discourse, between what remains and is discounted within western archival logic, resonates and informs many of the observations concerning duration and mastery made here. See Schneider, *Performing Remains*.
28 David Loy, "Saving time," in *Timespace: Geographies of Temporality*, eds. Jon May and Nigel Thrift (London: Routledge Press, 2001), 275.
29 Doane, *The Emergence of Cinematic Time*, 140.
30 Auslander, "Digital Liveness," 5.
31 Macdonald, "Acts of Holding," 44.
32 Miranda Pennell, "Some thoughts on 'Nowness' and 'Thenness,'" *The International Journal of Screendance* 2, no. 1 (2012): 76.
33 "Terrance Houle," HIDE: Skin as Material and Metaphor, accessed November 8, 2022, https://americanindian.si.edu/exhibitions/hide/terrance.html. Houle writes that many of his works "comment on the historical relationship between photography and aboriginal identity."
34 Garneau, "Extra-Rational Aesthetic," 17.
35 Laura Maria De Vos, "Spiralic Time and Cultural Continuity," *Transmotion* 6 (2020): 4. I was aware of my own absorption of this colonial narrative when, in the talk about the work afterwards, Houle described his clothing as being old in that it was his original pow-wow suit that he used to wear as a teenager. I realized that I had been thinking of his outfit as a costume, historical, the trappings of something lost.
36 *Friend or Foe* resists the "post" of post-colonialism, positioning it as something more akin to what Sandro Mezzadra and Federico Rahola describe as a "never-accomplished transition." See Sandro Mezzadra and Federico Rahola, "The Postcolonial Condition," *Postcolonial Text* 2, no. 1 (2006), https://www.postcolonial.org/index.php/pct/article/view/393/819.
37 Bracha Ettinger in Griselda Pollock, "Thinking the Feminine," *Theory, Culture & Society* 21, no. 1 (2004): 6.
38 *I made everything*, directed and performed by Anna Macdonald, 2019, https://vimeo.com/269609511.
39 Lisa Baraitser, *Enduring Time* (London: Bloomsbury, 2017).
40 Rosenberg and Ellis, "What Are We Doing?," 160. In the interview referenced in the introduction, Rosenberg calls for more people to state opinions and be less equivocal about the state of screendance. However, the authority to challenge dominant practice is perhaps more available to Rosenberg as a significant male academic and artist, than I. When I questioned the continuing emphasis on beauty within screendance in a piece of critical writing posted in an online screendance

forum, for example, I received immediate, defensive dismissal from several dominant male figures in the field.
41 My point is not to devalue these works but to suggest that using older women in screendance is not a kindness.
42 After Judith Butler and Barbara Bolt, my movement can be seen as a performative bringing into being of self, rather than a performance by an already finished, individuated subject. See Judith Butler, *Bodies that Matter: On the Discursive Limits of Sex* (New York and London: Routledge, 1993); Barbara Bolt, "Artistic Research: A Performative Paradigm?," *Parse Journal* 3 (2016): 129–42.
43 This point is made with reference to Adrienne Maree Brown's book *Emergent Strategy* in which she cites Angela Davies – "Radical simply means grasping things at the root" – from her "let us all rise together" address in Spelman college. See Adrienne Brown, *Emergent Strategy* (Chico, CA: AK Press, 2017), 35.
44 "Whiteness, as a set of power relationships structuring social life, is often not noticed by white people." See Royana Mitra, "Reflections on a Burning World," *Contemporary Dance and Whiteness*, June 5, 2020, accessed July 19, 2022, https://danceandwhiteness.coventry.ac.uk/blog/reflections-on-a-burning-world-by-royona-mitra/.
45 My understanding of this term comes from the writing of authors such as Resmaa Menakem and Kymberlie Crenshaw. See Resmaa Menakem, *My Grandmother's Hands: Racialized Trauma and the Pathway to Mending Our Hearts and Bodies* (Las Vegas: CRP, 2017); Kymberlie Crenshaw, *On Intersectionality* (New York: The New Press, 2017).
46 I am reminded here of Royana Mitra's blog on racial somatics where she notes the assumed levels of safety, often not available to people of colour, required by somatic practice. See Mitra, "Reflections on a Burning World."
47 A usefully provocative blog post on this is by The White Pube. See Zarina Muhammad, "Can White People Ever Be Radical?," *The White Pube*, April 4, 2021, https://www.thewhitepube.co.uk/canwhitepeopleberadical.
48 Singh, *Unthinking Mastery*, 174.
49 An exploration of transience-as-end and transience-as-change can be found in my PhD thesis. See Macdonald, "Acts of Holding."
50 Bench, "Complex Temporalities," 370.
51 Melrose & Sachsenmaier make some useful points regarding the way the expertise of dance, its mastery, is often undervalued as a knowledge form both within and beyond the field – see Melrose and Sachsenmaier, "Writing 'Practice.'"
52 Bojana Bauer, "When Train(ing) Derails," *Performance Research*, 14, no. 2 (2009), 74.
53 Kappenberg, "Does screendance need," 96.
54 Ann Cooper Albright, *Choreographing Difference* (Middletown, Connecticut: Wesleyan University Press, 1997), 74.
55 Garneau, "Extra-Rational Aesthetic," 21.
56 I first encountered this work in my role as a judge for a screendance festival where it was one of many works where the female dancers wore only underwear.
57 "DIVING INTO YOUR ABSENCE by Concha Vidal @ Brooklyn Film Festival," Brklyn Film Festival, accessed July 23, 2022, https://www.brooklynfilmfestival.org/film-detail?fid=1971.
58 Auslander, "Digital Liveness," 8.

Bibliography

Albright, Ann Cooper. *Choreographing Difference: The Body and Identity in Contemporary Dance*. Middletown, Connecticut: Wesleyan University Press, 1997.

Auslander, Philip. "Digital Liveness: A Historic-Philosophical Perspective." *PAJ: A Journal of Performance and Art* 34, no. 3 (2012): 3–11. https://doi.org/10.1162/PAJJ_a_00106.
Baraitser, Lisa. *Enduring Time*. London: Bloomsbury, 2017.
Bench, Harmony. "'Complex temporalities': digitality and the ephemeral tense in Adam H. Weinert's 'The Reaccession of Ted Shawn.'" In *The Routledge Dance Studies Reader 3rd edition*, edited by Richard Jens Giersdorf and Yutian Wong, 364–373. London: Routledge, 2018. http://doi.org/10.4324/9781315109695-32.
Bauer, Bojana. "When Train(ing) Derails." *Performance Research* 14, no. 2 (2009): 74–79. doi:10.1080/13528160903319570.
Bolt, Barbara. "Artistic Research: A Performative Paradigm?" *Parse Journal* 3 (2016): 129–142. https://parsejournal.com/article/artistic-research-a-performative-paradigm/.
Brown, Adrienne Maree. *Emergent Strategy*. Chico, CA: AK Press, 2017.
Butler, Judith. *Bodies that Matter: On the Discursive Limits of Sex*. New York and London: Routledge, 1993. https://doi.org/10.4324/9780203828274.
Butler, Judith. *Precarious Life: The Powers of Mourning and Violence*. London and New York: Verso, 2003.
Butler, Judith. *Notes Toward a Performative Theory of Assembly*. Cambridge, MA, and London: Harvard University Press, 2015. https://doi.org/10.4159/9780674495548.
Columpar, Corinn. "The Gaze as Theoretical Touchstone: The Intersection of Film Studies, Feminist Theory, and Postcolonial Theory." *Women's Studies Quarterly* 30, no. 1/2 (2002): 25–44. https://www.jstor.org/stable/i40000270.
Crenshaw, Kimberlé. *On Intersectionality*. New York: The New Press, 2017.
Cull, Laura. "Attention Training Immanence and ontological participation in Kaprow, Deleuze and Bergson." *Performance Research* 16, no. 4 (2011): 80–91. doi:10.1080/13528165.2011.606053.
Deleuze, Giles. *Cinema 2: The Time Image*. Translated by R. Galeta and H. Tomlinson. Minneapolis: University of Minnesota Press, 1989.
De Vos, Laura Maria. "Spiralic Time and Cultural Continuity for Indigenous Sovereignty: Idle No More and *The Marrow Thieves*." *Transmotion* 6 (2020): 1–42. https://doi.org/10.22024/UniKent/03/tm.807.
"DIVING INTO YOUR ABSENCE by Concha Vidal @ Brooklyn Film Festival." Brklyn Film Festival. https://www.brooklynfilmfestival.org/film-detail?fid=1971. Accessed July 23, 2022.
Doane, Mary Anne. *The Emergence of Cinematic Time: Modernity, Contingency, the Archive*. Cambridge: Harvard University Press, 2002.
Fraleigh, Sondra. *Dance and the Lived Body: A Descriptive Aesthetics*. Pittsburgh: University of Pittsburgh Press, 1987.
Garneau, David. "Extra-Rational Aesthetic Action and Cultural Decolonization." *Fuse Magazine* 36, no. 4 (2013): 14–23.
Heighway, Anna. "Understanding The 'Dance' In Radical Screendance." *International Journal of Screendance* 4 (2014): 44–62. http://dx.doi.org/10.18061/ijsd.v4i0.4530.
Houle, Terrance, dir. *Friend or Foe #1* (Calgary/Nelson). 2010–2011.
Houle, Terrance, dir. *Friend or Foe #2* (Colombia). 2012.
Kappenberg, Claudia. "Does screendance need to look like dance?" *International Journal of Performance Arts and Digital Media* 5, no. 2–3 (2009): 89–105.
Kozel, Susan. *Closer*. Cambridge, MA: MIT Press, 2007. doi:10.1017/S0149767711000076.

Lepecki, André. *Dance: Documents of Contemporary Art*. London: Whitechapel Art Gallery, 2012.
Lepecki, André. *Singularities: Dance in the Age of Performance*. New York: Routledge, 2016.
Loy, David. "Saving time: a Buddhist perspective on the end." In *Timespace: Geographies of Temporality*, edited by Jon May and Nigel Thrift, 262–280. London: Routledge Press, 2001.
Macdonald, Anna. "Acts of Holding: Dance, Time and Loss." PhD Thesis, Manchester Metropolitan University, 2019.
Macdonald, Anna. "Going Nowhere: Screendance and the Time of Dying." *International Journal of Screendance* 8 (2017): 11–28. http://dx.doi.org/10.18061/ijsd.v8i0.5350.
Macdonald, Anna, dir. *I made everything*. 2019. https://vimeo.com/269609511.
Macdonald, Anna. "Some thoughts about the Liquid body." *Movimiento en Movimiento*, no. 10 (2022): 26–29. https://issuu.com/yolanda.m.guadarrama/docs/revista_mov_en_mov_2022_parte_2.
Massumi, Brian. *Parables for the Virtual: Movement, Affect, Sensation*. Durham and London: Duke University Press, 2002.
Melrose, Susan, and Stefanie Sachsenmaier. "Writing 'Practice' /Practising/ 'Writing' (in the doctoral research context)." In *Researching (in/as) Motion: A Resource Collection – Artistic Doctorates in Europe*, edited by Vida Midgelow and Jane Bacon. Helsinki: Theatre Academy, University of the Arts Helsinki, 2019. https://nivel.teak.fi/adie/writing-practice-practising-writing/.
Menakem, Resmaa. *My Grandmother's Hands: Racialized Trauma and the Pathway to Mending Our Hearts and Bodies*. Las Vegas: CRP, 2017.
Mezzadra, Sandro, and Rahola, Federico. "The Postcolonial Condition: A Few Notes on the Quality of Historical Time in the Global Present." *Postcolonial Text* 2, no. 1 (2006). https://www.postcolonial.org/index.php/pct/article/view/393/819.
Mitra, Royona. "Reflections on a Burning World." *Contemporary Dance and Whiteness*. June 5, 2020. https://danceandwhiteness.coventry.ac.uk/blog/reflections-on-a-burning-world-by-royona-mitra/. Accessed July 19, 2022.
Muhammad, Zarina. "Can White People Ever Be Radical?" *The White Pube*. April 4, 2021. https://www.thewhitepube.co.uk/canwhitepeopleberadical.
Mulvey, Laura. *Death 24x a Second: Stillness and the Moving Image*. London: Reaktion Books, 2006. doi:10.3202/caa.reviews.2008.11..
Mulvey, Laura. "Visual Pleasure and Narrative Cinema." *Screen* 16, no. 3 (1975): 6–18. https://doi.org/10.1093/screen/16.3.6.
Nyong'o, Tavia. "Situating precarity between the body and the commons." *Women & Performance: a journal of feminist theory* 23, no. 2 (2013): 157–161. doi:10.1080/0740770X.2013.825440..
Parviainen, Jana. *Bodies Moving and Moved: A Phenomenological Analysis of the Dancing Subject and the Cognitive and Ethical Values of Dance Art*. Tampere: Tampere University Press, 1998.
Pennell, Miranda. "Some thoughts on 'Nowness' and "Thenness.'" *The International Journal of Screendance* 2, no. 1 (2012): 72–77. http://dx.doi.org/10.18061/ijsd.v2i0.
Peters, Gary. "Time to Die: The Temporality of Death and the Philosophy of Singularity." In *Making Sense of Dying and Death* Vol 1, edited by Andrew Fagan, 209–229. Amsterdam: Rodopi Press, 2004.

Pollack, Griselda. "Thinking the Feminine: Aesthetic Practice as Introduction to Bracha Ettinger and the Concepts of Matrix and Metramorphosis." *Theory, Culture & Society* 21, no. 1 (2004): 5–65. https://doi.org/10.1177/026327640404047.

Reynolds, Dee. "Kinesthetic Empathy and the Dance's Body: From Emotion to Affect." In *Kinesthetic Empathy in Creative and Cultural Practices*, edited by Matthew Reason and Dee Reynolds, 121–138. Bristol: Intellect, 2012.

Ridout, Nicholas, and Rebecca Schneider. "Precarity and Performance: An Introduction." *TDR: The Drama Review* 56, no. 4 (2012): 5–9. doi:10.1162/DRAM_a_00210..

Rosenberg, Douglas. *Inscribing the Ephemeral Image*. New York: Oxford University Press, 2012. https://doi.org/10.1093/acprof:oso/9780199772612.002.0004.

Rosenberg, Douglas, and Simon Ellis. "What Are We Doing?" *The International Journal of Screendance*, 10 (2019): 159–163. https://doi.org/10.18061/ijsd.v10i0.

Salazar-Sutil, Nicolas, and Sebastian Melo. "Exposed to Time: Cross-Histories of Human Motion Visualization from Chrono- to Dynamophotography." In *The Oxford Handbook of Screendance Studies*, edited by Douglas Rosenberg, 143–165. New York: Oxford University Press, 2016.

Schneider, Rebecca. *Performing Remains: Art and War in Times of Theatrical Reenactment*. Abingdon: Routledge, 2011.

Singh, Julietta. *Unthinking Mastery: Dehumanism and Decolonial Entanglements*. Durham and London: Duke University Press, 2018.

Smith, Jess. "Journeying the everyday of civic space: movement as method in socio-legal studies." *Journal of Law and Society* 48, no. 1 (2021): 59–73. doi:10.1111/jols.12334..

Sobchack, Vivian. *The Address of the Eye: A Phenomenology of Film*. New Jersey: Princeton University Press, 1992.

"Terrance Houle." HIDE: Skin as Material and Metaphor. https://americanindian.si.edu/exhibitions/hide/terrance.html. Accessed November 8, 2022.

"Terrence Houle – IMDb." IMDb. https://www.imdb.com/name/nm6364991/bio. Accessed July 22, 2022.

Vidal, Concha, dir. *Diving into your absence*. 2014. https://vimeo.com/102496100.

Vidal, Concha, dir. *Last Dance*. 2014. https://vimeo.com/81328805.

8

BILL ROBINSON

Icon of Dignity

Karla Etienne

Translated by Violette Drouin

> For our part, we know what distinguishes a brother. His dignity.[1]
>
> Dance is my medicine. It's the scream which eases for a while the terrible frustration common to all human beings who because of race, creed, or color, are 'invisible'. Dance is the fist with which I fight the sickening ignorance of prejudice.[2]

Though Bill Robinson, American tap-dance star, overcame many racial barriers, he has been accused by a number of people of only portraying submissive African American characters. He has been called an "Uncle Tom," and even the "epitome of Tom," and compared to a servant who is overly devoted, overly loyal, simple, and emasculated. In his analysis of the presence of African Americans in American cinema, *Toms, Coons, Mulattoes, Mammies and Bucks: An Interpretive History of Blacks in Films*, cinema historian Donald Bogle labels Robinson's role in these terms. He uses Robinson's various appearances in films to exemplify the stereotype of Uncle Tom.[3] Some also say that Bill Robinson does not deserve this label, given all the obstacles he overcame to be able to make it in Hollywood. For example, Robinson was among the first to dance without blackface. He also asserted his stage presence and his artistic agency by daring to perform solos onstage. These emancipatory gestures had an undeniable impact on African American communities, though they garnered less visibility than his onscreen performances in Hollywood films. The stage does not have the same immortalizing effect as cinema; it does not reach as large an audience as quickly and does not create the same sort of memories. As such, Robinson's bold stage performances had less of an impact on the collective imagination than film excerpts like the one examined here. Film also sometimes acts as witness to an era, as an artistic

DOI: 10.4324/9781003335887-11

and political archive. Is this why film has often seemed to me to be lagging when it comes to introducing emancipated Afro-descendant characters? Ava DuVernay, in her documentary *13th* (2016), discussing the links between race, justice, and mass incarceration in the United States, begins the film, and her argument, with an examination of *The Birth of a Nation*, a 1915 film directed by D. W. Griffith, in which the role of the Ku Klux Klan as a vigilante, racist lynch mob is validated and lauded.[4] For scholar Ann Murphy, presenting the white child star Shirley Temple and Robinson together onscreen was equally historic, since the film industry was far from racially neutral at the time.[5] For Murphy, the Robinson-Temple duo's presence in Hollywood cinema acts as an important, implicit shift in racial presence in film, transcending the era's norms of race, gender, and class. That being said, the analysis of the Robinson-Temple dynamic, though fruitful, is not what interests me here. Bill Robinson's presence itself strikes me as important. It seems even more admirable to me in light of the sociopolitical and cinematic context in which it takes place. Robinson's dancing body and what it evokes moves me and informs my own way of relating to the world. Beyond the story told in the film, it is the embodiment of emancipation that has a powerful effect on my own flesh.

Consequently, in this chapter, I am interested in discussing the emancipatory power of Bill Robinson's dance in the film *The Little Colonel* (1935), in which the dancer and distinguished actor, nicknamed Bojangles,[6] shares the screen with the young Shirley Temple. Thanks to its capacity to sublimate beings, dance has an intrinsic political power that I find important to highlight. The inner and spiritual strength that dance bestows upon its practitioners is essential and allows for a transgression of social roles. As a dance practitioner, and being particularly informed by African and Neoafrican traditions, I recognize the postures, the gestures, and the relationship to space that make Robinson's character a dignified person. This dignity not only prompts admiration due to the social and political context of the time and to the power relations that govern the protagonists, but also places him within a sphere of intrinsic and liberating resistance.

Dance and Racial Emancipation

Even today, any Afro-descendant person who enters the public sphere while living in a society where they are a minority has a dual task: to succeed and to uplift their compatriots. Doing well is not enough; one must become a hero, a figure of emancipation. A person who will not only excel in their field, but who will also make good pronouncements, who will honour their community, who will never give in. If by chance this person becomes too friendly with the majority, they will be called a sellout, a coon (a clown with bulging, innocent eyes), a "house negro." This last term, popularized by

Malcolm X, describes a person who, though enjoying certain privileges, validates the dominant class's degrading thoughts about them. The "house negro" does not work in the fields: he has clean clothes, he is well coiffed, he lives in the master's house, he speaks articulately, but nevertheless he remains a negro. Above all, his privileges become so valuable that rather than risk losing them, he prefers not to stand in solidarity with the members of his community.

The Black Lives Matter movement may have offered a respite since, confronted with the horror of George Floyd's murder, there was a certain legitimation of Afro-descendant people's fight for civil rights. At the time of this writing, three years later, nothing could be less certain. Our struggles remain fierce and the weight on our shoulders persists. If Bill Robinson was acting today in a film reflecting contemporary social codes, it is quite possible that the same debate would take place. Is his role one of submission? Does it allow for the emancipation of Afro-descendant people? But rewatching the film *The Little Colonel*, I remain amazed, moved, deeply affected by Robinson's presence onscreen. It is more than enough. I believe that Robinson's dancing has extraordinary power when it comes to putting forward an alternate reality that I feel down to my very cells. From that moment on, this new reality exists and propels me into my own strength. To me, Robinson's dancing seems timeless and universal; it straightens my spine.

In Afro-descendant families and communities, someone who "knows how to dance" will always receive enthusiastic approval from the group. Each moment spent dancing produces a feeling of pride, gratitude, and shared celebration. We recognize each other through dance. Dance celebrates the vitality and personality of each individual. In these circles, the importance of dance endures to this day. The cipher of street dancers, incidentally, comes to us from the same African tradition of celebrating each individual through dance. The dancers form a circle, and each person takes a turn improvising in the middle, giving free rein to their self-expression while demonstrating their skill; the others constantly encourage them to surpass themselves.

If dance has remained alive, it is because it celebrates, heals, and marks stages of life. It does so in an even more codified way in traditional African and Neoafrican contexts. Thanks to its fundamental nature, dance has survived in America despite centuries of enslavement during which drums were banned on plantations. It has survived despite long sea voyages where captive persons were forced to dance under threat of whips. Dance survived. More than that, it has been a source of survival, of resistance, and even of revolution.

Dance can be found in the history of the Haitian revolution, which led to the country's independence in 1804. The Bois-Caïman ceremony, on August 14th, 1791, played a crucial role in these events. That day, enslaved persons swore an oath to either free themselves or die. It was a Vodou ceremony, and

Vodou means dance, drumming, and ritual. Televised images showing anti-Apartheid protests in South Africa, especially from the late 1980s, are also etched into the memories of many people, myself included. Chants and repetitive dance steps were popularized in the West by Johnny Clegg, who was nicknamed the white Zulu. Here, too, dance characterizes struggle not as an ultimate battle, but as a way of being in the world, as an uplifting celebration. Capoeira, a Brazilian martial art, is also recognized as a dance born to resist the domination of white colonizers.

Many Afro-descendant people may be wondering what role dance plays in our day and age. In this era of modernity and urbanization, what is the meaning of the pleasure dance brings us? How does dance articulate itself as a source of survival and resistance? What ancestral power does dance hold and how is this power manifested? Robert Battle, artistic director of the Alvin Ailey American Dance Theater, said in an interview on his 2023 tour: "we have always survived with not just activism but humor, you know, with song, with dance. When you see people dancing together in spite of the weather, that, to me, is resistance."[7] It is possible to ask these questions of Bill Robinson's dance in *The Little Colonel*, in which he plays the role of an obliging butler alongside the clever little girl played by Shirley Temple. Can Robinson's dance truly offer an emancipatory counterpoint to the reductive representation that he portrays in his role as the servant?

Bill Robinson's Dance Beyond the Butler

In *The Little Colonel*, Bill Robinson plays the butler, Mr. Walker. He moves with surprising agility, particularly in the iconic staircase scene. When little Lloyd's (Shirley Temple) grandfather orders her to go up to her room and go to bed, she refuses, pouting. As the grandfather can become angry quite quickly, Walker feels the danger approaching, and asks Lloyd if he can show her something, a new way of climbing the stairs. He tells her to "just watch." Walker then dances for the better part of two minutes, ascending and descending the stairs with virtuosity and ingenuity. Lloyd then declares that she would also like to climb the stairs this way. Walker therefore teaches her a few dance moves. Placated and cheerful once more, Lloyd climbs the stairs, dancing up, down and back again, hand-in-hand with Walker. When the grandfather suspects too much fun is being had and asks from afar what is happening, the two protagonists run up the remaining stairs joyfully. Lloyd then goes to her room and agrees to prepare for bed under the maid's care.[8]

This scene highlights Robinson's capacity to foreground his humanity. In this sense, to me, the staircase dance is timeless. Even though YouTube, by making the film *The Little Colonel* available to me, allows me to watch the staircase dance multiple times in the comfort of my living room, as a dancer, I do not need to do so. The timelessness I feel springs partly from the fact that watching this dance scene was an embodied experience for me. It created enough vigorous kinesthetic traces in my memory. I even believe that it revived memories that I struggle to describe but that I feel to be simultaneously distant and very alive.

This is because Robinson manages to elevate the ordinary. With his nearly unmoving upper body, he ascends and descends the stairs with an ease that almost defies the laws of gravity. He gives off the impression of sliding from one step to another without the weight of his body holding him back. Thanks to his expertise in centering himself, his body exudes a sense of calm and groundedness that it would not do to disturb. His knees and ankles are limber and flexible, his pelvis grounded, his chest open and calm, his arms are supple and lightweight like two floating birds. His back is straight and graceful. His head is held high. He sings and his feet tap a multitude of rhythms that call out to each other and intermingle, while his upper-body posture remains stable. His polyrhythmic and vocal musicality engages those who watch and listen to his performance. He is just as close to the ground as he is to the sky, and his general posture exudes a presence and an elegance that transcends his character's subordination.

Robinson's remarkable capacity to move his legs about nimbly while his upper body remains relatively still requires precise isolation work. In order to simultaneously have such uprightness, agility of the lower limbs, and a chest that inspires generosity and trust, Robinson must fully inhabit his body and practice an energetic projection towards openness, while remaining centred. As such, Robinson is able to shatter the notions of space and time presented by the film's storyline. For me, he also embodies a refined labour of physical resistance, which offers a foundation for the mind's resistance. Murphy speaks of dance as a "counterforce."[9] By transcending the Christian mind-body dichotomy, this physical resistance becomes holistic, becomes a practice of spiritual liberty. Does not dance also allow for the expression of one's being outside the social self, of those characteristics of the self which cannot be expressed in words? Dawn Sardella-Ayres suggests that Robinson's performance, in and of itself, affirms emancipatory possibilities.[10]

For me, Robinson's dance is a gateway towards communication and empathy. Thanks to it, little Lloyd complies and goes up to her room with no fuss. The young girl, lost in an adult world, finds comfort and joy in Walker's presence. The grandfather, though he loves his granddaughter deeply, does not know how to express his affection for her, and limits himself to a patriarchal authority he believes to be necessary and appropriate in high society. Walker not only excels in his role as butler, he also displays emotional intelligence. Such emotional intelligence is linked to a high degree of artistic skill and to an evident capacity for transmission. Murphy describes Robinson as "the embodiment of mastery and knowledge [...] [a] black man [who is] the source of artistic and spiritual expertise."[11]

One thing I notice among Afro-descendant people in general is a culture of self-affirmation that challenges others' perceptions of us. We learn very early that no matter the degrading views others may have of us, no matter which social role we are assigned, we must remain proud. It is this pride that has allowed us to fight back against racial oppression and humiliation. It is also this pride that irritates police forces, that makes it so that black bodies must be beaten like dogs, as Ta-Nehisi Coates explains in his book *Between the World and Me* (2016).[12] This culture of self-affirmation is intrinsic to the practice of dance.

> You may write me down in history
> With your bitter, twisted lies,
> You may trod me in the very dirt
> But still, like dust, I'll rise.
> Does my sassiness upset you?[13]

This pride is more than a state of mind. It is an oral tradition of mental and embodied skill, passed down through generations, across oceans and continents. Some will say that there is little use for these skills in a world where only financial security and success seem to count, where too many black men and women endure humiliation and violence on a daily basis. Brenda Dixon Gottchild, in her book *The Black Dancing Body*, explains, with many examples and interviews, namely with choreographers, that the "black body" moves with disconcerting confidence. Confidence that rests on the presence of ancestors and on the strength of African cultural legacy.[14] Through dance, Bill Robinson presents an embodied counterargument that evokes hope in the face of dehumanization. What we want to see from Robinson is not what he offers us; he offers us other perspectives. He gives us the opportunity to open our minds to humanity.

His dance on the stairs is more than a pleasant moment of liberty; it is the indelible mark of a process of emancipation located beyond social codes. Robinson's dance informs and nourishes my motivations for choosing to dance and my own condition as an Afro-descendant woman. I go through life with my head held high, always. I go through life by maintaining an intimate relationship with dance; I aim for this relationship to be grounded, vigorous, a source of comfort and self-elevation. I know that I am supported by my ancestors. As Maya Angelou says, I never come alone, I am surrounded. As such, I never dance alone. Audre Lorde explains in her text *Uses of the Erotic: The Erotic as Power* (2003) that it is not only our actions that count, but also the joyful mindfulness and meaning they provide.[15] Experiencing the power of this emotion allows us to live and to show our dignity and strength to the whole world, since another relationship with it has become possible. Joy becomes a way of being, a profoundly transformative relationship to the self. For me, it is agility, grace, survival, and transcendence. That is why, in 2023, Bill Robinson shores up my strength.

Notes

1. Dieudonné Niangouna, *M'appelle Mohamed Ali* (Besançon: Editeur Solitaires Intempestifs, Collection Bleue, 2014).
2. Pearl Primus, quoted in Peggy Schwartz and Murray Schwartz, *The Dance Claimed Me: A Biography of Pearl Primus* (New Haven: Yale University Press, 2012).
3. Ann Murphy, "Bill Robinson and Shirley Temple Tap Past Jim Crow," in *The Oxford Handbook of Screendance Studies*, ed. Douglas Rosenberg (New York: Oxford University Press, 2016), 731–47.
4. *13th*, directed by Ava DuVernay (Kandoo Films, 2016).
5. Murphy, "Bill Robinson and Shirley Temple," 733.
6. Robinson earned this nickname thanks to his *joie de vivre* and unwavering enthusiasm. See SammyDavisJrVEVO, "Sammy Davis Jr – Mr. Bojangles (Live in Germany 1985)," March 17, 2017, YouTube video, 6:19, https://www.youtube.com/watch?v=-Fju4UajL7g.
7. Michel Martin, "Alvin Ailey's dance company marks 65 years," *NPR*, February 19, 2023, https://www.npr.org/2023/02/19/1158242069/alvin-aileys-dance-company-marks-65-years.
8. *The Little Colonel*, directed by David Butler (Fox Film, 1935).
9. Murphy, "Bill Robinson and Shirley Temple," 733.
10. Dawn Sardella-Ayres, "'What's goin' on around here?': Dancing Past Binaries and Boundaries in *The Little Colonel*," *Research on Diversity in Youth Literature* 3, no. 1 (2021).
11. Murphy, "Bill Robinson and Shirley Temple," 736.
12. Ta-Nehisi Coates, *Une Colère noire: lettre à mon fils* (Paris: Éditions Autrement, 2016).
13. Maya Angelou, "Still I Rise," Poetry Foundation, https://www.poetryfoundation.org/poems/46446/still-i-rise.
14. Brenda Dixon Gottchild, *The Black Dancing Body: A Geography from Coon to Cool* (New York: Palgrave Macmillan, 2002).
15. Audre Lorde, "De l'usage de l'érotisme: l'érotisme comme puissance," translated by Mahali C. Calise et al. in *Sister Outsider* (Carouge: Éditions Mamamélis, 2003), https://philo.esaaix.fr/content//audre-lorde/audre-lorde.pdf.

Bibliography

Agbor-Talor, Phylishia. "Bill 'Bojangles' Robinson (1878–1949)." BlackPast, March 13, 2018. https://www.blackpast.org/african-american-history/robinson-bill-bojangles-1878-1949/. Accessed February 15, 2023.

Angelou, Maya. "Still I Rise." Poetry Foundation. https://www.poetryfoundation.org/poems/46446/still-i-rise.

Butler, David, dir. *The Little Colonel*. Fox Film, 1935.

Coates, Ta-Nehisi. *Une Colère noire: lettre à mon fils*. Paris: Éditions Autrement, 2016.

DuVernay, Ava, dir. *13th*. Kandoo Films, 2016.

Gottchild, Brenda Dixon. *The Black Dancing Body. A Geography from Coon to Cool*. New York: Palgrave Macmillan, 2002.

Lorde, Audre. "De l'usage de l'érotisme: l'érotisme comme puissance." In *Sister Outsider*, translated by Magali C. Calise et al. Carouge: Éditions Mamamélis, 2003. https://philo.esaaix.fr/content//audre-lorde/audre-lorde.pdf.

Martin, Michel. "Alvin Ailey's dance company marks 65 years." *NPR*. February 19, 2023. https://www.npr.org/2023/02/19/1158242069/alvin-aileys-dance-company-marks-65-years.

Murphy, Ann. "Bill Robinson and Shirley Temple Tap Past Jim Crow." In *The Oxford Handbook of Screendance Studies*, edited by Douglas Rosenberg, 731–747. New York: Oxford University Press, 2016.

Niangouna, Dieudonné. *M'appelle Mohamed Ali*. Besançon: Editeur Solitaires Intempestifs, Collection Bleue, 2014.

SammyDavisJrVEVO. "Sammy Davis Jr – Mr. Bojangles (Live in Germany 1985)." March 17, 2017. YouTube video, 6:19. https://www.youtube.com/watch?v=-Fju4UajL7g.

Sardella-Ayres, Dawn. "'What's goin' on around here?': Dancing Past Binaries and Boundaries in *The Little Colonel*." *Research on Diversity in Youth Literature* 3, no. 1 (2021).

Schwartz, Peggy, and Murray Schwartz. *The Dance Claimed Me: A Biography of Pearl Primus*. New Haven: Yale University Press, 2012.

9

THE GHOST(S) OF ALICE GUY

Reminiscences of a Feminist Screendance Pioneer

Priscilla Guy

Translated by Alanna Thain

This chapter is driven by the question of the multiple points of view—in the sense of what is visible, as well as what has been overlooked—that have shaped screendance. This hybrid field's diverse corpus has been shaped by the fears, desires, and positionalities of artists, past and present. The male gaze[1] remains an important theme in feminist film theory, several decades after Laura Mulvey's initial formulation; it continues to inflect the conversation about the feminist roots of screendance and critical approaches to the field. The case of Alice Guy—the first female filmmaker in the world, at the end of the nineteenth century—brings into focus how the male gaze also creates blind spots: this pioneering filmmaker kept repeatedly disappearing from view throughout the history of cinema. Thinking of Guy's history in terms of the *gazes* of screendance highlights how women artists have appeared and disappeared from the cultural landscape and offers a pragmatic starting point for thinking about contemporary aesthetic and political issues. I propose to interrogate both the socio-economic conditions that influenced Guy's career and the aesthetic aspects of her body of work, to ensure that neither her art nor her history are left behind. Looking backwards at this dance of (dis) appearance is one way of taking the long view on the persistence of inequities and exclusions in screendance theory and practice. While Guy's work has not been prominent in screendance history, I argue that linking how screendance has been and still is marginalized as a field to Guy's sidelining as a major figure in cinema history might help us understand some biases at the core of gendered discriminations in the arts. Although it may seem paradoxical, writing Guy's legacy into a (marginalized) screendance timeline does help redress the recognition of her contribution while also shedding light on systemic problems.

The Irresistible Piano: Dance Like Nobody's Watching

In 1907, Alice Guy directed *The Irresistible Piano* in Paris, a short film just over four minutes long, in which members of a community (people at a dinner, textile workers, a police officer) are suddenly mesmerized by the music of a local pianist and start to dance randomly, as if under its spell. The dance movements in this film are incredibly surprising, funny, and captivating: each character seems to move with freedom in a disjointed manner, showing how they'd move if nobody was watching or as if they could not control their movements. Swaying pelvises, erratic torsos, and restless arms gradually but quickly go every which way in each small scene. Drawing on the appeal of music to provoke this erratic dance, Guy tackles how our modesty constrains our body from moving freely; she also addresses the social norms and codes that prescribe a certain way of moving. While all characters in the film appear a little terrified at how the music makes them move, they also eventually give into the moment and experience pure joy, all together. Indeed, at the end of the film, the different sub-groups assemble around the pianist in a hectic and chaotic dance party, joyfully bumping into each other and laughing. With humour, Guy interrogates our capacity to let go and proposes dance (and joy?) as a social bond that could bring us together, away from everyday preoccupations.

Alice Guy: Women's Screendance in the Light of an Invisiblized Origin

In 2023, well into cinema's second century following the invention of the cinematograph in 1895, the gender gap persists in how men and women are supported in the production, funding,[2] and recognition[3] (through awards) of filmmaking internationally, despite the introduction of quotas and other attempts to redress this imbalance in many areas of the film industry. The question remains about what place women can and should hold in the industry.

Returning to the early days of cinema at the end of the nineteenth century reminds us that in the beginning, there was Alice Guy (1873–1968). While she has been clearly established as the world's first female filmmaker, the debate still rages as to whether or not she was the first *fiction* filmmaker, preceding even Georges Méliès. For my purposes, the question of whether she was in fact the first fiction filmmaker doesn't matter. What is critical is that a woman has indisputably been part of the story of cinema since its earliest days, playing a critical role in its development. In the context of this book on screendance, Guy's legacy is crucial not only because of her historical importance to cinema itself, but also because she repeatedly filmed dance, staged women's bodies for the screen, and wrote and shot films that addressed marginalized gender realities. She also occasionally filmed herself as the protagonist of her own works.

I seek to re-inscribe Guy at the origin of a feminist history of filmmaking, and to reflect on the implications of her historical invisibilization in relation to current research in screendance studies. Her work has barely been considered by major screendance publications and books in the last two decades, both in and out of the academic field. I should highlight that French scholar Sophie Walon lists many examples of films attributed to Guy in her doctoral thesis on screendance (2017), shedding light on her contribution: *Leçon de danse* (1897), *Danse fleur de lotus* (1897), *Ballet Libella* (1987), *Danse serpentine par Mme Bob Walter* (1899), *Danses basques* (1901), *Danse mauresque* (1902), *Danse excentrique* (1902) and *Danse fantaisiste* (1902). However, the films cited above do not appear in the filmography of Walon's thesis, though they are mentioned in the text. Neither do they appear in the index, nor does the name of Alice Guy, who is also cited in the text. How can this erasure be understood, not only in Walon's thesis—which is only an anecdotal example—but in screendance research in general? It could be explained by the fact that Guy was not a dancer or a choreographer, and that her short films did not present choreographic research per se. And yet, screendance history has frequently appealed to visual artworks and experimental cinema productions that were not precisely choreographic, but that could nourish screendance research through a focused analysis: the Lumière Brothers, George Méliès and Germaine Dulac, for instance, are present in screendance bibliographies. Thus, the erasure of Guy's repertoire from screendance canons seems to stem more from systemic bias than from aesthetic issues.

Born in France in 1873, Alice Guy worked as a secretary for Léon Gaumont from the age of twenty-two. There, she quickly became interested in the emerging development of cinema and camera technology, and Gaumont allowed her to film her own short "views" in her spare time, on the building's balcony. It was in this context that she made her first fiction film (whose date is up for debate: some people claim that it was made in 1896, others after 1902). *La fée aux choux* (The Cabbage Fairy) exists in multiple forms in the archives, with different versions of the film identified by different titles. Since the early 2000s, there has been unprecedented interest in the career path of this pioneering filmmaker. Researchers have attempted to shed light on her historical importance, several books and documentary films have been devoted to her life, while memes, web-based content, and new video releases have restored her memory through popular media and social networks. Nevertheless, this current enthusiasm for Guy does not make up for her neglect for much of the twentieth century.

Long before this current wave of interest, Marquise Lepage, a Quebec-based filmmaker and researcher, broke new ground around Guy's forgotten career. After three years of studying film at the Université de Montréal in the 1980s without once hearing of Guy, Lepage came across her name in a book on early cinema. She was shocked to discover that Guy's body of work had been left out of the history she was taught and began a documentary project.[4] Six years later, in 1995, Lepage shared the fruits of her labour in the first ever documentary film about Guy: *The Lost Garden: The Life and Work of Alice Guy-Blaché,* produced by the National Film Board of Canada. This film traces Guy's career through television interviews, photo archives, and Gaumont production logs, including unpublished interviews with family members and personal correspondence. While occasionally some works have mentioned Guy's legacy[5] in the preceding decades, none offered such an in-depth incursion into her life and art to date. Lepage unearthed many aspects of Alice Guy's life and collected boxes of unpublished archival material, later depositing them at the Cinémathèque québécoise for other researchers to use. Lepage's film was followed by the publication of Alison McMahan's landmark book, *Alice Guy-Blaché: Lost Visionary of the Cinema* (2002), whose detailed analyses of films provides a deeper understanding of Guy's work. Indeed, it was as a researcher on Lepage's documentary that McMahan first discovered Guy's work, before deciding to pursue her own research project.

Initially, Lepage worked as an independent researcher, due to a lack of public funding.[6] Ironically, Lepage says she was refused funding due to Guy's obscurity, even as this very obscurity was Lepage's key argument for why this work was necessary. Lepage was told that if Alice Guy had been important to the history of cinema, her work would already be known. On the other hand, the director recalls that "[Alice Guy] had done so many things that it seemed incredible"[7] and that while proving her importance, the prolific aspect of her career made her journey almost difficult to believe. Eventually, several documents were unearthed and opened for the first time since the early twentieth century. Thanks to Lepage, Guy's own circle, including her family based in the United States, discovered whole swathes of her film output, and film libraries have since retrieved tons of material about her from storage. Lepage's meticulous work included correlating descriptions of the films in the catalogs and unidentified rolls of film in storage. Nevertheless, the impact of Alice Guy's decades-long obscurity remains difficult to reverse, despite monumental initiatives such as Lepage's and new waves of research on Guy in recent years. Whether in film schools, in the research community, or in the professional world, Alice Guy's name does not resonate like those of her male contemporaries. Redressing one's legacy is not only about the new or rectified facts that are brought to the conversation, but also about the *ghosts* that remain in the portrait. Guy's legacy, in the collective memory, is now about both her recovery and her previous absences. The former does not come without the latter, and thus reaffirms her specificity. No matter how much we revalue one's legacy, the lost years and the former confusion will remain as a filter that interferes with how we read the present.[8]

Amongst intellectuals and cinephiles alike, the controversy surrounding the legitimacy of Guy's legacy and the accurate identification of her output often seems to overshadow interest in her artistic contribution itself. Overlooking her aesthetics obscures her visionary spirit: her inventiveness has been engulfed by debate more concerned with the identification of her repertoire than with the nature of her artistic experimentation and the audacity of her contribution in a socio-historical context that did not facilitate it. However, many initiatives in the twenty-first century have contributed to a better understanding of Guy's art and continue to do so. Both McMahan's *Alice Guy-Blaché: Lost Visionary of the Cinema* and Jane M. Gaines's book *Alice Guy Blaché: Cinema Pioneer* (2009) have opened up the conversation by considering the content of Guy's films. Gaines's ambitious and ever-expanding Women Film Pioneers Project (WFPP)[9] also sheds light on films, aesthetics, and artistic visions developed by women in the early stages of cinema history, offering enormous amounts of resources to fight the minimizing of female filmmakers' work, notably that of Alice Guy's.[10] More than a simple catalog of profiles, the WFPP is also a critical tool. The project is described as "a search for 'women film pioneers' who challenged the established idea of the great 'fathers' of cinema. Since researchers found more women than anyone expected to find, one principle came to organize the project: *What we assume never existed is what we invariably find.*"[11]

Books and websites like WFPP's help demonstrate how Guy's work is relevant to the development of screendance and as a subversive cinematic poetics by pointing out Guy's approaches through several articles and discussions. For instance, Guy's interest in the way bodies moved on screen appears as a strong component in many of her cinematographic explorations. Reading across multiple films, McMahan argues that Guy's many cross-dressing appearances in her own films

> addresses the audience in different ways at each level of the narrative, and these differences demonstrate that she was very aware of what she was presenting when it came to gender identification and the place of each sex. Moreover, for her, these issues were part of a larger discourse on women's social agency.[12]

In particular, McMahan draws on the work of feminist film theorist Kaja Silverman to explore the notion of the productive gaze and describe *a posteriori* the complex strategies of engagement and identification at work in Guy's films. Silverman's productive gaze requires the audience to constantly and consciously reposition the locus of the gaze in relation to the accompanying power dynamics. According to McMahan, Guy encourages the construction of such a gaze through her tactics of cross-dressing and reversing gendered roles in her narratives, by avoiding a too-quick gendered identification with ambiguously presenting characters. Thus, McMahan considers Guy's work from perspectives neglected by twentieth-century historians. She observes how Guy uses cross-dressing to "interrogate, undermine and subvert the socially delimited concept of gender"[13] and, more specifically, the concept of woman. As Gaines points out, "since Guy herself is cross-dressing in *Sage-femme de première classe*, this film may invariably find its way into the queer film canon."[14] These analyses by McMahan and Gaines consider her artistic choices alongside their social and political significance.

With films on topics such as childbirth and adoption, Guy's works take a different look at contemporary women's realities that were of little interest to her male counterparts. In her films, women discover babies in the cabbage patch, dance in the snow, run a nursery for prospective adoptive parents, etc. Her career testifies to an unconventional artistic vision and serves as a starting point for screendance, women's cinema, and cinema in general, even today. It is necessary to take hold of this work in order to analyze and reflect on it as artistic content and not simply to debate it as historical documentation to be (in)validated.

Guy eventually moved to the United States, following her husband Herbert Blaché, who was also a filmmaker, and leaving behind her important role at Gaumont Studios. This move, necessitated by her marital situation, took place just as cinema was gaining critical momentum. It was a decisive turning point for Guy: not only did she leave behind her influential position just as cinema was taking off, but it appears that much of the work she produced between 1896 and 1907 was lost: poorly archived, attributed to others, or even destroyed. Though it is true that, at that time, the roles of each person working on a film and the question of final authorship were less hierarchical and distinct than today, this doesn't fully explain why such a large part of her repertoire is so muddled in the historical record. Although scholars agree that she left a prolific filmography, her catalog is said to contain between 150 and 1,000 films, which creates more than just confusion about her contribution to cinema and the volume of her artistic legacy. Given the difficulty in re-establishing her long neglected legacy, we might need to ask: what conditions have led to her absence in the historical record? How was Alice Guy removed from history, from the industry, from academic work? How was her obscurity a precursor to the male domination of the film world that still prevails today?

Between the development of cinema at the end of the nineteenth century and the way in which the dominant powers have seized upon it by opening up an unprecedented area of commercial cultural production, it is appropriate to ask what Alice Guy symbolically embodies. For it is not just a question of archival and identification problems, but a question of a woman's freedom in 1896; it is a question of the demand to follow her husband; it is a question of power issues, almost fifty years before women obtained the right to vote in France. Guy mentions in an archived interview in *The Lost Garden* (1995) that if she was able to make films and experiment with this technology, which was still artisanal at the end of the nineteenth century, it was because it was unthinkable at that time that cinema would become a powerful sphere. An interesting parallel can be drawn between Alice Guy's cinematic experiments at the end of the nineteenth century and women's experimentation with screendance. Indeed, unlike traditional fiction cinema, screendance is largely dominated by women: they are artists, directors, editors, academic researchers, festival directors, or producers. All this in a largely underfunded niche where the prospects for success in the commercial sense are limited. It is thus unsurprising that a large number of women are involved in the field. Here, the question of power is essential: screendance, as a space of expression and artistic practice, is not (yet) used for professional advancement, for international peer recognition, or for attracting major funding to produce work. The current state of screendance offers a space for exploration, research, and investigation, both technical and artistic, but it is not possible to parley this into a prestigious career in mainstream cinema. A colleague once remarked during a discussion about feminism and the strong presence of women in screendance that she felt it was quite useless to dominate a field of expertise that is perfectly invisible in spaces of power.

Thus, feminism, dance, and power intersect in Alice Guy's story, generating a surprising origin to fuel screendance research. The debates surrounding Guy's work are well known to many feminists and are increasingly circulating among the general public. Revisiting Guy's legacy and taking on the task of reconstructing the puzzle of her professional life is not just a work concerning history and the archives: it can be seen as a productive collective effort to rethink the present in the light of a revised past. For many decades, the focus on pragmatic details in studying Guy's work has obscured the conditions under which she was given the opportunity to create and the subsequent mechanisms by which she was erased from history. Shedding light on such mechanisms is crucial to understanding both dominant discourses in current cinema and the construction of the screendance field, in which visibility, power, and the important presence of women are not fortuitous. Indeed, as Donna Haraway argues, "evolutionary reconstructions condition our understanding of contemporary events and future possibilities."[15] I argue that better understanding Alice Guy's trajectory—through which women's narratives, bodily explorations, and gendered thematics are strongly present—is a key element to thinking about screendance today.

How to Erase a Woman?

How do you erase a woman? This question might sound dramatic, funny, and horrifying all at once. Yet systemic sexism has undeniably impacted women's ability to register in dominant narratives of cinema. Consciously or not, generations of historians have contributed to the erasure of the work of women artists. Ironically, such erasure leaves traces as the impassable gaps that delay the reintegration of such work within the dominant tradition. This is what keeps Alice Guy on the margins of history, despite the last decades of work dedicated to her restoration by several historians: she remains outside of the main narrative. Even when (re)discovered by subsequent generations, women artists receive only a tiny fraction of the recognition they deserve, and large parts of their history are lost forever. Gaines points out that even today, while "we know with more certainty what films she did make, her own historical non-existence makes it difficult to introduce her case, the case of a figure whose career has been radically revised over the century."[16] Gaines sums up the situation by recalling that Guy is absent "from early French history (Coissac, 1925), [that] she was later mistakenly described as an actress (Bardèche and Brasillach, 1938) and [that] films she most likely directed were attributed to others (Sadoul, 1948)."[17] Her *non-existence* weighs heavily in a historical account that cannot be easily rewritten. Moreover, restoring her place in film history also requires deconstructing false narratives about her life and accounting for a glaring lack of reliable documentation. Although Gaines fails to mention the contributions of Lacassin (1972) and Bachy (1993) who, in the second half of the twentieth century, contributed to reintegrating Guy into the history of cinema, it must be admitted that the damage done over more than fifty years is not easily erased.

Joanna Russ, in her book *How to Suppress Women's Writing?* (1983), identifies the most common ways by which women's work in the arts is rendered invisible. Several of Russ's examples are applicable to the case of Alice Guy: 1) denial of authorship—she did not make this film; 2) only crediting her in lesser roles—she is a secretary or an actress; 3) exclusion of her from the dominant tradition—she simply does not exist, or she is a "woman" filmmaker, singling her out from her male counterparts who are simply "filmmakers."[18]

The problems of identification, which may seem technical, partly explain Guy's absence from collective memory and the extraordinary efforts required to reinstate her in the history of early cinema. Nevertheless, it is important to recognize that such technicalities are anything but trivial; they help shore up systemic sexism, which operates by diminishing the importance of women's work. Whether by omission, diversion, or separation, women's work has often been subjected to such sexism. Lepage, the first filmmaker to take an interest in Alice Guy at the end of the 1980s and to open boxes of archives that had remained untouched for decades, would in her own turn be overlooked: although *The Lost Garden* contains information never before revealed and represented a colossal piece of research, it received little international media attention. Over the next twenty years, various documentaries revisited the narratives of Lepage's film without necessarily crediting her as a source, although many were based directly on her work.[19]

From Rigour to Recalibration

In a lecture at the Cinémathèque française in 2010 entitled "Alice Guy a-t-elle existé?" (Did Alice Guy exist?), Maurice Gianati carefully reviewed the repertoire of works attributed to Guy. Gianati's two-and-a-half-hour lecture is disingenuous, as the title itself is confusing and its methodology undermines its main subject. Gianati seemingly fails to realize that he is reifying the absence of this woman in mainstream history through his sensationalist title. Eliminating several films from Guy's repertoire for lack of sufficient documentation, Gianati also uses a title that suggests the elimination of the artist herself: did she even exist? This kind of joke also leaves traces that must be deconstructed in order to advance research: this talk, available on the web and widely distributed, is often cited in the rare academic contributions about Guy, despite its misleading title. While the example of Gianati's lecture may seem anecdotal, it does capture the challenges of (re)inscribing forgotten or ignored women in film history. Indeed, Gaines argues that, from a feminist perspective, the controversy surrounding Guy's films is perhaps "less important as a case of conflicting evidence than one of the power of French institutional denial."[20] Gianati sought reliable sources to identify which of the 1,000 films attributed to her Guy actually made. Unfortunately, Guy's writings and interviews on the subject confuse these efforts. Documents that could corroborate crucial information about her claims in these interviews, such as film titles, years of production, and identification of people on screen, are missing. Also, as several decades separate these rare interviews, discrepancies and contradictions are present in her comments and confuse the facts. For Gianati, this discredits Guy's own words. He suggested that Guy's potential motivation to backdate her first fiction film in order to seize the title of first filmmaker from Méliès makes her an unreliable source. Initially, Gianati's caution may seem understandable: it is a matter of basic rigour to corroborate evidence before making claims. Nevertheless, dismissing the only direct source—the filmmaker herself—in the face of a poorly documented historical account overlooks a critical resource, given the paucity of written material about Guy. The situation demands a different approach. It must be remembered that, at the time, Alice Guy shot her "views" as a side job to her work as a secretary at Gaumont, and that there were few protocols to archive this form of production.

Gianati's lecture makes one thing clear, at least: if Guy's interviews and the extant documentation do not identify with absolute certainty the films she discusses, they certainly don't confirm that she is lying, ill-intentioned, or wrong. Despite attempting to establish this, Gianati fails to prove such a thing. At best, he raises more doubts about Guy's authorship of certain works through a process of elimination but fails to reach any unequivocal conclusions.

Gianati certainly uses all the documented clues, from the type of machine to the type and length of the film, not to mention historical newspaper accounts, to deploy a logical methodology. However, this logic can only be based on what has been archived, and as we have been arguing, the historical archive is shaped by systemic sexism: cinema emerged in a social context that did not value women's work as equivalent to that of men. Thus, Gianati's illuminating attention to Guy's repertoire diminishes it by eliminating any film whose provenance he is unable to confirm. My point here is not to determine Guy's actual filmography or to debate the accuracy of the data Gianati has gathered, but rather to question the impact of bias in the way the dominant story is written. In short, Gianati's method is not wrong, but it is not *productive*, from a feminist perspective.

Reading Russ, we understand that few people of the intellectual elite consciously act in a sexist manner, but that the social context is far from neutral. Russ concludes that sexist behaviors are easily repeated, consciously or not, since to reproduce them it is "sufficient to act in an ordinary, accustomed, normal, even polite manner."[21] Gianati's preferred methodology does not resolve the enigma of Alice Guy's contribution; it simply allows him to dismiss the latter, by default. Under the pretext of rigor, he delves into the Gaumont catalogs and the logbooks of Alice Guy's subordinates to find written proof of the existence of her films. This documentation, written by men often under Guy's authority, is valued over the interviews given by the filmmaker. Although Alice Guy named what she considered to be her repertoire of works during her lifetime, her word is more questionable than the diaries that an assistant wrote decades earlier. It is true that exaggerating the importance of a historical figure is not a good strategy. Nevertheless, Gianati's approach undercuts feminist discourse at a moment when its impact is becoming ever greater in popular culture thanks to social movements, digital media, and accessibility of research via the web. Gianati's lecture feels like a backlash to this wider context, even as his conclusions remain partial and do little to contribute to the restoration of Guy's history.

I was struck by the parallels between Gianati's posture and the work of the researcher Frédéric Cavé. In a 2019 article entitled "Autour d'Alice Guy: sexe, mensonges et omissions" (All about Alice Guy: Sex, Lies and Omissions) published in the journal *Nonfiction*, Cavé attempts to demonstrate how the restoration of Guy has been partially reversed thanks to the proliferation of recent publications about her, to such an extent that it would be an exaggeration, even offensive, to keep speaking of her "erasure" from film history. Referring to two 2019 articles by Laure Murat and Emmanuelle Lequeux, published respectively in *Libération* and *Le Monde*, about the documentary *Be*

Natural (2019), Cavé argues that core problem with these texts lies in the "propagation of the thesis of Alice Guy's voluntary and obstinate erasure from the history of cinema," a posture he does not hesitate to call "an tired refrain bordering on martyrology."[22] Although historians François Albera and Laurent Le Forestier have already "responded to these articles" in which they criticize what Cavé calls the "dubious thesis" of Alice Guy's invisibilization carried by the film, the latter wishes to add his contribution to this discussion.[23] Like Albera and Le Forester, Cavé insists on pointing out contradictions, paradoxes, and exaggerations carried by the wave of enthusiasm around Alice Guy's redemption in cinema history. No doubt this celebration and even instrumentalization of Guy has at times included sensationalist media coverage. According to Cavé, the list of recent publications about Alice Guy is enough to undermine the argument of her invisibilization. Yet, if it is that easy to list all the books, articles, and documentaries on Alice Guy that exist, it is to say that there are not so many of them.

For Cavé, the damage done to Alice Guy's memory has already been rectified by the flood of interest in recent years. If gaps persist, Cavé explains, it is neither due to a lack of interest from researchers and historians nor to deny Guy's importance, but rather because of a lack of historical documents to promote Guy's work. By crudely reducing Guy's erasure to a question of technicalities, Cavé seems to suggest that Guy did not suffer an injustice, as those who dismissed her from film history did not act in bad faith. This focus on intentions erases systemic oppressions and distracts from real solutions available to us. Thus, rather than helping to deconstruct the mechanisms of sexism clearly at work in the film world and within institutions, Cavé joins his colleagues in opposing what he perceives as a real danger to film history. Cavé's list of publications rather confirms that Guy's redemption is just starting. While Cavé criticizes two female authors for "riding the #MeToo wave" and adopting an "opportunistic" attitude in promoting Guy in a mainstream publication, he does little better in coming to the rescue of historians faithful to a certain history of cinema.[24] While it is true that the two articles Cavé attacks do not show much depth or critical analysis, he himself attributes the documentary *The Lost Garden* to Guy's granddaughter rather than to Lepage, as do Albera and Le Forestier. In an article that aims precisely at denouncing the lie, at sorting out the sensationalist media hype surrounding Guy and her real heritage, the author shares erroneous information that will continue to circulate thereafter. This type of error contributes to the difficulty of redeeming women artists and their work.

Feminist researchers are working to reconstruct history despite gaps and incomplete archives by looking at things from new angles and developing alternative epistemologies to overcome these absences. What Guy's legacy needs is not Gianati's approach that attempts to limit the breadth of her repertoire nor articles like Cavé's that ridicule the choice to identify her erasure. Even when this erasure is sensationalized (by the mass media) or handled clumsily (in bad films), it still addresses the absence of women in the cultural landscape. A dozen books and films over the last twenty years retelling Guy's story is not enough to redress her erasure nor assess her impact. Simply naming such erasure does not, unfortunately, make Guy's legacy reappear. It is by questioning power structures and systemic sexism that it is possible to envisage, in the long term, a paradigm shift. But for this to happen, Guy's legacy would need to be taken seriously in all spheres of film—from education to academic research, distribution networks and mass media—and over time, not just in a handful of books or documentaries. Naming Guy's erasure is by no means "martyrology": the invisibilization of women in the film landscape is a well-documented fact, and Guy's remains a glaring case.

What feminism needs is bold, original research that fills the gap, leaping into other ways of mapping the works of forgotten women. Rethinking the impact of Guy's contribution from feminist perspectives gives us the opportunity to reflect not only on the aesthetic and archival aspects of her work, but also on the socio-economic conditions of its production and the inequalities faced by women. This "institutional denial" that Gaines describes refers to the difficulty that institutions, and many historians have in acknowledging the impacts of systemic sexism on women's cultural production, even today. Gianati and Cavé seek a "balance" that ultimately highlights their own reluctance to rethink history in light of new feminist research. Their claim to rigour instead reveals their rigidity in the face of paradigm shifts in the art world, and new approaches that allow for the study of women's contributions beyond documentation that has served to establish the prominence of their male counterparts to date.

Perhaps it is a refusal to accept Guy's existence and her work that perpetuates the backlash; perhaps it is a simple lack of collective imagination that continues to prevent women like Guy from taking their place. Of all the things that can be said about Lepage's excellent work, the most important qualities of her approach are precisely, on the one hand, her genuine affection for the feminist cause and the restoration of Guy, which drove her to carry out her rigorous research despite the challenges, and, on the other, her visionary intelligence. It takes a creative and intuitive artist to see beyond what was already probable or visible.

The Unthinkable Work of Women

Guy's work suffers from a lack of documentation but also from its very unthinkability. I borrow the concept of unthinkability from Gaines to account for a socio-political reality whose force takes precedence over what actually happened. In this sense, Guy's cinema is an event constituted and re-enacted by power issues, which are rooted in the gendered power relations of the late nineteenth century, the entire twentieth century and the early twenty-first century—tensions that, over time, have necessarily evolved, but not ended.

My foray into the discourses of Gianati and Cavé demonstrates that these issues continue to shape Guy's legacy. Gaines similarly invokes the structural limitations of French cinema that make Alice Guy's cinema virtually unimaginable. These traces of unthinkability, and their recirculation in the present, emerge from an implicit prohibition: who had the right to make films in 1896? The answer to this question must be formulated simultaneously in terms of multiple historical contexts, that is, taking into account the reality of 1896 as seen from our privileged position today, as well as our view of the present context, ideally from a critical and feminist point of view. The unthinkability of Guy's accomplishments permeate even her own discourse:

> [Guy] revises the story to fit the idea of authorial control while still downplaying what she was doing on the Belleville terrace, all the better to give the impression that she and her friends were totally unaware of the significance of their play.[25]

Guy rewrites a story where she reasserts her role, but in the only way that can be imagined: by making it a lucky, even naive event—in short, one that befits her status as a woman making films at that time. Paradoxically, it is by stripping herself of her artistic authority that she can try to recover it. Through likely unconscious gymnastics, she tries to make a place for herself by upsetting the narrative, while at the same time parroting the dominant discourse:

> In 1896, it was unthinkable that a woman would make the first work of narrative cinema, that is it was quite inconceivable before she made it, as she made it, and long after she may have made it. But it was not only that it was a woman making something that was so unthinkable; it was also what it was is that she had made … this making was not just inconceivable, it was also prohibited on multiple accounts—she was a woman, she was too young, and she held down a secretarial job.[26]

To give Alice Guy the title of pioneer (not just woman pioneer), despite a lack of certainty regarding her output, puts her at least on an equal footing with her contemporaries and has the effect of engendering a radical revision of the story of cinema. She should be considered amongst them, not on the margins, sidelined by the debate over the full extent of her repertoire.

On the other hand, I have considered Gaines's approach to the lack of clarity of Guy's role in film history: she proposes that such ambivalence actually amplifies her importance. To keep the debate around Alice Guy's achievements active, rather than attempting to solve an irresolvable enigma, would be more productive, historically speaking, than eliminating Guy for lack of empirical data. This does not mean crediting her for films we do not know she actually made. It means evoking her historical contribution despite our uncertainties, understanding these doubts through the lens of social and gender stigma, rather than marshalling them to delimit her contribution. We do not know whether Alice Guy made all of these films, but Gaines proposes that we ask: what if she did? This speculative position allows Guy to be part of the conversation and to gain a certain recognition.

The impact of Guy's restoration into the history of cinema, as seen from the angle of screendance, has several productive elements. It is a matter of inscribing the birth of screendance through the gestures of a woman, and through her visions of gendered relations and her innovative use of technologies that were still emerging. This transforms the origin of a history into one in which women have always been present. Amongst the very first gestures of cinema, there were those of a woman who was interested in bodies and images with a particular point of view, long before Maya Deren. Such knowledge is already transforming our understanding of film. Screendance has much to learn from the way Alice Guy was erased and continues to cause debate in the film industry. One could ask: how can screendance be not only an alternative site for women who can't find a place in mainstream cinema, but also a locus for change and transformation, a place where inequalities are carefully analyzed and radically addressed, so that the powers at play are used productively to reimagine past and present conditions of screendance making?

Notes

1 Laura Mulvey, "Visual Pleasure and Narrative Cinema," *Screen* 16, no. 3 (1975): 6–18, https://doi.org/10.1093/screen/16.3.6.
2 Founded in 2007, the Quebec-based organization Réalisatrices Équitables, dedicated to achieving equity in filmmaking, published statistics in 2021 that showed that, despite 15 years of hard-fought battles and political representation in Quebec, the majority of government institutions have still not achieved parity in the allocation of publicly-funded film subsidies: https://stats.realisatrices-equitables.com/.
3 In 2021, for example, French director Julia Ducourneau became only the second woman to win the Palme d'Or at the Cannes Film Festival in seventy-five years. In 2022, New Zealand's Jane Campion became only the third woman to win an Oscar for Best Director in ninety-four years.
4 Marquise Lepage, Zoom call with author, January 22, 2022.
5 Lacassin, Francis. " Une contre-histoire du cinéma" (1972); Bachy, Victor. "Alice Guy-Blaché: 1873–1968: la première femme cinéaste au monde" (1993).
6 Lepage, Zoom call with author, January 22, 2022.

7 Lepage, Zoom call with author, January 22, 2022.
8 In 2018, while I was a PhD candidate at the University of Lille, two fellow doctoral students in film studies in France only vaguely recalled having heard Alice Guy's name during their studies. While trying to obtain a copy of Lepage's 1990s master's thesis on Guy, produced in conjunction with her documentary, I discovered that it had never been digitized for online consultation, despite being a rare and important piece of academic research on this subject.
9 "About the Project," Women Film Pioneers Project, accessed April 2023, https://wfpp.columbia.edu/about/. In April 2023, 314 women's profiles were available on the website, which also featured many "short career profiles on single individuals, longer thematic peer-reviewed overview essays, and shorter multimedia posts, all by film scholars, film curators, archivists, and historians."
10 Alice McMahon, "Alice Guy Blaché," Women Film Pioneers Project, 2013, https://wfpp.columbia.edu/pioneer/ccp-alice-guy-blache.
11 "About the Project," Women Film Pioneers Project.
12 McMahon, *Alice Guy Blaché: Lost Visionary of the Cinema* (Continuum, 2002), 206.
13 McMahon, *Alice Guy Blaché: Lost Visionary of the Cinema*, 239.
14 Jane Gaines, *Pink-Slipped: What Happened to the Women in the Film Industry*. Women and Film History International Series (Champaign: University of Illinois Press, 2018), 70.
15 Donna Haraway, *Simians, Cyborgs, and Women: The Reinvention of Nature* (New York: Routledge, 1991).
16 Gaines, *Pink-Slipped*, 51.
17 Gaines, *Pink-Slipped*, 51.
18 Joanna Russ, *How to Suppress Women's Writing?* (Austin: University of Texas Press, 1983).
19 Lepage describes serving as a consultant for such works without her name ever appearing in the credits.
20 Gaines, *Pink-Slipped*, 64.
21 Russ, *How to Suppress Women's*, 18.
22 Frédéric Cavé, "Autour d'Alice Guy: sexe, mensonges et omissions," Nonfiction (2019), https://www.nonfiction.fr/article-10090-autour-dalice-guy-sexe-mensonges-et-omissions.htm
23 Cavé, "Autour d'Alice Guy."
24 Cavé, "Autour d'Alice Guy."
25 Gaines, *Pink-Slipped*, 65.
26 Gaines, *Pink-Slipped*, 67.

Bibliography

Bachy, Victor. *Alice Guy-Blaché: 1873–1968: la première femme cinéaste au monde*. Paris: Institut Jean Vigo, 1993.

Cavé, Frédéric. "Autour d'Alice Guy: sexe, mensonges et omissions." *Nonfiction* (2019). https://www.nonfiction.fr/article-10090-autour-dalice-guy-sexe-mensonges-et-omissions.htm.

Gaines, Jane M. *Pink-Slipped What Happened to Women in the Silent Film Industries?* Women and Film History International Series. Champaign: University of Illinois Press, 2018.

Haraway, Donna Jeanne. *Simians, Cyborgs, and Women: The Reinvention of Nature*. New York: Routledge, 1991.

Lacassin, Francis. *Pour Une Contre-Histoire Du Cinéma*. Paris: Union générale d'éditions, 1972.
McMahon, Alice. "Alice Guy Blaché." Women Film Pioneers Project. 2013. https://wfpp.columbia.edu/pioneer/ccp-alice-guy-blache.
McMahon, Alice. *Alice Guy Blaché: Lost Visionary of the Cinema*. London and New York: Continuum, 2002.
Mulvey, Laura. "Visual Pleasure and Narrative Cinema." *Screen* 16, no. 3 (1975): 6–18, https://doi.org/10.1093/screen/16.3.6.
Russ, Joanna. *How to Suppress Women's Writing?* Austin: University of Texas Press, 1983.
Women Film Pioneers Project. "About the Project." https://wfpp.columbia.edu/about/. Accessed April 2023.

10

IN A WORLD OF DANCING WAVES AND DIY ADDICTION

An Interview with Sonya Stefan[1]

By Priscilla Guy

Sonya Stefan is a media and dance artist from Canada who incorporates glitchy analog techniques such as 16mm and VHS, feedback and light refractions, and dance in her work. She has received numerous awards and is well known for her relationship to ethics in dance. Using her experience as a performer, choreographer, and filmmaker, she reflects in this interview on her relationship to self-representation. She talks about the productive choice to disappear from the image itself to appear differently, through waves and camera movement, for instance. Stefan's work has contributed to building screendance practices and discourses over the past twenty years in Montréal (Canada). She not only creates pieces but also approaches art-making from critical and political perspectives. Her relationship to lo-tech practices is developed consciously and adventurously, both as a counter-technique to dominant forms and as a gesture in itself that opens onto new artistic territories. Her films were screened as part of RIRH 2017, and she also participated in RIRH 2019.

Guy: I was interested to know how (or if) you see your work as "dance," even when there's no "dance," perhaps. Also, the idea of self-representation. Like Marie Menken—you never see her in the image, but she's using camera movement with a handheld camera so much that she's quite present in the film, in that way. How does it change your perspective of yourself in the film, if we see you, if we don't see you? Do you feel you're there? Do you feel it speaks to your image even when we don't see you? [...]

Stefan: It's funny because this year I've taken a step back, and was thinking about my trajectory, I guess, and at the beginning my body was in [my films] a lot. My body or my friends' bodies. At that time, I was thinking about fragmentation. I filmed [*Poisson* (2013)] with Audrée Juteau and her dog Sam. We had two GoPros, one on Audrée and the other on Sam. It was about the duet, the energy between them, the movement quality between them; instead of the camera being in a frontal position, the point-of-view was between Audrée and her dog Sam. And so, at the beginning, it was about how I could film something that represents how I feel as a dancer. How does it feel to move on stage with somebody else? How does it feel to look at that person and hear their breath and, you know, that energy in-between us? How could I do that? This footage, there were fast movement scenes that are difficult to watch because the camera movement is so lively. It was hard for me to watch it.

Then there was a period, five years later, where there were no bodies at all. I started to play with feedback. If you connect a recording camera to a television and you point that camera into the television, it sees itself, creating a never-ending loop (mise-en-abyme). It's a technique where an image contains a smaller copy of itself, constantly looping, an image within an image within an image, etc. There's a certain body that appears—an energetic body, that escapes its own boundary, escaping the physical, that is in constant motion. You can dance... a duet with the camera, moving, multiplying, melting, and becoming the light.

I was thinking about manipulation. How can you let this energy move and just live within its presence and sensations? Without shaping it, without forming it into something, without making it do something. I guess it was about power, now that I think about it. But also about how I understand my presence, when I'm the dancing or when I am engaged in a duet with the camera, or when I am a camera person recording. What do I see? What is this other space? What is the power dynamic? What if I remove the physical? And I become feedback? There's this "alien body" that exists, let's say, because the mise-en-abyme comes from machines so there is an unknown present. But I also feel I am in-between no matter what role I take.

Guy: It comes from your action too though...

Stefan: Yeah, so hence I never could remove myself quite from the situation, because the fact that I'm looking at it makes me a witness. I was thinking about aliveness, sensation, objects... I think for me it was more about collaborating with an entity with its own agency. I know that I'm addicted to older technologies because when I touch film objects, it always feels like there's a history or a presence within that object. It's gone through its own voyage, its own world, and once it arrives into my hands then we continue our duet. Energy, agency, and movement—these three things. When I was completing my MFA, a professor criticized me, saying, "Why don't you ever have a 'real' body in your work? Why isn't there ever something to hold on to?" I thought, "OK, maybe I'm rejecting my body," but I considered this illumination from the feedback a body. It didn't have to be in a recognizable form to be a body.

Guy: What previously made you have bodies, and especially your own body, on screen, like in that film with your daughter (*TurnOnTVDrinkCoffeeRehearseShow* 2011), where all the frames are fragmented? This had a lot of dancing, real bodies. So, was there a transition…?

Stefan: There was a transition. […] When I was very young and dancing, the feeling of being in my body and being connected to my body felt a certain way. And then, there was a point in my life where I started questioning the way I felt connected to my body: has that been taught to me? How do I understand that? What is my relationship with my body? Everything that I know about myself, I learnt it through movement. If we take away dance, even [when I was] younger, I loved riding my bike, I loved climbing trees; I was always this person who explored the world through a moving body. That's how I accumulate knowledge… through this moving body. And then the rejection came. I think the rejection came from disappointment.

Guy: Disappointment with the image, with the result…?

Stefan: The moment I see a body on screen, I understand it from the knowledge I was taught. How can I free myself from all these things that I've learned in my life? How can I be free and see possibilities that exist outside my own reality? Be very open and not have preconceived notions in my head? Does that make sense?

And then at one point I was like, OK, I can't, I can't do that. There's so many things that I must deconstruct in the way I think, in the way I see, and what I've been taught. I think that's when I broke away. I didn't want to look at my body or any other body. It's not because I disliked anybody's body. I'm in love with moving bodies of all sorts, and moving objects and moving plants, etc. I wanted to deconstruct my own biases and the only way I could think of doing it was to not have a body. So, I guess playing with feedback was the way to do it because it was an alien body. I started thinking, "What do I fear about my body and other bodies?" And, I guess, up to that point, I started thinking about pedagogy: how was I trained? What television did I watch? What did my parents teach me? What were the interactions with the men in my life? With the women in my life? You know, all those things, positive and negative. What did I read? What have I not read? At that point, as a dancer, I hadn't read a lot. My dance practice, up to that point, was mimicking my teacher's movement. I didn't question anything. I had a desire to widen that scope. And the only way I could do it, I guess, was to erase my body. To begin learning again.

Guy: But then you did not erase your presence.

Stefan: No! Because you can't. Can you?

Guy: Well, if you don't touch the camera and you don't…

Stefan: You still turn it on. And you have to bring it in the room!

Guy: Yes. But more than that, in your feedback work, you make yourself present by all the manipulations and the movement that you're performing behind the camera. Would you say it adds to your presence?

Stefan: Yeah. I mean, as soon as you manipulate the camera, move a camera, it's an extension of your body. It becomes your body. And watching camera movement, you get a sense of their rhythm, their speed, their energy. For example, I'm short. My camera often has the viewpoint of how I see the world, you know, and I usually look up to people. Everything seems bigger to me. [...] I remember the first time I experienced watching a Californian base jumper's GoPro footage; they jump and parachute off cliffs or large buildings to the ground. I remember, the experience was so visceral, I couldn't take it, but I realized, "Oh, I've never seen this before, I've never experienced this, this is so alien to see the world in this way." And so, I was thought, "OK, there's a certain way I see the world, the way I experience it." So, camera movement for sure, for me, is an extension of the body. There's no doubt about it.

Guy: And you feel it speaks more to who you are than, for instance, editing or other choices you have to make when you're behind the camera?

Stefan: I think editing is a very complicated question. Well, editing reveals what you believe in. How you choose to frame and knit things together—the relationship to sound, landscape, history, etc. Even if it's experimental, there's still a narrative that happens. It's how you understand the world, what type of cues you get from the society, whether it's, again, through sound or image, and how you place things side by side to each other. It's a narrative, no matter if it's experimental, it is a narrative.

Guy: Yes. It always seems to me that camera movement says a lot about how you experience the world, while editing says a lot about how you understand the world. As you said, it's more a series of decisions that you make, consciously or not. But it comes from a desire or an understanding of how things should be or could be. As when you're moving with a camera, decisions are coming from a different place. Or sometimes just the fact that your body moves a certain way, it's less, perhaps, intellectualized? They both speak about you, but in a different way.

Stefan: The camera is a body, but it's an intellectual body, though.

Guy: Why so?

Stefan: It's a hard question! [laughs]

Guy: I know, I know. It's just that I wouldn't say so, therefore I'm like, "Oh, well, maybe then?"

Stefan: Ok, how to explain it. I'm going to, of course, talk about Charlotte [my daughter]. When she was little, and I gave her a camera, she had a certain sense of movement, you know? She was very excited to run around the house quickly. There's this intelligence (intuition) in her body because she's curious: "I want to learn, what's here, what's there? I'm going to make a joke! Oh, listen to the sound!" You know, you can tell her brain is moving quick because she's learning... she's learning... she's learning. And then, let's go to the other side of the spectrum: we have a pro, they're doing a dolly-type movement; all very organized, very formal, and that's another intelligent (intuitive) body organizing the camera to move in a very fluid way, a body that has it all pre-planned. They're both different types of intelligence. With young Charlotte, you get a sense of her excitement, of her discovering the world. She is learning about the world through her body's intelligence (intuition), and she wants to take it in so fast, so fast. And then at the other end, "OK, this person has a calm body." You know, they planned it in their brain, doing the mechanisms of the movement—practiced it in a smooth way or with a body sway. For me, when I see things like that, the first thing I always think is, "Oh, that person moves more than I do." And it's like, "Oh, that's what it must feel to be in their body." Because that's not how my body feels. So that's an intelligent (intuitive) body because my body recognizes it is not like that other body, but that body is very interesting, how they do it.

Guy: I totally agree with that. I think it's because we've been using intelligent and intellectual. For me there could be a bodily intelligence, an understanding that is more visceral or intuitive, and then an intellectual body would be a body that learned to do the dolly shot.

Stefan: So that would be for me the intellectual body, and then the intelligent body would be my daughter as a young person, I guess.

Guy: But maybe it's both, maybe it's not so separate, but they have a different feel, how you describe them.

Stefan: Yeah. Because I think, "Oh, that's what it feels like to be in her body. Oh, she's in that state right now." But I'm not in that state. It's like me fitting inside of her body. And then the editing, I think it's more...

Guy: [...] You cannot be so spontaneous. It's something you have to learn. So it's already intellectual just because you have to learn it, learn the tools, the technology. And it's true that edits say a lot about what you think of the world, what you understand of the world. But with the camera, it can be like that too; if you learn a movement phrase with the camera, and then you learn it and then you construct it. And then you look at it. I think of your daughter: she was more in the experience of her body.

Stefan: She's in the moment. When I do camera movement—I practice it— I'm thinking about the process.

Guy: Maybe you went from intelligence to intellectual!

Stefan: I think so! I think that's what I did!

Guy: It's really interesting, that distinction.

Stefan: So, that's why I say editing for me is more complicated, because I think editing requires you making choices within both.

Guy: I was just about to say that, for me, it feels so intuitive, editing.

Stefan: It doesn't for me.

Guy: It's like, I have to first learn the tools, and then I can get more and more intuitive as I'm good with the tools. But with the camera movement, for me it feels like the intuition comes before you learn the technique, and once you learn the technique, you lose some of the intuition. And in editing for me it's the opposite: you get more freedom, more visceral choices available to you, when you know very well the language of editing and you can stop thinking about it and try.

Stefan: I feel like I'm in a cage when I'm editing.

Guy: Oh, yes?

Stefan: I do. I feel like the moment is gone because the moment is recorded. And then I start thinking of manipulation… Editing is complicated for me, personally.

Guy: And when you were editing images with your own body in it—did you actually?

Stefan: I did. I did it.

Guy: Was it more complicated if it was you?

Stefan: Yes, it was very complicated.

Guy: Why so?

Stefan: I think that my view on my own body was really skewed, really confused.

Guy: In life or in the film?

Stefan: In the film. In the film, I was trying to figure out what I understood about my body, I guess.

Guy: Was it more like nothing was good or everything could be good?

Stefan: I think it was… "Why does my body occupy this type of space?" Which requires certain rules in a variety of ways. I grew up in the 80s and the 90s, training was about "breaking down the body to build it back up." You know, to become a "trained body." I remember thinking about clothing, the costumes—my "dance costume," my "mom costume," my "intellectual costume." They're different versions of "me."

Guy: But then what was the—maybe you don't know—but what was hard when you were editing, for instance, that film with Charlotte? Was it that you were bored or that you were scared? Like, "Oh my, I don't want to screw it"?

Stefan: At the time, I was interested in repetition and mundane life tasks. I remember the aerobic part for me was training. It was all kinds of trainings that we can do, that we all do. Even if you're not somebody who's athletic or does movement, everybody goes through this formation thing.

Guy: And it's on television, so it's available to everyone to do that.

Stefan: And that was connected to my mom. If somebody becomes an engineer, you know, they go through their training, there's this idea of training the body, you know, to "become" something. And then the second part I know was mundane life, just the things we have to do. We come home, we feed ourselves. All those activities, which is another type of training. And then at the end, there was the dance, which was supposed to be… I guess I was thinking about the product. You know, you train to become a product or to be a product. Or to present a product to the world.

Guy: So you had some kind of a narrative already, so maybe editing was a bit formatted by the scenario, that borrows a bit from some fiction film?

Stefan: For Charlotte's voice, at the beginning, she was in the room while I was editing and asked a lot of questions. What I liked was that she was the critique, you know, she was questioning. I liked this aspect, she's a critic, she's very much the critique. And then in the second part I remember I liked that there were just household sounds. For example, there's certain sounds in that house that I am emotional and nostalgic towards because I've heard it every day. I'm in love. And then the end sequence, what does it mean when you consciously decide to put one thing together with another thing? You decide to put a body in a certain costume with a certain piece of music together. And it's not a clear narrative. What does it mean when you're engaged in something that you don't understand? So, is it bad that I'm part of something that I don't understand? Is it a good thing? Why accept being pulled along by the routine of it all? […]

Agency is definitely part of it. Agency, being in control of your own image. But then you're unsure of what you want to say. I guess it's like discovering—if I talk about my own body—discovering my own body again, as if I'm a child without somebody else telling me what to see. It proves to be quite difficult to do that. With that particular film, in the aerobics section, the instructor's name was Bess Motta, she did twenty-minute workouts on TV in the 70s. She was very sexy and had curly hair and was kind of the bad girl of the aerobics world, so I liked her—her voice is in the film. She would have the sing-song thing, you know, when she was telling you what to do. Did you do ballet training? You know, how they would bark things at you? So that was one thing that I really liked about aerobics, that there was this approach—"I'm going to sing to you the movement"—and so there was this playfulness about it. And I know that, that part of the video was something that I loved and that I wanted back. It's this idea of playfulness with my body, that it's just a body.

Guy: There is almost some self-mockery in the film also. It becomes a bit clownish at times. But you perform it with full dedication, no fooling around, you really do it. But then with the editing, you add a layer of humour.

Stefan: Yes, because there's this repetition. I remember that I wanted that aerobics section because I wanted it to be fun.

Guy: Playful.

Stefan: Playful, yes.

Guy: But at the same time, Charlotte's questions bring back some reality in it.

Stefan: Yes, it can't just be playful. There's always a dual thing happening. Always. No matter how much you want it to be something.

Guy: Even between your gaze and Charlotte's critique, there's another duality that is not you and you, but it's almost you and you because she's so... close to you. She's... kind of a product of you. [laughs] I don't want to call her a product but...

Stefan: [laughs] But yeah, it's true. It's also her seeing her mother in that way. I mean, it's not a big deal that she sees me that way. But she's also looking at me, looking, looking, looking, learning, learning, learning. That always crosses my mind. I don't know about you, but in dance that was my trajectory for sure: watching and learning. That's how we all were. I think people are still like that.

Guy: Are you hoping to learn something when you make a film? I mean, about yourself, to learn something about yourself?

Stefan: Well, I am finishing a film now that's taken ten years to make. There's *Flashdance* in there, there's Fred Astaire, there's a factory. And right now, it's just title cards with text—when I speak in the film, I speak in French because it's my second language, or third language. When I was a kid, I would always get comments like, "She doesn't speak well." Because at home we would speak a hybrid language. So, again, I guess it's about duality, so there's this idea of the body never being fixed in one point, it's always in-between. There's an in-betweenness, always. With *Flashdance*, when I was young, I really loved it, it was really cool. And now I understand it differently. The way in which she was framed in the movie, the way I saw her as a young child. And the way I framed her, you know, there's always this multiplication going on.

Guy: Different versions of yourself and your relationship to the film. Yes.

Stefan: There's like a multiplication of her body as well as a multiplication of my own body as a viewer. And then my mom... Just talking to her about her life, how she came here—the only reason I'm in dance is because she wanted to dance, she was never allowed, so then she did it through me. Again, there's a projection onto me. All our bodies are intertwined.

Guy: So to represent yourself is not different from filming your mother or your daughter.

Stefan: No. To represent myself means to represent anything and everything that's around me. My mom, my daughter, me.

Guy: Including your absence.

Stefan: Including my absence, yes! For example, when someone asks you to describe yourself, sometimes I'm unsure of how to do that. Does that make sense? So, I do know that in terms of representation, that was another thing too: it is important to see all the different types of bodies on screen. And then I thought, "OK, well, I can add to that conversation, I don't think it's that special, but it's present and it's fair."

Note

1 This interview was conducted on February 10, 2020, in person, in Montreal (Canada). It was held as part of Priscilla Guy's doctoral research on feminist screendance self-representation (Lille University, France). The interview has been lightly condensed and edited for clarity.

Bibliography

Juteau, Audrée. *Poisson*. 2013. Performance.
Stefan, Sonya. *TurnOnTVDrinkCoffeeRehearseShow*. 2011. 13:16 minutes.

PART III
Kinetics and Politics of Ephemerality and Ownership

11
"TAKE ME TO THE PLACE WHERE THE WHITE BOYS DANCE"[1]

Tom Hanks's Manchild

Addie Tsai

A Most Trusted American, a Most Likable Hollywood Star: Tom Hanks

Acknowledging the inevitable difficulty at locating the precise moment a televisual trope—especially one that reifies gendered and racial ideologies—cements itself into any popular culture, Black comedian Eddie Murphy recognized and brought to the forefront of American popular culture an attitude regarding cis white masculinity in his "White Man Dance" sketch included in the stand-up film *Eddie Murphy Raw* (1987). The sketch traveled beyond its emergence, especially when Black American actor Alfonso Ribeiro consciously borrowed from it in his own "white man dance" in the Black American network television sitcom, *The Fresh Prince of Bel-Air*, throughout its run from 1990–1996.

Contextualized by a stand-up career concretized and well-versed in homophobic content, Murphy hit on an ideology already cemented within the fears of white masculinity emerging for men in 1980s America—those of homosexuality and effeminization. These fears were particularly potent given the rise of homosexual masculinity in the mainstream exacerbated by the AIDS epidemic in the United States during the 1980s.[2] In *The Complexity and Progression of Black Representation in Film and Television*, David L. Moody borrows from E. Patrick Johnson's *Appropriating Blackness: Performance and the Politics of Authenticity*, when he concludes:

> The Reagan-led conservative administration in the White House during the 1980s paved the way for the reemergence of "family values," while simultaneously marginalizing those outside the heteronormative sphere

DOI: 10.4324/9781003335887-15

of family including gays, lesbians, single working women and single parents … Moreover, the insidious anti-gay pro-family sentiments promoted by the Reagan administration not only supported Whiteness as the master trope, but ironically also stimulated the career of a contentious Black comedian named Eddie Murphy. One could infer that Murphy's stand-up character during the 1980s became another minstrel cast member at center stage for the fulfillment of White political fantasies … Murphy had a large White constituency from the very beginning, and by adding homophobic dialogue to his repertoire, his stand-up act ultimately became commodified, and sold as amusement.[3]

In *Eddie Murphy Raw*, which opens with a sketch discussing his fear of gay men chasing him in anger due to the anti-gay jokes he included in his previous television special *Eddie Murphy: Delirious* (1983), the White Man Dance sketch can be read as burdened by an indictment on white masculinity, contextualized through a homosexual paranoia. As a point of comparison, one can note the difference in Murphy's depiction of white American men when compared with his sketch featuring Italian American men. In the sketch, he compares Italian American men to Black men, even referring to them as "n———s," while imbuing them with hypermasculinity in his physical impersonation, complete with an arched back and crotch grab. It is telling that in Murphy's view, Italian American men only visit nightclubs in order to get into physical altercations with other men, a gesture reinforcing their affirming masculinity, whereas white men attend nightclubs to "fail" at dancing—heads facing the floor, shoulders rolled forward, and arms swinging back and forth with snapping fingers; a familiar symbol also representative of the Black homosexual queen.[4] In other words, Murphy employed gestures possibly signifying effeminization and homosexuality in order to criticize white men's failure at traditional notions of American masculinity. The relationship Murphy explored between white masculinity and effeminization/homosexuality becomes even clearer when set apart by his hypermasculine depiction of Italian American men. By including in the same stand-up film a sketch of Italian American men, white American men who stand in as more ethnic than the generic white male, the generic white male dancer then can be read as further emasculated through this juxtaposition. Murphy pinpointed a very adept ideological relationship between white men's relationship to dance and their subsequent fear of being marked as homosexual or effeminate, which risked taking white men further away from their relationship to masculinity.

The White Man Dance trope—that white men are presented as unable (or unwilling) to dance well, in which the "misperformance" of "good" dancing is a comic mechanism, as proliferated throughout American popular media since the mid-1980s—is consciously in dialogue with the very movers who affirmed their masculinity in differing ways through the lens of dance. To name just a few examples, these movers include Steve Carell's Michael Scott (*The Office*), Matthew Perry's Chandler Bing (*Friends*), Jon Heder's Napoleon Dynamite (*Napoleon Dynamite*), comedy trio The Lonely Island, and Jon Cryer's Duckie (*Pretty in Pink*).

As will be illustrated in the following movement analyses of screendance texts that include Tom Hanks, it is their display of hegemonic masculinity that enables their dancing to be consumed by a mainstream audience.[5] However, in many of these sequences gender norms are troubled or questioned while traditional norms of masculinity are being represented. In the following sequences centering "everyman" actor Tom Hanks moving across American audiovisual texts, Hanks is able to destabilize ideas of white male dancing by pushing against the expectation of gender norms. But it is only because Hanks's hegemonic masculinity has already been established within American culture that it is "acceptable" for him to push against it in these mainstream American dance representations.

On May 20, 2017, Dwayne "The Rock" Johnson opens his monologue as weekly host of *Saturday Night Live* by discussing rumors of him running for President of the United States in 2020. Standing onstage next to actor Alec Baldwin, who received an Emmy for his recurring controversial impersonation of President Donald Trump for *SNL*, Johnson announces to erupting applause he's "all in." He continues his announcement, stating he has already selected his running mate, one who possesses the following qualities: "He's already very well liked, and like me, he's charming, universally adored by pretty much every human alive." As Baldwin grins and nods, implying that Johnson refers to Baldwin himself, Johnson instead introduces Tom Hanks as his running mate.[6]

Johnson's announcement of his campaign, later admitted a joke, was covered by many major news outlets in America such as *CNN*, *Los Angeles Times*, *USA Today*, and *Business Insider*, to name only a few. Although situated in comedy, Johnson's monologue introducing Hanks alludes to a common impression that Hanks has gradually imparted on the American viewing public, of him being portrayed as the most likable man in Hollywood and perhaps America. This 2017 claim of Hanks's trustworthiness was substantiated by an earlier 2013 *Reader's Digest* article titled "What Is Trust: The 100 Most Trusted People in America." In this text, the data from a poll conducted in collaboration with *Wagner Research* concerning what individual the public considered most trustworthy in America was compiled. The poll revealed Tom Hanks to be considered one of the most trusted men in America at that time.[7]

In this article I will analyze how Hanks's public images may have contributed to this feeling of trustworthiness by the general American public, and how these images helped form the public's shifting images of acceptable masculinity. To that end, I posit Hanks was considered to represent the "everyman American." Largely informed by scholarship from masculinities studies scholar Fred Pfeil, close readings are offered to demonstrate how Tom Hanks's dance sequences helped contribute to a new image of masculinity within American popular culture.[8]

Tom Hanks as Soft-Bodied, Disarming Nice Guy

To aptly situate Hanks's image as a mover over the last forty years in varying media, including film, television, and video, the first order of business is to contextualize Hanks's growing popularity in the 1990s as an example of an acceptable model of masculinity widely consumed by mainstream audiences of American popular culture. As masculinities studies scholar Fred Pfeil argues in his essay "Getting Up There With Tom: The Politics of American 'Nice,'" masculinities studies has dedicated much critical consideration towards "the outwardly hard-bodied, inwardly anguished, rampaging male as incarnated in the star image of Bruce Willis, Arnold Schwarzenegger, Mel Gibson, and/or Sylvester Stallone."[9] However, as Pfeil contends in his central argument, "a quite different version of masculinity has, in the form of the emphatically soft-bodied Tom Hanks, been taking up more and more room on the cultural landscape."[10] The soft-bodied archetype as a conscious resistance towards the beefcake, hard-bodied hypermasculinity that took hold of American popular cinema could be described as that which emblematized the nerdy, insecure, unathletic, awkward but charming underdog that began to rise in the 1980s and 1990s. Michael Kimmel, author of *Manhood in America: A Cultural History*, argues that the "wimp" archetype was born from the emasculation American men suffered via the loss of the Vietnam War at the end of the 1970s: "The wimp, for example, emerged in the early 1980s. Magazine articles and films had predicted that this new man—warm, sensitive, cuddly, and compassionate—would be the new hero of the 1980."[11]

Pfeil's following central question, then, opens possible insights into how Tom Hanks as the everyman might be read:

> And what, finally and not at all simply, are the implications of the construction and promotion of this particular [Hanks] rendition of white masculinity as the increasingly hegemonic alternative and/or complementary version to that of the rampaging "angry white male" victim, for those of us who still care and dare to dream of a world in which both the insidiously covert and brutally explicit coercions and exclusions of race, gender, and class might reasonably be regarded as nightmares of the past?[12]

With Pfeil's question in mind, this chapter seeks to explore what Tom Hanks and his particular brand of "trusting" white masculinity ultimately offers the

White Man Dance trope, and how, more importantly, dance is used as a mechanism to communicate this "alternative" but still hegemonic white masculinity.

Tom Hanks initially grew to popularity when he was cast as Kip Wilson in the short-lived television sitcom series *Bosom Buddies*, which aired on ABC from 1980 to 1982. Kip and his buddy Henry both work as advertising executives in New York City during the day, disguising themselves as women in order to obtain residence at the women-only Susan B. Anthony Hotel at nights and on weekends. The introduction to Tom Hanks via this televisual text is important in establishing the cis white man as an unintimidating antithesis of the hulking male stereotypes of the 1970s, such as Sylvester Stallone and Arnold Schwarzenegger. Not only does the show employ cross-dressing as a dominant theme throughout its run, but it also introduces male stars learning a great deal about presenting and being read, while also ultimately finding discomfort at disguising themselves, as women. Of course, part of the reason the gag works at both creating slippages within Kip and Henry's gender depictions and stabilizing their masculinity at the same time is because the audience never remains with "Buffy" and "Hildegard" for even an entire episode. Additionally, early in the first season, Kip and Henry are offered to the women as the brothers of Buffy and Hildegard, thereby lessening the amount of airtime that we see the women on camera, and offering a way for Kip and Henry to express and receive attraction from the other women in the hotel. Both main characters are posed as middle-management professionals constantly seeking both friendship and romantic relationships with women, depending on what role they perform in the show at the time.[13] As Pfeil argues, the comic engine employed in the cross-dressing performed on *Bosom Buddies*

> is played out in a slapsticky way that suggests quite the opposite of any actual incorporation of conventionally feminine psychological attributes, as in the case of our simultaneously feminized and hypermasculinized rampagers; the laughs are merely about how utterly unconvincing and uncomfortable the two guys are in wigs and women's clothes.[14]

I would also argue Kip and Henry exert their white male privilege in order to take residence from the women who actually deserve it and are disadvantaged in contemporary society; however, at the same time, they are never quite comfortable in the role they have opted to play. It is in the very obvious misperformance of their roles as imposters of cis women—and oftentimes their desire for women they need to convince of their "womanhood"—that their masculinity remains transparent and intact for the contemporary American viewer.

Bosom Buddies' pilot title sequence is unsurprisingly empty of scenes with either Buffy or Hildegard. It appears to be a buddy sitcom, and includes a montage of the two best friends sharing time together in a multitude of ways, all of which express some element of soft, but clear, masculinity, interspersed with comic sequences: Kip, in a dress shirt with the sleeves rolled up and long pants, riding a bicycle next to Henry trying to balance on a unicycle wearing a pink T-shirt and blue shorts that rest on the upper thigh; Kip and Henry running in the grass, clumsily sinking their feet into puddles, revealing a hint of the slapstick nature of the show; Kip and Henry playing basketball on a city court by themselves, Henry wearing a bright short sleeved shirt and long pants, while Kip wears the short shorts, in red, with a gray sweatshirt, Henry performing a victory dance when he scores a goal; Henry running to pay the meter of a parking spot while the two men, shirtless with undefined upper bodies, sun in the spot in pool chairs; Kip and Henry tossing an apple back and forth in front of an NYC brownstone. The opening sequence before the gag of the show is revealed (later on in the series, the opening is switched out for one that describes the premise of the show, using Hanks's voiceover to explain) intimates the dynamics the show will explore: the homoeroticism of the buddy comedy, the "soft-bodied" masculinity, and the light slapstick comedic tropes.

As Kip and Henry decide to crossdress in order to secure residence at the women's hotel, the misperforming is intentional. Both choose wigs remarkably close to their own hairstyle, especially Hanks, who keeps his hair thick and curly. Henry's wig is only slightly wavier and more voluminous than his actual hair. They take turns wearing a version of pink or blue, as well as other pastels. Their voices are not exceedingly changed to complete the disguise, just softened versions of their own. These "misperformances" are intentional so that the audience never loses sight of the men behind the disguise. Since early in the first season one of the men gets discovered in the apartment, the show creates a "new" set of characters—Kip and Henry, as the brothers of Buffy and Hildegard. These men then become the potential love interests for the women in the hotel, so that the audience always maintains a firm hold on the men's relationship within hegemonic masculinity, while, similar to other crossdressing films at the time, like *Tootsie*, we also see the men connect with their emotions and learn how to form friendships with women.

Although dance isn't integrated into the show often throughout its limited run, dance is employed in two specific episodes that address ideas around gender in interesting ways. In Season 1 Episode 7, "Beauty and the Beasts,"[15] Kip and Henry as Buffy and Hildegard agree to join the women in the hotel at a nightclub. Kip has already started to develop an attraction to one of the hotel's residents, Sonny Lumet, a breathy blonde reminiscent of Suzanne Somers's Chrissy Snow from *Three's Company*, a show running concurrently with *Bosom Buddies*. Although neither man is comfortable at the potential that men might want to dance with them in their disguises, Henry becomes comically insulted when they aren't asked to dance. Henry huffily laments, "I know what's going on here, and I don't like it. I know why. Because we're dogs. That's why no one's coming to ask us to dance ... Is it too much to ask for some hunk to buy me a drink or show me a little tenderness?" Kip tries to remind him why it's ridiculous to be insulted: "The clothes are a joke. This is a gag. We're playing 'let's pretend' remember?" Throughout the nightclub scene, Henry is hurt at being refused:

> What's it like on the dance floor? Buffy and I wouldn't know ... Not that we would care to know or would ever need to know at all ... Well, how would you like that! Again, we're rejected because we're not attractive! You think someone might want to consider there's a person in here. A person who has needs, who has feelings, who can give.

In the next scene, Kip swishes his hips around the apartment in his actual body and dress, playing with his nylons. "The point of the whole evening went right by you, didn't it? We're as guilty as any of those guys in the bar. This morning we gave a woman a job not because she had talent, but because she had a good body." Throughout the series Kip and Henry embody a vaudevillian duo, where Kip performs the "straight man," and Henry counters as "the banana man," but in this case Henry also offers a role as the more tender of the two, the more effeminate-coded in that regard. The sequence ends with Henry asking Amy to dance, who he initially sees as undesirable because she doesn't have the ideal body type, isn't blonde, and thus isn't seen as attractive. He then chooses to dance with Amy at the end of the night.

This scene recalls an interview that went viral in 2012, when Dustin Hoffman is interviewed about why he decides to perform the titular role of *Tootsie*, in which actor Michael Dorsey crossdresses as a woman to perform the lead role in a soap opera when he's unable to get cast as a man. *Tootsie* was released in 1982, the final year of *Bosom Buddies*' run, and with a very similar premise, addressing the way that men begin to disguise themselves as women in order to take positions and services from women they can't secure as men. In this interview, Hoffman explains that Murray Schisgal (the screen writer of *Tootsie*) asked him, "how would you be different as a woman?" Hoffman then went to Columbia Pictures and asked them to create a look that would enable him to successfully appear as a woman by any passerby. When Hoffman first saw himself on screen in this new look, he experienced an epiphany:

> When we looked at it on screen, I was shocked that I wasn't more attractive. I said, now you have me looking like a woman, now make me a beautiful woman because I thought I should be beautiful ... I would

want to be as beautiful as possible. They said to me, that's as good as it gets ... It was at that moment that I had an epiphany and I went home and started crying, talking to my wife. I have to make this picture. She said, why? Because I think I'm an interesting woman when I look at myself on screen, and I know if I met myself at a party, I would never talk to that character because she doesn't fulfill physically the demands that women have to have in order to ask them out. I said there's too many interesting women I have not had the experience to know in this life because I have been brainwashed. That was never a comedy for me.[16]

Of course, this confession from Hoffman is complicated in the era of the #Me Too movement, after writer Anna Graham Hunter stated that Hoffman groped her when she was seventeen on the set of *Death of a Salesman*, just three years after *Tootsie*'s release.[17] In both of these mediated moments, it is only through donning the disguise of women in order to take something from women at a time during which women are being given opportunities denied to men that men are able to come to terms with their own misogyny. Even though this sequence doesn't directly center Tom Hanks's movement, it opens ideas around white masculinity and the gendered nature of dance.

In the second season of *Bosom Buddies*, Henry teaches Kip to dance, and the show clearly enacts ideas around race, masculinity, and gender. In Season 2 Episode 3, "The Reunion,"[18] the show flashes back to the 1970s, the night of the senior prom at their high school. Kip (performed by Hanks), dressed in full hippie garb, admits to Henry, who has already dressed in his blue tuxedo, with a pink ruffled shirt, that the reason he plans not to attend the prom is because he doesn't know how to dance. Although Kip resists at first, with a joke playing off the stereotype that white people can't dance—"All rhythm has been bred out of my people"—Henry is able to convince him to learn in the school hallway outside of the auditorium, where the prom is taking place. Henry swishes his hips from side to side, teaching an awkward Kip to swivel his hips to a funk track. Henry's movements are fluid and certain whereas Kip's movements are exaggerated and stiff. Then Henry teaches a disco move to Kip: "Every once in a while, you just point." This is another moment of humor given that we're viewing this scene through a 1980s lens, in which this dance move has already gone out of fashion. As Henry continues to teach the 1970s pointing dance, he says, "Then you got to make these groaning noises, like Barry White," to which Kip responds by impersonating White, "Right on, right on," reinforcing this racialized relationship to dance. They continue speaking in "Barry White," which is playful and not *too* offensive, but still, like most comedy, sliding dangerously close to exploiting African American Vernacular English (AAVE) for appropriative measures. Kip then asks for a "killer move," and Henry, still speaking in "jive," replies, "I got it, baby," suddenly falling to his knees, coming up to one leg, standing in the opposite direction and then doing a quick turn to face the camera, all in rhythm. The live audience cheers. Kip attempts it, and although it's not quite as succinct as Henry's version, his variation maintains a smoothness, and so the lesson remains successful. The song changes to a jazzy instrumental, a slow dance. Kip becomes nervous again, unable to imagine slow dancing. Henry tries to bring Kip into an embrace, who backs up with expected homophobic panic, but Henry calms him down. The two come together, Kip wearing a disgruntled cringe on his face, and Henry places his head on Kip's chest, instructing Kip to "just sway." They begin to get closer and closer, gaining comfort in their dance. When a young woman in a pink dress comes to find Henry, Kip says nonchalantly, "Oh yes, I'm dancing with him," no longer self-conscious about the homophobic undertones of dancing with his friend, which, of course, becomes a comedic move as well. The woman makes an off-handed joke about her mother telling her not to trust a man who raises livestock, bringing the gendered attitudes around men and dancing full circle.

Although short-lived, *Bosom Buddies* addressed the shifting positions of men during this time in America with regards to gender relations. For example, because cis white men were no longer unequivocally known to be the sole providers in the household, they suddenly found themselves in a position where they were pressed to contend with this liminal position of being both financial equals and romantic partners with cis white women. White men in America were no longer able to feel secure in their position as the domineering providing lover; instead, they had to negotiate this liminal space of being both friend and lover simultaneously. Although the characters in *Bosom Buddies* are interested in being convincing as women, the men "misperform" the disguise for comic effect, their clumsy performance thus preventing not just the characters, but also the actors from being seen as homoerotic or transgender. Although celebrity culture and fandom was certainly not as prevalent in *Bosom Buddies*' 1980s as today given the intimate access due to the power and mobility of online spaces, the viewership understanding that Hanks and Peter Scolari (as Henry) were cishet men outside of this televisual text impacts the comedic comfort of the presentations. Further, neither Hanks nor Scolari were considered leading men at the time. Again, they were the emerging soft-bodied archetypes that pushed against the hypermasculine hard-bodied types: nerdy, unathletic, self-conscious, and awkward. In other words, their performance is not just successful but also Hanks and Scolari are cast because it is "convincing" that these men could embody both femininity and soft-bodied masculinity. It is also these same traits, that when Kip and Henry are alone in their apartment together, that get emphasized in their "bromantic" homosocial connection, not unlike a dynamic seen in the female-led *Laverne & Shirley*, which ran on the same network, ABC, from 1976 to 1983.

However, at the heart of *Bosom Buddies* and Hanks's embodiment of feminine identity lies an attempt to depict men struggling to navigate all of these new gender shifts indeed happening in America during the 1980s and early 1990s. Starting with Hanks's early role in this television show, an audience member can quite literally track an evolution of gender roles in American society and, in particular, American men's liminal space within traditional modes of masculinity, through Tom Hanks's expansive forty-year career. This early stage of liminality,[19] represented in Hanks as a not fully formed traditional masculine man, continues to shape Hanks's next performance in the film featuring his popular and oft-revisited dance, *Big*.

Tom Hanks as the Favorite Manchild

Over the past few years, many privately and publicly recorded moments of Tom Hanks dancing have reached viral status—such as when Justin Bieber shared a short iPhone video of Tom Hanks dressed as a rabbi dancing to Montell Jordan's 1990s R&B hit "This is How We Do It";[20] when Hanks's son Chet posted a video requesting his father perform the Dab, a dance move originating from Atlanta's hip hop scene;[21] or perhaps the most bizarre occurrence, when TMZ shared Hanks's appearance on a Spanish Univision show, during which Hanks danced goofily next to a weather woman, clearly unable to speak or understand the Spanish-speaking hosts.[22] Further, in response to Ellen DeGeneres's interview question on *The Ellen DeGeneres Show* regarding his apparent enjoyment of dance in various occasions on- and off-camera, Hanks offers the following disclaimer: "Understand, understand. I have a recessive dance gene, quite frankly because of my complexion. I like to say I'm a white boy from Oakland. But I *am* from Oakland, you see, so, we can, I believe you know what we can do."[23] This quote acknowledges the impression that white men are not expected to be able to dance (thus, his "recessive gene") while also inserting Hanks within a regional ("I am from Oakland") context of Black identity.[24] In other words, he asserts himself within two polar associations with race and dance, that of white masculinity and dance and that of Blackness and dance. Hanks places himself in yet another liminal space, that of gendered and cultural expectations of dance. This space is made evident when analyzing his first virally beloved dance, the rap-dance in the 1988 film *Big*.

Before conducting an analysis of *Big*, I would like to bring the reader's attention to the thirteenth chapter of the First Epistle in the New Testament of the Christian Bible, where Paul the Apostle warns his readers via a phrase often associated with dance: "When I was a little child, I talked and felt and thought like a little child. Now that I am a man I have finished with childish things." This biblical sentiment underscoring much of American culture enables an interesting reading of how an audience might relate to Hanks's performance in *Big*: Tom Hanks portrays a dancing boy-in-a-man's body, placing his character in yet another liminal space between the behaviors Americans then associated with either child or man. However, the fact that the audience not only felt comfortable with Hanks as a grown man performing a child's role once again shows the shifting relationship the American public was developing between their notion of traditional values and those that emerged in the 1980s.

The origins of the rap-dance Tom Hanks performs on *Big*, which he has been asked to perform on various talk shows over the past few years, is known most frequently as "Down Down Baby" and has become part of American popular culture lore. I was not able to find an established origin for the rap-dance; however, *Wikipedia* defines "Down Down Baby" as:

> a clapping game played by children in English-speaking countries ... Modified versions of the song have appeared in Little Anthony and the Imperials's "Shimmy Shimmy Ko-Ko Bop," Nelly's "Country Grammar," Simian Mobile Disco's "Hotdog," The Drums' "Let's Go Surfing," Carter USM's "Turn On, Tune In, And Switch Off," Bella Thorne and Zendaya's "Conscious Love," and the film *Big*.

Additionally, the *Wikipedia* entry includes lyrics first shown on a 1980s segment of the United States version of the children's television show *Sesame Street*.[25]

On October 25, 2016, Asian YouTube stars representing Wong Fu Productions remembered this twenty-nine second performance from *Big* so vividly they begged Hanks to perform it (along with Ron Howard dancing in the background) when they were given the opportunity to interview Hanks, accompanying him in the performance with glee.[26] Further, Hanks has informed audiences he inserted the rap into *Big* after watching his young son perform a version he learned at summer camp during the time of the film's shooting.[27] This rap-dance having come from Hanks's own child's game at a children's summer camp further demonstrates the liminality of this foundational dance in Hanks's early career. What is fascinating then is that this child's dance became one of the most frequently performed sequences from Tom Hanks's forty-year acting career.[28]

The film *Big* centers Hanks's character Josh Baskin, a thirteen-year-old who wishes on the arcade game Voltar to be big, after being too short for a carnival ride. It is an impulsive decision, made in the fear of being emasculated and embarrassed in front of his older female crush. Much to his horror, Josh wakes the next morning to find himself in the body of a man in his thirties. Like his previous character, *Bosom Buddy*'s Kip Wilson, Tom Hanks's Josh must also live in disguise, this time as a boy/man rather than as a man/woman. Again, just like in *Bosom Buddies,* only his best friend will ultimately know his secret. Desperate and afraid of his new circumstances, Josh sneaks into the gym where Billy is returning basketball equipment, a punishment for performing so badly during practice. It is here that he performs the rap-dance only the two of them know, a symbol of their intimate friendship, in hopes Billy will be convinced it is indeed Josh he sees before him in a transformed physiognomy.[29]

"Down Down Baby": An Analysis

The dance accompanying this twenty-nine-second rap sequence is composed mostly of simple pedestrian gestures and movements, many of which mime the words. The lyrics to this particular version of the rap are as follows:

> The space goes down, down baby. Down, down the roller coaster. Sweet, sweet baby. Sweet, sweet, don't let me go. Shimmy, shimmy, cocoa pop. Shimmy, shimmy, rock. Shimmy, shimmy, cocoa pop. Shimmy, shimmy, rock. I met a girlfriend—a triscuit. She said, a triscuit—a biscuit. Ice cream, soda pop, vanilla on the top. Ooh, Shelly's out, walking down the street, ten times a week. I read it. I said it. I stole my mama's credit. I'm cool. I'm hot. Sock me in the stomach three more times.[30]

From the jump, the lyrics themselves establish the boys' heterosexual identity and affirm their masculine positions. The song involves the recognizable markers of cishet teen masculinity: heterosexual partnering ("Sweet, sweet baby. Sweet, sweet, don't let me go"; "I met a girlfriend"; "Ooh, Shelly's out, walking down the street"), rebellion from one's mother ("I stole my mama's credit"), an affirmation of coolness or popularity ("I'm cool. I'm hot"), and an affinity for playful violence as connection between boys ("Sock me in the stomach three more times").[31] These lyrics, combined with the fact they are rapped (another signification of coolness, albeit appropriative of Blackness), signify an affirmation of white masculinity.

At the beginning of the dance, the camera remains on Billy in a medium close-up shot. With the back and side of his hair wet with sweat, his lips partly open, Billy maintains a scared facial expression as we hear Josh loudly rapping in the background. As Josh performs the first chorus to the rap, the camera switches back to Josh, framed so the viewer cannot see Josh's legs, thus allowing the viewer to only see Josh's upper body shimmy while he extends alternating arms and slightly rotates his upper body. Josh performs the rap with growing desperation as witnessed by his stressed facial expression, his voice growing in speed and intensity, and his breath becoming shorter and more audible.

As Josh continues performing the rap while walking up the few stairs between the two characters, he gradually lessens the distance between the two of them. It becomes clear Billy gradually begins to believe Josh based solely on his recognition that this dance is one only the two of them know. The camera focuses again on the tense muscles in Billy's face, which steadily relax as he begins to quietly sing the words under his breath while Josh continues his determined performance. When the camera shifts back to Josh rapping the words "a triscuit," Josh swings his arms faster, ending with a snap of his fingers and pointing in Billy's direction. His body does not twist but remains facing Billy who is now out of the audience's view. Most of the final visual phrases begin with Josh performing the gestures and the words and finish with Billy who finally joins him. By constructing a cinematic visual phrase beginning with Josh and seamlessly ending with Billy, the film illustrates how trust has been re-established between the two characters.

Josh, within his new transformed role as a grown man, has no job, no home ("big" Josh is forced to vacate his home when his mother believes him to be the "little" Josh's predator), and no money. Thus, Josh needs an ally in his newfound predicament, so it is of utmost importance he finds someone to believe in his transformation, a belief reached through the performance of shared childhood dance. Bringing the audience into perhaps their own associated memories of childhood, in which the importance of shared experiences creates a bond between children, allows the viewers to also trust the bond between Josh and Billy as the dance is performed. It is not only Billy who needs to be convinced of Josh; the audience, too, must be convinced that this man is still a boy. Josh performs the dance to convince Billy he is indeed his best friend, and Tom Hanks performs the dance to convince the audience he is believable as a thirteen-year-old boy.

In order to portray the emotional bond between the two boys, the camera largely focuses on the upper body and face for both characters throughout the scene. The emotive power enacted between the boys is highlighted in the intensity of their movements reflected in their faces, arms, and upper bodies. Further, Josh and Billy's postures are loosely held; their arms when extended retain a pedestrian amount of slack; and their fists when closed never fold into a tight or angry expression. By not focusing on the legs, hips, or the display of skillful, intricate footwork, a new technique for filming dance is thus employed that further solidifies a new image of the white male dancer as a non-dancer, one differing from the "beefcake" yet "professional" dancers of the late 1970s and early 1980s, like *Dirty Dancing*'s Patrick Swayze and *Grease*'s John Travolta, and from screendance and musical's long history of filming codified dance movement. The emphasis is displaced from the skilled technique of the trained dancer to the emotional intensity of the everyman dancer.

Instead of depicting the fear of two boys physically bonded, the bond is framed as a distanced portrayal of sensitivity and sweetness, once again establishing the image of the new 1980s man. *Big* depicts a new kind of intimacy through the genre of playful dancing. However, in this case, it is the image of two boys dancing on their own but in unison. The trend of the white male dancing as an individual is therefore established in *Big*. The mechanism of unison provides the viewer with a language that is only shared between the two "boys"; however, at the same time it also enables the viewer to see the different quality of the same movement performed by a young boy as well as a boy in the body of a grown man. The audience can therefore emotionally identify with the isolation that Josh feels and the platonic bond the dance establishes. Later in the film, a similar connection, and disjunction, is shown between adult Josh Baskin and his superior MacMillan when they dance-play "Chopsticks" and "Heart and Soul" on a large floor keyboard in the gigantic toy store F.A.O. Schwarz. It is yet another example whereby the film establishes a connection between two male figures through unison movement as it intersects with the liminal space between youth and adulthood. In this case, we see the distance between our secret knowledge of Josh's inside child and the access this child affords his supervisor, normally treated as unliked and inaccessible within his position of power.

Unlike the "Down Down Baby" sequence, the dance on the giant floor piano in the toy store seeks to connect two men through a universal experience of childhood. MacMillan, the owner of the toy company where Josh newly works, walks with Josh through their toy store, discussing ideas around toys. They come across an enormous piano on the floor. MacMillan is quick to dismiss it, but soon Josh inspires him to join in on a duet of "Heart and Soul." It's MacMillan who then suggests that they finish with "Chopsticks." By the time they perform the second song, they have an audience of onlookers, mostly children and their parents, who vigorously applaud. MacMillan is much older and although his movements start out more stiffly than Josh's, he also has a more fluid expression of the movements, using more of his upper body and hips to perform the notes than Josh, whose upper body is almost stoically still, with clean movements in his legs and feet. MacMillan, probably in his sixties, looks towards Josh at varying intervals for assurance and with excitement. Josh is so focused on the task that he rarely looks over, which continues the embodiment of Josh as a child in a grown man's body. We see, yet again, a duet being performed between two men that merges into unison, but in this case, Josh is seen as the younger of the two and is able to lead an older man into a dance of childhood.

A few scenes later in the film, director Penny Marshall uses movement between the two men in a very different way—one that empathizes competition and conflict, rather than connection, but still connected to ideas of masculinity and boyhood. Josh agrees to play racquetball with Paul, one of his new co-workers. Josh's agreement to this invitation is motivated by a desire to assimilate to his new adult life but also by his youthful innocence, as he's unaware Paul only seeks to connect with him out of a growing resentment for moving up the company chain so fast, with so little experience, as well as noticing that his previous girlfriend Susan has grown curious about the new employee. During the game, Josh calls Paul out on failing to abide by the rules that Paul had established at the beginning of the game. A sore loser, Paul refuses to concede, and denies it. We see young Josh's innocent face within this adult sequence as Josh calls Paul a cheater, which leads to a physical altercation between the two men. The two men run back and forth across the court as Paul, who in this ironic move on the part of Marshall, is seen as "the child" in this case, attempting to grab the ball from an unwilling Josh. Josh spirals his head down and away from Paul as he advances towards him, until Paul grabs his hoodie. Josh breaks away as he continues to alternate which hand holds the ball. Paul grabs the back of Josh's sweatshirt which results in a choreographic move as Josh spins around the axis of the sweatshirt that Paul holds, until Josh lies on the ground, grabbing the ball at the last minute.

This reigning image of Tom Hanks as not only the manchild but also as America's Hollywood everyman emerged in large part due to the popularity of *Big*, for which Hanks received his first Academy Award nomination. This chapter will end its examination of Hanks as an early pioneer of the White Man Dance trope, initiating the impetus of a new American masculinity, one sensitive, vulnerable, and unafraid to show emotion, even if that emotion involves a bond between two males, with an analysis of his performance in the music video for the female pop singer Carly Rae Jepsen's single "I Really Like You." To close, I will further explore this new liminal masculinity through Hanks's dance performance in this music video released thirty years later at the end of his ongoing acting career.

The Power of the Maybe: Carly Rae, Tom Hanks, and Bubblegum Pop

> *When Tom Hanks wakes up, it is still dark outside. The wall-to-wall windows in his bedroom reveal the bright cityscape of Manhattan. Hanks wakes up in song. It isn't his manly voice we hear, however, but the voice of bubble-gum pop singer Carly Rae Jepsen, whose hit "Call Me Maybe" took the world by storm. Hanks sings as he washes his face and brushes his teeth; walks the streets and greets his fans with high fives, autographs, and selfies; and makes calls on his cellphone in a cab and texts playful emojis back and forth with Jepsen. He continues to sing as he exits the cab and briefly meets with a director for the music video he's going to perform in with Jepsen. Hanks finishes the song with Jepsen in tow as they perform a flash mob synchronized dance joined by pop stars like Justin Bieber and a team of dancers behind them. As Hanks and Jepsen sing with the others, they chassé and shimmy down a cobblestoned path until the camera fades out.* [32]

Blog and online media network *Gawker*'s Emma Carmichael in "Have You Heard Call Me Maybe, the New Perfect Pop Song", regarding Canadian singer Jepsen's explosive hit song in 2012, "Call Me Maybe," declares:

> She's recorded a flawless pop song … We're fast approaching the phase in which we will be virtually incapable of escaping the song and its strident disco strings and that horribly catchy hook. Resistance is futile, people: As much as I want to hate this song, I have listened to it seven times today (maybe more like 10 times).[33]

The endlessly catchy pop melody of 2012 also spawned countless music video parodies and dance crew videos, including one performed by Marines stationed in Afghanistan that was revisited by actor Matt McGorry using the song "Hollaback Girl" during a flashback for his character on the Netflix series *Orange is the New Black*. For the music video for Jepsen's second hit single, "I Really Like You," she enlisted Tom Hanks to lip sync and dance, offering a gendered extension of Hanks's purposefully unsuccessful burlesquing of feminine impersonation introduced in his debut role in *Bosom Buddies*.

Unlike the dance sequence in *Big*, the music video for "I Really Like You" relies on the American public's forty-year familiarity of Hanks as a celebrity, combined with the popularity of Jepsen's previous pop sensation "Call Me Maybe." An important aspect of the quality of Hanks's lip sync, which contributes to the masculinity-affirming image of Hanks, is that, unlike many actors who perform cross-gendered lip sync in various popular cultural television moments,[34] Hanks does not burlesque femininity or perform a drag-inspired performance in his lip sync of this song. He also does not perform this lip sync in a camp aesthetic often associated with drag.[35] In this way Hanks can be viewed as troubling the signification of gender portrayal by underplaying the lip sync performance of Jepsen's bubbly high-pitched voice. The comic thrust of Jepsen's music video can be read to depend in part upon the comically stark contrast between Hanks's older, well established, masculine image and the high-pitched feminine characteristics associated with Jepsen's singing voice.

This disparity between the male/female representation in the video also contrasts Hanks's cross-dressing performance on the previously discussed *Bosom Buddies*, in which Hanks "misperformed" his character's imperfectly executed impersonation of female gender expression for comic effect. Additionally, the dance's simplistic construction aids in illustrating Hanks's seemingly organic and naturally masculine way of moving rather than overly articulated as within the burlesque mode. The video culminates in an image also relying upon Hanks's early work with *Big*, as the dance embodies a kind of childlike abandon, a dance party in the street among frolicking friends.

The fact that Justin Bieber, known for his set choreography in music videos and live performances, joins him at the end of the video, validates Hanks's accepted membership in American popular cultural dancing by white men despite the fact the dance itself is depicted as something the average person might do with their own friends rather than as a carefully choreographed performance such as one Bieber might perform on stage during a musical concert or a music video. However, what I find most significant in Hanks's work within this trope of white men dancing is his embodiment of white masculinity while working within these gender-troubling performances to question what it means exactly to be a white male moving in American popular culture.

In all of the moments analyzed in this chapter, Hanks is able to perform a more complicated relationship to masculinity because he not only remains in his own clear body, but in other bodies as well—in both *Bosom Buddies* and Jepsen's video he performs within the comic misperformance of a woman, and in *Big* we see him through the guise of both boy and man. Although the movements are not particularly difficult to execute, Hanks depicts them as natural and sincere, performing the movements from both sequences with a clear sense of rhythm and physical coordination. Not only that, Hanks also performs the moves confidently with apparent enjoyment. Because Hanks's masculinity is always already affirmed, the dance and bodies through which he performs them does not upset the balance. More to the point, there remains a masculine quality in the execution, and in all instances, Hanks is depicted as an everyman rather than a professionally trained dancer. Occupying a slightly more masculine version of what masculinities studies scholar Michael Kimmel refers to as the "Great American Wimp," an archetype of the "soft, cuddly man" ridiculed throughout the 1980s as American men suffered from emasculating defeat via the Vietnam War, Hanks appears nonthreatening and the dances he performs contribute to that image.[36] Hanks complicates the gender structures embedded within these texts via the liminality of gender performance in differing ways as discussed throughout this essay.

Notes

1 The Killers, "Where the White Boys Dance," track 7 on *Sawdust*, Island, 2006, streaming.
2 Many AIDS scholars have addressed this relationship; however, I find the episode titled "The Fight Against AIDS" in the documentary miniseries *The Eighties*, which premiered on CNN on June 9, 2016, to offer the most cogent depiction of the ways in which the AIDS epidemic caused widespread fear of homosexuality.
3 David L. Moody, *The Complexity and Progression of Black Representation in Film and Television* (Blue Ridge Summit: Lexington Books, 2016), 48.
4 E. Patrick Johnson, *Appropriating Blackness: Performance and the Politics of Authenticity* (Durham: Duke University Press, 2003), 66.

5 For a more thorough discussion of the difference between mainstream, indie, and niche audiences, particularly in film, please see Carrie Szabo's thesis, "Independent, Mainstream and In Between: How and Why Indie Films Have Become Their Own Genre" (2010), http://digitalcommons.pace.edu/cgi/viewcontent.cgi?article=1101&context=honorscollege_theses.
6 *Saturday Night Live*, season 42, episode 21, "Dwayne Johnson, Katy Perry," directed by Michael Lorne, aired May 20, 2017, on NBC, http://www.nbc.com/saturday-night-live/season-42/episode/21-dwayne-johnsonwith-katy-perry-289342.
7 Courtenay Smith, "Reader's Digest Trust Poll: The 100 Most Trusted People in America," *Reader's Digest*, May 7, 2017, https://www.rd.com/culture/readers-digest-trust-poll-the-100-most-trusted-peoplein-america/.
8 It's worth noting that as Tom Hanks ages, the public consumption of him changes as well. Tom Hanks and his wife, actor Rita Wilson, were two of the first celebrities to publicly announce that they tested positive for COVID-19. The American public, largely through social media, responded dramatically at the time, due to his "everyman" image, with hundreds of tweets that expressed the sentiment: "If Tom Hanks dies of COVID, the world is over!" At the same time, many people of color expressed anger at the privileged position Hanks had of receiving care while unable to fly back to the United States from Australia, as many people of color were prevented from the same level of care. As the American public contends with the growing untenability of life in the United States, figures like Tom Hanks will see what made them so likeable turn against their squeaky-clean image.
9 Fred Pfeil, "Getting Up There With Tom: The Politics of American 'Nice,'" in *Masculinity Studies & Feminist Theory: New Directions*. ed. Judith Kegan Gardiner (New York: Columbia University Press, 2002), 119–40.
10 Pfeil, "Getting Up There With Tom," 120.
11 Michael Kimmel, *Manhood in America: A Cultural History* (Oxford: Oxford University Press, 2011), 212.
12 Pfeil, "Getting Up There With Tom," 120.
13 It could be argued *Bosom Buddies* emerged from second-wave feminism during the late 1960s and 1970s. Largely provoked by Betty Friedan's 1963 text *The Feminine Mystique*, second-wave feminism was concerned with issues such as equal pay for women in the workplace, reproductive rights, sexuality, and custody and divorce rights. In terms of *Bosom Buddies*, white men are no longer the only bodies with recognizable "rights" as Kip and Henry must disguise themselves in order to gain residence in a hotel reserved for women. Additionally, their superior is also a woman, further promoting the new gender negotiations of the early 1980s white American male.
14 Pfeil, "Getting Up There With Tom," 121.
15 *Bosom Buddies*, "Beauty and the Beasts," Dailymotion, 25:02, January 15, 1981, https://www.dailymotion.com/video/x5v27gi.
16 Kurt Schlosser, "Dustin Hoffman's tearful 'Tootsie' interview about women goes viral," *Today*, July 9, 2013, https://www.today.com/popculture/dustin-hoffmans-tearful-tootsie-interview-about-women-goes-viral-6c10578440.
17 Benjamin Lee, "Dustin Hoffman accused of sexual harassment against 17-year-old," *The Guardian*, November 1, 2017, https://www.theguardian.com/film/2017/nov/01/dustin-hoffman-accused-of-sexual-harassment-against-17-year-old.
18 *Bosom Buddies*, "Reunion," Dailymotion, 25:11, October 22, 1981, https://www.dailymotion.com/video/x5v27hf.
19 First coined by folklorist Arnold van Gennep in the twentieth century, the term "liminality" originally signified a transitional stage in a participant's rite of passage but is now more popularly used to describe an individual's ambiguous state in the process of transformation. A more in-depth discussion of the term can be

found in Victor Turner's *The Ritual Process: Structure and Anti-Structure*, first published in 1966.
20 JBieberDay, "justinbieber: Haha Tom Hanks singing 'This Is How we do it' dressed like a Rabbi lol #thatdancetho," July 7, 2014, video, 0:14, https://www.youtube.com/watch?v=hyp_oBjfNLw.
21 Darnellkstewart0312, "Tom Hanks Does The Dab Dance," December 6, 2015, video, 0.07, https://www.dailymotion.com/video/x3s5udf.
22 ABC News, "Tom Hanks dio el tiempo con Chiqui," June 23, 2011, video, 0:42, https://www.youtube.com/watch?v=KTStOxAjtzg.
23 The Ellen DeGeneres Show, "Tom Hanks Brings the Funk," May 24, 2011, video, 2:32, https://www.youtube.com/watch?v=MzsBOER0gt0.
24 Oakland, California, has had a long and established Black community, which can be traced back to 1869, when it became the western terminus of the Transcontinental Railroad, which brought many Black Americans to Oakland for employment. By the 1980s, Black American residents outnumbered white residents. For more information, please see Angela Rowen's "Black Oakland's Story": https://oaklandherenow.com/blackoakland.
25 "Down Down Baby," *Wikipedia*, accessed July 1, 2022, https://en.wikipedia.org/wiki/Down_Down_Baby.
26 Ben Kaye, "Tom Hanks does the Big rap while Ron Howard dances in the background – watch," Consequence of Sound, October 25, 2016, https://consequence.net/2016/10/tom-hanks-does-the-big-rap-while-ron-howard-dances-in-the-background-watch/.
27 Matt Ralph, "Tom Hanks' Son Learned 'Shimmy Shimmy Cocoa Pop' Song At Summer Camp," Summer Camp Culture, October 16, 2016, http://www.summercampculture.com/tom-hanks-son-learned-shimmy-cocoa-popsong-at-summer-camp/.
28 BBC, "Tom Hanks does the 'Big' rap – Friday Night with Jonathan Ross – BBC One," May 8, 2009, video, 1:58, https://www.youtube.com/watch?v=p9z2hJwJuqg.
29 *Big*, directed by Penny Marshall (1988; Los Angeles, CA: 20th Century Fox, 2001), DVD.
30 *Big*.
31 *Big*.
32 Carly Rae Jepsen, "I Really Like You," March 6, 2015, video, 3:28, https://www.youtube.com/watch?v=qV5lzRHrGeg.
33 Emma Carmichael, "Have You Heard Call Me Maybe, the New Perfect Pop Song?," *Gawker*, March 9, 2012, http://gawker.com/5891935/have-you-heard-call-me-maybe-the-new-perfect-popsong.
34 See various lip sync battles performed by Jimmy Fallon and his invited guests on *The Tonight Show Starring Jimmy Fallon* (2014–18) as well as the cable television show these battles inspired, "Lip Sync Battle," which previously aired on the network largely targeting male viewers, Spike, and has since been moved to The Paramount Network (2015–18).
35 See Susan Sontag's essay "Notes on Camp," included in the collection of essays titled *Against Interpretation*, originally published in 1964.
36 Kimmel, *Manhood in America*, 212–13.

Bibliography

ABC News. "Tom Hanks dio el tiempo con Chiqui." June 23, 2011. Video, 0:42. https://www.youtube.com/watch?v=KTStOxAjtzg.
BBC. "Tom Hanks does the 'Big' rap – Friday Night with Jonathan Ross – BBC One." May 8, 2009. Video, 1:58. https://www.youtube.com/watch?v=p9z2hJwJuqg.

Bosom Buddies. "Beauty and the Beasts." Dailymotion, 25:02. January 15, 1981. https://www.dailymotion.com/video/x5v27gi.
Bosom Buddies. "Reunion." Dailymotion, 25:11. October 22, 1981. https://www.dailymotion.com/video/x5v27hf.
Carmichael, Emma. "Have You Heard Call Me Maybe, the New Perfect Pop Song?" *Gawker*, March 9, 2012. http://gawker.com/5891935/have-you-heard-call-me-maybe-the-new-perfect-popsong.
Darnellkstewart0312. "Tom Hanks Does The Dab Dance." December 6, 2015. Video, 0.07. https://www.dailymotion.com/video/x3s5udf.
"*Down Down Baby*," Wikipedia. Accessed July 1, 2022. https://en.wikipedia.org/wiki/Down_Down_Baby.
JBieberDay. "justinbieber: Haha Tom Hanks singing 'This Is How we do it' dressed like a Rabbi lol #thatdancetho," July 7, 2014, video, 0:14, https://www.youtube.com/watch?v=hyp_oBjfNLw.
Jepsen, Carly Rae. "I Really Like You," March 6, 2015, music video, 3:28, https://www.youtube.com/watch?v=qV5lzRHrGeg.
Johnson, E. Patrick. *Appropriating Blackness: Performance and the Politics of Authenticity*Durham: Duke University Press, 2003.
Kaye, Ben. "Tom Hanks does the Big rap while Ron Howard dances in the background – watch." Consequence of Sound, October 25, 2016. https://consequence.net/2016/10/tom-hanks-does-the-big-rap-while-ron-howard-dances-in-the-background-watch/.
Kimmel, Michael. *Manhood in America: A Cultural History*. London: Oxford University Press, 2012.
Lee, Benjamin. "Dustin Hoffman accused of sexual harassment against 17-year-old." *The Guardian*, November 1, 2017, https://www.theguardian.com/film/2017/nov/01/dustin-hoffman-accused-of-sexual-harassment-against-17-year-old#:~:text=Dustin%20Hoffman%20has%20been%20accused,inappropriately%20about%20sex%20with%20her.
Marshall, Penny, dir. *Big*. 1988; Los Angeles, CA: 20th Century Fox, 2001. DVD.
Michaels, Lorne, dir. *Saturday Night Live*. Season 42, episode 21, "Dwayne Johnson, Katy Perry." Aired May 20, 2017, on NBC. http://www.nbc.com/saturday-night-live/season-42/episode/21-dwayne-johnsonwith-katy-perry-289342.
Moody, David L. *The Complexity and Progression of Black Representation in Film and Television*. Blue Ridge Summit: Lexington Books, 2016.
Pfeil, Fred. "Getting Up There With Tom: The Politics of American 'Nice.'" In *Masculinity Studies & Feminist Theory: New Directions*, edited by Judith Kegan Gardiner, 119–140. New York: Columbia University Press, 2002.
Ralph, Matt. "Tom Hanks' Son Learned 'Shimmy Shimmy Cocoa Pop' Song At Summer Camp." Summer Camp Culture, October 16, 2016, http://www.summercampculture.com/tom-hanks-son-learned-shimmy-cocoa-popsong-at-summer-camp/.
Schlosser, Kurt. "Dustin Hoffman's tearful 'Tootsie' interview about women goes viral." *Today*, July 9, 2013, https://www.today.com/popculture/dustin-hoffmans-tearful-tootsie-interview-about-women-goes-viral-6c10578440.
Smith, Courtenay. "Reader's Digest Trust Poll: The 100 Most Trusted People in America." *Reader's Digest*, May 7, 2017, https://www.rd.com/culture/readers-digest-trust-poll-the-100-most-trusted-peoplein-america/.
The Ellen DeGeneres Show. "Tom Hanks Brings the Funk," May 24, 2011, video, 2:32, https://www.youtube.com/watch?v=MzsBOER0gt0.

12

TRACES, MEMORIES, AND REDISCOVERED GESTURES

A Creative Practice of Archiving and Sensitive Writing

Camille Auburtin

Translated by Cath Marceau

From the beginning of my documentary film project *Les Robes Papillons* (2020),[1] I choose not to position Alzheimer's at the center of this project. In fact, the disease is only a part of my grandmother's current circumstances, just as much as the century of history that this film takes us through. The film also incorporates different choreographic movements, from classical to contemporary, including modern dance and neoclassical ballet. It raises awareness about the evolution of bodies in dance and the journey of a woman, an artist in the fifties, then teacher, mother, and grandmother, with a life punctuated by compromises and unspoken sacrifices. At the project's origin, my questions are the following: How did two women, from different generations, successfully bond so strongly through dance? How did the second woman fashion herself in relation to the life and education of the other?

A History of Women

From my early childhood, I developed a bond with my grandmother Mimi, a choreographic artist and the builder of a family of dancers from which I am a direct heir. Mimi began her career at a very young age right after World War II. In 1946, she first danced at the Opéra-Comique National Theatre in Paris, before she worked at the Monte-Carlo Ballet, where classical dance was established in 1909 with Diaghilev's Ballets Russes, from 1947 to 1951.[2] She danced there for ten years with the greatest choreographers and ballet masters of her time: Nijinska (Nijinsky's sister), Balanchine, Massine, Dolin, Lichine, Skibine, and, of course, her mentor Serge Lifar. With a great deal of self-mockery, she nicknames herself the "*ballerina* of a bygone era" and says she belongs to the "old kneecaps club"! She is passionate about the evolution of bodies and the research on movement. When she became a teacher, for nearly forty years, she developed a resolute pedagogical approach inspired by contemporary choreographic practices. "Every human being has a dancer in themself," said Rudolf Laban.[3] For Mimi, students, children, have this dance in them. She favors individual relationships as the guiding principle of her pedagogical approach: "looking, feeling, listening, sensing," she would say! Her teaching, as well as her great and endearing commitment, has left an indelible imprint in her students' memory. She teaches many generations of students, many of whom are professional dancers nowadays. But beyond the bodies she trains, the technique she transmits, and the dancing she teaches, I interrogate the entirety of her legacy, activated and reactivated by various testimonials from her former students that I collected to make Les Robes Papillons.

As a child, I wanted to learn how to dance. Mimi naturally became my teacher. When I walked through the doors of the studio to take her lessons, I was a student amongst the others; she was "Madame Auburtin" for me as well. In private, even though the barriers fall to give way to intimacy, dancing is always there, and we continue dreaming of it together. She, little by little, became my coach, my confidante, a kind of model and heroine. I learned classical dance with her, between the pink studio of her private school and those she occupied at the Conservatoire National de Région de Metz. Later, it was also her who recommended the Rencontres Internationales de Danse Contemporaine (RIDC) Institute[4] in Paris to me, where I trained in contemporary dance, with her friend Françoise Dupuy (who passed away in 2022)[5] and the pedagogical team of her famous dance school. I completed a professional program there between 1995 and 1997.

Before me, Mimi felt this understanding and closeness through dance with her daughter Marjorie. Marjorie was also a professional dancer in many international companies and theaters, following which, like Mimi, she taught dance at the National Conservatory of Music and Dance in Strasbourg, France. The privilege of this understanding was, however, not reserved for our family. *Les Robes Papillons* not only evokes family memories, but also those linked to another family, that of dance. Throughout her entire life, Mimi cultivated a humanity, a particular and generous attention for each student. As a matter of fact, they all consider her as their "dance mom."

Genesis of a Gaze

I, too, am marked by her choreographic and pedagogical imprint. Between 1998 and 2000, interested in transmission, I enrolled in the State Diploma of Contemporary Dance program at the Pôle d'Enseignement Supérieur de

Musique et de Danse (PESMD) Bordeaux Aquitaine. I was not planning on becoming a dance teacher, but this training provided me with inspiring pedagogical tools. I appropriated them later by intersecting other practices with dance. Indeed, I am, ever since my adolescence, torn between dance and cinema, dancing and making films. In parallel to my dance training, and throughout my initial training, I pursued film studies. Through these studies, I notably discovered experimental cinema, video art, cinematographic forms at the intersection of visual arts, dance, and poetry, as well as, through a module on the anthropology of the body, a first approach to documentary cinema from Jean Rouch's ciné-trance.

I am interested in the representation of movement and bodies on screen, in the spaces they occupy, but also in choreographic composition through editing. For several years, I learned about the theory and analysis of the image, while exploring and exploiting it using movement, with my body, my camera, and my editing software. From 2009, living in Bordeaux, I made numerous filmic objects about dance, practice workshops, and mediation tools. Coming from a choreographic background, I am first interested in the camera in motion, in the physicality of the hand-held camera. I experimented with the framing of images, shot scale, static and dynamic shots, and I looked for what could connect me to the qualities of movements or motions in space, link me to the circulation of movement in the body, find the right distance between my body and those of the dancers to feel and sense the dance according to choreographic universes and images. It the end, it is by living the dance through the lens, then by composing choreographic writings through editing, that I gradually found the form of my own expression in dance.

The Memory of Movement in the Body

Following her retirement and the death of her husband, my grandfather Pierre Auburtin, a dancer as well, Mimi's health deteriorated. In 2012, she was officially diagnosed with Alzheimer's, which will, little by little, get the better of her autonomy. From then on, I came to see her in Alsace, and I wanted to stimulate her memory during each of my visits. I sought to slow down the process that is underway. Dance has, in general, the capacity to help sick or elderly people, by reactivating their joint mobility, by awakening their sensibility and their mind, by reconnecting them to their body. Dancing was Mimi's passion, her life and her profession. Stuck and dependent in this nursing home, it has disappeared from her life. She is now in a wheelchair, her whole body is in pain; her knees, her hips, her shoulders… "Dancer's osteoarthritis" too has spread throughout her body. When she wants to move around or simply move a body part, she needs arms, hands, another person for support.

It is also, in these moments, that physical contact and proximity help her to remember and reassure her. So there still exists in her a memory that calls upon the senses. If I stay far from her, she does not recognize me, she gets agitated. If I come closer, am against her, hug her, she relaxes and ends up recognizing me. What is transmitted by emotions, the sensed, is not forgotten. I feel that her status as a former dancer can allow me to go further, to search for what is deeply buried, underlying. I accept the support and care that has been chosen for her at that point, but I do not want to stop there. I have found a key to revive certain memories and want to try to find others, to continue this stimulation and to safeguard her memory. Dancing was our strongest bond. I realized that our communication still exists, and passes in part through the body. Behind the nebulous of the disease, something is still inscribed between us. With her consent, I filmed her, I filmed what we do together, and I recorded her speech.

In the beginning, my undertaking was motivated by the frustration of not being able to communicate with her anymore, by the refusal of the fatality linked to this disease as well, in addition to the will to safeguard and nurture what is left of our relationship. I did it for my family, for myself, and for her, in memory of our relationship and her history. Then, I realized that something else appears, fashions itself, takes shape. The family archive transformed itself into a film project: a documentary, a more universal dance film based on our intimate history. My aunt Marjorie was often present when I filmed my grandmother. She was the one who took care of her in Alsace at that time, as she lives only a few kilometers away from her nursing home. In this history of family and dance, the character of Marjorie finds her place in the narrative that I write, until she forms, with my grandmother and me, a choreographic trio that appears in the film. The documentary project germinates as I collect images during my visits.

A New Process of Creation

During this period (2013–17), and in parallel to this project, I regularly contributed to workshops in a prison in Bordeaux. I discovered participatory film practices through co-creation projects whose development is refined with each year. In the workshops, I conjoined several disciplines (body, image, text, sound, movement) in a process of exploration and creation. The workshop participants are thus all gradually led to be in front of and behind the camera. Cinema is a storytelling art, and it is also an art of emotions, of the visual and sonic sensed.

For each of these projects in a prison environment, I also brought setting and costume elements to dress and transform the spaces and bodies. The participants studied and explored the links between visual arts and dance, the power of the camera/dance relationship, the relation to the production of texts, to music, and to sound, and also discovered the technical aspects of these artistic practices. These devices are also sites of new and personal filmic compositions revolving around movement and dance. These incarcerated bodies enter the room isolated, fragmented, and erased. Little by little, some free themselves, express themselves and take in what the artist I am comes to share with them with a lot of openness, enabling maybe, for some, the opening of new windows into the world.

Between prison and outside society, there are ultimately more similarities than differences. The particularity of the prison space stems from its drastic nature. Putting cinema, dance, the arts to the test in prison is putting it to the test in our society as well. More broadly, these different artistic and human experiences can only be enriched by this meeting. Screendance, like any art, must be experimented on and must venture into the social space. It can help us reconstruct individual and collective narratives via movement, the body and the image. By means of these devices, I experimented and refined a process of creation enabling the mise en scène of personal histories, both imagined as well as representations of the real. It is in this manner that I advanced, almost naturally, towards documentary writing and *Les Robes Papillons*.

The Struggle Against Time

During each of my visits, I imagined devices to stimulate Mimi's memory. I wanted to go further, to share this history, to pay homage to her, and to dance one last time with her using this film. The devices then became increasingly cinematographic. I set up processes that would stimulate her senses and everything that could connect her story to dance and reveal memories, corporeal reactions, words… To do this, I used different media in my possession: her old performance programs, archival family films, dance photo archives, filmed interviews with dancers, her ballet costumes, but also music to which she has danced. On account of what this triggers, I intended to surpass what is offered to her on a daily basis and, thusly, awaken her memory. When I came to see her, I did her hair and make-up. It was also the small ritual of her daughter Marjorie's visits. Mimi has always been a very stylish woman, who has worn the same platinum blonde French twist all her life. The makeup also reminds her of the dressing rooms, the backstage before going on stage, the preparations before shows. While styling her hair, I attempted to evoke this, and I already sought to awaken her. Thus, she gets into condition, she is ready to get back on stage, and I then explored the slightest spark of dance that is still hidden in her.

I conceived the aesthetic universe of my film *Les Robes Papillons* "in motion." I wanted the global form of the film to serve the subject and its main concern. By motion, I mean the movements that occur in the image, the movements of the camera itself, and those created during editing. It is a film that blends writing and practices of documentary cinema and screendance. Documentary cinema offers a diversity of cinematographic experiences, at

FIGURE 12.1 Micheline Auburtin image from a Super 8 home movie captured by Michel or Pierre Auburtin in the 1980s
Source: Still from *Les Robes Papillons*.

times very experimental,[6] and it is exactly these films that nourish the composition research that I still pursue to this day.

With *Les Robes Papillons*, I undertook a new process of creation. Usually in my filmic practice revolving around dance, my approach is more instinctive, more spontaneous. And even though I always have a very precise vision of the experimental film project that I direct, the filmic narrative writing manifests itself at the time of editing. Hence, this being a first documentary film project, I benefited from regional support and assistance as an author.[7] These means allowed me to take the time essential to the adaptation of this other form of cinematographic writing. I initiated and subsequently continued it with Olivier Daunizeau, script doctor at the stage of the narrative and the film's narration, then with Laetitia Andrieu, author, actress, and dancer, for the writing of a voice-over that I wished to be sensitive and poetic, mixing real and imaginary memories.

The Issue of Memory

My film consequently follows a narrative path that rests on the real to tell the story of my grandmother and of our relationship. In 2012, my grandmother crossed a threshold. From then on, she is situated somewhere between dream and reality. On a daily basis, she sees things that do not exist, invents words, and no longer produces proper sentences. Mimi often has the impression that she has lived things that she has, in reality, dreamed. She confuses people she has met, or different eras, and also mixes up ballets characters with real people. I imagine the inside of her head as a big children's picture book that intermixes, on cut-up pages, the different body parts of several characters. So, echoing this, in the editing of the film, the archives are not assembled chronologically. The archive is treated as an experimental material that can be handled, transformed, and reinterpreted to rewrite history or, sometimes, to distance oneself from it. The editing is done by means of movement, accelerating, accumulating gestures and gazes, decelerating, repeating a loop, and drawing the spectator into their own reverie.

Between 2012 and 2017, I filmed digital images with my Sony HVR-Z7U HDV camera. They became my "archives of the present" in the film. They retrace, step by step, the progression of the disease and the last years in this nursing home. As soon as I visited her, I tried to look for emotions buried in her, to bring them out of oblivion. In *Les Robes Papillons*, when Mimi appears for the first time in her room in a Sélestat nursing home, she "listens to the wind" and "hears a flying cat."[8] These images that I kept of her, those in which she remembers while daydreaming about what surrounds her, reinforce all the poetry and fantasy that Mimi still had in her at that time.

I filmed her when her memories reappeared. These are sensitive and intimate moments that I captured with my camera. When I came to see and film her, I planned a device. But since my visits were spaced out in time, on account of the great distance between us (Bordeaux to Sélestat), I often found myself having to rebound from a device that does not work. What worked the previous time no longer functioned. The disease progressed, and I never knew how she would react. For instance, during a period when I came with my laptop with the intention of showing her images from a filmed interview with Frédéric Werlé, a former student of hers, who has become a great contemporary dancer and choreographer, Mimi had forgotten a lot of things. In this video, Frederic Werlé talks directly to Mimi. I attempted to revive my grandmother's memory, which at that point had declines considerably, by showing her these images and by making her listen to Frédéric's words:

> Madame, I did not make a career in classical dance, perhaps because I could not be a bald Prince Charming… but I absolutely wanted to pay homage to you and to insist on the positive contribution that you have afforded me through your teaching. I remember your patience waiting for my blossoming, my awakening. I remember your pink dance studio, rue du Pont des Morts in Metz…

At first, Mimi did not understand what I wanted to show her. It was as if she did not perceive the image or the computer placed right in front of her. So, I got a little closer to her, I held her shoulder and asked her to focus her attention on the voice that is speaking. Mimi calmed down, concentrated, and began to listen to Frédéric's voice. She didn't not move anymore, was no longer agitated, but was captivated by the sound of this voice that she tried to recognize. Then, when the sound of Frédéric's recorded voice disappeared and the image turned black, Mimi turned to me and asks, "How could I forget all of this? ... Do you realize? How could I forget?..."

But the next moment, she had once again forgotten everything; what she had just realized, what she had just said, seen, and heard.

These moments that I spent with her are related in the present tense in the film, not in the past tense. In the film, I transcribe the feelings that animated me at the time when I experienced and filmed them. In some cases, these moments are not exactly those I experienced, because sometimes showing them in a different manner, in a mise en scène, enables a better retranscription of the real. In these images, my grandmother's body is filmed as closely as possible. The framing is tight. There are, for example, close-ups of the details of her face, her wrinkles, her veins, her thin skin. The aging body is, for many people, disturbing, repulsive. Essentially, it announces the end of life, death. My gaze directed at this body is, on the contrary, tender. It emanates a certain beauty and poetry. This body whose curves, angles, solids, lines, textures, and reliefs draw a sensitive landscape: a body-landscape that I do not frame at a distance. I wanted the spectator to sense my physical proximity, my intimacy with my grandmother, because *Les Robes Papillons* is also the story of a relationship to the body. Showing this aging body in an almost abstract way, in extreme close-up shots, paradoxically creates an effect of distancing from my grandmother's physical state and avoids a certain voyeurism.

To shoot the last sequences with her in the nursing home, I was twice accompanied by another person working the camera. The first time by Christophe Hanesse, a cameraman friend, and the second time by the multidisciplinary artist Priscilla Guy. My grandmother's condition necessitated that I stay very close to her to support and stimulate her. I could no longer be alone, behind my camera. And at the same time, I could not have an imposing team or a complicated device to create these images in her small room either. It was necessary to be discreet, to be attentive, to have a smaller crew with reliable people; to be in an intimate relationship, calm and reassuring for her. For these images, I chose minimal technical equipment as well: a small Blackmagic Pocket Cinema Camera on which I had connected microphones to record sound. I continued to use this equipment for other means of mise en scène in the film: the incarnation of my grandmother in the ghost dress – in the pool and in the streets of Monaco, the memory of a dance by my grandmother's former students in Metz, and my solo of the reminiscences of this dance on the beach in Bordeaux, in a duet of with the camera and the director of photography. Hence, in order to succeed in capturing the character of my grandmother, the essence of her mobility, and the beauty of her aged body, it was necessary for the technical to be attuned to the sensible. The film's aesthetic universe is thus "in motion" because its form must serve the subject and its main concern.

The Hand Dance

Then, to evoke my past relationship with her when I was a child, I used family photographs taken by relatives. I selected in particular the ones where we are together, where our closeness and mutual understanding are perceptible, where the tenderness of her gaze on my younger self is visible.

I show these photos from a subjective point of view, as if the spectator could see them through my eyes, because it is actually my adult gaze in the present that remembers this past. The filmic device is simple and uncluttered. We see my hands going through these photos one after the other. The gestures of my hands are, however, precise and choreographic, reminiscent of the ancient tradition that dancers have to rehearse their steps, their movements. Like me, they use their hands to remember their movements, their dances. For *Les Robes Papillons*, I explored and composed a "hand dance," a mise en scène of these photographic archives, handled over a white

FIGURE 12.2 Camille's hands handling a family photo showing her as a baby and her grandmother Mimi, framed by Camille with a rostrum camera stand
Source: Still from *Les Robes Papillons*.

background, with a view from above using a static shot. My hands are, in fact, placed on a white table, and enter, slide, separate, show photos, get closer and further away from each other, or leave the frame of the image.

I was inspired by the minimalism of Yvonne Rainer's film *Hand Movie* (1966)[9] as well. The proposal of this film is powerful, at once extremely simple and utterly radical. The reference to this film marks another step since it is at once an innovative artistic proposal, a screendance of the artist who only films and mobilizes her hand in close-ups, all the while being an archive of her own life (as the artist was, in fact, sick and bedridden, unable to do anything else than to dance with her hands, vertically, in front of her hospital wall). I find it exciting that the constraints that projects or life impose upon us end up leading the artist further than they could have imagined. These constraints push us to advance towards the essential, to break out of our work habits, to eliminate the superfluous (technical, material), and to be more inventive, more direct, and simpler in order to obtain from the dream work what we imagine. During my projects in the prison, the constraints on bringing in equipment (camera, microphone, computers, tripods, elements of stage sets, lights) every day were numerous and significant. We had to regularly dispose of many ideas or objects that seemed important to us at the start. With Mimi, it is the limits of her aged and sick body that, in some ways, constantly narrow our playground, whilst opening up new imaginative territories to explore.

Unlike in *Hand Movie*, my hands get into motion with the photos in order to echo a tradition of memorization put into practice in classical dance, but this also resonates with the history of this film project and the moment when it was born. Indeed, one day, my grandmother, then greatly affected by Alzheimer's, remembered dances in her body when I put on musical pieces for her. The dance appears through her hands, which reproduce the choreography, but also in her whole body, which awakens, keeps time, and expresses the music. This mise en scène of my hands was also a matter of introducing myself. I open the film with my hands, at first without photos. My bare hands, which betray my emotion with a slight trembling, enter the frame, show themselves, turn around, open, offer themselves, and leave the frame again through the sides of the white background. When my hands return to the frame, it is to present my photos and tell their story. Several sequences made with this device punctuate the film, but each choreographic passage is different.

Hands have a very strong presence in the film, in these sequences of mise en scène of archival photographs but also when I am with my grandmother in the room of her nursing home or at the end of the film; hidden in the dunes and my yellow dress, my hands return again, this time to end the film. The objective of this motif was to propose an unusual approach for the mise en scène of the photographic archive, without getting lost in nonsense. The first shoot did not work when I moved on to the editing stage. I had an enormous amount of "parasitic" movements that prevented the sequence from working; I was making too many gestures, we did not see the photos, I was going a little too fast, and with my camera on a tripod, the image looked as if it were tilted. For this reason, with regard to gestures, I precisely choreographed these hand dances while I wrote the narrative and the form of the film. I redid two test shoots that we could test out directly in the editing. The sequence was satisfactory when, finally, I used a rostrum camera stand. This tool that makes it possible to create animations enabled, on the one hand, the obtention of the completely horizontal and level static shot that I was seeking and, on the other hand, allowed enough time for the spectator to contemplate the photographs presented as soberly as possible on the screen. The simplest things sometimes take longer to find.

I realized, as a result of these shooting experiences, to what extent the slightest flaw or excess element on the screen can prevent the reading of an image, pull us out of the narrative or the film. In these sequences of "hand dancing," in addition to the photographic archives that I collected from my family, there are also photographs of students spanning several generations and some rare black-and-white photos of Mimi from when she was a young dancer at the end of the late 1940s. These sequences allow me to re-examine each period of her life, to transcribe the atmosphere of an era, and to recount how much dance, but also transmission, was essential for her.

The Archive to Reactivate the Movement of the Present

Lastly, to evoke the past, in addition to the photographs, I had a considerable bank of filmic archives: archival Super 8 footage belonging to my family dating from the 1960s to the 1980s, but also videotapes in the rare Sanyo V-Cord[10] format, shot in the 1970s and 1980s. These images, captured with Super 8 cameras and video cameras, were of my grandfather, a dancer as well, and of my father, then a student of the fine arts, both also parents of students. We notably see, in these images, my grandmother giving dance lessons to her students in the 1970s and 1980s. Some archives are also in an audio format. All these sequences in the film in which my grandmother appears, at different times and in different situations, substantiate her. They underline her personality traits, since it is this living image of her that I wish to keep and incarnate in the film.

These video and Super 8 images are also part of popular culture: the spectator can easily project themselves into their own family archives, their personal memories, in the nostalgia of these moments engraved on film, and thus identify with them. These films are also the trace and the memory of an era. Apart from the image, which is a temporal marker in itself, what it contains also gives us information about a period or a historical context by means of numerous elements: the film's setting and its landscape (it can be entirely different nowadays), people's clothing, their haircuts, the furniture, the cars, the relationships between men, women, and children. Certainly, the present only exists in the moment. Afterwards, it is memories. If memories are a subjective fabrication of the real, is reality only what happens in the moment? To me, memories are in part interpretations or reinterpretations of what occurred that are specific to each person. We can therefore also think that everything is fiction or that everything is open to reinterpretation even when we employ physical archives of the real. It is difficult to be entirely and objectively faithful to what has already occurred.

At the same time, I also realized while watching my own family archives that, ultimately, in these Super 8 films, we do not really see everyday family life. I possess, like many families, films of the events that are milestones in our lives: Christmas in the snow, the arrival of spring for Easter, a wedding, the birth of a baby in the maternity ward, a child's first steps, summer vacations by the sea. The film protagonists are smiling, festive, tanned, dressed in their Sunday best. It is not a family's daily life but the mise en scène of the film of their life that they opt to make of it, long before the existence of social networks. These avenues to think about, interpret, and process these images of family archives are multiple.

Echoes and Resonances

For *Les Robes Papillons*, two very different films, which I consider to be masterpieces, have been a great inspiration to me in terms of the treatment of the archives. First, there is the British film by choreographer Siobhan Davies and filmmaker David Hinton, *All This Can Happen* (2012).[11] Like this film, which favors the use of archival images from the beginnings of cinema and photography, carefully selected, to create superimpositions, multiples, visual or sonic counterpoints, graphic abstractions or images that are more dreamlike by means of different effects, of filters or split screens, I wished to experiment experientially with/experience experimentally my own family archives to break out of their "classic" or "typical" mise en scène; to decontextualize them and to stay the course and achieve, with this material, a work of choreographic composition through editing. My idea, which I continue to explore in other projects, is to work the archives as a material that I can reinterpret, transform (with slow motion, freeze-frames, repetitions, fast-forwards), or explore in an abstract manner by playing with the movement (of the image, of the image's subject, of the camera).

The French documentary film *Groundswell* (2013) by Perrine Michel[12] has been a great source of inspiration as well. This film has as a starting point a BD – bouffée délirante.[13] A real personal experience that the director has lived through. In her film, she uses family archives, mainly photographs.

During her episodes, she writes her film and fantasizes about her memories linked to her personal photos. She reinterprets her own archives and, accordingly, constructs a disconcerting true-false documentary narrative, which she fully believes at that moment, leading us into the twists and turns of her psychotic episode. From this results a radical, violent, and troubling cinematic experience. She presents family images to us and constantly distorts their meaning, their context through her words and editing. She delivers herself in her own madness, and we lose ourselves with her until we are no longer able to differentiate the true from the false in her story. What impressed me a lot in Michel's work, besides her commitment, is her audacious writing work and its relationship to the body and to sensation. Her film's depth is sustained by the complexity, mastery, and fantasy of her extremely sensitive writing.

It is this film that made me want to enrich the writing of my own film as much as possible, by imposing the same work standards for the voice-over on myself. This preliminary writing process was essential to my creative process, enabling me to better define my film's main concern, its true subject, and its narrative form. It facilitated and accelerated the film's production by leaving very few grey areas at the time of editing. However, there was still a final writing phase at the time of editing. I had a comprehensively written film, but we tested and sometimes found other sequence arrangements. Moreover, the voice-over was written and pre-recorded, but when we layered it on the images, it was omnipresent throughout the film. There was a long process of pruning before we found the right balance between all the materials that compose the film (images, sounds, musical pieces... and silences).

Through this process of poetic writing, I interrogate her memory, the memory of a life but also that of our relationship, inhabited by dance. My grandmother is losing her language, and I search for and explore the words to portray her through dance, that which has always united us and that is still somewhere in her, even though the disease has taken over her.

How to Incarnate Mimi?

For this film, I chose the documentary form to write the narrative of my story on the screen. It was not so much a question of describing the daily progression of Alzheimer's or discussing the loss of a loved one head-on, but rather of understanding what an artistic and human legacy means. How does it reappear and in what forms? How can it be kept alive despite the loss, the mourning?

To portray my grandmother in the film, I consequently imagined several ways of representing her: through the images of her I have been able to film these last years, through older archival images, but also by staging fictionalized sequences with her or by means of other bodies that have danced with her (who were able to talk about that or revive her dancing for the film). I imagined sequences without her as well. The pink, vaporous dress, the film's golden thread – wandering in Monaco, or dancing underwater – is one such incarnation of my grandmother. It also echoes the film's title, *Les Robes Papillons*.

> Mimi wore long, large, flowing dresses. There was one she called her butterfly dress. It resembled the costumes composed of veils that the dancer Loïe Fuller[14] twirled at the end of the nineteenth century, immortalized by the Lumière brothers. When she wore it, she resembled a butterfly. Mimi renamed everything that surrounded her. Her car was her coach, her house her castle, and the memory room of her apartment in Metz was called St. Petersburg.[15]

When I visit my grandmother, I get her ready as if she were going to be on stage. Marjorie and I do her makeup, do her hair, change her clothes. I film this process because I want to capture the change, the moments when she comes back to life through this ritual. The original frame of the subject is raw, anchored in the real. The filmed space is principally her room, sometimes the corridors and certain common interior spaces of the nursing home, such as the dining room. But the frame does not allow to really see the space around her. And by incorporating mises en scène, I wanted to be able to move from documentary to fictionalized situations.

When I rely, in the narrative, on a mise en scène that comes close to fiction, it is to better narrate how Mimi's legacy continues on today and on the screen without her actually being present. I like to believe that it is never too late to tell someone's story, to know them, at the risk of resurrecting them, invoking their ghost. Only the power of the imaginary enables this. Sometimes, staging the real enables a better understanding of it and a faster advancement into reality.

In May 2016, I came to see her with music from *The Spirit of the Rose*[16] and the desire to stage her. This choreographic piece was also my first outing to a show, my first memory of ballet. I was five or six years old. I saw this show with Mimi at the Ballet du Rhin [Rhine Ballet] in Alsace in 1979 or 1980. I remember that the spectre was performed by a friend of my aunt Marjorie. He was very beautiful and, in my memories, he looked a little like Nijinsky's portrait from 1911; the one that Mimi had both in her dance studios and in her living room. As a child, the beauty of this portrait of Nijinsky fascinated me. When I visited my grandmother that day in Alsace, I was with Marjorie. We played this waltz that Mimi had so often danced and transmitted during her career. Mimi, who had dozed off, woke up. She immediately recognized this music. She remembered. Her eyes lit up suddenly. She hummed the melody, then she beat time, counted the beats. Next, her feet stirred. Her hands, but also her arms, rose. Her

FIGURE 12.3 Micheline Auburtin surrounded by her daughter Marjorie Auburtin and Camille in her nursing home in Sélestat, framed by Christophe Hanesse

Source: Still from *Les Robes Papillons*.

face brightened up, she closed her eyes. She relived the ballet and took my hands to dance with her. She sketched and named movements taken from the ballet, even though her body does not always follow as she wants.

We tried to assist her movements without guiding her. We initiated a kind of communication with her body. We were, the three of us, attentive to our sensations. This sequence traversed several phases from dream to reality, somewhat like the ballet of *The Spirit of the Rose*. The images that resulted from this staged moment, from that day spent improvising with her, ultimately became a central sequence of the film. It brings together all of my film's themes: memory, artistic transmission, family, and dance. In this film, what my grandmother passed on to me, I gather, interrogate, and transform it with the intention of being able to continue this transmission myself.

In another sequence of the film, there is this same principle of mise en scène, but this time without her, and instead with her former students. It is the memory of the Rachmaninov variation, a dance that my grandmother had choreographed for the girls over a prelude by this Russian composer whom she adored. I asked myself what was left of this variation of which we have no filmic trace: only a few photos and the body memory of her students who were fifteen years old at the time, and who are all about sixty years old nowadays. Some only remember one port de bras or port de tête, others sensations, others the variation more accurately. They, too, embody in a way what they have left of my grandmother, of her dancing, of their own dancing. *Les Robes Papillons* is also a film about dance, in another light. The film summons different forms of images and movements. It also renders visible other bodies issuing from this art, the dancers of the corps de ballet that the public forgets and often ignores in favor of the stars, all these dancers who, in time, fade into darkness.

Writing a Life's Movement

In *Les Robes Papillons*, even though the documentary narrative was prepared prior to the shooting and editing, I still employed the practice of screendance to imagine, throughout the project, the composition work for the body and movement in the film. I used it differently by adapting it to each image register of the film, so that it could create the movement on the screen.

The last sequence of the film is the ultimate appropriation of this work about movement. It is this narrative's epilogue. It takes place in front of the Atlantic Ocean, near Bordeaux, where I now live, while the film's prologue faces the Mediterranean Sea and the Opéra de Monte-Carlo. The film thus ends with a screendance sequence on a beach. This is my artistic proposal to leave the film, and it echoes the previous sequences.

The elaboration of this last sequence began with a residency at a Bordeaux Choreographic Center. My intention was for my work to resonate with the variation composed over Rachmaninov's music, a neoclassical variation that my grandmother's former students had just passed on to me and that I had filmed a few weeks before in Metz. I sought to learn it, then to transform it in this duet. I wanted to appropriate this choreography in order to make something else out of it based on my practice of contemporary dance and screendance. For the shooting, I wanted to work with a handheld camera and not to take the easy way out by using a camera stabilizer. These tools are, for me, the means to erase the physicality and the sensations of the camera's movement. The movement of the camera becomes smooth, perfect, aerial, and we no longer feel the human being behind the camera. I wanted the opposite effect, for us to feel the body of the director of photography in motion with me. I wanted to develop a "camera-contact" duet, seeking to work and master together the fluidity and the attentiveness to our movements with the camera.

The diversity of the short sequences that we succeeded in shooting with our bodies and the camera enabled me to play with recomposing and mixing them in the editing. The choices of cuts and camera movements harmonize with the bodies' choreography. Accordingly, in the film, the camera captures my movements on the fly but does not hesitate to follow its own path. It acts as a dancing eye, lingering for a moment on a detail of the space, on a hand or a body. It reacts to impulses, at the risk of finding itself on the ground and losing its bearings. The freedom of the handheld camera helps us glimpse the presence of the camera operator's body and immerses us in the sensations of movement. Facing the sea and the horizon, I run down the dunes. The sound of the ocean and the wind merge with my breath and the sounds of my gestures. The beach is deserted. I observe the coming and going of the waves, the water that sweeps up and withdraws from the sand, and I follow their rhythm. Little by little, this movement carries my body, and it is amplified.

This project has been a long time in the making and refers both to the dances inspired by the winds and waves of Isadora Duncan (whom my grandmother adored), but also to those inspired by Maya Deren's cinema, particularly in her film *At Land* (1944).[17] My grandmother became aquainted with Deren's work through my studies. These avant-garde artists also symbolize what my grandmother transmitted to me, what I made her discover, what we both loved, what intersected between us, what bonded us and interested us. Deren's films were created in the same era as when my grandmother was dancing at the Ballets de Monte-Carlo. I have a hard time realizing that they were nearly the same age, as their artistic worlds are so different! I wanted to confront my own influences from these avant-garde productions with my grandmother's classical universe.

The first dance book my grandmother gave me was a work by Isadora Duncan, *The Art of the Dance*.[18] I obviously had it in mind while making this film, because it is an integral part of her transmission. Mimi was a classical dancer who was nevertheless very open to modernity! Duncan made me dream and gave me inspiration for the sensations of the dancing body on the screen. How can the spectator perceive them, experience them, and how can I create an artistic proposal with these materials?

This last sequence on the beach is a purely sensitive proposal, an invitation to stretch out time, to prolong our dreams, our sensations, and the reminiscences of all these memories and all these dances that we traverse in the film. *Les Robes Papillons*: the history of dance that traverses a life history or a life history that traverses the history of dance?

Notes

1 *Les Robes Papillons*, directed by Camille Auburtin (France: Les Films du Temps Scellé, 2020).
2 Sergei Diaghilev and his Ballets Russes established themselves in Monte Carlo for two decades. From the principality, Diaghilev's Ballets Russes reformed ballet from its former classical school, with several arts following suit: music, painting, literature, and visual arts. When he died in 1929, the company was dissolved. Several personalities and choreographers revived it under various names. The Compagnie des Ballets de Monte-Carlo [Ballets of Monte Carlo Company] was created in 1936 by René Blum after his departure from Colonel de Basil's Ballets Russes de Monte Carlo [Russian Ballets of Monte Carlo] company. Sold in 1938 to American financiers, it was subsequently directed by Julius Fleischmann and Serge Denham (1938–42). The company resumed its activities after the war with Léonide Massine and Serge Lifar. It was bought in 1947 by the Marquis de Cuevas and detached from the Principality of Monaco in 1950. The reconstitution of a permanent company in Monte Carlo only took place in 1985.

3 Rudolf Laban, *La maîtrise du mouvement* (Arles: Acte Sud, 1994).
4 The Rencontres Internationales de Danse Contemporaine [International Contemporary Dance Encounters], located in Paris, France, is a professional training centre accredited by the Ministry of Culture. It offers state diplomas for dance teachers, pre-professional courses, amateur courses for adults, continuing education, and courses for children.
5 Françoise Dupuy (Lyon, 1925–Paris, 2022) was an iconic dancer and choreographer from the 1940s onwards, as well as a great teacher. With her husband Dominique Dupuy, she created the Ballets Modernes de Paris [Modern Ballets of Paris] in 1955, the festival des Baux-de-Provence [Baux-de-Provence festival] – the first festival entirely dedicated to dance – in 1962, and the RIDC Institute in Paris, the first dance school with a contemporary vocation in France. In the 1980s, she also held the position of dance inspector at the Ministry of Culture.
6 See filmmakers Chantal Akerman, Chris Marker, Johan Van Der Keuken, Naomi Kawase, Jean-Gabriel Périot Nicolas Humbert, and Werner Penzel.
7 I received support from the Bureau of Authors and Projects [Bureau des auteurs, des autrices et des projets] of the ALCA (Agence Livre Cinéma Audiovisuel en Nouvelle-Aquitaine [Book, Cinema and Audiovisual Agency in Nouvelle-Aquitaine]) and financial aid from the Grand Est Region/Cultural Agency Grand Est and the Nouvelle-Aquitaine Region.
8 *Les Robes Papillons*.
9 *Hand Movie*, directed by Yvonne Rainer (1966). This film was made with the technical assistance of choreographic artist William Davis. The artist's hand is shown in close-ups, in static shots, performing minimalist movements, such as spreading or wiggling her fingers, from behind, from the side, and from the inside, sometimes even to the point of going beyond the frame. The artist was immobilized in a hospital room following a surgical intervention.
10 V-Cord videocassettes are pre-VHS videocassettes. Those in my possession are V-Cord tapes from a Sanyo camera, produced and put on the market in 1974–76 before being withdrawn from the market.
11 *All This Can Happen*, directed by David Hinton, choreographed by Siobhan Davies (Siobhan Davies Dance, 2012). Adapted from the narrative of *The Walk* (1917) by Robert Walser. "A true masterpiece. *All This Can Happen* is the perfect expression of the meditation on the logic of life and its precious disorder. I know of nothing more complex, simple, archaic, postmodern than the vision evoked in this reflective film." Patrick Bensard, director of La Cinémathèque de la Danse du CND [the Dance Cinematheque of the National Dance Centre].
12 *Lame de fond*, directed by Perrine Michel (Hors Saison, 2013). "After her father's death, Perrine Michel returns to visit the family home that her mother is preparing to sell. Childhood memories soon give way to a feeling of oppression, and the creaking parquet lets out a terrible secret. Victim of a bouffée délirante, committed to a psychiatric hospital, the narrator then embarks on a path to remission that leads to the writing of the film…" Sylvain Maestraggi.
13 Bouffée délirante is acute short-lived delusional psychosis. "Bouffée délirante – symptômes, causes, traitements et prévention – VIDAL," Vidal, last modified May 12, 2023, https://www.vidal.fr/maladies/psychisme/bouffee-delirante.html.
14 *Danse Serpentine*, directed by Louis Lumière and August Lumière, choreographed by Loïe Fuller (Hors Saison, 1899). The serpentine dances created by Loïe Fuller were notably captured by all the first filmmakers of the end of the nineteenth century. In 1899, the Lumière brothers then hand-colored the film, highlighting the dancer's brilliant movements.
15 *Les Robes Papillons*.
16 *The Spirit of the Rose*, choreographed by Michel Fokine, interpreted by Tamara Karsavina and Vaslav Nijinski, the Ballets Russes de Monte Carlo, April 19, 1911.

17 *At Land*, directed by Maya Deren (1944). An experimental and dreamlike silent film, written, directed, and performed by Maya Deren. A woman stranded on a beach goes on a strange journey, and meets other people and other versions of herself.
18 Isadora Duncan, *Écrits sur la Danse* (Paris: Editions du Grenier, 1927).

Bibliography

Auburtin, Camille, dir. *Les Robes Papillons*. France: Les Films du Temps Scellé, 2020.

"Bouffée délirante – symptômes, causes, traitements et prévention – VIDAL." Vidal. Last modified May 12, 2023. https://www.vidal.fr/maladies/psychisme/bouffee-de lirante.html.

Deren, Maya, dir. *At Land*. 1944.

Duncan, Isadora. *Écrits sur la Danse*. Paris: Editions du Grenier, 1927.

Hinton, David, dir. *All This Can Happen*. Choreographed by Siobhan Davies. Siobhan Davies Dance, 2012.

Laban, Rudolf. *La maîtrise du mouvement*. Arles: Acte Sud, 1994.

Lumière, Louis, and August Lumière, dirs. *Danse Serpentine*. Choreographed by Loïe Fuller. Hors Saison, 1899.

Michel, Perrine, dir. *Lame de fond*. Hors Saison, 2013.

Rainer, Yvonne, dir. *Hand Movie*. 1966.

13
TERRANCE HOULE'S GHOST DANCING IN A WAGON BURNER LANDSCAPE

Jessica Jacobson-Konefall

Kainai artist Terrance Houle's audiovisual media works *Isstahpikssi (ghost)* (2013), *Wagon Burner* (2003), and *Landscape* (2007), in relation to the artist's Niipisiti (Kainai) and Saulteaux lifeworlds, redraw perceptual boundaries with dance. Houle's lo-fi films focalize light as does the Kainai creation story. His films, shimmering with light-based "imperfections," enact Kainai (re)creation. *Isstahpikssi (ghost)* tells the story of a medicine man, his image captured by a frontier photographer, after which images of Houle's family and community flicker and dance on the screen. Heart- and drumbeat syncopate the Kainai and Saulteaux narrative, foregrounding hapticity and the body. In *Landscape* Houle runs, during an outdoor game of cowboys and Indians with his young daughter, in his pow wow regalia. In *Wagon Burner* a Kainai youth, having set a toy wagon on fire, dances pow wow on the land. In the films, artist, family, ancestors, and community meet spectators through the dynamism of electrical energy and presence. Reiterating Kainai creation the films' dialogue of light and dark conjures the Ghost Dance, a Lakota and Saulteaux-led Indigenous movement against genocide. Finally, like the Ghost Dance, the films figure vulnerability, "the (re)creation of subject, relation, and world,"[1] as an aesthetic, embodied, and felt modality towards autonomy and change in a settler colonial context. Houle's lo-fi imaging technology resignifies light and language to treat with the living and dead in *Isstahpikssi (ghost)*, while *Wagon Burner* and *Landscape* posit other "genres of the human"[2] with gestures of motion from non-colonial worlds. *Isstahpikssi (ghost)* relays heartbeat and tempo to foreground the hapticity of racialized trauma. It figures the vulnerable and affectable liveliness of Kainai in relation to the sun and camera shutter, so that the medicine man's power and vulnerability shower me, as viewer, with Kainai resurgence and survivance. The

DOI: 10.4324/9781003335887-17

Wagon Burner's young man, in many ways at the mercy of colonial forces, restages his own power through the burning of a toy and by dancing pow wow beside it. The pow wow dancer in *Landscape*, a daddy "Indian" running from little girl "cowboy," also asserts power through play in response to vulnerability. I am vulnerable, in turn, to the artist's shifting of power on behalf of Houle's peoples. Houle models a lifeworld assertion of difference from prevailing structures of dominance. The lo-fi shimmer and flicker alerts me to the haptic materiality, not only of what I am seeing, but also of my own perception, as material *relationship* rather than visual mastery.

In responding to these works, I hope to perform what Susan Leigh Foster calls *writing dancing*. Thinking with these films my nervous system, my neurotransmitters, my soma respond, vulnerable to Houle's power to act, unlike the invulnerable and possessive structure of colonial society, Western Man's genre of the human.[3] To consider thinking as relational, dynamic, and vulnerable is to foreground that thinking, like dance, is undertaken by a body, in all its relations. I find it possible and even likely that the practice of writing is less consequential than dancing, in terms of the psychosocial shifts it can produce. Frantz Fanon calls "ontogeny and sociogeny"[4] the generational recapitulation of (especially racial) "identity," in/as the body, its disposition and perception of relation. Houle's works occasion a vulnerability in myself in a manner that Ferrarese argues is the starting point of the political, understood "as the advent of a world, the emergence of a relation, and the appearance of a political subject."[5] I am moved, in my body, by Houle's works. Vulnerability is the emergent voice of a needs-based discord with institutions and instituted reality. In response to Houle's artful films, I find my needs to be "response-able"[6] and to assert a humanity exceeding Western Man's enclosure. Houle's works convey scenes and dynamics of racialized trauma and racial capitalism. Cedric Robinson defined racial capitalism as the racism that was part of the emergence of capitalism at the start, as it emerged from European feudal societies that were already racialist within Europe, against gypsies, Jews, Eastern Europeans, Irish, etc.[7] Racial capitalism in North America can be understood as the deriving of wealth from racialized people, often Black people, by white people. Indigenous critiques of what Karl Max called "primitive accumulation" highlight not only the extraction of value from racialized labor but also from the land, what Indigenous peoples call non-human kin.[8] Peter Kulchyski describes this dynamic as the "racial reconfiguration and redistribution of wealth," and highlights how "Indigenous ways of life challenge dominant notions of wealth and poverty."[9] In this milieu, as art historian Tina Campt writes, I face "a choice: act or be complicit."[10] I feel invited, with Houle, to engage the past in dynamic and embodied ways that, like his figuration of dance, honor Indigenous resurgence and survivance.[11]

Isstahpikssi (ghost)

Isstahpikssi (ghost) tells the story of a medicine man, Houle's ancestor, who is photographed by a frontier photographer in the late nineteenth century. In the film his story is narrated by Houle's parents in their languages, Niitsiitapii and Saulteaux. English subtitles subtend the oral narrative but do not affect a full translation. I learn that the medicine man's great strength is that he could avoid capture. Following the medicine man's encounter with, and "capture" by, the photographer, he finds himself in an ambiguous location, spiritually and physically. At this point, a series of images of Houle's family and community, a photographic archive, appear on screen in an accelerating tempo, suggesting the medicine man's presence in the archive.

In *Isstahpikssi (ghost)* a heartbeat, highlighting the body, and tempo are central to its score. The film braids reference to the Lakota and Saulteaux Sun Dance with Chris Marker's 1962 sci-fi film, *La Jetée*. Still black-and-white archival images flash on and off the otherwise black screen. The score, by Houle and Dan Wilson, was meant to sound "synthy" and "spacey," for a "First Nations sci-fi" film, including drumming, vocals, synths, and image.[12] *Isstahpikssi (ghost)* is inspired by *La Jetée*, in a clear reference to dance, themes of time, memory, and perception, and the perceived illusion of cinematic movement.[13] Houle's is a story of technology and time travel from an Indigenous perspective, where a relationship to language, story, and land is iterated through energetic audiovisual means.[14] The work seems to summon spirits, a lifeworld. The Ghost Dance, an Indigenous resistance movement that emerged out of the Lakota and Saulteaux Sun Dance, echoes throughout it. Settlers banned the Sun Dance in 1883 as part of the effort to "civilize" the Indian and enclose their lands as private property. It continued surreptitiously. Due to the government ban, Houle's people, the Saulteaux, took the Sun Dance underground, dancing at night in basements or secretive places to avoid capture by Indian agents. Photos of the Sun Dance are not permitted.

Isstahpikssi (ghost) references the history of colonial images and their audiovisual recording technologies of image capture, connected to the visuality of the Ghost Dance, which sensorily worked with relations between living and dead. As in the work of many Indigenous theorists, the notion of a firm boundary between the living and the dead is overcome in Houle's work. The Zapatistas, for example, call upon their dead to lead them to the path: "'for everyone, everything' say our dead. Until this is so there will be nothing for us."[15] A quote from the historical archive describes:

> On January 1, 1889, Jack Wilson (or Wovoka), a young Paiute man, *had a vision during an eclipse of the sun* ... Revealed to Wilson was a place where his ancestors were once again engaged in their favourite pastimes, where wild game and abundant food were restored to the lands ... He

interpreted the vision as the coming of a new age, one where Native and non-Native people would (finally) live in peace. This was the birth of the Ghost Dance ... It was, quite possibly, the first pan-Indian movement in the United States.[16]

Settlers viciously repressed the Ghost Dance movement in the massacre of mostly women and children at Wounded Knee, where their remains were found frozen in the ground and photographed. The Ghost Dance provides an oppositional aesthetic grounded in ancient dynamics of the senses. Houle's film persists against figurative capture by Western Man by refusing sensorial enclosure.

Wovoka's vision of the eclipse of the sun as a source of light evokes the movement of the camera shutter, highlighted in *Isstahpikssi (ghost)*'s story of a medicine man, Houle's ancestor, whose picture is taken with a camera. In *Isstahpikssi (ghost)*, following his capture, Houle's family photographic archive flows, in rhythm to music, and overlayed by narration. *Isstahpikssi (ghost)* is clearly concerned with ethnographic entrapment and the photographic archive, as well as the role of Indigenous voices, practices, and relations in intervening in colonial dynamics of power in photography and visual culture. The work begins with a woman's voice, that of an elder (Houle's mother) who recalls, "This is the story of a great leader and traveler. This story takes place a long time ago when the world began to change [and tells of a] Medicine man with great power and wisdom."[17] The narration is offered in darkness, with guitar overlay, and tells the story of a medicine man whose power was so effective, he could walk through an enemy's camp and steal horses without awakening any of his adversaries. He was not seen. He had control over when he "appeared," how or even if he was seen.

Houle notes:

> My mother (Blackfoot) tells the story of a Saulteaux medicine man's life achievement then his capture, articulating the relationship to her husband's family and medicine. My Father's voice embodies his ancestor in his Saulteaux language, manifesting him through his language (giving voice). This is rooted as a Sci-fi story based on the true story of my ancestor in the photograph, who was on my father's Saulteaux side. It is in part a story of the medicine man's breach cloth told through Blackfoot (Niitsitapi).
>
> There is a part to this film that is completely oral in that one must learn three languages, to know the complete story: that of visual art, Niitsitapi and Saulteaux. My mother is telling a Saulteaux man's story but in Blackfoot while my father plays his ancestor. I stopped or broke up the English subtitles as I wanted to take away the control of the narrative from my audience and force them to listen...especially to the languages.[18]

This listening, a careful attentiveness, is sonic and somatic: what we hear as voices are material vibrations. To listen in the way Houle suggests, slowly, and in darkness, is to slow down, and be attentive to effect of sound and image on the body, what Campt calls "hapticity." Somatic abolitionist Resmaa Menakem argues this slowing down and listening attentively to the body is a key aspect of healing racialized trauma, defined as responses "embedded in the body as standard ways of surviving and protecting itself. When these strategies are repeated and passed on over generations, they can become the standard responses in individuals, families, communities, and cultures."[19] Menakem notes that this describes all trauma, but especially that of white body supremacy. There is no trauma, indeed, no modern phenomena, that escapes the materiality of racialization.[20] By enhancing Kainai and Saulteaux control of sonic, linguistic, and sensory bodily experience, Houle treats with the bodies of his viewers in ways that engage, as Fanon and Wynter argue, how race is affected in/as the (traumatized) body.

In *Isstahpikssi (ghost)*, and its trailer, I feel the frequencies of Houle's family and community relationships, which his score haptically enhances. After the first section of the work narrated by Houle's mother, I hear the medicine man ask, "Are you the man who has asked for me? ... Is that the object to take my shadow to print?"[21] The image is taken, and from this moment forward the archive of photographs of Houle's community flashes by. I hear fragments of the medicine man's voice, indicating he can't find where he is, where his spirit is. In the end he says, "I am a Medicine Man, I am here, waiting!"[22] In Houle's trailer for the film, beginning with "take my shadow to print?,"[23] the beat accelerates as family photographs flicker on the screen. I see family photos of people on the land, around tables, at the sink, in houses, in front of houses, on cars, in front of cars, in wagons, at dances, on military bases. The tempo moves faster. The photographs, less and less recognizable as individual images, become movement of light. I find that the tempo, speeding up, produces a kind of exaltation or anxiety. In colonial modernity the embodied tempo—the experience of indeterminate bodies—accelerates so that distinct histories are barely intimated. Campt, on the sound of images in photographic archives, writes,

> Listening to images is constituted as a practice of looking beyond what we see and attuning our senses to the other affective frequencies through which photographs register. It is a haptic encounter that foregrounds the frequencies of images and how they move, touch, and connect us to the event of the photo.[24]

I see shifts from tipi dwelling to reserve housing. I see connections to the past mediated by photographs. I see jobs in the Canadian military. To know Houle is to know that the men in his family have always defended, protected,

FIGURE 13.1 Terrance Houle. 2013. Film still. *Isstahpikssi (ghost) part 1*
Source: Courtesy of the artist.

and provided for their families, long before Canada was ever here. I see joyful longstanding attachment relationships that convey these histories, in multisensory modes, interrupted by generations of forced residential school attendance. I see innumerable beautiful moments. Truly, Houle's portrayal "engag[es] archives in a way that makes audible the quotidian practices of fugitivity they capture."[25] Against the aims of the Canadian state, against the state's laws, families and communities are happy together and love each other. They are Indigenous people. Campt resonates with Houle where she emphasizes hapticity, felt by the body, and "archival temporalities" beyond touch "link touching and feeling, as well as the multiple mediations we construct *to allow or prevent* our access to those affective relations in multiple temporalities."[26] Houle's manipulation of tempo speaks to somatic experience, of nervous system calm or activation, key to ontogeny or sociogeny.

Indigenous peoples' ongoing dynamics of attachment to each other, land, and lifeworld speak to viewers like me. Accessing these affective relations, I become vulnerable to their power, in that they act upon me, and I am somatically at their mercy.

Isstahpikssi (ghost) is connected to Houle's ongoing *Ghost Days* project, which he refers to as "an experimental art adventure with film/video, performance, photo, and music to conjure spirits and ghosts as audience and collaborators with the living."[27] The ghost in modernity has long signified unprocessed trauma, and the presence of what is repressed and cannot be allowed or dealt with. Discussing *Ghost Days* in an interview for *The Globe and Mail*, Houle offers these responses to the interviewer's questions:

> Is it a Seance of sorts?
> Well, I actually ended up working with a psychic last year. He would do psychic drawings, where he would draw higher selves and past lives. We started doing experiments in a garage, where I would play music for three hours, conjuring the music of people like Jason Molina and Hank Williams. We delved into a lot of turn-of-the-century ideas of seances.
> Is the performance similar to a religious experience?
> I don't want to equate it to a church. I want to equate it to a lodge, where the audience is participating in it as much as we are. We want them to feed off the energy that's coming into the room.
> What kind of state do you work yourself into?
> It's a healing state, where we're all together. I've found that people get emotional when they watch this. They feel a sort of reconciliation. I'm trying to raise colonial and Indigenous spirits, as well as non-colonial and non-Indigenous spirits, in an attempt to speak to them. That's what Indigenous people do every day.[28]

In somatic interaction with Houle's work, many histories come to life in my body. I think with theorist of vulnerability Estelle Ferrarese, who works in the traditions of Critical Theory, or the Frankfurt School. These thinkers wrote within histories of violence, and conditions of trauma underpin their interventions, including of the genocide of World War II. These traumatic histories of extreme violence sometimes become illegible as lived experiences, ghosts, and impulses as their theoretical works circulate in the white, Euro-American academy.

In response to Houle's work, I feel my own intergenerational trauma related to extreme violence, heteropatriarchy, class oppression, and genocides over hundreds of years of world capitalism. How do these traumas manifest as settler colonialism? The camera shot in *Isstahpikssi (ghost)* may signify trauma as a non-rational response "above all of speed and reflexivity,"[29] only retroactively justified through the prefrontal cortex "after that fact."[30]

According to Menakem, what Campt calls hapticity, or greater sensual and bodied perception, is needed for the healing of racialized trauma, and is available when I slow down, generating multiple temporalities of relationship, and become present to my own body, through practice, creating a "container" in which I can experience presence and co-presence safely and without reactivity.[31] I speculate that to heal this history will require numerous practices modelled by Houle's works, including being with the tempos of the body in its relations to the histories in which it is imbricated. The tempo of the film resonates in my body and affirms relationship.

In *Isstahpikssi (ghost)*, Houle references and embodies a Kainai creation story. In this way he haptically shifts a Kainai and Saulteaux world, its narratives and audiovisual praxis, into primacy against Western hegemonic genealogies. The story, wherein from the darkness comes light, highlights the relationship between energy, life, and light as central and elaborated. This emphasis also resonates with the origin story of the Ghost Dance, which appears as a prophetic vision of an eclipse of the sun. In the story, Kainai came from the Above People (Spomi'tapiiks), with emphasis on the role of celestial light in life on Earth, wherein light is part of the Kainai family. This Kainai creation story holds that Creator specifically names Earth or Ksahkomitapi to be the mother of all that he had created, "and all his creation would live off her. The Sun (Natosi) was created, and he was told that he would be the one to give light and warmth to everything. The Creator then told Natosi's wife, the Moon (Kokimmikisoom) that, along with all their children, the stars in the sky (Kakatosiiks), they would be the ones to give light at night."[32] This connection of celestial light to life, kinship, and nurturance secures what Winona LaDuke calls "continuous rebirth" at the basis of the Kainai people.[33] In the Ghost Dance vision, the eclipse of the sun suggests the movement of a camera aperture, as in *Isstahpikssi (ghost)*'s illumination of a photographic archive from this territory. When the photograph of the medicine man is taken in Houle's narrative, it is a new beginning, a (re)creation story, that recalls the Ghost Dance prophecy. After the camera shutter capture, the photographic archive of Houle's family presents the practice and power of each generation in persisting as Indigenous peoples following the "eclipse" and the re-emergence of/into the sun. A drumbeat or heartbeat gets louder as the photograph is taken. The woman describes, "it is as if it was an eagle or a star, and he is lifted by some unknown spirit." She narrates: "The medicine man could see the air around him, as colourful, like the spirits had taken him and he could see the world. He hit the ground, and everything went dark. Where am I? Why am I here?" he asks.[34] Medicine man, descended from the stars, like those in the Kainai creation story who dwell there in power, has fallen or been lowered from the sky. Again. A re-creation story. The blurry shimmer of lo-fi archival photographs, with their bright visual irregularities, foregrounds light and dark as perceptual dynamism, the movement of electrons as the dancing liveliness of ancestors and relations.

The woman elder (Houle's mother) comments that when the white man's camera box "flashes" the medicine man felt himself move with such force as he had never felt before. Now "aimless" the man speaks in a fragmented voice from an unseen place.[35] He doesn't know where he is or why he is there, whether he is a spirit, whether he is alive or dead. In the film, this disorientation complements photographs of family on the plains. His family members, members of his nation, pose together (on military compounds, in front of cars) while clearly exuding self-determination, loving their families, in their existence as Indigenous peoples. Campt writes, regarding Black portrait photography, of

> the quotidian practice of refusal...defined less by opposition or "resistance," and more by a refusal of the very premises that have reduced the lived experience of blackness to pathology and irreconcilability in the logic of white supremacy...nimble and strategic practices that undermine the categories of the dominant.[36]

Such poses and practices narrate survivance through Indigenous visual rhetoric. Medicine, with eagle spirit, or a star, falling from the sky, becomes dancing electrons, a source of light to make a home, coming down from the sky people, hitting the ground in re-creation. Electrons hold ancient medicine harnessed towards re-creation, through presence, mimesis, responsiveness, through Turtle Island and its illuminations, its power, Ininew rivers animating light in this room.

Wagon Burner and *Landscape*

Houle's project has been consistently responsive to forms of ethnographic entrapment, as in *Wagon Burner*. This work tells a story of destruction and re-creation. A Kainai youth approaches a plastic toy wagon on the grass, holds out his lighter for the camera to see, sets the wagon on fire, and dances around and above it in a dynamic assertion of self. Lo-fi shimmer, the degradation of the Super 8 film, makes it difficult to see through the distortion, emphasizing the film's materiality. *Wagon Burner* is droll. The wagon burner dances, makes his ground to stand on, and a low-key, flirtatious, funny, and extremely lo-fi aesthetic animates spiritual relationship. Like the reference to colonial photography in *Isstahpikssi (ghost)*, ethnographic entrapment arises in Houle's *Wagon Burner* in the form of the "frontier" or "prairie cowboy" toy wagon to which the child orients as "wagon burner." *Wagon Burner* is a well-known slur for Indigenous people from the plains. This boy, in fact a wagon burner, embodies and resignifies the trap or enclosure of the slur through autonomous Kainai values and orientations. Coloniality figures Indigenous identity as contained, primarily existing in relationship to settlers: "wagon burner." Houle figures settler colonialism as material practice of dispossession and representational discourse, a lifeworld, even, that can be embodied or challenged through play, and in dances that do or do not take place. Those who coined "wagon burner" banned the Sun Dance and enclosed people on reserves.

On ISUMA TV the work is described as follows: "a boy reclaims his identity through the simple act of destruction. The boy burns his wagon and dances to put out the flames. Houle's images tell a story older than colonization: the power of resistance and remembrance."[37] In this work, the story is one of a youth coming to create and know meaning. This process is self-led and spiritual, and Houle portrays it in an everyday, humorous, quotidian sphere that makes of the spiritual something accessible and present in the everyday practices, dispositions, and bodily comportments of Kainai youth. Through playful destruction and dance, the boy comes to know or reclaims what Leanne Simpson calls "whole body intelligence."[38] Menakem writes that somatic abolition involves bodily experiences of "moving, touching, holding, releasing, protecting, weeping, laughing, singing, or the cultivation of joy."[39] He further notes that these experiences are not "tools" but rather are *toys*—"something to explore, investigate, and perhaps share with others."[40] As Amanda Boetzkes writes of detritus, the meaning of the toy wagon, "comes from context and process, *energy expenditure* [like the sun, vitality], not content."[41] The toy, on fire, dances colonialism out of existence, replacing it with a sacred fire on the land, like there never was a wagon. This work is pedagogical, playing with disobedience and disregard for commodities, against coercion and authority as Western values (of play "nicely," "take care" of your toys). The boy makes something timelessly beautiful, fleeting, sacred, and grounded in land and intergenerational relationships that include the bison, through a subversive act of destruction.

Landscape, like *Wagon Burner*, restages and revises cowboys and Indians. In pow wow regalia, a play game of capture and agonism transforms histories of violence into love and intergenerational relationship. The film is shot in Nose Hill, downtown Calgary, in Alberta, Canada, an inner-city, a sacred place, and frequent site for ceremonies and teepee circles. Shot in Super 8, Houle positions the camera so that whenever he is on camera viewers can't see the city around him. He thus centers his body in a dialectical visibility with the broader civic body. In this green park, Houle, as a "lumbersome fearful" Indian, dramatically runs in slow motion. Nearly naked, he lumbers through the park in partial regalia. His belly sways freely until eventually he falls. Houle is shot in the back while falling; his daughter, dressed as a cowboy and riding a toy horse, has felled him. In this video, playing with contemporary signifiers of historical oppression, a father and a daughter make a home movie. The complex and entangled restaging of gender, power, and relationship in the choreography of this scene radically destabilizes the hegemonic visibility of these signifiers. By centering himself and his daughter in terms of their mutual perspectives in play, Houle choreographs an alternative to the "cowboys and Indians" mythos central to Calgary as a Western stampede town. I see lack of patriarchal authority, presence, and family togetherness as disruption of colonial insistence upon Indigenous disappearance. This kind of game conveys love, trust, and joy. Inhabiting "Cowboys and Indians" or colonial structures, parent and child in *Landscape* transform them.

Hapticity and Healing Antagonism

Houle's work functions in structural antagonism with a settler colonial lifeworld. I draw on the works of Menakem and Wynter to highlight how dynamics of oppression lived in/as the body structure nervous systems within the white body supremacy of settler colonialism. Menakem writes of somatic abolition, contending that racial oppression is caused by intergenerational trauma that recapitulates in ways decontextualized from its histories.[42] According to Menakem, modern Western political imaginaries, precluding ghosts, are borne of legacies of trauma.[43] Ferrarese notes that this Western "political" emerges in the vanquishing of vulnerability.[44] This invulnerability is a precognitive, somatic trauma response to violent oppressive hierarchies in tributary and capitalist modes of production, extremely intensified and accelerated in global capitalism. It has become, as Maori theorist Aileen Moreton-Robinson writes, whiteness as property. Ownership and control merge as dispositions of possession, what Moreton-Robinson calls "the white possessive" and Wynter names the "global bourgeois ethno-class."[45] Wynter writes of ways that bodies and nervous systems, neurotransmitters, recapitulate the Western Man as the Human and all others as "dysgenic" by degrees.[46] Working in photographic archives of the Black diaspora, Campt listens to images, where she feels an image's "frequency" as that of the relations the images exist within.[47] She argues that our bodily responses to images can be transformative if we "slow" down enough to "stay with the trouble"[48] they give us and, in Campt's words, "inhabit those feelings and responses."[49] How does the hapticity of Houle's lo-fi films impact me? Thus vulnerable, can I shift my own embodiment of racialized trauma?

I listen to Houle's mother and father speaking the story in *Isstapihsski* in Kainai, and I register the playing children and parents in *Wagon Burner* and *Landscape*. When I reflect on my own mother's voice, and myself as a child, I feel that my mother wasn't close with me. In her own words she can't tolerate intimacy or closeness. She does not have positive stories about her male ancestors, hailing from Eastern Europe as children deeply traumatized by

WWII. Their abuse gave her an autoimmune disease from which she almost died last year. Her live-in Latvian aunt regularly told the little girls that my grandmother was poisoning her, pretending to "be killed" by the children to control their behavior, and perpetrated more intimate harm than this. Raped by a family friend in elementary school, my mom found herself on a path to teen pregnancy and me. I followed a more extreme version of the same path. My father, adopted at birth, given up because his mother was a teenager, was "illegitimate," raised by Irish and Polish adoptive parents who grew up desperately poor in orphanages, prisons, or raised by nonbiological relatives. Serious drug and alcohol addictions characterize my family. My father is a psychopath. My brother has spent years in a maximum-security prison for aggravated assault and was diagnosed with conduct disorder. A mother myself, my grandmother has tried to have Child and Family Services remove my children from my care as recently as three years ago. A huge amount of trauma in my family flares into my somatic awareness every day, perhaps every moment, of my life. Materially, however, conditions are far better in my family than Houle's, due to what racial capitalism takes from him, to give to us.

Houle's work presents the activation of tempo and pacing, speaking sensorily to the most intimate histories of attachment as well as trauma, from the materiality of the body to the flickering camera roll. In his discussion of *Ghost Days* Houle gestures to practices of collaborative healing, such as seances and the Ghost Dance, and healing together—across difference—in a sort of reconciliation. His words connect to the dispositions of Cree-Métis-Saulteaux scholar Jas Morgan, who writes "Indigenous women and gender variant and sexually diverse Indigenous peoples, have consistently employed kinship and love within their communities in order to positively transform contemporary colonial realities for their kin."[50] They go on to say, "I am not describing a politics of recognition led by settlers or the state, but rather an ethical concept I experience within all facets of Indigenous life: being through kinship."[51] Their critique resonates with what Stolo scholar Dylan Robinson calls "The separation of kinship at the heart of settler colonialism."[52] I share that my own feelings of disastrous, cascading familial loss are triggered by viewing Houle's work. These feelings are muted and subordinate to the primacy of the sacred Kainai story, and the history, voice, presence, plenitude, and magnitude of Indigenous peoples' spiritual, cultural, and material histories within, before, and beyond colonialism. This lifeworld is an interesting context in which to encounter one's own unresolved and intergenerational loss. I wonder if this vulnerability is a kind of kinship.

Regarding what Houle calls non-Indigenous, non-colonial, and colonial and Indigenous spirits, Menakem writes that white bodies have colonized, oppressed, brutalized, and murdered Black and brown ones ... [before and during this period] powerful white bodies colonized, oppressed, brutalized, and murdered other, less powerful white ones. The carnage perpetrated on Blacks and Native Americans in the New World began as an adaptation and *massive, targeted intensification and expansion* of white-on-white practices.[53]

This brutalization created intergenerational trauma. Intergenerational trauma response figures as the world of Western Man: the Human, the settler, the nominal, the possessive, the reified, the nonrelational. Against this, Houle's dance, his performers, family, ancestors, and kin, among living and dead, moves.

I feel Houle's film's heartbeat in my body, an embodied relationship very thin in comparison to his familial and intergenerational connections, which are conveyed by both heartbeat and the beat of a drum. Traditions like collective dance—Inuit throat singing, Plains pow wow songs, group singing or dancing, call and response formats, and games—co-regulate and produce relational attachment in human nervous systems. These rituals implicate people and groups in a shared aesthetic and embodied experience. I think of the audible mother's heartbeat in the womb, and the generations held in one body, beating, vital. While the Ghost Dance draws on these ancient practices, it also draws forth a sense of a fragmenting lifeworld. Houle ushers the vulnerability of being at the mercy of colonial forces, somatically and aesthetically, to a new world of meaning experienced by me. His work speaks to the traumatic interruption of the Sun Dance and its dancers' lifeworlds as collective attachments. This trauma results in the unmet needs of peoples circumscribed by the world of the Western Man. Houle's film highlights the fragmentation of lifeworld through diegetic ambiguity. Whose heart is beating? Is it a drum? How do the images' movements syncopate with the beating, how does this change in the narrative, and what is the salience of these shifts in tempo that are felt in my body? How do the syncopations on the screen resonate differently with my nervous system as compared to that of another, or what is the collective effect in a room, across bodies, across difference? This open-ended presentation evokes the discomfort that marks the absent presence of secure attachment, certainly in my own life, named in the Saulteaux phrase "all my relations."

Houle's screen dance *relates*. It is animated with light that, for Kainai, the creator deigned first and most important after our mother, the Earth. This creation story highlights how Houle's works are manifestations of the ontological basis for Kainai ways of being, while materially relating these ways of being to the land through its own material dance, in the form of light. This is a dynamic staging of transnational relationship with the Cree or Ininew whose waters power my viewings. I return to Ferrarese's claims about vulnerability, and my intent to shed light on what writing dancing can mean within structural antagonism, within relationships structured in dominance yet holding potential for relation. Ferrarese writes of the political against Western conceptions, as emerging with vulnerability, as "a world, a subjectivity, and a relation, the emergence of which depends on the experience of living at the other's mercy."[54] Houle's work activates a Kainai world, agents, and relations. *Isstahpikssi (ghost)*, with the medicine man and the camera, with the elder's words and the family histories, with the electronic media that is powered by ancient rivers, speaks to a history of medicine and self-determination meeting trauma across and in bodies and lifeworlds. With tempo and beat *Isstahpikssi (ghost)* joins the play and dance in *Wagon Burner* and *Landscape* to suggest embodied healing and repair. It creates an aporetic moment imbued with fragmentation, abstraction, insecure attachment, and ancient and pre-figurative methods of regulating nervous systems, (re)creating attachment across the living and the dead. Houle's work engages dance to orient us towards the (re)creation stories of Indigenous peoples and speaks to what is both more and less than the Human and Western Man, what structuring in dominance has not totalized: being through kinship.

Notes

1 Estelle Ferrarese, *Vulnerability and Critical Theory* (Leiden: Brill, 2018), 1.
2 Alexander Wehelyie, *Habeas Viscus: Racializing Assemblages, Biopolitics, and Black Feminist Theories of the Human* (Durham: Duke University Press, 2014), 10.
3 Wehelyie, *Habeas Viscus*, 29.
4 Katherine McKittrick, *Sylvia Wynter: On Being Human as Praxis* (Durham: Duke University Press, 2015), 23.
5 Ferrarese, *Vulnerability and Critical Theory*, 1.
6 Marianne Hirsch, "Vulnerable Times," in *Vulnerability in Resistance*, ed. Judith Butler (Durham, NC: Duke University Press, 2016), 84.
7 Robin D.G. Kelley, "What did Cedric Robinson mean by Racial Capitalism?," *Boston Review*, January 12, 2017, https://www.bostonreview.net/articles/robin-d-g-kelley-introduction-race-capitalism-justice/.
8 Glen Coulthard, *Red Skin White Masks: Rejecting the Colonial Politics of Recognition* (Durham: Duke University Press, 2014), 18.
9 Peter Kulchyski, "Rethinking Inequality in a Northern Indigenous Context: Affluence, Poverty, and the Racial Reconfiguation and Redistribution of Wealth," *The Northern Review*, 42 (2016): 125–36.
10 Tina Campt, *Listening to Images* (Durham: Duke University Press, 2017), 28.
11 Leanne Simpson writes that "Resurgence has come to me to represent a radical practice of Indigenous theorizing, writing, organizing, and thinking, one that I believe is entirely consistent with and inherently from Indigenous thought." See Leanne Simpson, "Leanne Betasamosake Simpson: I am not Afraid to be Radical," *Indianz.Com*, June 17, 2018, https://www.indianz.com/News/2018/07/17/leanne-betasamosake-simpson-i-am-not-afr.asp. The Decolonial Dictionary defines "Survivance," following Anishinaabe scholar Gerald Vizenor, as naming the conjunction between resistance and survival – calling attention to the fact that not only have Indigenous peoples survived the genocidal ambitions of settler colonialism, but have continued to enliven their cultures in fluid, critical and generative ways.

The term thus resists the static overtones of "survival" and instead emphasizes the ways in which Indigenous peoples have created counter-poses/positions to those that are marked out for them by the settler-state through stereotypes, popular culture, and national mythology. See "Survivance," *The Decolonial Dictionary*. April 15, 2021, https://decolonialdictionary.wordpress.com/2021/04/15/survivance/.

12 Terrance Houle, in discussion with the author, November 12, 2019.
13 Uriel Orlow, "Photography as cinema: *La Jetée* and the redemptive powers of the image," *Creative Camera*, no. 359 (August–September 1999): 14–17.
14 When I refer to energy, I refer to the hydropower that comes from dammed Ininew rivers in my province. Audiovisual media are in relationship with Indigenous lands in many ways, and centrally through the energy that animates them.
15 ZNLA, cited in Denise Ferreira da Silva, "Reading the Dead: A Black Feminist Reading of Global Capital," *Otherwise Worlds: Against Setter Colonialism and Anti-Blackness*, eds. Tiffany Lethabo King, Jenell Navarro and Andrea Smith. (Durham: Duke University Press, 2020), 38.
16 "Ghost Dance: Activism. Resistance. Art. – Announcements – Art & Education," Ryerson Image Centre, September 18, 2018, https://www.artandeducation.net/announcements/108334/ghost-dance-activism-resistance-art (my emphasis).
17 Houle, *Isstapiksi (ghost)*.
18 Houle, in discussion with the author, April 2, 2022.
19 Resmaa Menakem, "Healing Racialized Trauma Begins with your Body," *Resmaa Menakem: Embodied Anti-Racist Education*, November 17, 2020, https://www.resmaa.com/somatic-learnings/healing-racialized-trauma-begins-with-your-body.
20 Wehelyie, *Habeas Viscus*, 12.
21 Houle, *Isstapiksi (ghost)*.
22 Houle, *Isstapiksi (ghost)*.
23 Houle, "Isstahpiksi trailer," Vimeo, February 24, 2013, https://vimeo.com/60364433.
24 Campt, *Listening to Images*, 13.
25 Campt, *Listening to Images*, 13.
26 Campt, *Listening to Images*, 98 (my emphasis).
27 Houle, "GHOST DAYS: CVD 19 Series," *Luma Quarterly*, no. 21 (2020), https://lumaquarterly.com/index.php/issues/volume-six/021-summer/ghostdayscvd19series/#text-2.
28 Brad Wheeler, "Terrance Houle Conjures Spirits with Ghost Days Performance," *The Globe and Mail*, August 9, 2017, https://www.theglobeandmail.com/arts/art-and-architecture/terrance-houle-conjures-spirits-with-ghost-days-performance/article35932000/.
29 Menakem, *My Grandmother's Hands: Racialized Trauma and Pathway to Mending Our Hearts and Bodies* (Las Vegas: Central Recovery Press, 2017), 9.
30 Menakem, *My Grandmother's Hands*, 9.
31 Menakem, "Unlocking the Genius of Your Body," *Resmaa Menakem: Embodied Anti-Racist Education*, December 18, 2020, https://www.resmaa.com/somatic-learnings/unlocking-the-genius-of-your-body.
32 Creation story retrieved from the website of the Blackfoot Crossing Historical Park, https://blackfootcrossing.ca/wordpress/?s=creation.
33 Winona LaDuke, *Our Relations: Struggles for Land and Life* (Cambridge: South End Press, 1994), 41.
34 Houle, *Isstapiksi (ghost)*.
35 Houle, *Isstapiksi (ghost)*.
36 Campt, *Listening to Images*, 33.
37 "Wagon Burner," Isuma TV, May 15, 2007, http://www.isuma.tv/en/imaginetive/wagon-burner.
38 Simpson, "Land as Pedagogy," *Decolonization: Indigeneity, Education & Society* 3, no. 3, (2014): 7.

39 Menakem, "Unlocking the Genius."
40 Menakem, "Unlocking the Genius."
41 Amanda Boetzkes, *Plastic Capitalism: Contemporary Art and the Drive to Waste* (Cambridge: MIT Press, 2019), 30.
42 Menakem, *My Grandmother's Hands*, 44.
43 Menakem, *My Grandmother's Hands*, 52.
44 Ferrarese, *Vulnerability and Critical Theory*, 11.
45 Aileen Moreton-Robinson, *The White Possessive: Property, Power, and Indigenous Sovereignty* (Minneapolis: University of Minnesota Press, 2015); Sylvia Wynter, "Unsettling the Coloniality of Being/Power/Truth/Freedom: Towards the Human, After Man, Its Overrepresentation – An Argument," *The New Centennial Review, Coloniality's Persistence* 3, no. 3 (2003): 260.
46 Wehelyie, *Habeas Viscus*, 36.
47 Campt, *Listening to Images*, 10.
48 Donna Haraway, *Staying with the Trouble: Making Kin in the Chthulucene* (Durham: Duke University Press, 2016).
49 Tina Campt, *A Black Gaze: Artists Changing How We See* (Durham: Duke University Press, 2017), 37.
50 Lindsay Nixon, "Visual Cultures of Indigenous Futurism," *Otherwise Worlds: Against Settler Colonialism and Anti-Blackness*, (Durham: Duke University Press, 2020), 333.
51 Nixon, "Visual Culture of Indigenous Futurism," 333.
52 Dylan Robinson, "Critical Conversations 2021: Dylan Robinson: The Museum's Incarceration of Indigenous Life," *Critical Conversations*, University of Saskatchewan, March 5, 2021.
53 Menakem, *My Grandmother's Hands*, 35.
54 Ferrarese, *Vulnerability and Critical Theory*, 81.

Bibliography

Boetzkes, Amanda. *Plastic Capitalism: Contemporary Art and the Drive to Waste*. Cambridge: MIT Press, 2019.
Campt, Tina. *Listening to Images*. Durham: Duke University Press, 2017.
Campt, Tina. *A Black Gaze: Artists Changing How We See*. Durham: Duke University Press, 2020.
Coulthard, Glen. *Red Skin White Masks: Rejecting the Colonial Politics of Recognition*. Durham: Duke University Press, 2014.
Ferrarese, Estelle. *Vulnerability and Critical Theory*. Leiden: Brill, 2018.
Ferreira da Silva, Denise. "Reading the Dead: A Black Feminist Reading of Global Capital." *Otherwise Worlds: Against Settler Colonialism and Anti-Blackness*, edited by Tiffany Lethabo King, Jenell Navarro and Andrea Smith, 38–51. Durham: Duke University Press, 2020.
"Ghost Dance: Activism. Resistance. Art. – Announcements – Art & Education." Ryerson Image Centre. September 18, 2018. https://www.artandeducation.net/announcements/108334/ghost-dance-activism-resistance-art.
Haraway, Donna. *Staying with the Trouble: Making Kin in the Chthulucene*. Durham: Duke University Press, 2016.
Hirsch, Marianne. "Vulnerable Times." *Vulnerability in Resistance*, edited by Judith Butler, 76–96. Durham, NC: Duke University Press, 2016.
Houle, Terrance. Isstapiksi (ghost). 2013.

Houle, Terrance. "Isstapiksi trailer." Vimeo. February 24, 2013. https://vimeo.com/60364433.
Houle, Terrance. *Landscape*. 2007.
Houle, Terrance. *Wagon Burner*. 2003.
Houle, Terrance. "GHOST DAYS: CVD 19 Series." *Luma Quarterly*, no. 21 (2020). https://lumaquarterly.com/index.php/issues/volume-six/021-summer/ghostdayscvd19series/#text-2.
LaDuke, Winona. *Our Relations: Struggles for Land and Life*. Cambridge: South End Press, 1994.
Kelley, Robin D.G. "What did Cedric Robinson mean by Racial Capitalism?" *Boston Review*. January 12, 2017. https://www.bostonreview.net/articles/robin-d-g-kelley-introduction-race-capitalism-justice/.
Kulchyski, Peter. "Rethinking Inequality in a Northern Indigenous Context: Affluence, Poverty, and the Racial Reconfiguation and Redistribution of Wealth." *The Northern Review*, 42 (2016): 125–136.
McKittrick, Katherine. *Sylvia Wynter: On Being Human as Praxis*. Durham: Duke University Press, 2015.
Menakem, Resmaa. "Healing Racialized Trauma Begins with your Body." *Resmaa Menakem: Embodied Anti-Racist Education*. November 17, 2020. https://www.resmaa.com/somatic-learnings/healing-racialized-trauma-begins-with-your-body.
Menakem, Resmaa. *My Grandmother's Hands: Racialized Trauma and the Pathway to Mending Our Hearts and Bodies*. Las Vegas: Central Recovery Press, 2017.
Menakem, Resmaa. "Unlocking the Genius of Your Body." *Resmaa Menakem: Embodied Anti-Racist Education*. December 18, 2020. https://www.resmaa.com/somatic-learnings/unlocking-the-genius-of-your-body.
Nixon, Lindsay. "Visual Cultures of Indigenous Futurism." *Otherwise Worlds: Against Settler Colonialism and Anti-Blackness*. Durham: Duke University Press, 2020.
Orlow, Uriel. "Photography as Cinema: La Jetée and the Redemptive Powers of the Image." *Creative Camera*, no. 359 (August–September 1999), 14–17.
Robinson, Dylan. "Critical Conversations 2021: Dylan Robinson: The Museum's Incarceration of Indigenous Life." Critical Conversations. University of Saskatchewan, March 5, 2021.
Simpson, Leanne. "Land as Pedagogy." *Decolonization: Indigeneity, Education & Society* 3, no. 3 (2014): 1–25.
Simpson, Leanne. "Leanne Betasamosake Simpson: I am not Afraid to be Radical." *Indianz.Com*. July 17, 2018. https://www.indianz.com/News/2018/07/17/leanne-betasamosake-simpson-i-am-not-afr.asp.
"Survivance." *The Decolonial Dictionary*. April 15, 2021. https://decolonialdictionary.wordpress.com/2021/04/15/survivance/.
"*Wagon Burner*." Isuma TV. May 15, 2007. http://www.isuma.tv/en/imaginenative/wagon-burner.
Wehelyie, Alexander. *Habeas Viscus: Racializing Assemblages, Biopolitics, and Black Feminist Theories of the Human*. Durham: Duke University Press, 2014.
Wheeler, Brad. "Terrance Houle Conjures Spirits with Ghost Days Performance." *The Globe and Mail*. August 9, 2017. https://www.theglobeandmail.com/arts/art-and-architecture/terrance-houle-conjures-spirits-with-ghost-days-performance/article35932000/.
Wynter, Sylvia. "Unsettling the Coloniality of Being/Power/Truth/Freedom: Towards the Human, After Man, Its Overrepresentation – An Argument." *The New Centennial Review, Coloniality's Persistence* 3, no. 3 (2003): 257–337.

14

DESIRE TO HEAL; DESIRE TO BE SEEN; DESIRE TO DANCE

An Interview with Kijâtai-Alexandra Veillette-Cheezo[1]

By Priscilla Guy

Translated by Alanna Thain

Kijâtai-Alexandra Veillette-Cheezo is a filmmaker and journalist based in Montreal, descended from a Québécois mother and an Anishinaabe father. Their short films speak to Indigenous realities in Canada from a personal point of view, weaving together political concerns with their singular point of view. Interested in taking on all roles in the production of a film, they use self-representation as a way to connect with others; talking about their own experience is, for them, a way to open up dialogue by touching people's hearts. Also an activist, and passionate about journalism, Veillette-Cheezo uses words and images to create bridges between communities, to support their Indigenous peers, and to stop the erasure of their culture in the context of colonial violence. By using a DIY approach to filmmaking, they offer a touching and unique window through which audiences from diverse backgrounds can relate to and take responsibility for how to support Indigenous struggles.

Guy: I'm very interested in your relationship to the image, your body in the image, but also in the rewriting of the image in your work, that is to say [your way] of bringing new images into the imaginary through an activist's lens. At what point did you choose to be the subject in some of your works, the subject or the filmed object, or the filmed body, the material of creation? How did this come about?

Veillette-Cheezo: I had stopped making films for a long time. [...] I was lost for several years, then I started making film again. I thought I needed it, especially to express myself and externalize what I had inside me. Because we live in a society, in an era, where we have to repress everything, all our

DOI: 10.4324/9781003335887-18

emotions. [...] And I hadn't done that for years. So, with my first film, *Kijâtai*,[2] made with Wapikoni Mobile,[3] I just needed to get everything out of my head. And it was good for me. That's also what Wapikoni is about: being able to reappropriate the tools of cinema and express our Indigenous realities. What we feel. And also, it has a very therapeutic side because for a long time Indigenous communities were silenced. A certain image of ourselves was imposed on us, if you watch John Wayne Western films, for example. Wapikoni is a way to reappropriate these representations that exist in the media. It's happening more and more these days, and it's great to see. To be able to express ourselves, and then show our own stories. I just finished a film, I called it *Odehimin*,[4] which means "strawberry" in Anishinaabe, but it also means "heart berry," because the strawberry is heart-shaped. *Odehimin* also links us to the earth because the strawberry is like a representation of the fact that it links the sun to the earth. And I wanted to incorporate that, to address my heart. With this film, this time I needed to talk about my body. To talk a little about the relationship I have with my body [... I] wanted to show that it is possible to be in harmony with our body, to love our body. And that it's normal not to love ourselves too, it's a part of who we are, human beings. So, I made a video about it, with drums and my voiceover. Especially with everything that's going on right now [social uprisings, the #MeToo movement, anti-racist and decolonial struggles, the COVID-19 pandemic], I thought it would be nice to find myself again. With the pandemic, we were isolated, and we found ourselves face to face with ourselves... I was very, very busy before, I kept myself busy with activism, my involvement and everything. And the pandemic put me on pause, and I found myself alone. That's when I saw that I had to speak. I had to speak about what was inside me. And it did me good to make this new film with Wapikoni.

Guy: Speaking for yourself also brings you back to activism and in the desire to support people who are close to you.

Veillette-Cheezo: Yeah, if I go back to *Odehimin*, I did a lot in this film: I shot it and also filmed myself, I filmed myself in the river too, with a tripod and everything. I'm also in a project right now that includes training, and we had an exercise at one point to find our inner motivation. I went to see my mother and my sister, who were around a lot when I was little. When I told [my sister] what I thought was my inner motivation, she said, "Yes, that's exactly what I was going to say." I said I wanted to make the people around me happy. That I wanted to reach out to people, to connect with them. And she said, "You did exactly that when you were a little baby, you were always smiling." I was always making faces to make people laugh. It made me feel better because I feel like I'm starting to reconnect with myself and understand what I want to do in life. And that's kind of what I wanted to do with *Odehimin*, because I see that there are a lot of people who don't feel good about themselves. I know it, I feel it. I know what it is. And then, also, one thing that affected us, amongst Indigenous people, is that many women have experienced sexual violence. And not just women actually. But we don't talk about it much. We're talking about it a bit more these days. It's not fun, but I would say it's important that we talk about it, whereas before, we didn't talk about it. So, I just wanted to join other people to show that it's still possible to heal. But it's one step at a time. Just to show that they are not alone. That's how I started to have the fire again, to want to make films, by watching other films, for example at Wapikoni. I saw other people who were going through the same things as me. And I thought, "Wow, I'm not alone." That helped me to continue. I want to be able to transmit that feeling through the films as well.

Guy: Yes, it's also true that your film *Kijâtai* is really welcoming. You directed it, and ultimately it's also about you; it's your name, but it welcomes others. In any case, when I look at it, it welcomes me, because there is mystery, but also a clear message, which is not ambiguous or vague. Not everyone is capable of doing that. To have both: a very assertive message and, at the same time, space in which to breathe and feel welcomed.

Veillette-Cheezo: That's why I like to use images and sound, because it allows me to express something that I can't necessarily express with words.

Guy: But you use words too.

Veillette-Cheezo: Yes, I use words anyway, but in a different way. In *Odehimin*, I wrote a text and then I recorded it as a voice-over. I wanted to try to use the words from beginning to end, to make a kind of poem [...].

Guy: Earlier you spoke about your relationship to the body and how it is present in your work on screen. I'm really curious to know more about this scene in the river, where there is a tripod and no one behind it. I've also filmed myself this way, and it's strange: when we film ourselves, we are sometimes before a tripod with nobody behind, because we are the ones who start the recording and then we come back in front of the camera. So, there is someone, there is a look, that of the camera on the tripod, but there is no human being. What does this work mean to you?

Veillette-Cheezo: I felt more comfortable this way, especially for the type of images I wanted to film. I wanted to film myself, not completely naked, but I wanted to film at least parts of my body. At one point, for an hour, there were two people picnicking nearby, but I wasn't completely naked, I had a light black dress on. But when the two girls left, I felt more free to continue filming. Before that I was still filming, but I was a bit distracted by the gaze of the two girls, even though they seemed to be concentrating on what they were doing. So, I tried to focus on myself, because that's an exercise too. For a long time, like many people, I attached a lot of importance to the gaze of others, and I wanted to try to get rid of that a little. The camera for me is like a third eye. It's like my "other eye." So, I felt like I was just with myself because the camera is me too. I was very comfortable filming the images, but if there was someone else to help me film, I don't think I would have been as comfortable.

Guy: That brings me to another question: the relationship to the control of the images, that is to say, what we decide to do in the image as a performer; how we decide to frame ourselves as a "cameraperson"; how we decide to edit it, as an editor? There are three levels of power, of control. What is your relationship to this: performing, filming, editing? Have you always worked like this? Are these new roles for you?

Veillette-Cheezo: For the creation of *Odehimin*, I wanted to be more structured, and I realized that this was not my way of doing things. Because I was trying to write the text first, rather than after filming everything. But in the end, I think I had to experience the images I filmed to know how to use the text. I already had the film in mind, I hadn't made my technical edit, but I had a lot of things, images that I wanted to use. So, I took many, many shots. Until I ran out of batteries in my camera. And then, what I love doing most is editing. That's where I have fun. Since I was a little kid, I've been using my computer, making films, and I love editing, because it's another way of telling a story or telling a perspective, showing a certain perspective. If someone else had edited my film, it would not have been the same story at all. For example, with *Kijâtai*, it took me a long time to find out how I wanted to put these images together. And at one point, I knew I wanted to talk about my father and my mother, and then I thought of the messages they left me on my phone. It kind of shows the relationship I have with them. How do you show that everything is intertwined? I try to show a bit of how I feel: I hear my mother talking to me, my father talking to me. It's a bit like that for everyone: we are influenced by the people who raised us. This time, I wanted to show who I am. But at the same time, am I defined by my parents? In any case, it's still a lot of questions!

Guy: When you look at the images of yourself, do you discover things about yourself? Or are you not surprised, because it's a subject you know?

Veillette-Cheezo: No, I don't think I was surprised. For *Odehimin*, I knew what I was getting into, I knew what I wanted to do. At one point I had started my editing, I had just shot the footage in the river. So, I took my tripod and went to shoot other images, because I could see in my head what I needed. And then that's what I shot. So, I wasn't surprised when I filmed or when I saw the images. Especially when you film your own images, you know what you are filming. It's more when others film me that I'm surprised, I think, "Ah, ok, that's how they see me." But when I film myself, I know what I'm doing, what I see. With a digital camera I can see what I'm filming at the same time, it's fun.

Guy: Do you ever think about what you don't want to do? Or do you just think about what you want to do? I know that often I don't want to reproduce a certain cliché. Except that sometimes, when you think about what you don't want to do, you end up reproducing it. When you talk about decolonizing the gaze, do you say to yourself: "I don't want to go towards such and such images"?

Veillette-Cheezo: I try above all to be authentic. [...] For clichés, I don't know. I try to be myself as much as possible. When I create, I create. [laughs] It's a funny thing to say. I think first of all about the message I want to convey. Then I don't think about what I don't want to do. I have the impression that would take me in another direction. But it's more important to focus on what you want to do. The image you want to present. For a long time, my mother brought me up like that too: just think positively, that's how you'll attract things into your life. So, I always had a positive way of thinking too.

Guy: Is it political for you to film yourself, rather than filming others? Do you approach it in the same way?

Veillette-Cheezo: It depends on what you want to say. I think I'll borrow the words of Mélissa Mollen Dupuis: "If I could, I would just be an artist. But I have to be an activist too."[5] I think that, as a woman, just the fact that I was born as an Indigenous woman, I feel like I already had, not that obligation, but let's say that mission. To have to fight for my rights and also to make people aware of this reality. There is still a lot of awareness to be raised around Indigenous realities. And as women, we also have a lot to pass on. But if I film myself, as opposed to filming someone else, I think that... it still depends. I know that when I film myself, it's more artistic, but there is still a little political undertone. With *Kijâtai* I talk about the transmission of cultures, and also a little about the fact that I don't speak my own language. It's another way of conveying the fact that there is a break in the transmission of cultures. It's a quest for identity between Native and non-Native, because in fact I am both. So, I don't know if it's more activist. I think in everything I do, it took me a long time to realize that I was an activist, because it's always been a part of my life...

Guy: ...By default?

Veillette-Cheezo: Yes, like when I started speaking in front of people. It's now something that's part of my daily life, but I didn't realize it, so now I'm trying to talk about it more. I haven't been able to do much lately with the pandemic as I was living further away, but now that I'm in Montreal I'll be able to get more involved. I would like to add something about *Odehimin*. I arrived there, near the river, and I was in my "moon time" (menstruating). I had prepared myself, but it wasn't enough... so I had to film in the water all the time! As a woman, I was filming myself, and I was like... I don't know, but in Indigenous culture, when you have your period—why is it hard for me to say? It's still a taboo thing. [...] And that's what I was trying to show in the film, that we don't have to be ashamed of our bodies. And I was in perfect harmony with nature. We are very powerful when we are in our moon time. We are more connected with the spirit world, if I remember correctly. So, I thought it was really good that I was connected with everything! I don't show it in the film [that I am menstruating], but...

Guy: ...But you know it, yes.

Veillette-Cheezo: Yes, I know it. So again, it's a way for me to express myself. When I see the images, I see that I am completely interrelated with all the elements of nature. And also with myself in the water. There were also fish that came to nibble at my feet. There were ducks around me. It was a really beautiful place; the weather was good. I really enjoyed it. When I look at this film, I think of the filming I did.

Guy: I wonder what your relationship to dance is.

Veillette-Cheezo: I want to start dancing again! Sometimes I dance just to... I don't know.

Guy: You know, between the drums, the music, the images and the editing... Everything in your films is related to dance: the body, the music, the sounds, the rhythm.

Veillette-Cheezo: When I hear the sound of drums, when I hear music, I want to dance, then I dance. I think it's something that I denied myself for a long time, because I hid behind... let's say, the fact that my body is bigger. I mentioned above the problem of sexual violence, and I experienced it when I was young. And I have internalized the male gaze, which I cannot get rid of. I have the impression that sometimes I hide behind the idea that I am less desirable. So, I've stopped dancing. But I would like to start dancing again.

Guy: Do you consider your films to be dance?

Veillette-Cheezo: I didn't think about it at all, but now that you mention it, it's true that I use rhythm a lot. One time someone saw me dancing, I went to an Indigenous show, and I was dancing, and they said, "Wow, you have rhythm." So, when other people say it, I see it. Especially in *Kijâtai*, I don't know, I jump in the water! And in *Odehimin*, I use my body a lot.

Guy: Yes, in *Kijâtai* too, the editing dances the body in a way that makes the body appear and disappear from the frame. Very simply, too. But it's true that it feels like you didn't dance when you were shooting, but when you began to edit, it started to dance.

Veillette-Cheezo: Yes, I make my images dance. That's what I like most about editing. I would like to be more comfortable with my body so I can dance. But I think I'm getting there, with the film I made, *Odehimin*, it helped me deal with a lot of things. The fact that I'm going to release the film, make it public. There are parts of my body that I have never shown to anyone. Like my belly: I wear crop-tops, but I hide the whole lower part of my belly, you know?

Guy: It's rare that we show those parts too. The neck, the throat, we're more used to it, but the belly for women, it's less... Guys are always bare chested, and sometimes I think about it, and I think, "Wow, that's funny, I can't imagine that in my body, baring my belly or chest all the time."

Veillette-Cheezo: That's why I wanted to be partly naked in my upper body in my film. Because I also talk about being "two-spirited," in my film, it is very present. I want to show that I consider myself "two-spirited" and that we could remove this sexualization of women's breasts. But I think it's going to take some time before that happens.

Guy: Yes, it's impressive the pressure on women's bodies. There's a desire to feel strong and daring, to present the body, and at the same time, there are a lot of wounds and barriers. And that doesn't mean that it's not possible to change our ways of seeing and feeling, but I have the impression that for many women, we still have to break down these barriers before we can do what we want... All these barriers, that you have to go through just to bare your breasts. [...] Do you have the impression that the camera, and then the screen, allows you, in a controlled setting, to explore what you can't explore in everyday life?

Veillette-Cheezo: Yes. The camera allows you to see things in a different way. To show that it's normal, that it's beautiful to normalize things. When Safia Nolin did it [stripping],[6] many people were scandalized. I think it was good to use the camera to show that. That it's normal, that it's us. Just to stop being ashamed of our bodies, and then to love them, above all.

Notes

1 This interview was conducted on September 11, 2020, on Zoom. It was held as part of Priscilla Guy's doctoral research on feminist screendance self-representation (Lille University, France). It has been lightly edited for clarity and relevance.
2 *Kijâtai*, directed by Kijâtai-Alexandra Veillette-Cheezo (Wapikoni Mobile, 2019).
3 Co-founded in 2003 by Manon Barbeau, the Atikamekw Nation Council, and the First Nations of Quebec and Labrador Youth Council, with the support of the Assembly of First Nations and the collaboration of the National Film Board of Canada, Wapikoni Mobile was launched in 2004 as part of the Présence Autochtone festival in Montreal. Since then, Wapikoni Mobile has been touring Indigenous communities and offering First Nations youth workshops that allow them to master digital tools through the production of short films and musical works. At each of its stops, "filmmaker-accompaniers" welcome around thirty young participants in training at every stage of the production process. See https://evenementswapikoni.ca/.
4 *Odehimin*, directed by Kijâtai-Alexandra Veillette-Cheezo (Wapikoni Mobile, 2020).
5 Mellissa Mollen-Dupuis is a renowned indigenous activist and mentor for many folks from a younger generation who are getting involved in defending Indigenous heritage and culture in Québec, Canada.
6 In 2019, Quebecois singer and songwriter Safia Nolin released a music video in which she appears naked, fighting dominant beauty standards that value only narrow types of beauty ideals and that shame overweight women. See Radio Canada, "Safia Nolin nue dans un vidéoclip pour promouvoir la diversité des corps," *Radio Canada*, August 13, 2019, https://ici.radio-canada.ca/nouvelle/1258776/safia-nolin-nue-videoclip-lesbian-breakup-song-diversite-des-corps.

Bibliography

Radio Canada. "Safia Nolin nue dans un vidéoclip pour promouvoir la diversité des corps." *Radio Canada*. August 13, 2019. https://ici.radio-canada.ca/nouvelle/1258776/safia-nolin-nue-videoclip-lesbian-breakup-song-diversite-des-corps.

Veillette-Cheezo, Kijâtai-Alexandra, dir. *Kijâtai*. Wapikoni Mobile, 2019.

Veillette-Cheezo, Kijâtai-Alexandra, dir. *Odehimin*. Wapikoni Mobile, 2020.

PART IV

Technology; Technics; Tenderness

15
FROM _ RYAN CLAYTON TO _ EMILIE MORIN

Ryan Clayton and Emilie Morin

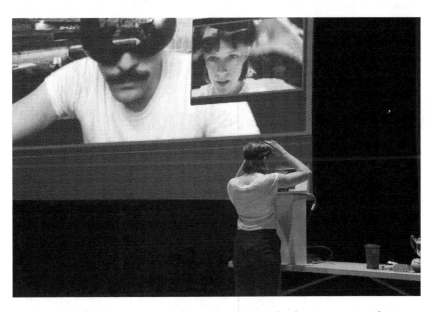

FIGURE 15.1 *SkypeDuet* performed at Regards Hybrides International Forum, Montreal (QC), Canada in November 2019
Source: © Omer Yukseker.

DOI: 10.4324/9781003335887-20

FIGURE 15.2 *SkypeDuet* performed at Hexagram GALA, Montreal (QC), Canada in December 2021
Source: © Caroline Pierret.

Part 1

SkypeDuet Description

SkypeDuet is a twenty-minute Skype dance choreographed for a live audience. A bit of context is that this performance was created and choreographed by us (Emilie Morin and Ryan Clayton) in 2018. When we stage this performance, one of us performs in a space with a live audience and receives a Skype video call from the other performer in a room with no audience. The video call occurs on a laptop in view of the performer, and the laptop's screen is reproduced via large-scale projection behind the performer with a live audience. Both of us, as tele-present and present performers, enact a choreography exploring the limits and space of a Skype conversation, reflecting on its capacity to create and inform virtual worlds. The choreography is broken into three discrete sections with an established choreography of movement and vocalization. Within three of these sections are also several previously agreed-upon times deliberately left open for improvisation by the performers. The performance works through these sections, ending with a short discussion about the weather between performers just before the Skype call ends and the performance concludes.

SkypeDuet Genesis

Performing for and with Each Other through the Screen via Skype

We first started this project by meeting via Skype video calls twice a week during the summer of 2018. As we collaborated, we began performing for and with each other, unconcerned with an exterior audience. It was a very organic process as we developed the separate segments that make up the Duet. One of the first topics we explored was the different kinds of spaces and their connections, whether ideal rooms, actual rooms, workspaces, public or private, and of course, virtual spaces. We worked with OBS, a software that allows us to play with multiple video effects during a Skype conversation, to create and utilize a chroma key effect. This effect and our discussions around it formed a whole section of work where we can virtually be in the same room, having the same room as the background, while being in separate geographic locations. This illusion effect continued a more conceptual discussion around the spaces we create in real life and the ones we imagine, and how they harmonize or confront each other but are always in conversation.

It was fascinating to play with how our bodies react to the ideal/real/virtual spaces we created and encountered in the performance. We had fun witnessing how our bodies were connecting from one non-mediated space to the other through the flatness of the screen. For instance, we explored how to move the body from one space to the other, from one side of the screen to the other, from real to virtual. The relation of ideal/real/virtual spaces resonated with "bodies." We discussed the ways we imagine our body or picture the parts of it that are invisible. For instance, we talked about visualizing the interior of one's own body and how medical imagery can give us a glimpse of how that interiority appears. These images are in conversation, sometimes in vivid contrast, with how we actually *feel* the interior of our body.

An animated series of Magnetic Resonance Imaging (MRI) images of one of the performers appears in one of the sections of *SkypeDuet*. The MRI is a carpet[1] on which Emilie dances, repeating gestures: bouncing on her pelvis, hands, and knees; stopping; sitting still; floating her arms and legs, slowly letting them touch the ground and lying down. As Emilie executes the repetitive dance, she answers Ryan, who, just before, was talking about imagined and real spaces. Emilie says how imagined spaces and the ones people do inhabit in reality remind her of how she thinks about her body. She talks about how she imagines her dancing body as she moves and what it looks like from another exterior perspective. She speaks about the labour of dancing, intrinsically linked with practice and repetition. Her physical endeavours, repetitive gestures, and audible breath highlight Emilie's statement. She mentions how there is a gap, sometimes, between the expected body's performance and the result. She talks about how her real body will inevitably fail and that she needs to feel at peace with that. These considerations around ideal/real/virtual bodies stem from a dance performer's perspective. The imagined body is in action, and the idea of "failing" lies in the possibility that the real, able body does not execute to perfection what was imagined. The physical labour necessary to the performance, and the exhaustion that emerges from it, is mirrored by the exhaustion of the technologies we use in the performance: Skype itself, our smartphones, and laptops will eventually "fail" too.

Adding a Third (Exterior) Audience Present in the Room with One of the Performers

In July 2018, we had the opportunity to present a version of our performance to an external audience. Emilie was in Oaxaca, Mexico, for a screendance residency at CaSa—Centro de las Artes de San Agustín Etla. She was present in the room with the audience and Ryan was joining via Skype, calling from a residency in New York City. We projected the Skype conversation on a TV screen; the public could watch Emilie live in the meeting room with them and watch the screen. We also presented the duet at Flux gallery in August 2018. Ryan was live with the audience, and we projected the conversation with Emilie in her apartment in Montreal on a gallery wall.

Having an exterior audience changed the performance. The live audience modified the performer's attention, the attention shifting and splitting, divided between the interaction with the remote performer onscreen and, less obviously, between the exchanges with the external audience, acting on a subtle mood level in the room. The remote performer has to be careful of their actions as they have repercussions on the performer present live with the audience. With the exterior audience, there is less room for the unexpected. A prescient example of this would be when we were rehearsing *SkypeDuet* with no audience, just the two of us running through the piece.[2] In the first section, we improvised our actions as long as we stayed in front of our camera for the green screen effect to work. Improvising, Ryan started to tape his goggles and face, making Emilie break out of character and laugh. This action would have been perhaps goofy but extremely difficult to read for an outside audience, as this specific (funny) action exits the limits of what we want to say with *SkypeDuet*. Indeed, the stakes are different from one version to the other: when performing with and for one another, *SkypeDuet* is more exploratory. The playfulness is still present with the exterior audience, though we can't deviate entirely from the structure.

The exterior audience also impacted the kind of movements that we did in the performance. When performing for just one another, we choreographed the movements for the screen. They needed to be modified when we included the third audience, as the latter have their perspective on the same labour. Our focus on the movement was then to make the choreography more visible in "space" vs in "screen."

SkypeDuet Evolution

Adapting to the Technology Updates: SkypeDuet and Our Lives in the Digital Covid-19 (Post)Pandemicene

In the first written statement that accompanied *SkypeDuet* in 2018, we wrote: "The malleability of the performance is crucial to us, because it speaks of the constant dialogue between spaces, that have become increasingly more present, with the rise of virtuality's potential."[3] We did not know at the time that this statement would be so prescient of the unprecedented and overwhelming transfer of our social interactions occurring digitally during the first lockdown period of the Covid-19 pandemic and subsequently as people adapted to the use of these more commonly used digital spaces in their everyday lives. After the arrival of the pandemicene, it became increasingly obvious that the performance of *SkypeDuet* would need to change. It has now been adapted for Zoom as people have become more comfortable with that digital venue. During the first lockdown of the pandemic, Skype updated, creating problems for our performance as we could no longer be side by side on the screen. Its interface of buttons and controls became more visible, no longer auto-hiding after a few moments. The adaptation to Zoom has allowed *SkypeDuet* to live on as the world and technology change. We have noticed that its meaning has changed for our audiences. Before the pandemicene, the idea of performing with telecommunication technology was novel. Post-pandemicene, it has become almost banal, as what feels like hundreds of live streaming and hybrid performances were developed and perfected during the lockdowns. Instead of novelty, our performance now asks questions about the relationship with our screens and how these relationships have changed within the pandemicene.

Part 2

De: Ryan Clayton <surplusorgans@gmail.com>
Envoyé: 8 juillet 2020 10:41
À: Emilie Morin <mieliemorin@hotmail.com>
Objet: Hey Friend

Okay, I know I said I would email you two days ago, and two days before that I said I would send this same email. But here we are today with an actual email and not a promise of one, so clearly some progress is being made. The problem, you see, is that every time I go to sit down and write to you, the 100 other distractions my computer is capable of producing swarm through and around my attention, letting me easily wander off from what I initially sat down to do.

A list of things I looked at between the next paragraph and this one:

Textures for a metal walkway
A press release about UK's offer to HK BNO holders
Changed the song on my Spotify playlist
Water material node trees for Blender

It seems weird to be writing about our performance now. We performed to a room full of people, sitting shoulder to shoulder, and we shared a meal afterwards! I don't think we could do any of those things right now, but I look forward to doing them again.

I remember the feeling of isolation and wanting to connect, to be in the space with the audience after the performance ended, and being excited to bike to the venue and meet the audience. It was particularly odd that, when I did arrive, several people expressed their surprise that I was in Montreal and was able to arrive at all—that the telecommunication technology was not used out of necessity, but rather as a material.

This is fine, of course. No one was sad to meet me! But that realization leads to an important aspect of our performance, that of using a tool against its purpose. Through our embodied gestures, Skype is unable to communicate meaning, obscured and indiscernible as the interior of our bodies.

Hope you're doing well in Gaspésie, we just lost power so this will get to you when power (and the internet) return.

Ryan

De: Emilie Morin <mieliemorin@hotmail.com>
Envoyé: 13 juillet 2020 9:42
À: Ryan Clayton <surplusorgans@gmail.com>
Objet: Hey Friend

Hey, I know I didn't mention when I would get back to you and answer the first entry to our email correspondence, but it seems I went over my own various deadlines. Days went by and I kept thinking: "this morning, right after coffee, I will write my response," or I was running and saying to myself, "this afternoon, the first thing I will do is answer Ryan." But it never actually happened.

So I decided I would write Monday morning right before our Skype meeting. I thought it was a mental deadline I could not *not* meet. I guess I didn't want to tell you in person, even if you'd understand, that: "I haven't written my response yet, but it'll happen when, or when, or when…"

The kids downstairs are making a lot of noise as they're playing and of course this agitation is affecting my writing.

Before I started to write, I:
went for my daily morning run
swam a tiny bit in the river
drank my coffee
had breakfast
and here we are

The idea that, through our gestures, Skype can no longer communicate meaning is appealing to me. However, maybe Skype does still communicate meaning, just not in the way it conventionally does. What are Skype's conventionalities? Perhaps a detailed definition of what the platform means to us is necessary.

About the obscurity and indiscernibility of our bodies:

The indiscernible was first used to qualify our gaze and now has expanded, in our minds, to our entire bodies. The opacity of our mind, rather than the opposing transparency of the platform, is one way to work against Skype's purpose. I remember Bart Van den Eyden,[4] dramaturge, with whom I had a meeting before we started to create *SkypeDuet*. He said that, for him, Skype wasn't about the visual but about communication, and that the visual was just a plusvalue, not the core of Skype's purpose. In a way, while performing *SkypeDuet* we emphasize the usage of the visual components of Skype, and therefore deviate from its mission. Through visual optimization, we as performers become more opaque in meaning.

Once, it was that Skype was used for long distance communication, but in our new reality of the pandemicene, distance is no longer the reason to choose a device for remote communication. I don't mean to say that we've gotten to a point where we use Skype solely for the purpose of communication while in isolation, but that its conventional and alternative uses are intertwined, and that those uses will shift with societal transformations.

In the book *Touch: Sensuous Theory and Multisensory Media*,[5] Laura U. Marks defends a writing practice that speaks of embodied art processes involving new media and technologies. But she asserts that what is most striking to her is when the writing isn't always able to achieve the translations of these sensuous artistic manifestations.

I think this could inform our thinking: translating our process of *SkypeDuet* into writing is our aim, despite translations' imperfection, and despite our awareness of our own inability to completely achieve the task.

That's all for now. Looking forward to talking to you in a few hours:)
Emilie

De: Ryan Clayton <surplusorgans@gmail.com>
Envoyé: 9 novembre 2020 19:52
À: Emilie Morin <mieliemorin@hotmail.com>
Objet: Re: Hey Friend

Okay, okay okay. This gap is embarrassing. It has been 4 whole months since I got back to you! I can't believe it. So much has changed in the last 4 months for me personally, with very little meaningful change happening in the world at large (except that good news yesterday!).

We have continued to spend uncountable hours on Skype, Zoom, Facebook Chat etc. etc. etc., and their meaning, instead of becoming clearer, becomes more and more obscured. It's almost as if the more you stare at an interface, the more invisible it becomes. I think that is where that dramaturge was wrong about visuality being plusvalue. I think it *is* the value, the non-verbal communication being so valuable as I talk. I can see the person across the city, across the world, react in close to real time to my words, and those reactions change what I say. Without the visuality I wouldn't know to alter my tone to change my context or to take a break from the conversation, but I am always staring at the representation of the person, not the interface. I think that is the difficulty of our performance: to center our bodies (what Skype wants us to do), while drawing attention to the interface (what Skype does not want us to do).

I look forward to spending more time speaking to the interface with you.
Ryan

De: Emilie Morin <mieliemorin@hotmail.com>
Envoyé: 15 novembre 2020 17:32
À: Ryan Clayton <surplusorgans@gmail.com>
Objet: Re: Hey Friend

Hey,
I am happy that we can continue this conversation.
I am also very fond of it happening through writing.
Guess it's because it gives me a break with visuality.
Or maybe it doesn't…
I mean it is a text-based technology, so it gives me a break from images, from online meetings, but not from the screen.

***

A few thoughts in response to "spending more time speaking to the interface with you."
One colleague told me about this study stipulating that on Zoom, we spend a lot of energy compensating for the lack of non-verbal language. It

comforted me, as I am spending all my time web-conferencing and am feeling exhausted.

Your idea about the non-verbal brings new light to this, where a shift of attention needs to be made in order to adapt to the interfaces' particular ways of presenting non-verbal communication.

If I still consider the image a plusvalue to Skype, it is maybe because the quality of the image is mediocre, and Skype's focus isn't on improving the quality of the visual. But, in our conversation, are we using "plusvalue" with consideration to its dimensions of productivity and effectiveness, or to its intrinsic relation to capitalism? And what about "value"? Are we considering a "value" a feature which allows us to increase our non-verbal communication efficiency, when such a feature stems from a consumer technology? Skype's inherent consumerism plays both in and against our favor: as users/consumers of the platform, we can expand the potential of the valuable visuality although we can't completely escape the capitalist flow produced by the "plusvalue". What does it mean, now, in our pandemicene day and age ;) to divert Skype's purposes, when the application and its users are facing such uncertainties? It feels like we're in the same boat: us (critiquing) and them (the object of our critique).

Have you noticed how Skype has changed its visual features and toolbar to copy zoom? I wonder how this is related to the brand's idea of what it is selling. Is Skype thinking more of becoming a platform for web-conferencing? Was that always the case? How will our *SkypeDuet* unfold under these new conditions?

You can't actually get rid of the tool bar on Skype now with the new update. It's always there, privileging the communication features of the product instead of its former visual slickness.

I wonder how that speaks to the simultaneous invisibility and opacity of interfaces you were mentioning. I feel the tool bar is very visible, very "in the way" of the visual aesthetic of *SkypeDuet*, for instance. I feel it is very opaque, in the sense that the opacity is imposed upon us. We don't know what the effects of spending exponentially more time on these different interfaces will have on us, and we don't know how to make our experience and its opacity our own.

***

I wasn't sure what you meant when you said the world changed very little in the last few months, but your life changed a lot in comparison. Were you ironic? I am genuinely asking:)

I also didn't know what event you were referring to when you said "except that good news from yesterday". I guessed it was the news of the democratic party being declared winner of the presidential election by most media, but now I am unsure.

***

I have noticed my gaze deviates from the screen, beyond the computer's metallic frame, more and more when I am in online meetings. This deviation is an escape from all that staring I need to perform—that we all need to perform. Staring is the new "reading of the room," and gaze deviation beyond the screen is the new *être dans la lune*.[6]

Indiscernible.

Emilie

De: Ryan Clayton <surplusorgans@gmail.com>
Envoyé: 15 décembre 2020 19:20
À: Emilie Morin <mieliemorin@hotmail.com>
Objet: Re: Hey Friend

The conversation continues in ebbs and flows, dribs and drabs, as I carve out moments between engagements. It seems so hard these days to carve out a moment for something that doesn't seem like it has a definite deadline. Without a looming, missable moment, it feels like I retreat into lethargy and distraction. Well, no longer. I will write this email today, just as I promised.

I am stuck on you noticing that Skype has removed the ability to hide its interface. This seems to be in line with Zoom and Jitsi, where you are always made aware that what you are viewing is "live" and not recorded. This imposition of a user interface seems to be a way to affirm the veracity that the person you are talking to is there with you live, and that people are reacting to each other in real time. I guess when we are all forced to do this day-in and -out, having this tiny visual reminder is useful, otherwise we might start to doubt the "realness" of every conversation we have on these platforms.

***

I think if we have unproductive conversations, that is perhaps the way to utilize the plusvalue of the image in Skype's interface. We add live video feeds because it increases non-verbal communication tenfold. On business calls, it adds value in perhaps a capital sense; I might be able to sell you a bigger car or convince you to invest in my company by reading your non-verbal cues. The image facilitates a quicker movement of capital, which is perhaps in part why it was developed. But how we choose to use Skype to deploy this plusvalue means we can reallocate this value from "speedier movement of capital" to something else. Users of Skype are lucky that they want to connect in a real way that is in line with the desires of the program to speed up the movement of capital. If we wanted to disconnect, to become unaligned, I can't see a way to do that within Skype. We would have to turn it off, no? This leads me to agree with the ones who critique (you and me) and the program itself are in the same boat, the critique circle is completed. The only way to get off the ride is to turn it off.

***

The world is always changing, of course. It just seems kind of stuck in the larger picture right now, while the tighter frame has been full of change. I'm occasionally ironic, I suppose, but in general I try to avoid it. An overreliance of irony eventually leads down an alleyway which causes too many layers to build up, and you can no longer find the layers of sincerity.

***

I have three monitors in my office. When I turn my gaze from the conversation's monitor, it drifts into a new one.
Ryan

De: Emilie Morin <mieliemorin@hotmail.com>
Envoyé: 4 Jan 2021 12:22 PM
À: Ryan Clayton <surplusorgans@gmail.com>
Objet: Re: Hey Friend

An imposition of the interface:
I had a meeting this morning with three other artists on Google Meet. Google Meet offers the option of my own square on the meeting grid to be minimized. This way, I can remain in my corner. From there, I can still look discreetly at myself, and have my eyes mainly focused on the person speaking. On Zoom, if the person speaking has their square right beside mine on the grid, it is a nightmare to keep my gaze on them rather than on myself, hence the fear of missing out on what could happen to my own visual representation.

At the beginning of my morning meeting on Google Meet, one of the other artists had issues with their internet connection, and notified us they might cut off sometimes, punctuating their verbal explanation with fake freezing faces to illustrate the potential. They were also saying that they could only see me, and not the other two participants in the meeting, which led to these two participants turning off their cameras—despite the fact that the one saying they could only see me was already just seeing me, and now I, as well, could not see the other two participants.

Later on, the participant saying they might freeze or cut out *did* freeze and cut out. This was uncanny, as their earlier imitation of being frozen and cutting out was slightly different, but not that far from the real, "virtual" glitches. I'm not sure where I am going with this, but it seems like an idea for an online performance: the "realness" of the imperfect interface versus the performance of faking its potential failure.

***

Pets can also act as signs to affirm the "realness" of the virtual interaction.

For instance, my cat always ends up showing her face to the screen when I am in virtual meetings. She loves the screen. And she can't fake it, or fake anything, as she has no interest in social niceties or for the business of meetings.

Perhaps pets, and their inappropriate visit to your desk, should be mandatory for any virtual meeting, in an attempt to affirm their "realness".

***

I was reminded recently by Zab Maboungou, a choreographer and philosopher, that dance is all about the management of immediate time.[7]

This conception of time is very organic—it's about sensation, it's about the body's capacity to relate to its present and to its immediate space and time.

Immediacy has been replaced by instantaneity: a time that I am always running after, that I am just missing by a fraction of second, and that is demanding my urgent and constant reaction, as fast as my thumbs can tap on the luminous digital surface.

Emilie

Notes

1 Live, Emilie is dancing on a green fabric that acts as a green screen. On screen, with OBS producing the chroma key effect, the animated MRI appears, and Emilie looks like she is dancing on it (see Figure 15.2).
2 A run through is a common term used in live arts meaning going through the entire performance to remember the actions and cues, but without being fully engaged physically.
3 Emilie Morin and Ryan Clayton, "*SkypeDuet* Written Statement" (unpublished manuscript, DISP 615 Directed Studio Practice course, Concordia University, August 18, 2018).
4 The meeting with Bart Van den Eyden took place in May 2018, in the context of *Les Cliniques dramaturgiques*, an initiative organized by Festival TransAmériques that focused on helping artists solve a question by "matching" them with an appropriate expert. The meeting with Bart happened just before Ryan and I started our creative process. The questions I worked through with Bart explored ways to shift from the common usages of Skype while using it as a performative platform. Bart used his years of experiences as a dramaturg for stage work and implemented his expertise onto our creative process around telecommunication technology. Through this short conversation, Bart helped us to move towards questioning the edges of the affordances of Skype.

5 Laura U. Marks, *Touch: Sensuous Theory and Multisensory Media* (London: University of Minnesota Press, 2002), IX.
6 "Être dans la lune" is a common French idiom, translated literally into "Being on the moon." It refers to the state of a person losing its focus while busy at a task and zoning out.
7 Zab Maboungou, "La notion de temps en danse" (online lecture, Katya Montaignac and Regroupement québécois de la danse, December 11, 2020).

Bibliography

Maboungou, Zab. "La notion de temps en danse." Online lecture at Katya Montaignac and Regroupement québécois de la danse, December 11, 2020.

Marks, Laura U. *Touch: Sensuous Theory and Multisensory Media*. London: University of Minnesota Press, 2002.

Morin, Emilie, and Ryan Clayton. "*SkypeDuet* Written Statement." Unpublished manuscript, DISP 615 Directed Studio Practice course, Concordia University, August 18, 2018.

16

FILMING CONSCIOUSNESS

Between Phonesia® and Talking Camera—Organological Cinema

Anatoli Vlassov

Translated by Cath Marceau

> Cinema is characterized by the coinciding of the film's flux and the spectator's consciousness, and by the phenomenon of the adoption of the film's time by the consciousness of which it is the object.[1]

In the summer of 2015, while on vacation at a friend's in Majorca, I suggested to my daughter Tess Vlassov that we make a short talking dance film together. It was not the first time I had involved my daughter in my choreographic or filmic works. Creating with my child has always been a way for me to meet her anew. Creation is a form of play, an experience that permits, with its ups and downs, the discovery of the other on a journey made of shared trials. Such life lessons remove us from familial conditioning and reweaves new ties of kinship between us. This regeneration of the bonds that unite us allows us to become conscious of each other as more autonomous individuals. Creation is, moreover, a constructive game since its goal is to create a common object. A tangible object, an object that would not have been there if we had not played together. A newly created object, materialized, that we will be able to revise (*revoir*) at a later time. In short, the creation of a common work. A work that inscribes our encounter in matter and in time, leading to a new awareness not only of the other but also of us, of what we have created together. Beyond a simple game, the different co-creations with my daughter have been moments of privileged encounter for me, the co-construction of a new common consciousness. A space of complicity and encounter that only emerges if the process of creation has been set in motion, the process of a common becoming.

But let us come back to this performative film that I proposed to shoot alongside my daughter and that I later titled *Phoné-Scopie*.[2] To do so, I suggested a game to her: to go through a garden together with two GoPro

FIGURE 16.1 Tess Vlassov and Anatoli Vlassov, *Phoné-Scopie*, 2015, photo from a shot of the film
Source: Anatoli Vlassov.

cameras on our heads while talking continuously. I wanted our words to flow continuously and our gestures to be more or less influenced by the path of our bodies. So, Tess and I devised a precise itinerary in advance for our two different routes, composed in such a way that our respective paths would intersect and separate; following its steps, one would perform a solo for the other and vice versa. Two frontal cameras placed on our respective heads filmed us simultaneously and reciprocally. The result was a duo of gazes, mobile and speaking, moving within a given area. At times in parallel, at times separately, at times face to face, at times side by side, two distinct paths cross and separate; two cameras film two itinerant gazes and record the respective talking dances. The two different images thus captured were edited into a split screen (screen divided into two parts) where we see and hear the two protagonists simultaneously. A face-to-face between father and daughter gaining awareness of each other.

But what does the film spectator perceive in this encounter between father and daughter? Can the film ultimately capture this interfamilial realization of consciousness? And, finally, is it possible to film consciousness itself?

Creating Temporal Objects that Develop Freedom

Human consciousness functions like cinema. This idea from the philosopher Bernard Stiegler is based on how consciousness, like a film, consists of a montage. Stiegler specifies that this consciousness, made of one's attention to the present moment, "is situated between retentions (memory) and protentions (projection, expectation, desire) that it links by being receptive to what happens in the 'now.'"[3] It is thus a montage in the present moment between what is retained from the past (retention) and what is expected from the future (protention). Film functions exactly in the same manner, that of a montage between different temporalities of a story that is told, condensed into an average length of an hour and a half. It is for this reason that consciousness and film have the capacity to tune in to each other when one (consciousness) follows the other's unfolding (film). This synchronization is what particularly interests me, since it is precisely because of, or by virtue of, this synchronization that cinema has such an influence on human consciousnesses. However, it is not only film that has this power of action. A piece of music, dance, a performance, or a lecture also have this capacity to influence consciousnesses since their very functioning implies that a human consciousness follows them in time. This is why Stiegler groups all these artifacts under the term "temporal object." Unlike a usual object, the temporal object is an object "whose flow coincides with the flow of the consciousness of which it is the object."[4] Stiegler also specifies that this synchronization carries a risk of abuse of power, since "temporal objects enable, by the same token, the modification of these processes of consciousness, and up to a certain point, their influencing, even their control."[5] He underlines that in an age of massive production of temporal objects, the danger lies in an "industrial temporalization of consciousnesses" that leads to a "general synchronization of the temporal flows of consciousnesses"; a phenomenon that easily leads to a standardization of minds.

As Walter Benjamin writes in a short and masterly text, "The Work of Art in the Age of Mechanical Reproduction," songs, films, shows, and all other temporal objects influence our consciousnesses, with the risk of turning them into homogeneous masses.[6] Stiegler underlines that, on a collective scale, consciences "end up being synchronized to such an extent that they have lost their diachrony, that is to say their singularity, and, at bottom, their freedom."[7] The artistic, but also political, question I would like to ask here is: how do we create temporal objects that allow (or even develop) this freedom of perception? Temporal objects that leave enough room for the spectators' consciousness so that they each keep their interpretative singularity. Temporal objects that do not synchronize every consciousness in the same manner but open them up towards an emancipatory diversity. Where freedom, like consciousness, also becomes a process and not an end in itself.

FIGURE 16.2 Tess Vlassov and Anatoli Vlassov, *Phoné-Scopie*, 2015, photo from a shot of the film
Source: Anatoli Vlassov.

The Spectator Synchronizes Themselves with the Performer's Modified Consciousness through the Film

And what if, to produce such a temporal object, it was necessary to film consciousness itself? Not just any consciousness, but consciousness as a process, that is to say, as an act of liberation from its habitual codes. This is not about filming a consciousness altered by this or that drug, passively undergoing what is different in its experience. It is rather about filming a consciousness whose alteration is activated voluntarily and performatively by the protagonist themselves. Such a modified consciousness is in fact performed in our screendance *Phoné-Scopie*. In this game of wandering in a garden, Tess and I use a performative technique that I call *Phonesia*®, which is a re-articulation of the structural links between gesture and speech. It is thus by transforming the habitual relationships between body and language that we modify our consciousnesses during the performance. My hypothesis is that, while watching these films in which these processes of modification of the performers' consciousnesses are captured, the spectator will be able to experience, by synchronizing themselves with the performers during the film, the modification of their own consciousness.

Phonesia® as Technique and *corpArleity* [8] as a Site of Consciousness Re-articulation

If consciousness functions like cinema and cinema like consciousness, then *Phonesia*® functions at once like cinema and consciousness. It is a practical ability of montage for talking dancers and non-silent ones. It is a performative montage between the sensible and the intelligible that a performer executes in their corporeality or, rather, what I call their *corpArleity*, as a field of experience that emerges when a *Talking Dancer* practices *Phonesia*®. In "*CorpArleity*, Field of Experience for a *Talking Dancer*,"[9] an article written in the context of a research-creation collaboration with Julie Reshé, a Ukrainian philosopher and psychoanalyst, I develop this new way of defining the human body as a site of encounter between several forms of life: human, linguistic, and choreographic. I write, "*corpArleity* is thus this site of crossing and circulation where the real and the imaginary, the physical and the semantic meet and express themselves in a dense network of interdependence and exchanges."[10] When a performer practices *Phonesia*®, they have, accordingly, a field of experience (*corpArleity*) at their disposal where they can act on networks of interdependence between these gestures and words. In everyday life, when we speak, certain words correspond to certain gestures, each one being entangled in a meaning we wish to express. By disarticulating these habitual correspondences between words and gestures, the performer acts upon what links these actions to these words, thereby changing their consciousness of the relationship between their doing and saying. Does such a process not resemble the functioning of human consciousness? It would perhaps be between the experience and the reconsideration of this same experience that human consciousness is formed and evolves.

If *Phonesia*® enables the modification of consciousness through the rearrangement between acts (dancing gestures) and a distancing from these same acts (spoken words), it also provides tools to be capable of doing so intentionally. In the article "Phonesia,"[11] I have described some of its tools already (*Hole, Injector, Contaminator, Illustrator, Echo, Torsion, Parallel*...)[12] that enable one to act on logo-somatic arrangements. The *Talking Dancer* executes a montage between their words and their danced movements, a montage similar to that which cinema operates between sounds and images. In "Transmutation of the Gesture and the Sign – from Eisenstein to Kabuki and from *Phonesia*® to Godard," Dominique Chateau and I draw a parallel between these two forms of montage, cinematographic and phonesic. In it, I refer to video editing software: "where the editor mixes two tracks, AUDIO and VIDEO, the *Talking Dancer* does not mix two, but three tracks: DANCE as a set of possible movements, VOICE as a set of sounds produced by the vocal apparatus, and WORD as a set of meaningful words that they utter."[13] Still, the difference between the cinematographic and phonesic editors is the fact that one manipulates sounds and images that they have not experienced, whereas the other operates with words and gestures that concretely run through them. In their own experience at once sensible and intelligible, the phonesic editor has direct access to an act-speech montage and, as a result, to the experience of their own consciousness. With the tools of *Phonesia*®, they can act, with their danced gestures, on the structure of the spoken language they are using in that very moment; they have the capacity to influence their speech with these gestures (the reverse is also possible – with their words, they can act on their gestures). If we further develop the idea invoked at the beginning of this text, that ordinary consciousness is a montage between memory (retentions) and expectations (protentions), then phonesic consciousness is also a temporal montage (that of the present between the past and the future) where gestures and words successively play the roles of retention and protention. When it is a gesture that is retained in the performer's attention (gestural retention), the words are expected (verbal protention), and when words are retained by the protagonist instead (verbal retention), the gestures are expected (gestural protention). More concretely, retaining a gesture or a word is either to slow down their flow or repeat them on a loop. For example, in the film *Phoné-Scopie*, these moments are clearly visible when the protagonist swings in a hammock (see Figure 16.2): the repetitiveness of the corporal rocking allows the performer to retain her gesture in time (gestural retention), then the protagonist's attention awaits the word (verbal protention) that will thereafter superimpose itself onto the retained gesture (in terms of phonesic tools, this case is the application of an *Injector* effect that enables the introduction of an utterance within a flow of silent dance). Hence, in turn, the somatic and the semantic are edited via the circulation of the performer's attention in a perpetual flow of arrangement and rearrangement of acts and words. It is indeed this process of montage between the sensible and the intelligible that occurs in ordinary consciousness: only in the phonesic state is this process voluntarily intensified.

Dominique Château glimpses this similarity related to montage between *Phonesia*® and film in the history of the very appearance of cinema: "A number of characteristics of *Phonesia*® evoke considerations that we encounter in montage theory since its origins, some time after the advent of cinema."[14] Indeed, in his theory of montage, Russian filmmaker and theorist Sergei Eisenstein, inspired by the form of Japanese live performance called kabuki, invents a concept that he calls "monistic ensemble" to denote how "[s]ound-movement-space-voice here *do not accompany* (nor even parallel) each other, but function *as elements of equal significance*."[15] Even before the advent of sound film, Eisenstein already anticipated with this concept the power of sound latent in silent film. Accordingly, the monistic ensemble accords with that of *corpArleity* in the sense that danced movements are as important in their significance as the meaning of the spoken words. This egalitarian consideration of danced gesture and spoken word allows the *Talking Dancer* to defuse the power of words with respect to their claim to imposing exact meanings – whereas the intent behind a gesture remains open to interpretation to a greater extent. *CorpArleity* thus offers a site where the meaning of words counts as much as their sound, just as the movement of the body is as meaningful as the weight of words. A synesthesia transpires in *corpArleity* then, one that would renounce any form of hierarchy between the senses and sense. Château underlines, moreover, that in the monistic ensemble "signs transmute into one another and the garland of these signs which are put on an equal footing develops according to ceaseless transmedial

FIGURE 16.3 Tess Vlassov and Anatoli Vlassov, *Phoné-Scopie*, 2015, photo from a shot of the film
Source: Anatoli Vlassov.

FIGURE 16.4 Tess Vlassov and Anatoli Vlassov, *Phoné-Scopie*, 2015, photo from a shot of the film
Source: Anatoli Vlassov.

operations."[16] And it is precisely these garlands lit by *corpArleity*, interlacing the signs of dance and those of speech, that interest us here. These garlands that I call *Sens-Ations* and that I have already defined in the article "*Sens-Ations* Machine: When Sense Meets Sensation" as "channels in which a signification can transubstantiate by transmuting itself into sensation and vice versa."[17] Channels enabling transfers between doing and saying—and from which consciousness, as I hypothesize above, emerges. We can observe an example of the manifestation of a *Sens-Ation* in the film *Phoné-Scopie* when the performer feels that he has touched a tree involuntarily while in motion and verbalizes this fact at that very moment (see Figure 16.3). I will not consider this consciousness here as something stable and perennial, but rather as a succession of ephemeral events; consciousness akin to these garlands of lights that turn on and off when saying transmutes into doing (and vice versa), propagating a wave of modified consciousness. The hyphen of this neologism *Sens-Ation* is this sparkling light of a consciousness that emerges when we practice *Phonesia*®.

Capturing *Sens-Ations*

Here, we have reached one of the issues, this time cinematographic, at stake in the film in question, namely capturing these notable *Sens-Ations*. It is a matter of filming the *Talking Dancers'* modified consciousness by capturing the moments when their gestures and words mutually transmute into one another. In our context, this question returns to the following one: how to record the sound of speech and the image of the dance, organized by this actualized consciousness with its sap that circulates between gesture and utterance, between action and thought? Which filmic devices could render this back-and-forth movement between the visible of gestures and the audible of speech sensible?

Organological Cinema

To answer these questions, I present the concept of *Organological Cinema*. To do so, I draw on Stiegler's theory of *general organology*.[18] Derived from Greek, the term *organon* means tool or instrument, and *organology*, in musical contexts, refers to the study of musical instruments. For Stiegler, general organology studies organs from the anatomical parts of the human body to technical fields and social organizations. Organs are the instruments that sustain human life as well as its evolution, as much on an individual scale as on a collective one. The Ars Industrialis website claims that general organology studies "a transductive relationship between three types of 'organs': physiological, technical and social."[19] Transductive, in that this relationship enables the propagation and the amplification of an activity or another between the different organological scales. A circulation that is necessary because it responds to a problematic: that the human body and its anatomical organs have been stabilized for several millennia already, whereas its exosomatic organs (technical and social) do not cease to evolve. It is thus important, in this relationship between the endosomatic and exosomatic organs, for a form of circularity to be activated, since exo-organs are also what Stiegler calls *pharmakon*. This is a Greek notion referring to something that is at once a poison and a remedy, meaning that, depending on its use, it can be toxic or salutary. This ambivalence arises notably from the widening gap between the endo- and exosomatic organs; nowadays, the technological leap is too sudden and too steep to be easily assimilated (humanity has already experienced this kind of gap at the time of the appearance of the printing press, for instance). In this situation, technological and institutional organs tend to predominate over psychosomatic and social organs; new possible fields of human exploitation open up—the case of the GAMA companies[20] is, in this regard, symptomatic. It is therefore important for psychosomatic organs not to be short-circuited by those of digital technologies in order for them not to remove human beings from their flesh-and-blood involvement in their own becoming. For if this incorporation is not activated, there is likely to be a kind of frustration and a feeling of powerlessness at the level of the individual—what Stiegler also calls proletarianization.

The individual's antidote against this proletarianization lies not only in the preservation of their practical and theoretical knowledge (which they have a tendency to hand over to machinery), but also in a constant evolution of this same knowledge. This is what differentiates the notion of "individual" as a fixed totality from that of "individuation" as a process that does not cease to evolve. Borrowing the term "individuation" from Gilbert Simondon, Stiegler sees in this phenomenon a "formation, at once biological, psychological and social, of the always unfinished individual."[21] And that is where the organs take on all their importance: it is in conjunction with them that the individual acquires the techniques for being-in-the-world and participates fully in what happens to him. In this sense, *Organological Cinema* is a cinema that turns all its attention to different organs, anatomical as much as technical, and works so that human beings can develop their individuation in a context where technology takes up more and more space.

Hence, referring to the film *Phoné-Scopie*, I would like to expose three principles without which *Organological Cinema* cannot exist:

1. The film's protagonists must perform their individuation.
2. The film is divided into three levels of organs: somatic, semiotic, and technological.
3. The protagonists' individuation must be filmed following three chiasms: intraorganic, interorganic, and paraorganic.

Principle Number 1—The Film's Protagonists Must Perform Their Individuation

Organological Cinema endeavors to draw the contours of cinema where film protagonists practice their own individuation and share it with the spectators via the screen. Individuation is considered here first as becoming conscious of biological, psychological, and social automatisms, and secondly a modulation of these automatisms for the purpose of their transformation (deautomatization) for metaphysical or aesthetic reasons. For instance, individuation in the case of the film *Phoné-Scopie* takes place due to *Phonesia*®, a technique of deautomatization of the relationships between gesture and speech that enables their re-automatization within new arrangements. *Phonesia*® thus allows consciousness to continually become through its own modulation. And, as I have already postulated above, it is in performing this process of consciousness modulation that the film's protagonist, via synchronization,

FIGURE 16.5 Tess Vlassov and Anatoli Vlassov, *Phoné-Scopie*, 2015, photo from a shot of the film
Source: Anatoli Vlassov.

enters a state of cohesion with the spectators' consciousness, while modifying it in their turn during the film. This is how the artist-performer of *Organological Cinema* activates the transductive movement I described previously and produces what Stiegler calls circuits of transindividuation. That is, the protagonist propagates the effect of their own individuation throughout the collective, creating a wave of social individuation.

Principle Number 2—The Film is Divided into Three Levels of Organs: Somatic, Semiotic, and Technological

To film the protagonists' individuation, *Organological Cinema* rests on Stiegler's theory of *general organology*, in which what we name "organ" extends from physiology to the social, along with the technical. *Organological Cinema* will thus consider as organs not only the parts of the human anatomy, but also the symbolic systems that the filmed protagonists make use of, as well as the technological instruments with which this film is made.

Organological Cinema consequently distinguishes three levels of organs:

1. Somatic organs (anatomical organs of the protagonists)—in the case of *Phoné-Scopie*, the heads of the two protagonists play the role of somatic organs.
2. Semiotic organs (the language, dance, *Phonesia*®, or other semiotic techniques that the protagonists employ in the film)—in the case of *Phoné-Scopie*, it is *Phonesia*® that plays the role of a semiotic organ as a montage between dance and speech.
3. Technological organs (cameras, microphones, and all the technological instruments necessary in order to make this film)—in the case of *Phoné-Scopie*, the two GoPro cameras play the role of technological organs.

This organological perspective of the relationship between human beings and their technologies is not new in cinema; it has even been present since its beginnings. Dziga Vertov, for one, a Soviet avant-garde filmmaker and theorist, in his 1923 manifesto *Kino-Eye*, considers the camera's kino-eye as his superior organ that has a capacity for movement that exceeds that of his anatomical eye: "I am in constant motion, I draw near, then away from objects, I crawl under, I climb onto them."[22] To make his films, he places his mechanical eye in places that are as unusual as unforeseen, such as, for example, as close to the protagonists' faces as possible, or on cars, trains, and even planes. As he travels a lot to film a multitude of newsreels, he strives in this manner to capture "life as it is."[23] These images are then shown in skillful and complex montages with different rhythms, effects, and camera movements, opening the way for what would later become a new genre of cinema: that of documentary film. As such, we can see that using and considering differently the relationship between human beings and their technology not only produces a new way of filming, but also an entire new cinematographic movement. Through his organs that become his tools, Vertov performs his individuation and expands it around him up to the collective (transindividuation).

This process of propagation, from individuating individuation to collective individuation, is possible due to the fact that, in individuating, human beings create around themselves a milieu or rather what Stiegler calls (extending Simondon's thinking) an associated milieu.[24] Stiegler first defines the word "milieu" both as a milieu around the individual (environment) and a milieu between individuals (*medium* as in intermediary). These two meanings of the notion of milieu enable the definition of individuation (the singular becoming of an individual) and transindividuation (a collective becoming). The importance of this double sense lies in the fact that it is about an in-between space, a mi-lieu that is at once "neither inside nor outside."[25] It is thus a place that makes a third one appear between two others, a transitional space between the individual and the environment, between one individual and another. And it is this intermediary space of circularity between organ and tool that is the very site of the becoming, that is, of the appearance of the technique that is individuation itself. This mi-lieu, this third place, is the space where tools become organs and organs become tools; from then on, techniques of individuation appear. These techniques of individuation correspond to the ceaseless movement of tool incorporation and decorporation. In other words, the technique as operative consciousness surfaces within a dynamic in which technical instruments become exosomatic organs or, on the contrary, where somatic organs become techniques. For instance, throughout the film *Phoné-Scopie*, a GoPro camera (technical instrument) becomes a kind of third eye (exosomatic organ). Or, when the young performer begins to dance with her head while knowing that it is holding the camera, it is her head as a somatic organ that becomes a technical instrument (see Figure 16.4). Another important aspect occurs when symbolic organs become semiotic prostheses. For example, the fact that in the film we would stop speaking for short moments while continuing to move means that we were transforming our symbolic organ (spoken language) into a prosthesis. Defining organs as prostheses enables us to attribute the possibility of attaching themselves to and detaching from a human body to them, thereby creating a maneuverability of possible assembly between its different organ-instruments. In this regard, *Organological Cinema* enables this prosthetic dynamic of articulation between different types of organs. This dynamic offers the possibility of reducing the misalignment between the different types of organs by adding more transductive movement to it, the one that makes the circulation of creative gestures between the different levels of organs within transindividuation circuits more fluid.

FIGURE 16.6 Tess Vlassov and Anatoli Vlassov, *Phoné-Scopie*, 2015, photo from a shot of the film
Source: Anatoli Vlassov.

Principle Number 3—To Film the Protagonists' Individuation Following Three Chiasms: Intraorganic, Interorganic, and Paraorganic

To capture the transductive gestures between the different levels of organs, *Organological Cinema* will place these cinematographic sensors in three directions: firstly, it will film the organs themselves by getting as close as possible to their movement. For instance, in *Phoné-Scopie* each protagonist films the other's head-organ. Inversely, it will also film from these same organs, seeking in this way to capture their autonomous movements. For example, in *Phoné-Scopie* each protagonist films from their own head-organ. Then, thirdly, it will capture the interactivity between these different types of organs (somatic, semiological, and technological). In *Phoné-Scopie* the protagonists capture with their cameras-microphones-heads the interactivity between dance, speech, and framing.

To capture this milieu of organs, *Organological Cinema* will rest on three types of chiasms: intrasensory, intersensory, and parasensory,[26] and transform them into intraorganic chiasms, interorganic chiasms, and paraorganic chiasms:

1. Intraorganic chiasm: capturing towards and from organs. Filming not only the organs as such but mainly their dance—that is to say, to capture a process of individuation of the human subject, the bearer of this organ. To film from the organs is to film their individuation by placing the filmic sensors on the organs themselves during their dance. Dancing is considered here as the individuation of an organ, that is to say, the activation of consciousness particular to itself.
2. Interorganic chiasm: capturing the translation between the different somatic organs. To film between organs consists of capturing certain moments during which an action transfers from one somatic organ to another: the moment, for example, when the gesture of an organ-arm is translated into a sound from an organ-mouth.

3. Paraorganic chiasm: capturing the transmutation between somatic, semiotic, and technological organs. This chiasm is in line with the issues raised earlier in the text, namely those related to the capturing of *Sens-Ations*, that is, the moments when signs from a somatic organ (arm, mouth, whole body...) transmute to a semiotic organ (language, dance, song...) and vice versa. For instance, when the body's movements link up with the meaning of the spoken words or when the singing voice links up with the danced gesture, or the singing voice links up with the camera's movement.

Talking Subjective Camera

Let us then return to the film *Phoné-Scopie* and to the capturing of *Phonesia*® as well as of its invisible network of *Sens-Ations*—where the audibility of the mouth joins the mobility of the body. To capture this interstice between the audibility of words and the visibility of the dancing body, I placed a (GoPro-like) frontal camera at the end of an organ that is, this time, the head. A "superior" organ of the human body that interested me based on the fact that it unites the visibility of the eye and the audibility of the mouth. In cinema, filming from the head is a method called "subjective camera" that brings us to the heart of the action through its jerky movements, linked to the movement of the protagonist. However, while the use of frontal cameras is very widespread in videos of extreme sports, and while the effect of subjective camera is often used in cinema as much as in screendance, it is very rare for a subjective camera also to record the speech of the protagonist in action. And, yet the subjective camera proves to be very useful in capturing an emotional, even a sensory, state of the character. Consequently, would a talking subjective camera not be an interesting contribution to fiction cinema and especially to screendance? Is capturing the verbalization of a dancer's sensible experience during their dance—sensible experience being one of the most sought-after elements in contemporary dance—not a way to make the spectators feel what happens in the sensory world of a dancer in action to a greater extent?

In the video's capturing of *Sens-Ations*, it is therefore precisely the appending of the voice to the image of a subjective camera that interested me to capture at once the camera bearer's mobile gaze and their speech; to capture flows in the interstices between a scopic receptor-organ (eye) and a verbal transmitor-organ (mouth). In this regard, a subjective camera becomes a talking one, since while capturing an image, it also captures the voice.

Let us see then how, in *Phoné-Scopie*, the talking camera not only enables the sharing of the dancer's sensibility during their dance, but also glimpses a whole choreography of *Sens-Ations*. The film begins around a garden table, with the two performers (Tess and myself) facing each other, so that the two

FIGURE 16.7 Tess Vlassov and Anatoli Vlassov, *Phoné-Scopie*, 2015, photo from a shot of the film
Source: Anatoli Vlassov.

cameras would film both the shot and the reverse shot of the same scene. The spectator then witnesses the same action, filmed at once from the space of the foreground and that of the background. *Phonesia*® begins. The speech of the protagonists begins with descriptions of what is happening at this moment. The simultaneous speakers start by counting together, then describe their respective faces. Then, staying face to face, they leave the table and move in parallel, while continuing to talk to each other simultaneously. When leaving the table, one of the protagonists slightly changes the subject of his speech, by pronouncing the words "to leave far away," whereas the other protagonist continues in the descriptive mode regarding what is happening at the moment. So, what we see on the screen is that the two protagonists continue to travel through the same space while the direction and meaning (*sens*) of the flows shifts. Saying "to leave" while leaving the table maintains the direct relationship between action and word meaning; adding the words "far away" to the words "to leave" forms the beginning of a detachment of word meanings in relation to space and makes the dialogue veer towards a semantic virtuality. Then, later, this virtuality "returns" to concrete space when some exchanges of words specify a common destination to our respective courses.

But let us return to the third "parasensory" chiasm that represents a direct and chiasmatic connection between perceiving and saying. Michel Bernard calls it "the operative Word," defining it "as a change in 'the flesh' of the sensory body into that of language, conceived as a reversibility of the sensory and the said."[27] That is to say that saying and feeling mutually influence and transform each other. Bernard thus specifies that the "sensing which presents that [universal] voice [of Nature] to us is wrought, just as much as speech and writing, by the act of self-projection into the virtual or, as linguists might say, by *disengaging* [or *shifting out*], in other words by the desire for utterance."[28] Linguists name "disengagement" a moment when the meaning of words is virtualized outside the real situation of the human subject towards another time or space.[29] In other words, it is a moment when the human subject begins to talk about a different context than the one in which they are

FIGURE 16.8 Tess Vlassov and Anatoli Vlassov, *Phoné-Scopie*, 2015, photo from a shot of the film
Source: Anatoli Vlassov.

physically located. On the contrary, engaging is a similar, but opposite, operation, that of bringing the meaning of words closer to one's real situation in the present. In this dynamic of engaging and disengaging, the protagonist creates a form of elastic space between the real of their presence and the virtual of their speech. This elastic space between gesture and speech is precisely that which enables the appearance of the *Sens-Ations* whose existence I track down. In *Phoné-Scopie*, if we follow the direction and meaning of the two protagonists' flows of speech, we can perceive that they constantly perform disengagements and engagements between the meaning of words and the actions they execute. They oscillate between the meaning of their words and the sensations of their acts, while establishing bridges between the real and the virtual of their performative acts. These are actions of transmutation of gesture into language, of an anatomical organ into a semantic one – which reverts to the third principle of *Organological Cinema*: to capture the mi-lieu of organs following the paraorganic chiasm.

Disengaging and Engaging for a Consciousness of the Spectators

If, on a film's performative level, the dynamic of engaging and disengaging is articulated between the performers' statements and actions, the filmographic aspect also follows this same dynamic. Engagement and disengagement materialize there due to a split screen, a union of two shots into one: that of the shot and the reverse shot. Indeed, the paths that the two protagonists take during the film meet and separate several times, while the spectator sees these two routes simultaneously on the screen. When their paths meet, an engagement between the different images on the screen takes place, and when their paths separate, a spatial disengagement of one of the two split-screen shots from the other occurs. Hence, while in the real space of the performative act the performers' two routes split, in the virtual space of the screen these paths are united. There is therefore a constant dynamic of drawing-closer and distancing between the real of the action and the virtual of the screen. In his 2004 film *Notre Musique*, Jean Luc Godard states that "the truth has two faces," before continuing, "[s]hot and reverse shot. Imaginary, certainty. Real, uncertainty. The principle of cinema: going to the light and directing it onto our night. Our music."[30] While he says these words, the spectator can observe a lamp swinging from the ceiling in a room plunged into darkness, from the left to the right of the screen. It is as if in order to compose "our music" it is necessary to establish a relationship of oscillation, a back-and-forth movement between shadow and light, between real and virtual, between truth and doubt. In this sense, the performative film *Phoné-Scopie* is within the purview of this issue (and by this fact *Organological Cinema*), setting up an entire dynamic network of tension and loosening not only between utterance and gestuality, but also between the two images activated by the split screen. This double polarization opens up the perception of this temporal perfo-filmic object towards a possible interpretative diversity. It proposes a synchronization with an entire palette of diverse movements in an elasticity of drawing-closer and distancing between acts, tongues, and images to the spectators' consciousness. From performance to film, where organs film and cameras speak, the spectators compose their own cinema.

Notes

1 Bernard Stiegler, *Technics and Time, 3: Cinematic Time and the Question of Malaise*, trans. Stephen Barker (Stanford University Press, 2011), 87.
2 *Phoné-Scopie*, directed by Anatoli Vlassov (2015; Montreal: Festival Rencontres Internationales Regards Hybrides [RIRH], 2019), accessed February 27, 2023, https://vimeo.com/205013955.
3 Bernard Stiegler, "Le cinéma des consciences," Art Press, 2002, accessed February 27, 2023, https://www.artpress.com/2002/02/01/bernard-stiegler-le-cinema-des-consciences/ (Marceau's translation).
4 Stiegler, "Le cinéma des consciences" (Marceau's translation).
5 Stiegler, "Le cinéma des consciences" (Marceau's translation).
6 Walter Benjamin, "L'œuvre d'art à l'ère de sa reproductibilité technique," in *Œuvres III* (Paris: Éditions Gallimard, 1939), 110 (Marceau's translation).
7 Stiegler, "Le cinéma des consciences" (Marceau's translation).
8 In French, this term combines "corporéité" (corporeality) and "parler" (talking).
9 Julie Reshé and Anatoli Vlassov, "Recherche-Création-Publics / Language as a parasite in the brain of a child or critical perspective on postmodern linguistic relativism / corpArléité champ d'expérience pour un *Danseur Parlant*," *p-e-r-f-o-r-m-a-n-c-e* 6 (2022), accessed February 27, 2023, http://www.p-e-r-f-o-r-m-a-n-c-e.org/?page_id=5836 (Marceau's translation).
10 Reshé and Vlassov, "Recherche-Création-Publics" (Marceau's translation).
11 Vlassov, "La Phonésie," in Julie De Bellis, Marion Fournier and Karine Montabord, *Panorama du métier de danseur*, Pantin, February 2018, Paris: Centre national de la danse. https://docdanse.hypotheses.org/files/2018/05/atelier_2017_juin.pdf.
12 These are different effects that I apply in the articulation between dance and speech (the following examples only describe these interactions in one direction,

but the opposite direction is also possible): effects of rupture (HOLE) when dancing stops while speech continues; of injection (INJECTOR) when, conversely, while dancing continues in silence, speech occurs all at once and continues with the dance; of repercussion (CONTAMINATOR) when vocal timbre influences danced gestures; of prolongation (ILLUSTRATOR) when dancing illustrates vocal sound; of delay (ECHO) when danced gesture illustrates the projected voice, but with a delay; of deformation (TORSION) when dance deforms orality; of complete independence (PARALLEL) when word flow is completely independent of the dancer's movements. In addition, there are other effects that operate more precisely on the semantic dimension, such as those of swallowing (LOGOPHAGIA), when the dancer pronounces words as if he were swallowing them, or of splitting (SYLLABIA), when the syllables of words are repeated, or of propagation (POLYSEMY), when the same word, repeated, changes meaning when articulated with different gestures.

13 Dominique Chateau and Anatoli Vlassov, "Transmutation du geste et du signe. D'Eisenstein au Kabuki et de la *Phonésie* à Godard," *Penser/Créer en déroute* (Paris: PUF, 2023) (Marceau's translation).
14 Chateau and Vlassov, "Transmutation du geste et du signe" (Marceau's translation).
15 Sergei Eisenstein, *Film Form: Essays in Film Theory*, trans. and ed. Jay Leyda (Harcourt Brace Jovanovich, 1977), 20.
16 Chateau and Vlassov, "Transmutation du geste et du signe" (Marceau's translation).
17 Vlassov, "Machine à *Sens-Ations*: quand le sens rencontre la sensation," *L'Art tout contre la machine* (Paris, Éditions Hermann, 2021).
18 Stiegler, "Organologie générale," *Ars Industrialis*, accessed February 27, 2023, https://arsindustrialis.org/organologie-g%C3%A9n%C3%A9rale (Marceau's translation).
19 Stiegler, "Organologie générale" (Marceau's translation).
20 GAMA /GAFA/ GAFAM: an acronym of the initials for Google, Apple, Facebook (now Meta), Amazon and Microsoft. See "GAFA," *Le dico du commerce international*, https://www.glossaire-international.com/pages/tous-les-termes/gafa.html.
21 Stiegler, "Individuation," *Ars Industrialis,* accessed February 27, 2023, http://arsindustrialis.org/individuation (Marceau's translation).
22 Dziga Vertov, *Kino-Eye: The Writings of Dziga Vertov*, ed. Annette Michelson, trans. Kevin O'Brien (University of California Press, 1984), 17.
23 Vertov, *Kino-Eye*, 71.
24 Stiegler, "Milieu," *Ars Industrialis*, accessed February 27, 2023, https://arsindustrialis.org/milieu (Marceau's translation).
25 Stiegler, "Milieu" (Marceau's translation). Mi-lieu in the original French evokes both a "mid-place" or an in-between.
26 Michel Bernard, *De la création chorégraphique* (Pantin, Éditions du Centre national de la danse, 2001), 97. Here, I borrow the three chiasms developed by Michel Bernard, for whom *intrasensory chiasm* encapsulates the double aspect—active and passive—of feeling (seeing-seen, touching-touched, hearing-heard, etc.); *intersensory chiasm* intersects the senses in a synesthetic manner; and *parasensory chiasm* closely connects perceiving and saying (Marceau's translation).
27 Bernard, "Sense and Fiction, Or the Strange Effects of Three Sensorial Chiasms," trans. Anna Pakes, *Paris 8 Danse* (2019), 3, https://hal-univ-paris8.archives-ouvertes.fr/hal-02292135.
28 Bernard, "Sense and Fiction," 3. The last line of what appears in Bernard's original text that Vlassov quotes—"Le désir d'énoncer, c'est toujours un débrayage"—would be closer to "The desire to enunciate is always a disengagement" (Marceau's translation).

29 See Jean-Marc Lemelin, "L'analyse du langage," accessed February 27, 2023, http://www.ucs.mun.ca/~lemelin/sens.langu.htm (Marceau's translation).
30 *Notre Musique*, directed by Jean-Luc Godard (2004) (Marceau's translation).

Bibliography

Benjamin, Walter. "L'œuvre d'art à l'ère de sa reproductibilité technique." In *Œuvres III*. Paris: Éditions Gallimard, 1939.

Bernard, Michel. *De la création chorégraphique*. Pantin: Éditions du Centre national de la danse, 2001.

Bernard, Michel. "Sense and Fiction, Or the Strange Effects of Three Sensorial Chiasms." Translated by Anna Pakes. *Paris 8 Danse* (2019). https://hal-univ-paris8.archives-ouvertes.fr/hal-02292135.

Château, Dominique, and Anatoli Vlassov. "Transmutation du geste et du signe. D'Eisenstein au Kabuki et de la *Phonésie* à Godard." *Penser/Créer en déroute*. Paris: PUF, 2023.

Eisenstein, Sergei. *Film Form: Essays in Film Theory*. Edited and translated by Jay Leyda. Orlando: Harcourt Brace Jovanovich, 1977.

"GAFA," Le dico du commerce international, https://www.glossaire-international.com/pages/tous-les-termes/gafa.html.

Godard, Jean-Luc dir. *Notre Musique*. 2004.

Lemelin, Jean-Marc. "L'analyse du langage." http://www.ucs.mun.ca/~lemelin/sens.langu.htm.

Reshé, Julie, and Anatoli Vlassov. "Recherche-Création-Publics / Language as a parasite in the brain of a child or critical perspective on postmodern linguistic relativism / corpArléité champ d'expérience pour un *Danseur Parlant*." *p-e-r-f-o-r-m-a-n-c-e* 6 (2022). Accessed February 27, 2023. http://www.p-e-r-f-o-r-m-a-n-c-e.org/?page_id=5836.

Stiegler, Bernard. "Organologie générale." Ars Industrialis. Accessed February 27, 2023. https://arsindustrialis.org/organologie-g%C3%A9n%C3%A9rale.

Stiegler, Bernard. "Individuation." Ars Industrialis. Accessed February 27, 2023. http://arsindustrialis.org/individuation.

Stiegler, Bernard. *Technics and Time, 3: Cinematic Time and the Question of Malaise*. Translated by Stephen Barker. Stanford: Stanford University Press, 2011.

Stiegler, Bernard. "Le cinéma des consciences." Art Press. February 1, 2002. Accessed February 27, 2023. https://www.artpress.com/2002/02/01/bernard-stiegler-le-cinema-des-consciences/.

Stiegler, Bernard. "Milieu." Ars Industrialis. Accessed February 27, 2023. https://arsindustrialis.org/milieu.

Vertov, Dziga. *Kino-Eye: The Writings of Dziga Vertov*. Edited by Annette Michelson. Translated by Kevin O'Brien. Berkeley: University of California Press, 1984.

Vlassov, Anatoli, dir. *Phoné-Scopie*. 2015; Montreal: Festival Rencontres Internationales Regards Hybrides (RIRH), 2019. Accessed February 27, 2023. https://vimeo.com/205013955.

Vlassov, Anatoli. "La Phonésie." *Panorama du métier de danseur*, Pantin, CND (Centre National de la Danse), (February 2018), 38. https://docdanse.hypotheses.org/files/2018/05/atelier_2017_juin.pdf.

Vlassov, Anatoli. "Machine à *Sens-Ations*: quand le sens rencontre la sensation." *L'Art tout contre la machine*. Paris: Éditions Hermann, 2021.

17
THE MATTER OF ANALOGUE MEDIA TECHNOLOGIES IN SCREENDANCE, POST MARTIN HEIDEGGER AND POST HITO STEYERL

Claudia Kappenberg

A Technological Long View

In the editorial to *Technē/Technology: Researching Cinema and Media Technologies – Their Development, Use, and Impact* (2014), Ian Christie, Dominique Chateau, and Annie van den Oever note how film theory has, almost since its inception, been dominated by questions of technology. Each significant technological invention and transition ushered in a new set of questions for film theorists and philosophers, whose history in turn has come to reflect the history of the technologies themselves.[1] In other words, sequential technological developments have given way to an increasingly varied pool of available media as well as related theories, forming a pluralistic technoverse with a somewhat bewildering range of technical and creative choices. The contemporary art world of the late twentieth century and artists working in media largely responded in two different ways, either turning towards older and analogue technologies such as Super 8 and 16mm film, analogue video, and magnetic audio tape, or embracing the digital realm. Writing for *Artforum* in 2012, British critic Claire Bishop was highly critical of what she described as an ongoing preference for the analogue, noting that contemporary art has been surprisingly "unresponsive to the total upheaval in our labour and leisure inaugurated by the digital revolution."[2] While some may use digital technologies in some form, she argued, few confront its impact on how we think and see today, refusing "to speak overtly about the conditions of living in and through new media."[3] Canadian scholar Katharina Niemeyer was more forgiving, describing this preference for the analogue as a double helix-type phenomenon, whereby artists respond with slower technologies to the ever-increasing speed of the digital realm.[4] The selection of creative technologies is compounded by a widespread realization that technologies overall not only help us to make the world in our image, a dominant belief of the nineteenth and twentieth centuries, but that they entail environmental exploitation and destruction on a global scale. As argued by Laura Marks, digital media are also toxic to the planet's natural environment and digital technologies have a big and growing carbon footprint.[5] Considering these complexities, many questions arise for contemporary artists about the choice of technology for the realisation and presentation of work and about their practical and creative impact. For contemporary screendance practitioners and theorists, the question of technology is relevant particularly in the context of discourses on materiality and corporeal selves. After all, technologies determine parts of the process of making, shape the content and provide the interface with which a work addresses the audience. The large majority of screendance artists embraced digital video and digital editing as soon as it became available, attracted particularly by the ease, flexibility and relative low costs of digital means of production. However, the image quality of the archival film stills in *Snow* (Hinton and Lee, 2003) and *All This Can Happen* (Hinton and Davies, 2012) ensure the work's sensorial qualities and immediacy. Lucy Cash's use of 16mm footage in *How The Earth Must See Itself (A Thirling)* (2019) emphasizes the specific qualities of the location as well as the physicality of the bodies on site, while the digital editing reinforces the materiality of the 16mm used. A common concern appears to be a desire to reach out to audiences and to engage their embodied selves, and analogue technologies may have more to offer here than is generally assumed, in view of the mediated and homogenized, if not illusionary or fake, contemporary experience particularly in the global North.

Technē, Poiēsis, and Enframing

A significant historical text in the debates on the creative uses of audio-visual media is German philosopher Martin Heidegger's essay "The Question Concerning Technologies," originally published in 1957.[6] The late 1950s are considered as the beginning of the digital revolution, that is, a shift from mechanical and analogue technologies to digital computers and digital information storage. 1957 was also the year of the first digitally scanned photograph, of a young child, by Russel Kirch on a Standards Eastern Automatic Computer (SEAC). This digital revolution had been preceded by a wider proliferation of technologies in the 1930s, which had in turn reignited debates over the effects of machines on everyday life, perceived in part as a means to progress and in part as destructive force and threat to culture as well as to all that secured individuality. As Benoît Turquety notes in an essay on the relation between cinema and technology, the key question was, "Is the machine liberating, a source of well-being and an embodiment of progress? Or is it enslaving, imposing its rhythms to [sic] the worker and its obtuse materiality [sic] to the thinker?"[7] Heidegger's text speaks both to advances of technologies as well as to concerns with the instrumentalized as well as instrumentalizing modern existence, which, in the mid-twentieth century, appeared to have lost sight of what "being" might be in the broadest sense. As Robert Sinnerford notes in his review of Heidegger's essay, "the motivation and aim of Heidegger's questioning of technology is largely ethical, in that it aims to clarify how we should best live in a free and fitting manner within our technologically disclosed world."[8]

Heidegger's essay also featured in the second issue of *The International Journal of Screendance*, an issue dedicated to significant theoretical texts that continue to bear relevance for contemporary screendance theories and practices. Interested in bringing Heidegger into the debates, dance scholar Ann Cooper Albright contends that this essay is still useful to reflect on how moving image technologies might be affecting how we see the world today, on and off screens, and how the proliferation of screens itself may affect how we think about movement and ourselves.[9] If time and space can be collapsed at will within the screen space, how does this impact on how we relate to real space and time "in real life"? Or, what happens when we translate bodies and faces into pixels and what might be achieved or get lost in this translation? This chapter first draws on Heidegger to reconsider the relation between enquiring bodies and technological exploration in screendance. It subsequently turns to the writing of Hito Steyerl to explore how artists can maintain a criticality if they use the same audio-visual technology and produce the same kind of image quality as commercial media and the corporate market economy. The chapter, furthermore, considers two analogue film projects to investigate how they engage the corporeality of their audiences and what this might offer to screendance practices.

Accessing Heidegger's writing is not easy though, as his terminology and neologisms are awkward even in his native German and a translation into English does not simplify matters. The first argument in his essay differentiates between what Heidegger calls the essence of technology and technology as a thing, meaning machines, computers, and modern science. Technology as a thing, he argues, is largely based on thinking in terms of means and ends and has led to a proliferation of machines that aims for total mastery, assuming a ubiquitous availability and manipulability of matter and the natural environment. In this construct of means and ends, Heidegger remarks, technology is instrumentalized and put at the service of wealth creation.[10] Accordingly, human activity at large as well as the natural environment have come to be perceived in terms of what they can contribute, more or less reduced to a use-value and resource of some kind instead of being considered for themselves and in themselves.

Aside from critiquing this instrumentalizing modern context, Heidegger proposes that in its essence technology can "bring about" or reveal aspects of the world, even contending that a certain use of technology can help to reveal precisely the constraints of the instrumentalising regime. To build this argument, Heidegger returns to the Greek term *technē*, which, he writes, is related to the word *epistēmē*: "Both words are terms for knowing in the widest sense. They mean to be entirely at home in something, to understand and be expert in it."[11] *Technē* thereby refers to a knowing that comes from a process of revealing rather than designating something that is already known, and it is also different to making in the sense of manufacturing. Technology is therefore a process of revealing that relates to *poiēsis*, that is, poetry, signalling a poetic bringing-forth or revealing. Heidegger furthermore proposes a particular notion of causality; instead of a bringing about or effecting in the sense of *causa efficiens* [meaning efficient cause as in traditional causality], he advances an interpretation that is more akin to being responsible for or being indebted to.[12] Heidegger writes: "The principal characteristic of being responsible is this starting something on its way into arrival," in the sense of "an occasioning or an inducting on going forward."[13] The verb "to occasion" thereby describes a process of presencing, meaning that something is arising out of itself and has the capacity to reveal in terms of what the Greeks call *alētheia* and the Romans *veritas*, that is, truth or knowing.[14] As Albright notes, this truth and knowing is "not a passive recognition of what already exists, but rather a method of bringing forth, of revealing."[15] In other words, the categorical distinction between the essence of technology and technology as a means to an end distinguishes between the process of occasioning, on one hand, and a deterministic, instrumentalized manufacturing on the other. It also implies an artistic agency with a sense of a responsibility for an occasioning or bringing forth, despite potentially instrumentalizing constraints.

Thinking further about the conditions of the artist/maker, Heidegger introduces the notion of "enframing." In general, the instrumentalizing modern credo of productivity has enforced a process of "enframing" by which matter and the environment are framed as a "reserve." A river for example becomes a water-power supplier or a "standing-reserve," losing its status as object and disappearing "into the objectlessness of standing-reserve."[16] Crucially, this enframing challenges humans as well as they are expected to undertake the ordering of what is designated as reserve. Heidegger is highly concerned about this demand on individuals, noting that people could potentially be subsumed by a system from which there is no escape. Nevertheless, Heidegger contends that there is still the question of "how we actually admit ourselves into that wherein enframing itself essentially unfold", meaning that we do have some agency in how we respond to and engage with the expectations that are placed on us.[17] Whilst accepting that the individual is part of the system and cannot stand outside of it, he/she "becomes one who listens, though not one who simply obeys."[18] Heidegger therefore sees a possibility of choice and freedom and this possibility is dependent on grasping the essence of technology and its distortion, that is, its potential enframing of reality in terms of resources. Heidegger is therefore clear that it is not technology per se that is the danger and notes that, to the contrary, the essence of technology and its capacity of bringing-forth is mysterious. It is the force of the enframing that constitutes the danger if it is not recognized.

Heidegger is, however, not entirely consistent in his argumentation and wavers at times about the possibility of artistic agency and criticality. At a later point in the essay he borrows from a poem by German poet Hölderlin from the early 1800s to resolve this complexity: "But where danger is, grows / The saving power also."[19] A saving power, that is, a power of recognition, emerges precisely when one experiences the process of enframing, and out of this situation truth can emerge. Heidegger concludes that "the closer we come to the danger, the more brightly do the ways into the saving power begin to shine and the more questioning we become."[20] Heidegger thereby conceives of the possibility that a questioning of the impact of modern technologies is possible, precisely because everything and everyone is so deeply implicated in the enframing and the instrumentalization. A creative use of technologies therefore potentially allows for the unmasking of the distorted functioning of modern technologies themselves and reveals what is at stake within the frenzied modern world. While Heidegger has generally not written much about media and film, this argument affirms the role of cinema as an artform in the mid-twentieth century along with photography, and further implies that as an artform rooted in technology it is particularly well-equipped to represent the times.

Heidegger's notions of *technē*, *poiēsis*, and *enframing* also help to break down the dichotomies that have for some time marked the fields of dance and screendance studies, whereby live dance and live bodies have been seen as other to technology. As Albright notes, the essay helped her to understand "the inherent interconnectedness between dance and technology, including the ways that dance techniques are, in fact, examples of very effective technologies of the body."[21] Albright is effectively arguing that the creative process of the filmmaker with his/her audio-visual technologies can be seen as a parallel process or an extension of body technologies and dance research, constituted through physical abilities and sensorial faculties, corporeal intelligence, and movement vocabulary. Ann Dils notes in the same journal issue that she had for some time resisted the engagement with moving image technologies in dance and distrusted the idea of capturing of movement through audio-visual media, but has come to view these technologies differently through Heidegger's essay.[22] It is worth noting that the term "capturing," frequently used in dance-tech discourses for the documentation and reproduction of movement through audio-visual means, is somewhat problematic if not misleading in that it implies a catching, seizing, or arresting of movement that sets up a binary between the technologies used and the bodies in movement. The notion of capturing movement is, however, as old as film, evident for example in the machine used by Étienne-Jules Marey in 1882, which was described as a "chronophotographic gun!"[23] Pre-cinematic technologies therefore introduced a notion of shooting and left a legacy that continues to mark contemporary perception. Screendance discourses should nevertheless shake off this antagonistic construct and argue instead that an engagement with moving image technologies can be conceived as a continuation of the processes and enquiries of moving bodies and of their own techniques. Rather than thinking in terms of binaries, and following Heidegger, we can posit a kinship between bodies and technologies, by which dance is technology and technology is dance, if we understand both as means to reveal and explicate the world..

The Poor Image

Another publication by Martin Heidegger entitled *Discourse on Thinking* (1959) was published a couple of years after the essay on questions concerning technologies.[24] As Robert Sinnerbrink notes, in this second text post-war Europeans are described as being at the mercy of proliferating mass media, encountering "a generalized condition of 'homelessness' and an existential 'worldlessness.'"[25] Heidegger laments: "Hourly and daily they are chained to radio and television. Week after week the movies carry them off into uncommon, but often merely common, realms of the imagination and give the illusion of a world that is no world."[26] His, illusion of a world that is no world, implies a proliferation of absences, theorized later in the 1980s by Jean Baudrillard as a systematic simulation of reality that has become endemic in many contemporary Eastern and Western cultures.[27] The commentary also echoes Heidegger's concerns in "The Question Concerning Technologies," imparting a sense that the media have become a key part of the process of enframing, controlling the lives of people by providing them only with illusions. Half a century later this argument finds a perfect complement and counterargument in Hito Steyerl's *The Poor Image* (2009), which offers a passionate endorsement of the proliferation and circulation of low-resolution images and a celebration of the power they hold through their transience and digital characteristics.[28]

The motivation for Steyerl's text is also an ethical one, much like Heidegger's, in that the author searches for a way to resist being subsumed by capitalist values and to live freely within a class-based, corporate market economy. But instead of resisting the mediation of the everyday, Steyerl swims with the tide and embraces all things digital, pointing to the subversive power that resides within the digital image itself: "The poor image is a copy in motion. Its quality is bad, its resolution substandard. As it accelerates, it deteriorates. It is a ghost of an image, a preview, a thumbnail, an errant idea, an itinerant image distributed for free."[29] Heidegger's world "that is no world" meets Steyerl's ghost images; however, she celebrates the digital uncertainty and bastardized existence of the poor image as a counter movement to the information capitalism and persistent class system. Bypassing traditional structures of entitlement and wealth, poor images generate an alternative audio-visual economy and empower grassroot communities. Nevertheless, Steyerl also acknowledges that the poor image is not entirely immune to being subsumed into a commodity culture that thrives on compressed attention spans and quick gratification. She notes that this awkward, ambivalent position and combination of political alternative with cultural indulgence perfectly reflects the modern condition:

> The poor image is no longer about the real thing—the originary original. Instead, it is about its own real conditions of existence: about swarm circulation, digital dispersion, fractured and flexible temporalities. It is about defiance and appropriation just as it is about conformism and exploitation. In short: it is about reality.[30]

Interestingly, the confused posture of both defiance and appropriation, conformism and exploitation echoes Hölderlin's comment, that "[w]here danger is, grows [t]he saving power also."[31] While digital technologies and platforms are that which underpin large swathes of the commodity culture, they are also tools with which to unmask and critique the very same system. They are a means to secure freedom of expression.

At a first glance Steyerl's strategy might seem opposed to Heidegger's philosophy but she performs what he had envisaged: "the closer we come to the danger, the more brightly do the ways into the saving power begin to shine and the more questioning we become."[32] In Heidegger's words, Steyerl is after all "one who listens, though not one who simply obeys."[33] The impact and role of technologies in cultural production and reception therefore no longer divide along obvious differences and high-tech or low-tech alternatives; production and reception are enmeshed and play out within the same domain. Heidegger and Steyerl effectively echo one another and demonstrate a continuation of concerns in their argumentation and approaches.

In screendance the digital turn has also facilitated different developments, on one hand leading to higher production values with increasingly spectacular locations, virtuoso camera movements and editing, and on the other significantly expanding access and affordability through readily available digital tools. Online platforms like TikTok have also facilitated the proliferation of poor-image screendance so to speak, a curious mixture of assertion of self through infinite copying of moves and scenarios, frequently looking more like thumbnails rather than artefacts. The question concerning technology that remains to be explored in this world of ubiquitous and enmeshed technological circulation, and that will be addressed in the following sections, is the role of analogue technologies and photochemical inscription. Are they by and large remnants and technical ruins, anachronistic and nostalgic indulgences as critic Claire Bishop maintains, or do they have a role to play?

Of Materiality

The differences between analogue and digital technologies are interesting for contemporary screendance practices as they each assist or compromise the director/filmmaker/choreographer in different ways. At the same time, their impact on the audience's viewing experience also depends on the wider cultural context. For example, the original Film Notes to Shirley Clarke's *Bridges-Go-Round* (1958) propose that "the monumental bridges spanning New York Harbour dissolve into flattened abstractions that seem to sway with the music," emphasizing a dissolution of the structures into visual patterns.[34] But looking back at the film in 2023, the sense of materiality of the 16mm film is hard to overlook with its grainy structure and soft focus, and now appears to lend a sense of weight to the images that might not have been felt had the footage been generated with digital technologies. This sense of weight possibly makes a link between the architectural structures in the images and the bodies of the viewers, a phenomenon that those working with digital media sometimes seek to re-create via digital filters, grading, and effects. Also, the fragility of the film strips and their potential for various kinds of deterioration evoke the precariousness of physical existence that are often filtered out of the modern mediated environment. As will be discussed in more detail later, digital media generally include error correction and so, in the medium term at least, tend to be more resilient and less subject to the acquisition of artefacts. The fragility of analogue film therefore suggests that celluloid film could lend itself to filmmaking projects that seek to distance themselves from the instrumentalization of modern existence and support those endeavours that seek to "bring forth" or evoke alternative narratives. Such a reading of analogue image qualities, according to a Heideggerian take on modernity, could also explain the tendency in screendance to film within old buildings or industrial ruins, whereby the quality and texture of the decaying walls compensates in some ways for the perfection of the digital image where footage has been acquired on a digital medium. This notion of compensation could in turn be extended to the glitch technique deployed by numerous digital artists, whereby the digital glitches seemingly counteract the inbuilt error correction, an aesthetic that could again be interpreted as some kind of attempt to metaphorically address real materiality. Considering the various methods of compensation in aesthetics and postproduction one might therefore conclude that it does not matter whether something is actually made with analogue or digital media and that the digital can compensate in various ways for whatever analogue inscription offers, but this is perhaps misleading.

Analogue film has a materiality, which means that we can see the thing itself, that we can hold a film loop up against the light and see the sequence of frames, and we can also look into an analogue video cassette and see and touch the tape. Furthermore, the processing in analogue technologies is similar to our own way of perceiving in that the input is proportional or similar to the output, a parallel that facilitates our identification with how they operate. Dropouts and signs of decay, perhaps visible as scratches and blotches on the celluloid images or noticeable as interference in analogue sound recording, demonstrate that these technologies can age and become distressed, visibly or audibly, adding to the sense that they have a corpus not unlike us, subject to the laws of physics. Existing within the same paradigm, writes Laura Marks, analogue media reinforce a sense of kinship with our sensorial selves, reminding us of our own vulnerability and mortality.[35] By comparison, the encoded digital images and sound are made up of virtual pixels written in combinations of 0 and 1 and have a more complex and tenuous connection to the physical world and to our material bodies, depending, for example, on the means of storage and the means of display. Nevertheless, in her essay "How Electrons Remember," Marks argues also that electrons and photons, the smallest particles in a digital image, have an ability to remember.[36] This raises the possibility that there might be some kind of synergy also between our corporeal selves and digital technologies, or that we might be able to project something of our own diverse forms of embodied memory and capabilities onto digital entities. Marks's later study on touch and haptic visuality furthermore demonstrates that certain haptic video images also facilitate a bodily relationship with the viewer, despite their flatness and electronic otherness.[37] In other words we cannot simply contrast analogue and the digital domains, but there is little doubt that analogue technologies mirror our sensorial and material selves more easily than digital technologies.

Marks therefore raises the question as to "what becomes of materiality in the transition from analogue to digital?," a question that is timely also with regards to the renewed theoretical engagement with matter and materiality in contemporary philosophy, political theory, and cultural studies.[38] In their introduction to *New Materialisms, Ontology, Agency, and Politics* (2010), Diana Coole and Samantha Frost write that "we unavoidably find ourselves having to think in new ways about the nature of matter, and the matter of nature," acknowledging that "the myriad of available analogue and digital technologies can facilitate this complex rethinking."[39] Screendance could conceivably play a significant role in this renewed engagement with "the real" and with related concerns about body, agency, and sustainability, and analogue technologies could be a useful tool in this endeavour.

Bye Bye Super 8

In January 2010, Kodachrome stopped developing the Super 8 film K40, which had arguably become the most successful colour home movie film of all time, recognizable through its iconic colour palette. Filmmaker Johan Kramer used Kodachrome's last twenty-five boxes to make portraits of twenty-five eight-year-olds. The resulting twenty-five film loops were projected side by side, on twenty-five Super 8 projectors in a piece called *Bye Bye Super 8 – In Loving Memory of Kodachrome* (2011).[40]

Kramer also edited a short film combining K40 Super 8 clips from his own childhood, found footage, and brief snippets of the twenty-five selected children, declaring in subtitles that he wanted to give the other children the same childhood memory he had.[41] The edit begins with images of himself, perhaps about eight years old, coming in or out of the family home and playing football in the garden. In this section, the soundtrack combines the purring of Super 8 footage with gentle happy music. It is summer and big orange subtitles say: "Hello. This is me. This is my childhood." Scenes of playing with what is probably his sister, other children and walking the countryside are subtitled: "Happy memories. All shot on Kodachrome. The most popular family film ever." Giving a brief sense of K40's history the subtitles say that the film stock became available in the 1950s and was used by millions of amateur filmmakers until the 80s, when video was introduced. The subtitles also note that the end came in 2010 when the last lab stopped processing the films. At this point the music becomes more melancholic and is accompanied by children whispering about things being beautiful, while the images show more snaps of his and other families in nature and on holidays. Subsequent clips of the selected twenty-five children emphatically waving to camera and found footage of whole groups of people waving to camera are subtitled: "This is my way of saying good-bye to Kodachrome," and "Farewell to Kodachrome," as well as "You'll live forever," gradually blurring the distinction as to whose voice this is and who or what they address. The soundtrack with string instruments of this later section emphasizes a sense of longing and loss. Today this film is most likely seen on Vimeo, digitized and available for viewing online.

The installation of the main project with twenty-five film loops projected side by side will have been an interesting physical and sensorial experience, not least for the noise generated by twenty-five projectors and the regular purr of the film strips running through the gates. Considered from the perspective of screendance, there is an interesting interplay between the movement on and off the projected images as the whole setup is performing, extending the screendance from the images to include the machinery and the film loops themselves as well as the viewers as they walk along the twenty-five rotating filmstrips. The installation makes visible the particular relation to time in analogue technology as it holds within its celluloid strips the images of the children, materializing their image, whilst also projecting them onto the walls of the space where they are dematerialized again, reinstating the transience of the original instant. This play creates a very particular synergy with the wandering public, who are there as solid bodies but are present only for an instant. Perhaps part of the magic of the analogue is this kind of transcendence of boundaries between the permanent and the instant, the material and the immaterial, something which digital projects cannot provide in the same way. The installation at Kunsthal Rotterdam ran for twelve days and the film strips will also have accumulated a considerable amount of dust and scratches in the process, some loops possibly snapping and needing repair, altogether asserting something utterly "real" and at a grand scale. Such large-scale installations are a rarity in the canon of screendance, but the combination of analogue media and noisy apparatus offers an experiential intensity that could be very interesting for screendance projects in the quest for a renewed engagement with the nature of matter.

Numerous film theorists have explored the relation of analogue media to time and place, fascinated by film's photographic nature as photochemical image that determines its material bond with the world and its time signature. As German film theorist Siegfried Kracauer argued in 1963, any such recording, as photography or celluloid film, is "essentially associated with the moment in time at which it comes into existence."[42] Photographic representation thereby ensures the engagement of film with real-life material, although any resemblance is understood to be both mimetic and potentially alienating or confrontational, as well as contingent. These considerations are at the core of extensive debates about what is described as indexicality, the particular quality of the photochemical image to be an imprint, a trace, and to therefore have a direct and irrefutable connection with the time and place in which it was taken. According to Kracauer, there is a sense that the analogue is touching the real by dint of the trace it holds within itself, which is in excess to its capacity for image making and representation. In an essay on the relation of analogue photographs to history David Green and Joanna Lowry similarly observe that it is not just the analogue image or its status as a trace of that moment in time that matters, but that the image asserts itself also by the sheer fact that it was taken there and then. Green and Lowry therefore argue that there is a performativity at play and that these photographic images "point to the real" even though any representation is always partial.[43]

As Mary Ann Doane points out, this discussion on indexicality gains momentum again in response to the rise of digital media, providing a means to distinguish between one and the other.[44] Significantly, digital technologies do not inherently expose their functionalities and do not inherently show signs of use regardless of how often they have been copied and displayed. Digital images are designed to be flawlessly reproduced within a system that is regulated by binary quantization and predictability. Artist Parker Heyl writes that

> [w]hen digital data is copied, error-checking bytes are used to verify that every signal came through the wire correctly, [...] exactly identical to its copy with no variation, despite the fact that it is being transmitted via the messy world of continuously flowing electrons, analogue circuitry, copper wires, and satellite signals. The elimination of error (and uniqueness) from a digital reproduction is made possible by quantization, as electrical signal noise is made irrelevant [...]. [Images] render with perfect consistency, regardless of the place or time [they are] viewed. This contributes to the feeling of time standing still or the destruction of presence.[45]

Flawless and disembodied, digital media are not able to mirror our geospecific lives in the same way as analogue media except through the screens and devices that translate the data into analogue signals. Drawing on Henry Giroux, Heyl argues that our posthuman subjectivity is "ultimately void of geospatial culture, instead defined by a virtual world which is fully monetized under the illusion of escapism."[46] Curiously there appears to be little concern in the wider screendance discourse over these aspects of digital media even though much of the work tries to assert geospatial specificity, time and again seeking out locations in remote mountains or busy city intersections. Kodachrome became a popular medium for home movies precisely because of its indexical relation to the recorded instant and the specific and identifiable colour imprint, a phenomenon that Doane has described as "the sheer affirmation of an existence."[47]

The combination of individual children as protagonists and adults as chorus in *Bye Bye Super 8* gives the scenes an epic, cinematic edge and choreographic approach that also speaks to the wider significance of home, family and childhood. Not surprisingly, Kodachrome film stock facilitated decades of recording particularly of family events and their every-day lives by amateur filmmakers and family members. While Kramer paints a particularly "rosy" and happy picture of childhood with its freedom of movement and beautiful nature, the film evokes more generally a sense of loss and posits that something personal will be less shareable due to the demise of Kodachrome. Kramer's subtitles however also claim "[y]ou'll live forever," possibly directed at the celluloid film, which has after all a lifespan that exceeds those of humans, or it could be directed at the children who, by dint of having been recorded on celluloid by Kramer, will now live forever as if by proxy.

While celluloid film promises a sort of immortality, it is also marked by imperfections and by "happy accidents" that function as a marker of authenticity. Kramer said himself about filming with analogue film: "Digital is perfect, but I like imperfection. With analogue there is always an element of serendipity involved. When I shoot analogue, I can never really be sure what it covers and how exactly it will turn out. Sometimes, the picture actually turns out way better than I expected."[48] This sense of authenticity accounts for the current popularity of Super 8 as well as the later VHS format, a magnetic video technology that also provided less than perfect images. Italian researcher Giuseppina Sapio undertook a study investigating the use of media in conventional home movies. She found that quite a few families compensate for the sense of the dematerialization of contemporary, high-resolution digital media by adding special effects such as grain and vintage filters to digital recordings to make the images "warmer."[49] According to Sapio, the added grain provides an "idea of symbolic continuity [in] the reservoir of family images," potentially compensating even for the dematerialization of the traditional model of family, its roles, and its values.[50] This retro style in digital home movies is however not an isolated phenomenon and part of a wider cultural trend and "retromania" in music, fashion, and art. As Sukhdev Sandhu writes in a review in *The Guardian* of a book titled *Retromania*, retromania is an expression of a need for "safety and succor, especially when life – life under capitalism – feels concussive, brutalising."[51]

Amateur films about family life could be considered as an analogue screendance archive that speaks directly to our corporeality and reflects our need to assert both individuality and continuity. When Marks asks, "what becomes of materiality in the transition from analogue to digital?,"[52] we could ask more specifically: what becomes of our primal embodied selves and experiences in the shift to digital technologies? Analogue media can touch on something or bring into play something about self, identity, agency, and community that is rooted in a contingent and imperfect physical world. It is a constellation that does not easily translate into a digital nowhere in which quantization and fidelity automatically eliminate variations and differences. So what if screendance artists use analogue media and push the technologies themselves to work with and expose contingent materiality?

Priya

Priya is the name of a 16mm film that had a long gestation. In 2002, London-based filmmaker Alia Syed worked on a project called *Eating Grass* (2003) with cinematographer Noski Deville, filming the kathak dancer Priya Puwar.[53] Interested in abstracting the near infinite rotation of the dancer,

Syed decided to film the scene from above with Puwar turning on the spot. Syed recalls:

> We discussed how to obtain an aerial view, so Noski rigged up the camera attaching it to the ceiling on a rope. We then tightened the rope and the camera slowly unfurled with the dancer underneath; once the camera had got to its lowest point, the weight and the velocity of the camera made it twirl back up again. The shot was designed so that the dancer and the camera were twirling around in the same direction, but as the camera went down, it spun in the opposite direction, so within the same shot the movement shifts into two opposing ways. This has a visceral effect on the viewer partly because it's difficult to understand - it's almost like something's swimming against a current, but also because, in actuality, there are two opposing forces at play.[54]

Despite the successful camera work Syed decided at the time not to use the shot because the dancer, trained in classical Indian dance, had worn a classical and somewhat stereotypical white dress for the shoot, which was not what Syed had been looking for.

After making another project, *A Story Told* (2008), edited on computer and installed with different types of projections and monitors, Syed felt the need to return to the materiality of film and to further investigate its relation to time: "When I was making *A Story Told* I missed the smell and the touch of film. When you are editing, you mark the film with a Chinagraph pencil, you then clean off all the marks, traces of dust, keeping the film as clean as possible, but I now realised that the dirt was an index of the films journey through time."[55] Syed proceeded by making a print of the shot with Puwar and burying it in her garden, leaving the print in the ground for a whole year. When digging it up, most of the image had disappeared, and after washing the print there was nothing left at all; the celluloid was blank. Syed persevered and buried prints for three, six, and nine months, developing a system by which the whole scene was divided into sections of equal durations and put back together with filmstrips from the variously composted prints. After projecting and videoing the messy 16mm edit and exhibiting it as video at the Talwar Gallery in Delhi, Syed realized that the piece was losing everything in the transfer to digital. As she could not send the edited piece to a lab for printing due to the dirt and soil that was part of the imagery, she made an optical print herself, frame by frame, eventually finishing the film in 2011. Reflecting on this process Syed writes:

> *Priya* needs to be shown as a 16mm film, it's about 16mm film. It's a representation of a twirling dancer, which is a performance, but you're also aware of the performance of the camera particularly when it shifts

direction. Meanwhile, the chemical nature of film performs through its own breakdown and the apparatuses became apparent through their juxtaposition.[56]

Saying that the project is about 16mm film means that the materiality matters, not only as actual object that could be buried and put together in new ways, but in terms of what the piece was doing as a work of art. The materiality of film had been of interest to a whole generation of artists, making and showing their work at the London Film-Makers' Co-op between 1966 and 1998, for example, more often than not in order to deconstruct the cinematic apparatus and to challenge and expand what film could be.[57]

For Syed this exploration of the materiality of film in *Priya* was an exploration of the parallels between the speed of the movement in the image and the corresponding material deterioration of the celluloid itself. The combination foregrounded duration against or alongside a gradual breakdown and the eventual reconstitution of the image – and of the dance – towards the end of the film. Now only ever shown and projected as a 16mm film, this experience of time and process is reinforced by the sound of the projector with its continuous purring and the regular movement of the film strip running through the projector. Syed writes:

> Film is an immersive experience, and I like to think of that immersive experience as a holding or an embrace – where you're held within a moment not necessarily directed. There's a holding of attention as opposed to a directing of attention. "Priya" is the name of the dancer but it also means "beloved." So there's also this idea of desire – the desire to recognize and to hold on to an image, precisely because the image disappears.[58]

Syed reflects on the power of the image to hold the viewer's attention within the space and time of the projection and compares it to an embrace, that is, a corporeal experience of being with another, yielding to and accepting this other. As a celluloid filmstrip that is projected through space, there is indeed another presence, which fills the space visually and aurally and which has perhaps also a sense of weight and tension and a smell. In the embrace the viewer can give in to the magical brilliance of the screen image, lose herself in the light, or allow the image to become her. The dancing Puwar spins the viewer with her through the continuity of her turning. However, when the image disintegrates, losing its contours and becoming random blotches of colour, it pulls the viewer into the visual disarray that has no structure and no direction. Still held within the glow of the disappearing image, the viewer can only endure and wait and witness, until the forms and the figure return. The end and the resolution of this holding comes when the last click of the projector signals the last frame. The beloved is playing a cheeky game here, teasing the viewer with her brilliance and then vanishing. However, when she returns the viewer is also reconstituted and returned to her own seated, material self.

The film draws the spectator into a tension between the different modes of production, the technical, the audio-visual and the organic, even charting the seasons in which the film strips were buried as evident in the red and orange stains of beetroots, mangoes, and other kitchen scraps, forming a diary of what Syed was eating at the time. Through the particular earthy hands-on process of making, the materiality of the celluloid and its fragility come to constitute the image, taking over the pictorial plane. *Priya* is therefore an acknowledgment of change over time, which pervades the whole apparatus and engulfs the viewer, matter, and machine. Perhaps this is the ultimate antidote to the spaceless and timeless digiverse, in which everything is possible most of the time. The film *Priya* runs its course, slowly and surely, and there is no escape; it is a matter of limitations, imperfections, and snags.

Once upon a time, in 1935/36, Walter Benjamin stated that "[f]ilm is the art form that is in keeping with the increased threat to his life which modern man has to face."[59] At the time Benjamin was concerned about the constant change and increasing speed of modern life and how this impacted the individual, and he found the constantly moving filmstrip to be as shocking as the world around him.[60] Today, in 2023, the celluloid filmstrip pushes against the increasingly dematerialized and virtual spheres, offering instead a respite of human and more-than human dimensions in which the viewer finds an echo of her own matter, her own ageing and imperfections. *Priya* is a screendance in which the technologies partake in the essential aspects of the embodied nature of living and where the technologies are undergoing the same ebb and flow as the content.

Epilogue

There is no doubt that the essence of technology harbours within itself the growth of the saving-power, to use Heidegger's terminology, and this applies in different ways to both analogue and digital technologies. While digital media are convenient and offer huge opportunities for connectivity and exchange, there is a role for analogue media as well for hybrid projects in which digital processes are complemented by analogue, tactile, and sensorial output. As Heyl notes, "[b]y opposing a future that is corporatized in a touchless ether, we can rebuild a technotopia which augments the real rather than replaces it."[61] A screendance technotopia can be a sphere in which technology is dance and dance is technology, and perhaps we may even invent new analogue technologies that bring us back to the matter of matter. Analogue technologies facilitate a bringing-forth that is commensurate with real time and real space, bound by the same laws of physics. They facilitate an occasioning with which we can "question the presumptions about agency and causation implicit in prevailing paradigms [that] have structured our modern sense of the domains and dimensions of the ethical and the political."[62]

There is, however, also a question of whether our daily interactions with the virtual, binary sphere might on some deep level promote binary thinking more generally, possibly impacting on all of human activities. The dynamic of a binary system was brilliantly enacted in *Star Trek: The Next Generation*, Season 1, Episode 14, "11001001," broadcast in 1988, in which the Bynars, a race of cybernetically enhanced humanoids and inhabitants of the planet Bynaus, are called upon to upgrade the computer system on Starship Enterprise.[63] Interconnected with a master computer, the Bynars live in pairs that are physically symmetrical and have thought patterns and ways of speaking that closely resemble binary code, thinking in terms of "yes" or "no." A reviewer of the episode for Tor.com comments that "[m]ost impressive is director Paul Lynch's maintaining of the binary theme. We see people in groups of two—not just the Bynars, but Yar and Worf, Data and La Forge, Picard and Riker. Of particular note is the way Picard and Riker move in near-perfect unison when they try to take the ship back."[64] This choreography of the Starship crew suggests that humans might be highly susceptible to binarization. In real life, the app Tinder has also adopted a yes/no approach in its core mechanics, as users swipe right to accept someone and left to reject them. Since the launch of Tinder in 2012, the gesture of swiping right and swiping left has even become a pop cultural artefact along with the thumbs up/thumbs down binary, which has permeated much of the internet and social media, potentially contributing to an increasingly worrying polarization of entire populations.[65] Real world interactions generally offer many more differentiated responses, more often than not formed of processes that unfold over a period of time and are less delineated than their online equivalents. The film *Priya* takes 11 minutes and 36 seconds to gradually dissolve and reconfigure the figure of the spinning dancer, forming a screendance that is all about process and duration, a space-time without definable boundaries.

Notes

1 Ian Christie, Dominique Chateau, and Annie van den Oever, "Editorial," in *Technē/Technology: Researching Cinema and Media Technologies – Their Development, Use, and Impact*, ed. Annie van den Oever (Amsterdam: Amsterdam University Press, 2014), 9.
2 Claire Bishop, "Digital Divide: Contemporary Art and New Media," *Artforum* 51, no. 1 (2012), https://www.artforum.com/print/201207/digital-divide-contemporary-art-and-new-media-31944.

3   Bishop, "Digital Divide."
4   Katharina Niemeyer, *Media and Nostalgia. Yearning for the Past, Present and Future* (Basingstoke: Palgrave Macmillan, 2014), 2–6.
5   Laura Marks et al., "Streaming Carbon Footprint," School for the Contemporary Arts, Simon Fraser University, accessed January 16, 2023, https://www.sfu.ca/sca/projects—activities/streaming-carbon-footprint/.
6   Martin Heidegger, "The Question Concerning Technologies," in *Basic Writing, Martin Heidegger*, ed. David Farrell Krell (London: Routledge, 1993), 311–41.
7   Benoît Turquety, "Toward an Archaeology of the Cinema/ Technology Relation: From Mechanization to 'Digital Cinema,'" in *Technē/Technology*, 52.
8   Robert Sinnerbrink, "Technē and Poiēsis: On Heidegger and Film Theory," in *Technē/Technology*, 69.
9   Ann Cooper Albright, "The Tensions of Technē: On Heidegger and Screendance," *International Journal of Screendance* 2 (2012): 21. https://doi.org/10.18061/ijsd.v2i0.
10 Heidegger, "The Question Concerning Technologies," 312.
11 Heidegger, "The Question Concerning Technologies," 318–19.
12 Heidegger, "The Question Concerning Technologies," 314, 316.
13 Heidegger, "The Question Concerning Technologies," 316.
14 Heidegger, "The Question Concerning Technologies," 318.
15 Albright, "The Tensions of Technē," 22.
16 Heidegger, "The Question Concerning Technologies," 324.
17 Heidegger, "The Question Concerning Technologies," 329.
18 Heidegger, "The Question Concerning Technologies," 330.
19 Heidegger, "The Question Concerning Technologies," 333.
20 Heidegger, "The Question Concerning Technologies," 341.
21 Albright, "The Tensions of Technē," 22.
22 Ann Dils, "Moving Across Time with Words: Toward An Etymology of Screendance," *The International Journal Of Screendance* 2 (2012): 24. https://doi.org/10.18061/ijsd.v2i0.6890.
23 For a detailed account of the history of pre-cinematic machines and Marey's photographic gun, see Pasi Väliaho, "Marey's Gun: Apparatuses of Capture and the Operational Image," in *Technē/Technology*, 169–76.
24 Martin Heidegger, *Discourse on Thinking* (New York: Harper & Row, 1966).
25 Sinnerbrink, "Technē and Poiēsis," 65.
26 Heidegger, *Discourse on Thinking*, 48.
27 Jean Baudrillard, "Simulacra and Simulation," in *Selected Writings*, ed. Mark Poster (Stanford: Stanford University Press, 1988), 166–84.
28 Hito Steyerl, "In Defence of the Poor Image," *e-flux Journal*, no. 10 (2009), https://www.e-flux.com/journal/10/61362/in-defense-of-the-poor-image/.
29 Steyerl, "In Defence of the Poor Image."
30 Steyerl, "In Defence of the Poor Image."
31 Heidegger, "The Question Concerning Technologies," 333.
32 Heidegger, "The Question Concerning Technologies," 341.
33 Heidegger, "The Question Concerning Technologies," 330.
34 "Film Notes: Shirley Clarke's Bridges-Go-Round (1958)", National Film Preservation Foundation, https://www.filmpreservation.org/dvds-and-books/clips/bridges-go-round-1958. Accessed June 17, 2023.
35 Laura U. Marks, *Touch: Sensuous Theory and Multisensory Media* (Minneapolis, London: University of Minnesota Press, 2002), 148.
36 Laura Marks, "How Electrons Remember," *Millenium Film Journal*, no. 34 (1999): 66.
37 Marks, *Touch*, 7–12.
38 Marks, *Touch*, xxii.

39 Diana Coole and Samantha Frost, "Introducing the New Materialisms," in *New Materialisms: Ontology, Agency, and Politics* (United Kingdom: Duke University Press, 2010), 6.
40 "Bye Bye Super 8," Halal, accessed November 15, 2019, https://halal.amsterdam/item/bye-bye-super-8/; Penny Lee, "Bye Bye Super 8 film project branding," Behance, accessed November 15, 2019, https://www.behance.net/gallery/51023003/Bye-Bye-Super-8-film-project-branding.
41 *Bye Bye Super 8*, directed by Johan Kramer (2010; Chelsea Pictures, 2011), https://vimeo.com/23007405.
42 Siegfried Kracauer, *The Mass Ornament: Weimar Essays*, translated and edited by Thomas Y. Levin (Cambridge, MA: Harvard University Press, 1995), 54.
43 David Green and Joanna Lowry, "From Presence to the Performative: Rethinking Photographic Indexicality," in *Where Is the Photograph?*, ed. David Green (Brighton, UK: Photoworks/ Photoforum, 2002), 60.
44 Mary Ann Doane, "The Indexical and the Concept of Medium Specificity," *Differences: A Journal of Feminist Cultural Studies* 18, no. 1 (2007): 130.
45 Parker Heyl, "Analogue Future: Materiality in the Digital Arts," Design for Performance and Interaction, The Bartlett School of Architecture, University College London, UK, November 30, 2018, http://www.interactivearchitecture.org/analog-future-materiality-in-the-digital-arts.html.
46 Heyl, "Analogue Future"; Bradley Evans and Henri A. Giroux, *Disposable Futures: The Seduction of Violence in the Age of Spectacle* (City Lights Open Media: City Lights Publishers, 2015).
47 Mary Ann Doane, "Indexicality: Trace and Sign: Introduction," *Differences: A Journal of Feminist Cultural Studies* 18, no. 1 (2007): 3.
48 Johan Kramer, "Johan Kramer: Camera Dream," interview by Linda Zhengová, *GUP Magazine*, accessed January 22, 2023 https://gupmagazine.com/interview/johan-kramer-camera-dream/.
49 Giuseppina Sapio, "Homesick for Aged Home Movies: Why Do We Shoot Contemporary Family in an Old-Fashioned Way?," in *Media and Nostalgia*, 44.
50 Sapio, "Homesick for Aged Home Movies," 46, 49.
51 Sukhdev Sandhu, "Retromania: Pop Culture's Addiction to its Own Past by Simon Reynolds –review," *The Guardian*, May 29, 2011, https://www.theguardian.com/books/2011/may/29/retromania-simon-reynolds-review.
52 Marks, *Touch*, xxii.
53 *Priya*, directed by Alia Syed, performances by Priya Puwar (London, UK: 2012).
54 Alia Syed (filmmaker), in discussion with Ella S. Mills, April 17, 2018.
55 Syed, in discussion with Ella S. Mills.
56 Syed, in discussion with Ella S. Mills.
57 A.L. Rees, *A History of Experimental Film and Video* (London: British Film Institute, 1999).
58 Syed, in discussion with Ella S. Mills.
59 Walter Benjamin, *Illuminations* (London: Pimlico Editions, 1999), 243.
60 Dominique Chateau, "The Philosophy of Technology in the Frame of Film Theory: Walter Benjamin's Contribution," in *Technē/Technology*, 34.
61 Heyl, "Analogue Future."
62 Coole and Frost, "Introducing the New Materialisms," 6.
63 "Star Trek: The Next Generation" 11001001 (TV Episode 1988) – IMDb," IMDB, https://www.imdb.com/title/tt0708668/.
64 Keith DeCandido, "Star Trek: The Next Generation Rewatch: 11001001," Tor.com, June 23, 2011, https://www.tor.com/2011/06/23/star-trek-the-next-generation-rewatch-q11001001q/.

65 Josep Ferrer, "Swipe left, swipe right – but why? The real story behind Tinder's most famous gesture," UX Collective, September 27, 2022. https://uxdesign.cc/swipe-left-swipe-right-but-why-tinder-ux-ui-simple-dating-mobile-app-swiping-design-4d2295d80407.

Bibliography

Albright, Ann Cooper. "The Tensions of Technē: On Heidgger and Screendance." *The International Journal of Screendance* 2 (2012): 21–23. https://doi.org/10.18061/ijsd.v2i0.

Baudrillard, Jean. "Simulacra and Simulation." In *Selected Writings*, edited by Mark Poster, 166–184. Stanford: Stanford University Press, 1988.

Benjamin, Walter. *Illuminations*. London: Pimlico Editions, 1999.

Bishop, Claire. "Digital Divide: Contemporary Art and New Media." *Artforum* 51, no 1 (2012). https://www.artforum.com/print/201207/digital-divide-contemporary-art-and-new-media-31944.

"Bye Bye Super 8." Halal. https://halal.amsterdam/item/bye-bye-super-8/. Accessed November 15, 2019.

Chateau, Dominique. "The Philosophy of Technology in the Frame of Film Theory: Walter Benjamin's Contribution." In van den Oever, Annie, ed. *Technē/Technology: Researching Cinema and Media Technologies – Their Development, Use, and Impact*, 29–49. Amsterdam: Amsterdam University Press, 2014.

Christie, Ian, Dominique Chateau, and Annie van den Oever. "Editorial." In van den Oever, Annie, ed. *Technē/Technology: Researching Cinema and Media Technologies – Their Development, Use, and Impact*, 9. Amsterdam: Amsterdam University Press, 2014.

Coole, Diane, and Samantha Frost. "Introducing the New Materialisms." In *New Materialisms: Ontology, Agency, and Politics*, 1–43. United Kingdom: Duke University Press, 2010.

DeCandido, Keith. "Star Trek: The Next Generation Rewatch: 11001001." *Tor.com*, June 23, 2011. https://www.tor.com/2011/06/23/star-trek-the-next-generation-rewatch-q11001001q/.

Dils, Ann. "Moving Across Time with Words: Toward An Etymology of Screendance." *The International Journal Of Screendance* 2 (2012): 24. https://doi.org/10.18061/ijsd.v2i0.6890.

Doane, Mary-Ann. "Indexicality: Trace and Sign: Introduction." *Differences: A Journal of Feminist Cultural Studies* 18, no. 1 (2007): 1–6.

Doane, Mary-Ann. "The Indexical and the Concept of Medium Specificity." *Differences: A Journal of Feminist Cultural Studies* 18, no. 1 (2007): 129–152.

Evans, Bradley, and Henri A.Giroux. *Disposable Futures: The Seduction of Violence in the Age of Spectacle*. City Lights Open Media: City Lights Publishers, 2015.

Ferrer, Josep. "Swipe left, swipe right - but why? The real story behind Tinder's most famous gesture." *UX Collective*, 2022. https://uxdesign.cc/swipe-left-swipe-right-but-why-tinder-ux-ui-simple-dating-mobile-app-swiping-design-4d2295d80407.

Green, David, and Joanna Lowry. "From Presence to the Performative: Rethinking Photographic Indexicality." In *Where Is the Photograph?*, edited by David Green, 47–60. Brighton, UK: Photoworks/ Photoforum, 2002.

Heidegger, Martin. *Discourse on Thinking*. New York: Harper & Row, 1966.

Heidegger, Martin. "The Question Concerning Technologies." In *Basic Writing, Martin Heidegger*, edited by David Farrell Krell, 311–341. London: Routledge, 1993.

Heyl, Parker. "Analogue Future: Materiality in the Digital Arts, Design for Performance and Interaction." The Bartlett School of Architecture, University College London, UK. November 30, 2018. http://www.interactivearchitecture.org/analog-future-materiality-in-the-digital-arts.html.

Kracauer, Siegfried. *The Mass Ornament: Weimar Essays*. Translated and edited by Thomas Y.Levin. Cambridge, Massachusetts: Harvard University Press, 1995.

Kramer, Johan, dir. *Bye Bye Super 8*. Bye Bye Super 8. 2010; Chelsea Pictures, 2011. https://vimeo.com/23007405.

Kramer, Johan. "Johan Kramer: Camera Dream." By Linda Zhengová. *GUP Magazine*. https://gupmagazine.com/interview/johan-kramer-camera-dream/. Accessed January 22, 2023.

Lee, Penny. "Bye Bye Super 8 film project branding." Behance. https://www.behance.net/gallery/51023003/Bye-Bye-Super-8-film-project-branding. Accessed November 15, 2023.

Marks, Laura U. "How Electrons Remember." *Millenium Film Journal*, no. 34 (1999): 66–80.

Marks, Laura U. *Touch: Sensuous Theory and Multisensory Media*. Minneapolis: University of Minnesota Press, 2002.

Marks, Laura U., Stephen Makonin, Radek Przedpełski, and Alejandro Rodriguez-Silva. "Streaming Carbon Footprint." School for the Contemporary Arts, Simon Fraser University. https://www.sfu.ca/sca/projects—activities/streaming-carbon-footprint/. Accessed January 16, 2023.

"Film Notes: Shirley Clarke's *Bridges-Go-Round* (1958)." National Film Preservation Foundation. https://www.filmpreservation.org/dvds-and-books/clips/bridges-go-round-1958.

Niemeyer, Katharina, ed. *Media and Nostalgia. Yearning for the Past, Present and Future*. Basingstoke: Palgrave Macmillan, 2014.

Rees, A.L. *A History of Experimental Film and Video*. London: British Film Institute, 1999.

Sapio, Giuseppina. "Homesick for Aged Home Movies: Why Do We Shoot Contemporary Family in an Old-Fashioned Way?" In Niemeyer, Katharina, ed. *Media and Nostalgia. Yearning for the Past, Present and Future*, 39–50. Basingstoke: Palgrave Macmillan, 2014.

Sandhu, Sukhdev. "Retromania: Pop Culture's Addiction to its Own Past by Simon Reynolds – review." *The Guardian*, May 29, 2011. https://www.theguardian.com/books/2011/may/29/retromania-simon-reynolds-review.

Sinnerbrink, Robert. "Technē and Poiēsis: On Heidegger and Film Theory." In van den Oever, Annie, ed. *Technē/Technology: Researching Cinema and Media Technologies – Their Development, Use, and Impact*, 65–80. Amsterdam: Amsterdam University Press, 2014.

"Star Trek: The Next Generation" 11001001 (TV Episode 1988) – IMDb." IMDb. https://www.imdb.com/title/tt0708668/.

Steyerl, Hito. "In Defence of the Poor Image." *e-flux Journal*, no. 10 (2009). https://www.e-flux.com/journal/10/61362/in-defense-of-the-poor-image/.

Syed, Alia, dir. *Priya*. Performances by Priya Purwal. London, UK, 2012. https://vimeo.com/132308381.

Turquety, Benoît. "Toward an Archaeology of the Cinema/ Technology Relation: From Mechanization to 'Digital Cinema'." In van den Oever, Annie, ed. *Technē/ Technology: Researching Cinema and Media Technologies – Their Development, Use, and Impact*, 50–65. Amsterdam: Amsterdam University Press, 2014.

Väliaho, Pasi. "Marey's Gun: Apparatuses of Capture and the Operational Image." In van den Oever, Annie, ed. *Technē/Technology: Researching Cinema and Media Technologies – Their Development, Use, and Impact*, 169–176. Amsterdam: Amsterdam University Press, 2014.

van den Oever, Annie, ed. *Technē/Technology: Researching Cinema and Media Technologies – Their Development, Use, and Impact*. Amsterdam: Amsterdam University Press, 2014.

18
MOVING MIRROR: SCREENDANCE AS PERFORMANCE METHODOLOGY

An Interview with Nadège Grebmeier Forget

By Alanna Thain

FIGURE 18.1 *Inside-Outside, Off & On* (2020)
Source: Image credit: Adrián Morillo.

For more than a decade, Nadège Grebmeier Forget has been testing the edges of the image through the generation of experimental zones of intensity. Through performance that produces live action screendance and the occupation of the screen as a moving mirror, her use of lo-tech and intimate, at-hand technologies, especially Photo Booth, have developed a movement practice relevant to the digital age. This is a practice of intensities and repetitions, working with a massive personal archive of production in parallel with the database of pop cultural gestures and images. Grebmeier Forget's practices of auto-archiving inform both her performance and media practice and trouble that distinction. Her approach remixes the tactics of screendance for the mobile media of the twenty-first century. Her video *Some Kind of Game* (2020), produced as a Facebook livestream during the first weeks of the pandemic, maps and charges the feedback loop between performer and her image, social media and self-representation, and the contagious tremble of pandemic bodies captured and confined in anxiety, restriction, and the need for connection.[1] For two hours, she manually looped "Some Kind of Game" by Against All Logic in a hyperkinetic and evolving negation of exhaustion and relentlessness, one of the first works to showcase how screendance, reimagined, might sustain itself and its audience as a tactic of survival. Her work has frequently confounded the spectacularity of dance on screen by reorienting questions of visibility as an exploratory terrain of the artist's own body. In *Rendering on View (Betty Rowland Meets Angela Aames)* from 2017, the artist "reperformed" an imitation of a burlesque dance by Rowland and other iconic and feminized movements, breaking the screenic dyad that would make her moves just a poor copy, and exploring what it is we want from pop culture. *Inside-Outside, Off & On* (2020) blows up the screen's enclosures, transferring capture from a webcam to an unstable and large reflective surface where we witness the artist at work. Recomposing her image in real time, Grebmeier Forget shifts the potential of lo-tech creation from the easily at-hand to the atmospheric intimacies of the laptop's roving eye.[2]

Thain: Screendance is a place where many women artists describe finding some kind of liberation, from formal dance training and its gendered expectation, or from mass cultures and mainstream cinema's images of women and techniques of representation. Your work often plays with the legacy of the erotic and idealized representations of women, using duration and mediation in surprising and challenging ways to turn these into moving material, rather than fixed images.

What makes it possible for you to work with images that often come with a tremendous amount of baggage, expectation, cliché? What attracts you to these and what are your techniques for making them playable? In both your performance and image-making practices, you're always working with a lot of layers, whether the material layers or whether you're trying to evoke memories on top of the live or recorded images, often drawn from pop culture, on the part of viewers. For me, this produces a kind of affective *discretion*: I never feel like there's going to be one singular moment of revelation of the real thing, the real truth, the real inner essence. But it's also not postmodern in that sense of there's nothing but layers. Every layer is also a recreation of everything—a composite editing in real time. Every time something is removed, or something is added, it's like, now *that's* the thing.

Grebmeier Forget: *Moshi Moshi* (2011) is the first thing I did with a mediation, which was actually my first performance in front of a live, in-person audience... In certain regards to what you are saying, I'm thinking a lot these days of how my practice speaks about self-isolation and feels as such mainly in its process of becoming manifest. There's a lot of introspection. A lot of inner work that requires a certain amount of alone time, that is maybe a little longer than what I would "naturally" be comfortable with... I need to cultivate a certain kind of state that I don't particularly like. And at the same time, it needs so much of others to exist—in other words, the context of the viewer—to actually have a significant impact on my understanding of the (my) world and practice. When I naturally started performing during my studies, I instinctively went towards the camera. Even during my bachelor's, I was doing a lot of things for the lens, but it was very still, and it wasn't in a live feed format. You know, you're a certain age and you're looking for something, and it started to be a lot about like self looking for self. I began with simple questions: What does that mean? How can I frame it (that feeling of searching for what the self means and is)? How can I be comfortable with it, my body and surroundings: aka Life? In the case of *Moshi Moshi* at VIVA! Art Action (the performance festival in Montreal I was unfolding this work in), I was too shy to perform in front of people. So, I said, "Perfect—I'll use a camera and I'll go trap myself in this box and I'll film it. Done." It was super impulsive. "Oh, I'll do this, and I'll feel better." But then it escalated, because I started really being interested in the types of images and tensions that this methodology was producing and how there is a sort of privacy that is not visible onscreen. And my pleasure is there. In the invisible.

I think my liberation is produced by a certain self-referential quality in my work; there are so many images that create stress on our bodies and worth, where you can compare yourself indefinitely and you are drawn more and more towards the outside. I find when I look at myself in action, I know that my body holds all of that outside, so my job as an artist (and woman) is to dissect; finding myself through myself instead of trying to compare what I do (or am) to a hypothetical better other. When you stick to what is unique in your internal core, then (comparison) just becomes unnecessary, superficial...

When speaking to the idea of the erotic, in *Re-Reflecting On...* (2016), I was five hours under a table (filming myself with Photo Booth). But everything that's

FIGURE 18.2 *Re-Reflecting On…* (2016)
Source: Image credit: Paul Litherland.

going on would be projected. I didn't have much space to move, so I had to always be holding the camera on my toe and thinking very quickly about where to find beauty. I'm still trying to always be a perfect image, right? That mind flow of not thinking, but just doing, is very liberating and satisfying. A sensual and organic searching. And you don't find that often in life, where you can just let go and concretely feel extreme self-satisfaction. In that moment of challenging myself, I enjoy (re)discovering the images that inhabit me, in the moment of their reproduction and afterwards as well. The element of surprise in your own language is really magical, to me at least!

Thain: This sense of constantly being in a relay of generating and recomposing your own image is part of why I think of you as a real remix artist. Watching your work, I feel the liveliness of that; you're not remixing something that is an original or something that's elsewhere. It's like the remix *is* the work, the remix *is* the practice, it's *the* thing.

Grebmeier Forget: Yeah… On the other hand, I have this obsession of trying to be original or trying not to be a spoof of myself. Unfortunately, it creates a lot of stress because I'm known for this thing you speak of, but how can I try to do something that refers to this, refers to the experience of it, but not actually fall into the expectation of it? I'm trying to break this self-imaging all the time. And by doing that, I find it reinforces my way of working, and the way society functions (under pressure)—it creates another type of image that is perhaps oddly more real/bad, but that permits movement. Maybe this idea of dance for screen is linked to this idea of images that are always moving. Like there's never a moment where I'm actually still and saying absolutely yes to everything I do or sense. I hold poses, states, but I am not trying to say: "This means this or that. This is very meaningful."

Thain: There's an intensity to those kinds of stillness and those kinds of pauses. Little repetitions and loopings are a lot of what you use in your work.

Grebmeier Forget: Well, would you say that there is no narrative? It's like I was practicing, practicing or trying to find an idea. Searching. To be honest, I never do a whole run. I'm never quite sure what the actual performance will be. So, I practice being free and just experimenting. This creates an archive of fragments in me. I play with this idea of what I can or cannot remember of the fragment. What creates a sort of intrigue is I'm actually doing the action until the end, and then when I lose interest, I let it go. There's no conclusion, I'm not going anywhere with it, most of the time. If you observe the strategies I use the most in my practice, put it all together, it's always this: spaces in time filled or forgotten. I always describe my work as like a ball that is constantly rolling, you know, instead of an arc that's trying to meet a sum of what a "good" performance could be…

Thain: I'd like to talk specifically about some of the lo-tech methods you use, like Skype and Photo Booth, for example, to create spaces for choreography and performance. Photo Booth as a tool is both like and unlike other kinds of cameras. What is the appeal of these tools for you, and what do they allow you to do?

Grebmeier Forget: I use basic technologies: the computer, the projector, my cell phone, I used a GoPro once and I think I like them because they're always on your body in some ways (like the phone). I see it as an extension of my brain/eyes. Who are you the most in relation with in your life? Pretty much your handheld or "ear-budded" phone and laptop! They're in your bed, they're in your bathroom, the laptop and phone cameras are very intimate things… At some point, I just said, "Well, I'm going to use this tool that I already have instead of spending too much money on a new one." That's it. There is an immediacy in using these tools that I like and that requires me to stay in the moment, not think about what I need to do afterwards for it to be art. What I capture is what it is, and performance is also that: accepting a certain irreversible time frame.

I also like that it archives everything on its own; I don't have to deal with hierarchy, it just ends up being full of everything. It mixes my life and my work, and I'm ok with that. It collapses all moments into one, turning my bank of possible images into something quite infinite and malleable.

Thain: Coming back to that idea of an archive of fragments, it's also very much about the connections of the fragments, like seeing at a glance where you were at in your life.

Grebmeier Forget: Of course. As I was saying, these simple tools create a timeline of memories. I go back through Photo Booth and pictures on my phone and don't have to spend much time with the pictures or captions to remember where I was in my life at that moment. And there's a charge there. I'm not just for me. I like this idea of always having some sort of presence, viewing/framing of myself for others, which is why Instagram started being a thing where, yes, I'm alone, I'm always isolated, but there is this present thing that's always watching or creating true or false memories. My Photo Booth is a lot of that. I can go through it and re-embed myself in some sort of emotion that I created or that spontaneously came up while at home or working in the studio and then the new piece will be embedded with that ambiguity. Everything is embedded with something of the past, or something of the present, and most likely fantasy.

I think that is why I was working at some point with mimicking my own reproductions. For these reasons, I often make the archive present because I feel like the performance isn't a still moment for me. It's all about the buildup of getting there. And there's a lot of interesting things that happen in trying something out, even if they're not conclusive, so often I'll be referring to my own experiences and kind of snipping out pieces I like. Self-reproducing and editing.

It's an archive and it's a tool, but it's also very private because the laptop is constructed to face you. If you turn it around, your laptop is actually non-functional. It's like a channel, right? I'm trapped in it: it's a relationship and it's a mirror and it's a lot of things. You can't frame in many ways with all these simple tools; there's always the same self-focused angles embedded within their structure. So often people will say, "Oh, you're really obsessed with your crotch," for example. But literally I have two options, either my face or like this part of my legs because it can't really go lower because then you'll see my boring keyboard and the type/brand of computer I'm using. [Going through my archive] I really noticed a distinct pattern; there are honestly only so many angles you can work with, if you don't use an external webcam. I must like the constraint of it as well.

But really, I mainly use it as a studio tool. If I'm in a place where I'm going to prepare a performance, I just turn on the camera and film myself being in the space. It's a trace of my presence, it's an external presence. I can then look at whatever I filmed when I'm calmer, because I tend to do very short and intensive studio times. I then have a better sense of what the public will be (maybe) seeing. A lot of the time I objectify my own self as a way of editing: "Oh, I like it when I move like this, when I don't see my face. Maybe this is too much." I recompose the image and the possible actions.

Thain: For you, does that set the parameters of the stage? When you're thinking about performance, when you're thinking about framing, you've got this box of the screen to work in as much as you have this space to work in.

Grebmeier Forget: Knowing the relationship with the screen allows me to work through my shyness by avoiding the awkward dynamic of wanting to visually engage the public. I never look people in the eyes and try to make them feel or understand something. I'm always deliberately staying very concentrated on the tasks at hand because I'm actually seeing the performance while you're seeing it, and I can only manipulate the image like a sculpture if I do this studio work beforehand.

Thain: Are you seeing or are you reacting? Are you able to have enough distance from also having to do and make that you can be a little distant and actually see what the images are like, or are you always playing with it more immediately, like in a mirror?

Grebmeier Forget: It's odd. I hardly see myself anymore. What I'm seeing is a shape: there's a square and I'm trying to fill the square. It's like I'm interacting with the flow of images that I'm seeing not necessarily with myself: I'm filming here, I'm looking there, so I'm not even attentively observing what it is I'm doing. So, there's something about that I find fascinating; I have to be very present and at the same time very absent. I'm a machine. I'm actually working and feeling a lot, so I'm always super tired afterwards. I'm doing something physical, but also very mental; I find working with and for images is hard. As you say, responsive. Actually, the tiredness I feel is really about how you can think very fast about making-thinking, what is being produced and what is being questioned, live. Because of my own anxiety, I unfortunately need that pressure to be able to be free within a limited time, or else I start overthinking. Overthinking makes you lose all the interest because that's when it's contaminated by life, right?

Thain: That kind of constraint—of the box in the corner or on the screen, or under the table—how does that happen in a work like *Inside-Outside, Off & On* in the context of *Allegorical Circuits For Human Software #2* (2020)? In that work, you did a live and live-streamed performance in the public outdoor plaza of Montreal's Darling Foundry, working with an enormous and flexible mirrored material. This creates a funhouse mirror effect that you repeatedly play with as it distorts the reflection and warps your body image and the surrounding street. You also use a laptop with a webcam, and the funhouse effect continues as the laptop is both also a kind of mirror, and also reflected in the image. It is almost impossible to place the idea of the "screen," and instead, you create a live-action zone for screendance that undoes any binary distinction of body and technology. At one point you even pull the mirror over yourself and the camera like a blanket, creating a wild image that is both enclosed and full of refraction and vortexes. In this work, can the camera be a box, perhaps that is also a portal for you, that allows you to find a space to move within?

Grebmeier Forget: At the Darling Foundry; there was no way for me to be anchored. It was very difficult for me to think through. It was so big, with the sky above! When I added the elements of the image workings, I really felt I could suddenly focus and create a sort of bubble around me. And because I'm tapping into that more centered energy, I think people feel it, you're not just seeing a body that's wandering around. You are seeing a space within a space. That's a muscle you really have to exercise.

Thain: That bubble—that's a little bit what I was trying to describe when I said there's a kind of discretion to your work that I find very powerful.

Grebmeier Forget: As I was saying earlier, I deliberately don't create contact. I'm actually doing, I'm not showing. I'm doing the action, the task at hand that I gave myself to do, and you're actually watching somebody doing, not acting to be something else or incarnate some other person. That really shifts presence a lot. You make that bubble felt. I think that's challenging a lot of times for audiences. You transfer that space that you managed to create; you sort of say without words: "this is a zone in which these things are possible and it's a little bit up to the you (the audience) to figure out your own way to share that with me. I'm not there just to be consumed." It's about sharing responsibly.

Thain: You said, when you're looking at your own image, "I'm not even looking at myself. I'm looking at shapes." Much of the kind of analysis of women looking at themselves is in terms of narcissism or ego. This isn't the feeling that I get from your work. There's a real inhabitation of the image; the world of the mirror as well. Some of this is as you said, that sense of "I'm working." You're not posing, you're not an object: you're working, and you feel the work. That's one of the reasons why I see dance so much in your practice, because dance is an art without an object, right? So, it is the working, the working of the body.

Grebmeier Forget: I see what you mean. There is some sort of trust in the inner knowledge that dancers have, much more than visual artists sometimes. And also, the importance of the body as a source of answers, of memory, of feelings, of a lot of things. And I think although I work a lot with objects and things outside of myself, I try to make my body as visible as possible, in feeling it when I'm working and knowing when maybe something is not right. I'm not just in my head.

Thain: When in many works I see you playing with your own image, or images from the pop culture archives, they don't feel precious but instead full of the pleasure of the playable. Nothing feels fetishized or perfected. You had that one image of you dressing up like Marilyn Monroe, where it's also for you, it's not about matching up to a particular kind of image. In fact, presented via Photo Booth, we see an archive that undoes the idea of a single, still image, and instead see all the multiple versions as well. There is something about pop culture that asks us to participate in it. How do you take up that invitation to participate?

Grebmeier Forget: This image is from a series that came out of the performance archive produced during *Hier est Aujourd'hui* (VU PHOTO/Mois

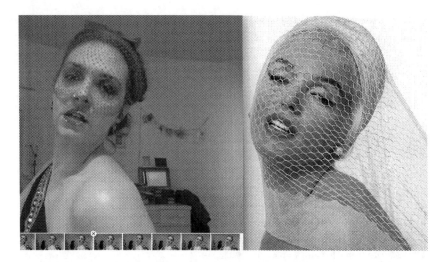

FIGURE 18.3 *Stilled as Marilyn stilled by Bert as Marilyn Behind a White Veil (March 6)*, from *Hier est Aujourd'hui* (2016)
Source: Image credit: Nadège Grebmeier Forget.

Multi, 2016). Without remembering, I had screenshotted a bunch of situations across thirty-one days. I find this to be a great photo series because it really talks about my way of working and what the work is actually doing and talking about. Pop culture often makes me think of my mom. Or more of like a memory of my mom and all her sisters obsessing with TV and classic romance movies. My mom is from California, so until I was twelve, I was going to California during the summer. *I Love Lucy, I Dream of Jeannie*, all these 1950s American things are part of my background and I've always admired that aesthetic of the American dream, which is over the top… it's so polished and it's so gendered, so much so that it's a caricature. So, you could do what you want with this caricature. I think that's oddly the point. If I incarnated it exactly, it's not interesting. It stays flat. But if I take my feel of it, then I'm making it my own. You wouldn't even see the reference if I didn't give you my point of view. Pop culture, it's everywhere in everything we do… it's an atmosphere. When you said it's like a moving mirror, yes, it's always present. You're just seeing it in different angles, lights, and it always loops back at you.

Thain: Pop culture is animated by us and our energy as well.

Grebmeier Forget: It exists because we're putting importance on it.

Thain: But what that importance is and what that value is also up for negotiation, right? What are you interested in in these images? Why are they compelling to you? What happens when you play with them?

Grebmeier Forget: I find them dreamy, like you want to be this not-so-impossible thing so badly. There is a pull there and I hate! Every time I look at images like this, there's a sensual attraction and like a type of beauty that's between refinement and playfulness. A femininity and a childlike aspect. There are always two things going on when I'm attracted to an image. It has to ignite excitement and some sort of more gross feeling, like envy, that I can then work with.

Thain: When you're working in this mode, you're using Photo Booth, you're always, as you said, composing an image. So, are images a part of the body for you? In screendance, there's a concept called kinesthetic empathy, that when we watch dance on screen, for example, our bodies are kind of moving with the image... [it's] contagious. Could an image be part of the body?

Grebmeier Forget: I do feel okay when you say image as the body. I'm conscious of the type of body I have and the image I send as just a person... the type of code I am in the world. The objects I choose, I know they respond to me in some sort of vibe; there is a link. My body adds something to the object and the object adds something to me and it becomes one. And because they fit together suddenly, there's a perfect image that appears and suddenly disappears very quickly. I'm interested in those micro moments, which are closer to photography actually, that are fleeting.

Thain: Pop culture serves as a kind of moving mirror, in that it doesn't just tell us how to look/move/feel, but we appropriate these images and can make them material to expand our ideas and the lived reality of our bodies, gender, self-image, etc. So, the focus would not just be on your re-appropriation of these images, but on the act of mimetic reproduction, first of other women's images, and of your own. Could you discuss this action of re-performance as a re-play, in relation to your project developed for *I've Only Known My Own* (OPTICA, Montreal, 2017)?

Grebmeier Forget: In that group show of performance artists (*I've Only Known My Own 2016–2017*), the curator was thinking about the traces of performance. What remains and how can that be like retranslated? [The show happened] in two parts: one in Houston, one in Montreal. The Montreal version—composed of an installation *Walls of Wind: The Mirroring and Rendering* and a performance *Rendering On View (Betty Rowland Meets Angela Aames)* —was supposed to translate what we had done in Houston, [where there] was this room, like an old yoga studio, all mirrors. I had created three panels and the panels were all the size of the door and the two windows. There was like this little installation and I performed in private. The panels covered the windows and the door. And then the people who were watching perform the storytelling for me; their job was to recount what they had seen after the fact. One of the panels then became a stage for them to recount the encounter to the public. But what happens is that the person recounting doesn't really recount the truth. She talks about her experience, what she remembers, what it makes her think of, about her life. [The spectators are] puzzling out my performance through the memory and subjectivity of the chosen viewer. And that's what I actually thought was the most important. To underline the work at play in the subjectivity of reception.

For the Montreal version, I tried to mirror that space by memory. The Houston performance I did in private, my face is always looking into the mirror. So, they never saw my face directly. In the Montreal iteration, I tried to do the inverse. If I was looking at the mirror, I was looking at the public, and then I was trying to redo by memory the audio recording of the Houston performance and the recountings I was listening to, what they were saying, and re-translating what they were translating themselves.

This was done at the beginning of my performance; I am listening to what they are saying and I'm re-saying it out loud. "So, she crossed the room. She looked at this, I fell on the floor, blah, blah, blah. I was thinking of the cream I used to hydrate my hands, it smelled of vanilla." I'm really listening to it and then I react to it with the objects I brought [in Montreal]. As I said, it's based on the collective memory—of that reading and of what I remember doing for them too. It seems convoluted because it is! It's about showing the loop of self-reflexiveness.

Thain: And then what was that experience like for you, looping all of these different kinds of memories and recordings, without just taking one as the "real" archive? Did you feel the pressure to be accurate in representing this? What became the goal for you?

Grebmeier Forget: The initial encounters felt more pressure to be accurate then I did. I used a strategy where I film myself live and confuse the story with other elements I get on the internet. I was looping other narratives, such as videos, found and created on the spot. I was browsing, going back and forth between videos, and trying to imitate the videos and possible realities. The truth was not that important to me. Are archival documents really the ultimate truth of the past anyways?

Thain: That sense again of mirroring the play with the archive of pop culture is really interesting in that work.

Grebmeier Forget: I have an archive and I don't put so much importance on it. It's often a repetition of the same things over and over again, but different… for me, it's like, how can I constantly change something banal… the interaction with it, but also how people watch it unfold. And so, I give myself a lot of constraints in reaction to them. I'm like, "okay, I'll use these two videos, I'll be projected, and I'll use these objects." And then I just play in that moment. My documents are shifting materials. Starting points more than final ones.

Thain: Earlier you said that when you're in performance, you're like a machine.

Grebmeier Forget: It's because I get in my zone and I try not to think, I just do. Maybe that's why I feel like a machine.

Thain: Does that feel okay to you? You're watching the screen imitating it. The audience also is seeing that. This disjunctive gaze is to me, a signature of your work, and part of what makes it feel so relevant to an era of intimate self-surveillance and to technologies like Photo Booth.

Grebmeier Forget: I'm framed in a screen looking at the screen. It doesn't feel that different to me from being trapped on a video call. It's like I go in under, I become calmer. I'm trying to be very conscious of what I'm doing. There's a care in that, how I'm trying to care for what I'm doing, for the situation.

Thain: Care also means caring for yourself and caring for others. It's not just about "you give the audience something" or "you protect yourself from them." Care is also about negotiating that vulnerability; that's when it becomes interesting.

Grebmeier Forget: But I have a hard time looking at the documentation of me working, the official documents of my performances if they are filmed by an other; I generally enjoy discovering the still images the chosen photographer has produced, but the moving images feel totally empty and irrelevant to me.

Thain: You just want to film your own body, your own self.

Grebmeier Forget: My art is about showing what I want to show the way I want to show it and understanding the world around me. It's the only time I can actually apply some sort of hyper-control tangibly.

Thain: That's a word that I wanted to ask you about: does control matter to you?

Grebmeier Forget: I think you can only lose control if you have control

Thain: Can I ask a question about *Some Kind of Game*, which was first a Facebook live stream, and then a video? This was a two-hour livestreamed performance, where you animated the space of the screen with your intensive, shaking movements repeatedly interrupted as you reset the song and drew objects and images into the frame, using your own body as a hybrid camera/editing system to create changes in scale, live cuts, to film and edit in the same gesture, all while watching yourself onscreen along with the live audience.

Grebmeier Forget: It is wonderful. I love this performance so much. It's my favorite, because I just turned the camera on and did it. A venue didn't ask me anything. I felt like I needed to do it. It was urgent. And I acted upon that gut feeling with no doubt.

Thain: March 25, 2020. Twelve days…

Grebmeier Forget: After the lockdown… I didn't think about the pertinence of it at first. It was on Facebook, for my online community and, like I said, I just did it. And then, I had so much positive feedback from it; a lot of people suddenly wrote to me with very personal and significant reactions to it. So, I watched it myself a week later. Then I really listened to it and saw what they were seeing/feeling. And I find that beat [of "Some Kind of Game"

FIGURE 18.4 Still from *Some Kind of Game* (2020)
Source: Image credit: Nadège Grebmeier Forget.

by Against All Logic] was really helpful in spreading my impulse across platforms and bodies. And the shaking: it really made and added impact in that moment. It's hard to transcend something so pure after that, even if it comes from your deep self…

Thain: Here you've set yourself up for a spontaneous performance… you've worked so many times with this format, collapsing proximity and distance, [creating] a space to move in that is spontaneous and yet feels so familiar to your practice. I think this duality of familiar but in the process of changing is what people were able to respond to. And this was really early on in what would be our life for two years. Really early on, you got it, and you were like, "you can live like this." It felt very reassuring, actually. It was like, you can be alive even in this.

Grebmeier Forget: The pandemic interrupted the flow of my practice and deeply changed my perception and the role I want my work to have in my daily life; all my production until the pandemic had been framed a certain way in my personal space, in my private apartment. And so, after that significant time framing my solitude (as I had always done subconsciously even before COVID) right now. I need air, I need people, I need to shift towards something less familiar, less commonly isolating.

Notes

1 This video, as well as extensive documentation of all the works discussed here, is available on the artist's website: http://www.nadege-grebmeier-forget.com/.
2 This interview was conducted in person June 20, 2023, at Grebmeier Forget's studio and continued via email. It has been edited for clarity and content.

Bibliography

Grebmeier Forget, Nadège. *Moshi Moshi*. 2011. Performance. http://www.nadege-grebmeier-forget.com/performances/moshi-moshi/.
Grebmeier Forget, Nadège. *Re-Reflecting On…*. 2016. Performance installation. http://www.nadege-grebmeier-forget.com/performances/re-reflecting-on/.
Grebmeier Forget, Nadège. *Hier est Aujourd'hui*. 2016. Performance installation. http://www.nadege-grebmeier-forget.com/performances/hier-est-ajourdhui/.
Grebmeier Forget, Nadège. *Rendering on View (Betty Rowland Meets Angela Aames)*. 2017. Performance installation. http://www.nadege-grebmeier-forget.com/performances/rendering-on-view/.
Grebmeier Forget, Nadège. *Some Kind of Game*. 2020. Live-streamed performance. http://www.nadege-grebmeier-forget.com/performances/2020-some-kind-of-game/.
Grebmeier Forget, Nadège. *Inside-Outside, Off & On*. 2020. Performance. http://www.nadege-grebmeier-forget.com/performances/2020-inside-outside-off-amd-on/.

INDEX

7 *Fragments for Georges Méliès* (Kentridge), 91
13th (DuVernay), 154

activism, 11, 41, 156, 245, 246, 249; glitch, 11
affect, 8, 15, 20, 31, 40, 50, 53, 88–92, 93, 95, 97, 108, 110, 134–42, 144–46, 232–34, 310
agency, 11, 16, 27, 28, 32, 33, 35–36, 38, 39, 56, 64n9, 153, 165; nonhuman, 35, 39
Ahmed, Sara, 95, 96
Albera, François, 171
Albright, Ann Cooper, 145, 288, 289–90
Alcoff, Linda Martín, 50
alienation, 18, 90
Allegorical Circuits for Human Software #2 (Grebmeier Forget), 314
All This Can Happen (Hinton), 220
analogue media, 20, 286–302
Andrieu, Laetitia, 214
Angelou, Maya, 158
animation, 2–3, 10, 12, 30, 79, 87, 91, 92, 97, 219
Apariciones (Caycedo and Magalhães), 79, 80, 81
Aquarium (Hamalian), 79, 80, 81
archive, 9, 13–14, 148n27, 154, 163–64, 168, 170, 215, 218–21, 230–33, 235, 238, 315, 318; analogue, 298; digital, 13–14, 21, 114–16, 119, 123–24; expanded, 10, 16–17; of fragments, 312–13; limitations of, 16, 171; photographic, 217–19, 230–32, 235, 238; somatic, 17–18, 91, 94; unruly, 4
At Land (Deren) 5, 225, 227n17
Auslander, Philip, 136, 138, 146

ballet, 17, 33, 91, 120–22, 183, 209, 213, 222–24, 225n2
Battle, Robert, 156
Baudrillard, Jean, 291
Bauer, Bojana, 144
Believe (Lees), 75
Bench, Harmony, 136, 144
Benjamin, Walter, 270, 301
Big (Marshall), 17, 198–203, 204, 205
Birth of a Nation, The (Griffith), 154
Bishop, Claire, 286, 293
Bixler, Litza, 6
Black Lives Matter, 94, 155
body, the 4–5; avatar; mutability of, 15; unruly; as technology, 4; virtual. *See also* embodiment
Boetzkes, Amanda, 237
Bogle, Donald, 153
Bolt, Barbara, 149n42
Bosom Buddies, 193–98, 199, 204, 205, 206n13
Boudry, Pauline, 92–93; *Moving Backwards*, 90, 92–94
Brakhage, Stan, 98
Bridges-Go-Round (Clarke), 293

Brouillard (Larose), 97–98, 101n44
Brown, Adrienne Maree, 149n43
Brum, Leonel, 3
BTS: "Black Swan," 120–24. *See also* K-pop
Bush, Kate: "Wuthering Heights," 10, 25–26, 28, 35–38, 41, 42n19
Butler, Judith, 94, 147n9, 149n42

Campion, Jane, 174n3
Campt, Tina, 229, 232–35, 238
canonization, 7, 13, 113–14, 115, 121, 123–24, 166, 296
capitalism; 46–48, 50, 52, 55–56, 60, 64, 99, 229, 234, 238–39, 263; racial, 229, 239, 298
care, 6, 9–10, 11–12, 17, 18, 19–20, 39, 92, 138, 156, 195, 212, 217, 319
Carmichael, Emma, 204
Carnet de voyage (Labrecque), 105–106, 108
Carroll, Noël, 6
Cash, Lucy: *How the Earth Must See Itself (A Thirling)*, 287
Castile, Philando, 98
Cavé, Frédéric, 170–71, 172, 173
Chace, Marian, 72–73, 82
Chairy Tale, A (McLaren), 95
Château, Dominique, 272–73, 286
Cho, Michelle, 119
choreographic software, 10
choreography: and Bieber, Justin, 205; and BTS, 115–22; as control, 33–35; in *I Got You*, 75; invisible, 108; in *Landscape*, 237; in *Les Robes Papillons*, 218, 224; lo-tech, 312; in *Moving Backwards*, 93, 94; in *Phoné-Scopie*, 280; in *SkypeDu*et, 256, 259; in *Star Trek: The Next Generation*, 302; in *Un Ballo in Maschera*, 85, 86; in "Wuthering Heights," 10, 25–41
Christie, Ian, 88–89, 286
cinema. *See* film
Clarke, Shirley: *Bridges-Go-Round*, 293
Clayton, Ryan: *SkypeDuet*, 19, 256–59; *Spectre that Animates Our Bones, The*, 1–3
Clegg, Johnny, 156
Coates, Ta-Nehisi, 158
Cocteau, Jean, 96
collage, 2, 30

collectivity, 8, 10, 18, 27, 30, 33, 35–36, 38, 73, 92, 240, 270, 275, 277–78
consciousness, 20, 50, 268–83
control, 4, 10–11,13, 17, 20, 28–30, 32, 33–40, 57, 89, 91, 99, 104, 134, 142, 144, 173, 183, 231–32, 238, 248, 291, 319; limits of, 10–11, 145, 162
Coole, Diana, 294
Covid-19 pandemic, 13–14, 62, 72, 114, 116–18, 121–22, 126n11, 206n8, 246, 249, 259, 261, 263, 309, 320
Cull, Laura, 134
Cullors, Patrisse, 94
cultural studies, 5, 9, 294
curatorial practice, 70, 73–74, 78–79

D'Aloia, Adriano, 73
dance history, 113–14, 124
dance movement therapy (DMT), 72
Danse Serpentine (Lumière Brothers), 163, 226n14
Daunizeau, Olivier, 214
Davies, Siobhan, 220, 287
Davis, Angela, 149n43
de Burca, Benjamin, 3
DeFrantz, Thomas, 36
Deleuze, Gilles, 65n15, 89, 92
Demolition of a Wall (Lumière Brothers), 12, 87, 88–89, 91, 97–98, 100n11
Deren, Maya, 90, 174; *At Land*, 5, 225, 227n17
Derrida, Jacques, 11, 51
desire, 12, 16, 32, 46, 53–55, 60, 64n9, 92, 114, 133, 142, 146, 245–51, 269, 284n28, 300; queer, 53
Deveril, 6
Deville, Noski, 298
Dialghilev, Sergei, 121, 225n2
digital media, 4, 33, 170, 287, 293–94, 296–98, 301
Dils, Ann, 290
Dimech, Alkistis, 53–54
Distribution, 172
Diving into your absence (Vidal), 15, 35, 142–46
DIY culture, 2, 4–5, 6–7, 9, 10, 11, 16, 18, 29, 45, 54–55, 56, 58, 107
Doane, Mary Ann, 138, 296, 297
Donath, Judith, 74, 82
Don't Miss It (Tedholm), 80, 81
Dozier, Ayanna, 98
Ducourneau, Julia, 174n2
Dulac, Germaine, 163

Duncan, Isadora, 225
Dupuis, Mélissa Mollen, 249, 251n5
Dupuy, Françoise, 210, 226n5
DuVernay, Ava: *13th*, 154

Eddie Murphy: Delirious, 190
Eddie Murphy Raw, 190
Edison, Thomas, 87, 88
editing, 13, 18, 33, 38, 57–58, 79, 89, 104, 106–107, 108–10, 180–83, 211, 213–15, 219, 221, 224, 248–50, 287, 299, 310, 313, 319
Eisenstein, Sergei, 272, 273
embodiment, 2, 9–11, 17, 30, 50, 52, 55, 58–59, 72, 75, 154, 157, 198, 202, 205, 238, 287. See also body, the.
empathy: kinesthetic, 8, 11–12, 70–78, 82, 90, 317
En deçà du reél (Labrecque), 105, 108
ecological collapse, 46, 59–63
Ettinger, Bracha, 139
everyday, the, 7–8, 86, 88, 97, 104, 137, 237, 291

fan culture, 5, 14, 28–30, 32–35, 40, 43n41, 115–17, 120, 126n10, 126n11, 197; labour of, 42n35
Fanon, Frantz, 229, 232
Faz Que Vai [Set to Go] (Wagner and de Burca), 3–4
feminism, 167, 172, 206n13
Fernandes, Brendan, 2
Ferrarese, Estelle, 229, 234, 238, 240–41
film: actualities, 88; amateur, 295, 297, 298; and consciousness, 20, 50, 268–83; documentary, 3, 17, 18, 88, 154, 163–64, 170–71, 209, 211–14, 220–22, 224, 277; early, 87–88, 164, 168; editing, 13, 18, 33, 38, 57–58, 79, 89, 104, 106–107, 108–10, 180–83, 211, 213–15, 219, 221, 224, 248–50, 287, 299, 310, 313, 319; experimental, 214; history, 16, 89, 168–71, 174; Hollywood, 191, 203, 153, 154; materiality of, 10, 106–107229, 236, 239, 287, 293–94, 298–300; organological, 20, 268–83; westerns, 246; women's, 166
Flashdance (Lyne), 184
Flip/Bend 1 (Forrest), 94, 96, 97, 101n44
Floyd, George, 155
FOMO (fear of missing out), 13, 116

Forrest, Nik, 95; *Flip/Bend 1*, 94, 96, 97, 101n44
Foster, Susan Leigh, 18, 229
fragmentation, 30, 91–92, 134, 178–79, 213, 232, 236, 240–41, 312
Fraleigh, Sondra, 136
Friend or Foe (Houle), 15, 135, 137–39, 141, 142, 144, 146, 148n36
Frost, Samantha, 294
Fuller, Loïe 222, 226n14

Gaines, Jane M., 165–66, 168–69, 172–74
Galbraith, Patrick W., 31–32
Garneau, David, 135, 137, 145, 147n15
Gary, Ja'Tovia, 98–99, 101n44
Gaumont, Léon, 163–64
gaze, the, 7, 10, 31, 40, 53–54, 90, 139, 145, 146n5, 161, 165–66, 210, 216–17, 247, 250, 319; decolonizing, 15, 249
gender, 16–17, 35, 96, 122, 165–66, 173–74, 191, 193–98, 204–205, 206n13, 238, 309, 316–17; and caricature, 316; and discrimination, 161, 162, 163; and violence, 18. See also masculinity
Gennep, Arnold van, 206n19
gesture, 13, 27–30, 35–39, 55, 58, 81–82, 86, 94–95, 104, 108–109, 138–39, 154, 174, 190, 200–201, 215, 217, 219, 225, 239, 257, 260–61, 269, 217–74, 276, 279–82, 284n12, 302
Ghost Dance, 87, 228–31, 235, 239–40
Gianati, Maurice, 169–73
Giersdorf, Jens Richard, 123
Giroux, Henry, 297
Giverny Document, The (Gary), 99, 101n44
Giverny 1 (Gary), 98
Glass, Alice, 46, 50, 53–54, 56, 58–59; "Love is Violence," 11, 45–46, 50–54, 56, 58–63
glitch, 35, 38–41, 99, 293; activism, 11; as dance, 5, 38–41
Gottchild, Brenda Dixon, 158
Graham, Martha, 120–21
Grebmeier Forget, Nadège, 308–20: *Allegorical Circuits for Human Software #2*, 314; *Hier est Aujourd'hui*, 315–16; *Inside-Outside, Off & On*; 309, 314; *Moshi Moshi*, 310; *Rendering on View (Betty Rowland Meets Angela Aames)*, 309, 317 ; *Re-Reflecting On…*, 310–11; *Some Kind of Game*, 319–20

Green, David, 296
Groundswell (Kramer and Thrash), 220–21
Guattari, Felix, 92
Gündüz, Zeynep, 27
Guy, Alice, 152–74

Halo, Laurel, 33
Hand Movie (Rainer), 218, 226n9
Hanks, Tom, 17, 191–94, 196–99, 201, 203–205 206n8
hapticity, 228, 232, 233, 235, 238
Haraway, Donna, 6, 16, 167
Heidegger, Martin, 20, 288–91, 292
Heyl, Parker, 297, 301
Hickok, Gregory, 71–72
Hier est Aujourd'hui (Grebmeier Forget), 315–16;
Hinton, David: *All This Can Happen*, 220; *Snow*, 287
Hoffman, Dustin, 195–96
Hölderlin, Friedrich, 290, 292
HOME (Larsson), 80, 81
hospitality, 10, 11, 13, 17, 45; and private property, 47–50; and sex, 50–56
Houle, Terrance: *Isstahpikssi (ghost)*, 228, 230–36, 241; *Landscape*, 228–29, 236–38, 241; *Wagon Burner*, 228–29, 236–38, 241
How the Earth Must See Itself (A Thirling) (Cash), 287
Hunter, Anna Graham, 196

I Got You (Yagaboo), 95
I made everything (Macdonald), 15, 135, 140–42, 145, 146
images: low-resolution; and the body, 317
immediacy, 266, 287, 312
Indigeneity, 135, 137, 139, 228–41, 241n11, 245–47, 249, 251n3
Inside-Outside, Off & On (Grebmeier Forget), 309, 314
Irresistible Piano, The (Guy), 162
Isstahpikssi(ghost), (Houle), 228, 230–36, 241

Jepsen, Carly Rae: "I Really Like You," 17, 203–205
Johnson, Dwayne "The Rock," 191
Johnson, E. Patrick, 189
Journey to the Moon (Kentridge), 91
Jowitt, Deborah, 33

Kappenberg, Claudia, 134, 144
Kentridge, William, 90–92, 101n44; 7 *Fragments for Georges Méliès*, 91; *Journey to the Moon*, 91; *More Sweetly Play the Dance*, 91, 101n44
Kim, Suk Young, 116, 117
Kimmel, Michael, 192, 205
kinetics, 12, 31, 33, 71, 107
kinship, 18, 235, 239, 241, 268, 291, 294
Kijâtai (Veillette-Cheezo),18, 246–47 248, 249, 250
Kozel, Susan, 136
K-pop, 13–14, 115, 117, 119, 122
Kracauer, Siegfried, 33, 296
Kramer, Johan: *Bye Bye Super 8—In Loving Memory of Kodachrome*, 295–97
Kulchyski, Peter, 229

Laban, Rudolf, 14, 124, 210
labour, 13, 34, 56–57, 85, 96, 98, 123–24, 140–41, 157, 164, 257–58, 259, 286
Labrecque, Manon, 13, 104–10; *En deçà du reél*, 105, 108
LaDuke, Winona, 235
La fée au choux (Guy), 163
La Grande Dame (Larose), 97
La Jetée (Marker), 230
Lame de Fond (Michel), 226n12
Landscape (Houle), 228–29, 236–38, 241
Larose, Alexander: *Brouillard*, 97–98, 101n94; *La Grande Dame*, 97; *Ville Marie A & B*, 97
Last dance, The (Vidal), 143
Latour, Bruno, 27
Lecavalier, Louise, 7
Lees, James: Believe, 75
Le Forestier, Laurent, 171
Lepage, Marquise, 163–64, 168–69, 171, 172; *Lost Garden: The Life and Work of Alice Guy-Blaché, The* (Lepage), 164, 167, 168, 171
Lepecki, André, 90
Lequeux, Emmanuel, 170
Les Robes Papillons (Auburtin), 209–10, 213–17, 220, 222–25
liberation, 15, 271, 309, 310
Li, Michael, 25, 26, 28
Little Colonel, The (Butler), 15, 154–56
liveness, 13, 14, 117, 119, 136, 144, 146
Lorde, Audre, 158
Lorenz, Renate, 90, 92–93; *Moving Backwards*, 90, 92–94

Lost Garden: The Life and Work of Alice Guy-Blaché, The (Lepage), 164, 167, 168, 171
lo-tech creation, 4–5, 6, 7, 8, 9, 19–20, 21, 87, 94, 96, 104, 309, 312
love, 46, 48, 51–52, 54, 56, 58, 72, 78, 91, 157, 179, 183, 237, 238, 239, 246, 251
"Love is Violence" (Glass), 11, 45–46, 50–54, 56, 58–63
Lowry, Joanna, 296
Loy, David, 138
Lumière, Auguste, 12, 87, 88, 163, 222, 226n14
Lumière, Louis, 12, 87, 88, 163, 222, 226n14

Maboungou, Zab, 266
magic, 12, 71, 88, 90, 96–97, 296
Malcolm X, 155
manifestos, 6, 7, 119–20, 277
Manovitch, Lev, 86–87
Marey, Étienne-Jules, 291, 303n23
Marks, Laura U., 261, 287, 294, 298
Marx, Karl, 56, 229
masculinity; 14, 17, 18, 118, 189–205; white, 17, 189–90, 192–93, 196, 198, 200, 205; toxic, 14, 118
Masilo, Dada, 91
Massumi, Brian, 136
mastery, 11, 14–15, 133–37, 139–42, 144–46, 146n5, 147n10, 148n27, 149n51, 157, 221, 229, 288
materiality, 10, 50, 106–107, 229, 232, 236, 239, 287–88, 293–94, 298–301
Matsutoya, Mari, 33
McLeod, Ken, 36
McMahan, Alison, 164–66
McPherson, Katrina, 6
mediation, 11, 19, 20, 37, 48, 291, 309–10
Méliès, Georges, 90–91, 162, 163, 169
Melrose, Susan, 144, 146n5, 149n51
memory, 9, 13, 15, 16, 17, 18, 91, 92, 114, 117, 120, 157, 163–64, 168, 171, 210–16, 219, 221–23, 230, 269, 272, 294–95, 315, 316, 318; bodily, 17, 18; collective, 164, 168, 318
Menakem, Resmaa, 232, 235, 237, 238, 239
Menkman, Rosa, 35
Mezzadra, Sandro, 148n36
MikuMikuDance (MMD), 10, 28–41
mimesis, 40, 236, 309
modern dance, 33, 120–22, 209

montage, 194, 269, 271–73, 277
Moody, David L., 189
More Sweetly Play the Dance (Kentridge), 91, 101n44
Moreton-Robinson, Aileen, 238
Morgan, Jas, 18, 239
Morin, Emilie: *SkypeDuet*, 19, 256–59; *Spectre that Animates Our Bones, The*, 1–3
Moshi Moshi (Grebmeier Forget), 310;
"Mos Thoser" (Foodhouse), 59
motion capture technology, 2, 3, 27
movement: reverse, 12, 87, 89, 92, 94, 97, 98, 100
Moving Backwards (Lorenz and Boudry), 90, 92–94
Mulvey, Laura, 146n5, 161
Muñoz, José Esteban, 66n39, 93–94, 96, 97
Murat, Laure, 170
Murphy, Ann, 154, 157
Murphy, Eddie, 189–90
music videos, 10, 11 17, 27–30, 33, 36–38, 41n7, 42n19, 50, 57, 115, 119–21, 123–24, 203–205, 251n6

Niemeyer, Katharina, 286
Nolin, Safia, 251, 251n6
Notre Musique (Godard), 283

ocularcentrism, 10
Odehimin (Veillette-Cheezo), 18, 246, 247, 248, 250, 251
Oever, Annie van den, 286

Parviainen, Jana, 136
Paual Nunes, Ana, 3
pedagogy, 5, 6–7, 13–14, 21, 114–15, 118–19, 123–24, 179, 210–11, 237
performance: gender, 205; mis-, 17, 190, 193, 205
Pfeil, Fred, 192–93
Phoné-Scopie (Vlassov), 268–83
Phonesia ®, 271–74, 276–77, 280–81
Piñata (Rodriguez), 80, 82
play, 5, 11, 21, 53–54, 57, 109, 117, 141, 173, 202, 229, 237, 268, 318
Poisson (Stefan), 178
popular culture, 4–5, 7–8, 9, 16, 21, 122, 124, 170, 189, 192, 199, 205, 219
posthumanism, 10, 27, 29, 35, 38, 40–41, 297
precarity, 15, 134–38, 141–42, 145, 147n9

property: intellectual, 34; private, 11, 46–50, 52–53, 55–56, 60–61, 63–64, 64n8, 64n9, 230; and whiteness, 238
Priya (Syed), 298–302

queerness, 4, 8, 11, 12, 46, 53, 59–61, 90, 93–97

race, 17, 117, 153–54, 192, 196, 198, 232. *See also* Indigeneity; whiteness
Rahola, Federico, 148n36
Rainer, Yvonne: *Hand Movie*, 218, 226n9
reanimation, 12, 13, 17, 89, 107
Reason, Matthew, 74
refusal, 4, 12, 39, 93, 99. 139, 172, 212, 236
relationality, 27, 35, 37, 96
remixing, 5, 8–9, 13, 14, 20, 99, 311
Rendering on View (Betty Rowland Meets Angela Aames) (Grebmeier Forget), 309, 317
representation, ; limits of, 8
Re-Reflecting On... (Grebmeier Forget), 310–11
Retornar (Soler), 11, 45–46, 60–63
Reynolds, Dee, 74, 78, 82
Ribeiro, Alfonso, 189
Robinson, Bill, 15, 16, 153–59
Robinson, Cedric, 229
Robinson, Dylan, 239
Rosenberg, Douglas, 6, 15, 133, 134, 148n40
Rouch, Jean, 211
Russ, Joanna, 168, 170
Russell, Legacy, 11, 39, 41

Sachsenmaier, Stefanie, 146n5
Sandhu, Suhkdev, 298
Sapio, Giuseppina, 298
Sardella-Ayres, Dawn, 157
Schneider, Rebecca, 85, 136
screen: and the body, 36, 41, 179, 184; as dream space, 73; and flatness, 256; as mirror, 20, 314; as mise-en-abyme, 50, 53, 56, 58, 60; and pedagogy, 14, 118; space, 12, 38, 90, 282, 288, 319; as window, 10, 37
screendance, 4–12, 70–71, 73, 115; and analogue media, 298; as anarchival, 86, 94, 96, 100; cinematography of, 280–82; as countertechnique, 7; and the digital turn, 292–93, 309; and emancipation, 15, 154–55, 158; ethics of, 7, 177; feminist, 161–74; and futurity, 46, 59, 62–63; and hospitality, 10, 11, 45–64; industrialization of, 56–58; and kinesthetic empathy, 8, 70–79, 82, 90, 317; and mastery, 133–146; origins of, 13; as pedagogy, 5; politics of, 7, 17; remixed, 9–10; and reverse motion, 86, 89, 90; and sociality, 213; and technology, 20, 287–88, 301; temporality of, 18, 86, 89; and unlearning, 7, 11
self-representation, 13, 104, 106–107, 177, 245, 249, 309
settler colonialism, 3, 98, 234, 237–39, 241n11
sex, 11, 34, 46, 50–51, 53–57, 64, 65n25; and violence, 247, 250
sexism, 167–68, 170–72
sexuality, 17, 96, 189–90, 200, 205n2, 206n13, 239; homo-, 189–90, 205n2; hetero-, 200; two-spirit, 251. *See also* queerness
Sicinski, Michael, 101n44
Siegert, Bernhard, 39
Silverman, Kaja, 165
Simondon, Gilbert, 90, 275, 278
Simpson, Leanne Betasamosake, 237, 241n11
Singh, Julietta, 133–34
Sinnerbrink, Robert, 291
Skype, 3, 19, 20, 256–64, 266n4, 312
SkypeDuet (Clayton and Morin), 19, 256–59
Sloterdijk, Peter, 2
Snow (Hinton and Davies), 287
Sobchack, Vivian, 136
social media, 11, 14, 21, 35, 55, 100, 115, 206n8, 302, 309. *See also* Skype; TikTok; Tinder; Twitch; Zoom
Some Kind of Game (Grebmeier Forget), 319–20
special effects, 12, 86–90, 95, 298
spectacle, 31, 38, 55, 87, 88, 89, 98, 117
spectatorship, 8, 20, 55, 71, 74–75, 78–79, 276–77, 280, 283
Spectre that Animates Our Bones, The (Clayton and Morin), 1–3
Spinoza, Baruch, 2, 65n14
Spirit of the Rose, The (Weber), 222–23
spontaneity, 181, 214, 313, 320
Star Trek: The Next Generation, 302

Stefan, Sonya, 177–84; *TurnOnTVDrinkCoffeeRehearseShow*, 179
Steyerl, Hito, 288, 291–92
Stiegler, Bernard, 269–70, 275, 277–78
Strategic Retreat (Renzi), 80, 81
Still, Judith, 48
Story Told, A (Syed), 299
Syed, Alia, 298–301; *A Story Told*, 299; *Priya*, 298–302

tap dance, 153
technology; 286–93, 301; analogue, 20, 296; and the body, 15, 85, 93, 94, 99, 314; as dance, 20; digital; DIY, 4; domestic, 19; fixity of, 12; and glitch, 35; lo-fi, 16, 19, 228; and progress, 20; telecommunication, 259, 260, 266n4
Temple, Shirley, 15, 154, 156
temporality, 15, 59, 92, 134, 138–40, 146n5
TikTok, 43n41, 55, 292
Tinder, 302
Tohline, Alexander, 89–90, 96, 99, 100n11
Tootsie (Pollack), 194–96
Torun, Lisa, 85
trauma, 13, 18, 99, 228–29, 232–35, 238–41
Tuck, Eve, 94
TurnOnTVDrinkCoffeeRehearseShow (Stefan), 179
Turquety, Benoît, 287
Twitch, 3

Un Ballo in Maschera (Shonibare), 85
uncanny, the, 2, 26, 30, 40, 96, 265

Veillette-Cheezo, Kijâtai-Alexandra, 18, 245–51; *Kijâtai*, 18, 246–47 248, 249, 250; *Odehimin*, 18, 246, 247, 248, 250, 251

Vergès, Francoise, 94
Vertov, Dziga, 277–78
Vidal, Concha, 135, 142–46; *Diving into your absence*, 15, 35, 142–46; *Last Dance*, 143
video: aesthetics of, 58; affordances of, 4; analogue, 286, 294–95, 298; circulation of, 113–14; fragility of, 104; instructional, 26, 36. *See also* music video
video games, 10, 11, 31, 36, 46, 60
Ville Marie A & B (Larose), 97
violence, 13, 18, 39, 46, 51–52, 53, 59, 86, 91, 118, 158, 200, 234, 237, 247, 250; colonial, 18, 46, 59, 86, 245; sexual, 247, 250
virtuality, 88, 96, 281
visibility, 5, 10, 90, 115, 123, 140–41, 153, 167, 237–38, 263, 280, 309
Vizenor, Gerald, 241n11

Wagner, Bárbara, 3–4
Wagon Burner (Houle), 228–29, 236–38, 241
Walon, Sophie, 163
Warren-Crow, Heather, 33
Werlé, Frederic, 215
Wheelchair Dance (Tamura), 75–76
whiteness, 17, 133, 190, 238. *See also* masculinity: white
Williams, Sarah, 94, 95
Wills, David, 86
Women in Cities (Trump), 80–81
Wong-Merseau, Amélie, 3
Wynter, Sylvia, 232, 238

YouTube, 3, 10, 17, 26, 28, 29, 36, 37, 42n15, 113, 117, 118, 119 122, 124, 156, 199

Zoom, 3, 118, 121, 259, 262, 264, 265

Printed in the United States
by Baker & Taylor Publisher Services